Charles Allen is best known as a historian of British India and for such books as *Plain Tales from the Raj* and *Soldier Sahibs: The Men Who Made the North-West Frontier*. However, he has also travelled extensively in Tibet and the Himalayas and has written a number of books on the region, including *A Mountain in Tibet*, *The Search for Shangri La* and, most recently, *The Buddha and the Sahibs: The Men Who Discovered India's Lost Religion* ('a marvellous book . . . colourful, informative and splendidly readable', Saul David). In researching *Duel in the Snows* he covered as much of the invading army's route to Lhasa as political constraints set by the government of the Tibet Autonomous Region allowed.

DUEL IN
THE
SNOWS

*The True Story of the Younghusband
Mission to Lhasa*

Charles Allen

JOHN MURRAY

First published in Great Britain in 2004 by John Murray (Publishers)
A division of Hodder Headline

Paperback edition 2004

3 5 7 9 10 8 6 4 2

A CIP catalogue record for this title is available from the British Library

ISBN 0 7195 5429 2

Typeset in Monotype Bembo by Servis Filmsetting Ltd, Manchester

Printed and bound by
Clays Ltd, St Ives plc

Hodder Headline policy is to use papers that are natural, renewable and
recyclable products and made from wood grown in sustainable forests. The
logging and manufacturing processes are expected to conform to the
environmental regulations of the country of origin.

John Murray (Publishers)
338 Euston Road
London NW1 3BH

In the Year of the Wood-Dragon the first part of the year protects the young king. Then there is a great coming forward of robbers, quarrelling and fighting, full of many enemies. Troublous grief by weapons and such-like will arise. The king, father and son, will be fighting. At the end of the year a conciliating speaker will vanquish the war.

Prophecy from the Tibetan Almanac for
the Year of the Wood-Dragon,
beginning mid February 1904

Contents

Illustrations

Line drawings in the text

The author and publishers would like to thank the following for permission to reproduce illustrations: Plates 2, 5, 10, 11, 12, 13, 15, 18, 21, 23, 27 and 32, Director of the National Army Museum, London; 3, 4, 8, 9, 22 and 29, Oriental and India Office Collection at the British Library; 6 and 20, Royal Norfolk Regiment Museum; 7, 14, 26, 28 and 30, Royal Geographical Society, London; 16, 19 and 24, Royal Fusiliers Museum; 17, Royal Engineers Library; 25, Gurkha Museum. Plate 1 is taken from Dr L. A. Waddell, *Lhasa and its Mysteries*, 1906, and plate 31 from Perceval Landon, *Lhasa*, 1906.

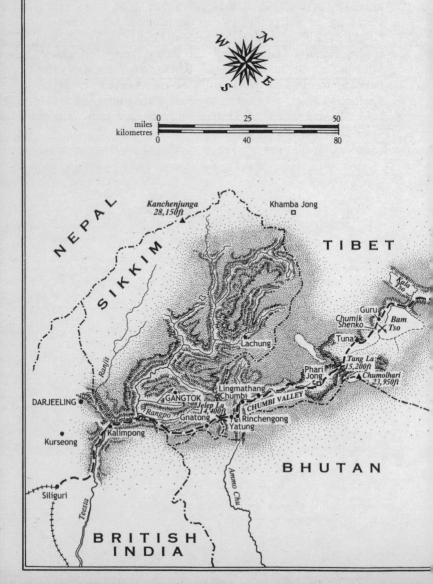

THE ROAD TO LHASA
1903–1904

miles
kilometres

NEPAL

SIKKIM

Kanchenjunga
28,150ft

Khamba Jong

TIBET

Gala Tso

Guru

Chumik
Shenko

Bam Tso

Tuna

Lachung

Tang La
15,200ft

Phari
Jong

Chumolhari
23,950ft

Lingmathang
Chumbi

DARJEELING

GANGTOK

Rangpo

Jelep La
14,400ft

CHUMBI VALLEY

Gnatong

Rinchengong

Yatung

BHUTAN

Kalimpong

Kurseong

Ranjit

Teesta

Ammo Chu

Siliguri

BRITISH
INDIA

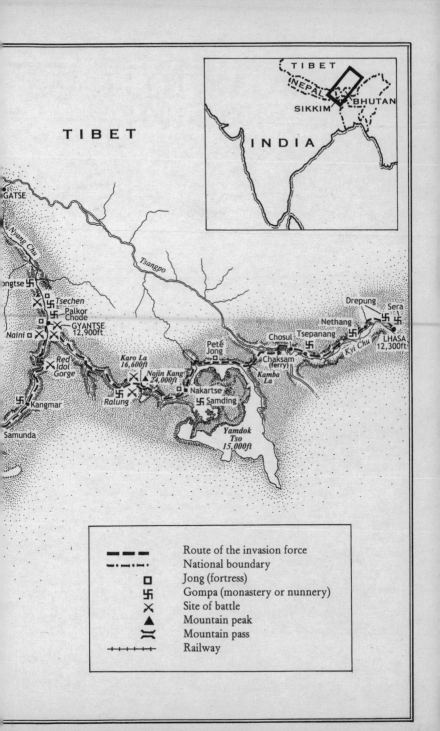

TIBET

GATSE

Nyang Chu

Tsangpo

ongtse
Tsechen
Palkor
Chode
GYANTSE
12,900ft
Naini
Red
Idol
Gorge

Kangmar

Samunda

Karo La
16,600ft
Nojin Kang
▲ *24,000ft*
Ralung

Peté
Jong

Kamba
La

Nakartse
Samding

Yamdok
Tso
15,000ft

Drepung
Sera
Nethang
Chosul
Tsepanang
Chaksam
(ferry)

Kyi Chu

LHASA
12,300ft

TIBET
NEPAL
SIKKIM
BHUTAN
INDIA

Route of the invasion force
National boundary
Jong (fortress)
Gompa (monastery or nunnery)
Site of battle
Mountain peak
Mountain pass
Railway

Foreword: The Younghusband Mission

THIS IS the story of the British invasion of Tibet in 1903-4, told as far as possible in the words of those who were there.

The official reasons for this invasion were almost entirely bogus; indeed, as one reads through the secret and private correspondence of the time exactly one century later, one is struck by how history repeats itself: how easily intelligent and otherwise honourable men allow their judgement to be clouded once they have set a course of action they believe to be morally right – and how far they will go to deceive both themselves and others. But in this case the bogey was not 'weapons of mass destruction' but Russia's perceived ambitions in the East. What began as the Tibet Frontier Commission and grew into the Younghusband Mission was imperial Britain's last throw of the dice, a hangover from the 1890s when vast swathes of Africa and other tropical regions were brought under the protection of the Crown by empire-builders such as Cecil Rhodes and Frederick Lugard. As was so often the case in such adventures, it was initiated largely by one man; in this instance, Baron Curzon of Kedleston, in the peerage of Ireland, appointed by the Queen-Empress Victoria as her Viceroy in India in 1898. George Nathaniel Curzon had long been obsessed with Russia's relentless advance into Central Asia, and feared that a Russian invasion of

British India was predestined. In 1900 these fears became focused on the neighbouring country of Tibet and the person of its spiritual leader, the thirteenth incarnation of the lama known to his countrymen as Gyalpo Rinpoche, 'Blessed Protector', and outside Tibet as the Dalai Lama.

Bypassing the Chinese Government, which had its own representative in Lhasa in the form of a Resident known as the Amban, Curzon sought to enter into direct negotiations with the Dalai Lama, ostensibly on the subject of trade. His overtures were twice rebuffed.

Acting on the advice of his state council and national assembly, the Dalai Lama declined to have any dealings with the British Government in India. Advised that the Buddhist faith was under threat from the British, he sent an emissary to the court of Czar Nicholas II, a Buddhist lama of Siberian origins named Agvan Dorjieff, already known to the Government of India's Directorate of Criminal Intelligence and suspected of being a Russian spy. Dorjieff's appeal for Russian protection was met with polite evasions, but his warm reception at the Peterhof in October 1900, followed by an equally cordial audience of the Czar at his palace in Yalta a year later, reinforced Curzon's belief that the Dalai Lama was about to enter into a treaty that would end Tibet's neutrality and place it firmly within the Russian camp.

Caught up in the mire of the Boer War, Lord Salisbury's government in England had no time for a further entanglement that might involve both Russia and China. However, in the summer of 1902 a peace treaty was signed at Vereeniging in South Africa and a new administration took office under Arthur Balfour, an old friend and ally of Curzon. Then in August of that year the British Minister at Peking telegraphed to Whitehall the twelve clauses of a secret agreement said to have been drawn up between China and Russia, by which the former relinquished her interest in Tibet to the latter in return for Russian support in maintaining the integrity of the Celestial Kingdom. Both powers were quick to deny the existence of any such understanding, but in London and Simla (British India's summer capital between mid April and September) it was widely agreed that some sort of secret treaty had been arrived at by which Tibet had been made over to Russia.

Lord Curzon had no doubts in the matter. 'I am myself', he wrote in November 1902, 'a firm believer in the existence of a secret understanding, if not a secret treaty, between Russia and China about Tibet; and, as I have said before, I regard it as a duty to frustrate their little game, while there is still time.' In January 1903 Curzon sent a long despatch to his constitutional superior in London, the Secretary of State for India, arguing for a mission to be sent to Lhasa to deal directly with the Dalai Lama. For two months the Cabinet equivocated, having received further assurances from Russia that she had no designs on Tibet. Curzon then proposed a more modest course of action: the despatch of a Tibet Frontier Commission to a place just inside the Tibetan border where a British representative could meet with Chinese and Tibetan delegates and discuss the issue of trade. He suggested Khamba Jong, a fortress about eighty miles due north of Darjeeling and half a day's march inside the Tibetan border.

On 29 April Curzon received a telegram from London authorising the mission – but to Khamba Jong only, and no further. The jubilant Viceroy began at once to lay his plans.

The events that followed are told here chiefly through the diaries, letters and memoirs of the men on the ground. They were mostly British military officers. Some – like the junior subaltern Frederick Marshman 'Hatter' Bailey of the 32nd Sikh Pioneers – were field officers commanding Indian troops or Nepali Gurkhas. Others had graduated to the more exclusive ranks of the Indian Political Service and were present as 'politicals', most notably Colonel Francis Younghusband, the most senior of the Tibet Commissioners, whose name soon became synonymous with the Mission. A third category of eye-witnesses was made up of non-combatants such as Doctor Austine Waddell, a colonel in the Indian Medical Service, who was selected for the Mission not for his medical skills but because he was British India's leading – if not sole – Tibetologist. Others in this category were Perceval Landon, Edmund Candler and Henry Newman, newspaper correspondents representing respectively *The Times*, the *Daily Mail* and Reuters. On their return to India they and other participants published accounts of the Mission, so that by the end of 1905 every bookshop window in Britain must have been packed with literature about Tibet and the Younghusband Mission, nearly all richly illustrated with photographs.

Few military endeavours of comparable size can have been as well documented by its participants as the Younghusband Mission. Many officers took with them one or other of the new lightweight hand-held Kodaks, together with their easily portable rolls of film. At least one officer had a Panoram Kodak camera that took 2¼ inch by 7-inch negatives and covered a 142-degree field of vision; another man, Claude White, came armed with a folding-stand plate camera that produced landscape images of the highest quality. All were acutely aware that they were intruding into a remote, mysterious and much romanticised cul-de-sac hitherto barred to outsiders that was, in the words of the expedition's instigator, 'The one mystery which the nineteenth century has still left for the twentieth to explore.' Quite remarkably in the circumstances, telegraph and express postal services were established between the Tibetan plateau and the Indian plains. Although the press reports were doubly censored, officers' letters were not, so that private correspondence surviving from the expedition is, by and large, frank and revealing – as are the diaries.

Four companies of the 1st Battalion of the Royal Fusiliers took part in the latter stages of the invasion, the only sizeable British Army contingent present. The National Army Museum and the headquarters of the Royal Regiment of Fusiliers in the Tower of London have between them six diaries, of which three were written by what were known then as BORs or British Other Ranks, giving us a rare glimpse of the thinking of the ordinary British soldier on the campaign.

Despite the richness of source-material, the voices of the greater number of participants remain all but unheard. This almost silent majority was made up, on the one side, of the sepoys, porters, transport drivers and camp-followers who constituted the bulk of the British invasion force; on the other, of the native peoples of the Tibetan plateau and the central Himalayas who found themselves affected by this extraordinary – and, for many, fatal – eruption into their lives. In the case of the Tibetans, only faint echoes of the event have been preserved. However, it is now possible for Western visitors to retrace a large part of the invading army's route to and from Lhasa, although few vestiges of its passing remain – and even fewer local memories. The Tibetans are a forgiving people, and they have moved on. Ironically, it is the Chinese rulers of Tibet who seem determined to remember the British intrusion and to make political capital out of it – most notably at what has been designated the 'heroic city' of Gyantse, whose fortress was shelled and then dynamited by General Macdonald in 1904, and then again dynamited by the Chinese in 1967. Visitors who tour Gyantse's restored and once more magnificent rock citadel today should be sure to spare a few minutes to inspect its 'Museum of Anti-British' before climbing to the summit of the fort, where a memorial stone erected by the Government of Gyantse County in 1997 proclaims in English: 'The place of jump in cliff that against British hero martyrs. Eternal glory to the hero martyrs of jump in cliff!' Presumably the accompanying Chinese and Tibetan inscriptions put it rather better.

Several secondary accounts of the Younghusband Mission have been written, most memorably Peter Fleming's *Bayonets to Lhasa*, published in 1961, and Patrick French's definitive biography of its leading character, *Younghusband: the Last Great Imperial Adventurer* (1994). A number of histories and biographies have also dealt with the subject and its major protagonists in passing. All, without exception, have accepted the self-serving line first given out by Sir Francis Younghusband and his many contemporary admirers and reinforced half a century later by Peter Fleming, who mounted a vigorous defence of his hero based on the private letters made available to him by Sir Francis's daughter Eileen (later Dame Eileen) Younghusband, and on the testimonies of a number of surviving officers. Yet in the sub-tropical jungles of Sikkim or on the pine-clad slopes of the Chumbi Valley, on the wastes of the Chang Tang and on the long, rocky road to Lhasa the situation was far more tangled than we have been led to believe, and this is where I have tried to focus – rather than on the political heights of Viceregal Lodge and Snowdon in Simla, Government House in Calcutta, the Foreign Office in Whitehall, the Winter Place in St Petersburg, or even the Potala Palace in Lhasa.

In seeking to give a more human perspective of events I have used wherever possible the written words of the participants themselves, as set down in private letters and diaries, in the belief that they contain if not always the most honest version of events, then at least something of the writers' thinking when they wrote them. Of the two leading protagonists in this adventure, one – Francis Younghusband – was determined from an early age to make his mark both as a man of action and a man of letters; he was a compulsive writer who used his private as well as his official correspondence as political instruments, and he was blessed with a large circle of friends and admirers. Peter Fleming drew extensively on his private papers and so I have felt no qualms in doing the same. By Fleming's account, Younghusband was the hard-done-by man of action while his opponent – James Macdonald, the officer who commanded the escort to the Tibet Mission – was one of the two deep-dyed villains of the piece: 'One of the most contemptible men who ever wore the king's uniform.' The other was the Secretary of State for India, St John Brodrick. My difficulty has been that Macdonald was a man of few words, spoken or written, and fewer friends. Although described as a great scribbler of notes, he left behind nothing in the way of private papers, so that his thoughts and actions have had to be viewed for the most part through the writings of his critics. I have restored some balance to this unequal equation, not to invite controversy but because the surviving evidence has led me there.

Here and elsewhere, wherever the private word is lacking I have turned to the published: the considered version of events that its author wished to leave on the record. Some of these published accounts were written many years after what the Tibetans knew as The Year of the Wood-Dragon (1904), with all the obvious attendant drawbacks, but it is also true to say that in some cases their authors no longer felt bound by the constraints that had caused them to pull their punches at the time: an example is the overlooked autobiography of the Reuters correspondent Henry Newman, written in 1937. A select cast-list of the players in this sideshow of the Great Game is appended at the end of the book, together with a glossary and bibliography. When quoting extracts from diaries, letters and journals, I have in a few instances corrected punctuation in the interests of clarity – most notably in the case of Royal Fusilier Private Sampson, whose approach to punctuation mirrored that of James Joyce when writing *Finnegan's Wake*.

To avoid confusion I have stuck with Tibetan personal and place names as Anglicised a century ago. Thus, the mountain known to the Tibetans as Jomo Lhari is here set down as it was known to the British, Chumolhari; the pass properly known as the Dzelap La is here called the Jelep La; and so on. A short list of the more correct versions of names encountered is included in the Glossary, set down as spoken and not in accordance with modern academic rules for transliterating written Tibetan. Travellers to Tibet should be aware that the country has always enjoyed a bewildering excess of names for places and people – to which the present rulers of the Tibet Autonomous Region of China have added by allocating new and often arbitrary Chinese place-names. Readers unfamiliar with the language will find it helpful to understand that *jong (dzong)* means both citadel and county; *jongpen (dzongpon)*, fortress commander and district governor; *gompa (gonpa)*, monastery; *la*, pass; *tang*, plain; *chu (chhu)*, flowing water; *tso (tsho)*, lake; and *ri*, mountain. The Tibetan word *lama*, incorrectly used by the British to describe all Tibetan monks, means a guru or religious teacher and is used only for very learned monks or high incarnations. No one word in Tibetan describes all the male occupants of a monastery. The novices and uninitiated lower orders are known as *trapa*; a fully ordained monk is a *gelong*; and *geshe* describes a monk with superior spiritual qualifications. *Ani*, thankfully, serves to describe every sort of nun.

Charles Allen,
Combe Florey,
September 2003

I

The Morning of 12 December 1903

O<small>N THE</small> borderland between Tibet and the modern Indian state of Sikkim the first peak to catch the rising sun is always the 24,000-foot snow pyramid of Chumolhari, followed moments later by the several summits of the still higher Kanchenjunga massif, seventy miles to the west. The next to be lit up are the higher points along the mountain chain that links these two giants to make up one segment of the Central Himalayan Range, the great barrier that both guards the Tibetan plateau from the Indian subcontinent and provides a natural border.

Only at one place is this mountain rampart vulnerable: immediately to the west of Mt Chumolhari, where the line of the Tibetan frontier dips to the south in a sharp V. Here the border follows the crests of two ridges radiating south-east and south-west from the Central Himalayan Range to form a triangle of land, a wedge known to the Tibetans as Dromo and to Indians as the Chumbi Valley. It can be entered from neighbouring Sikkim and Bhutan by way of a number of passes, one of which is the 14,300-foot crossing-point known as the Jelep La, the Lovely Level Pass.

In midwinter, sunlight strikes the narrow saddle of the Jelep La about an hour after sunrise. As on every mountain crossing in these parts, the highest point on the pass is marked by a cairn of stones over which flutter strings of Tibetan prayer-flags, originally dyed in bright primary colours – yellow, green, red, white and blue in ascending order – but soon bleached grey and shredded by the wind. On 12 December 1903, as the sun's rays lit up the cairn and then extended down the ridge's southern slopes they began to illuminate an army: first the scouts and advance guard, then the main body of three thousand fighting men, clambering up the steep mountain side in single file.

As well as his sidearm and twenty rounds of ammunition, every man carried in his pack four days' rations and one thick quilted cotton rug folded over and sewn to make a 'sleeping-bag'. In addition to his service dress he wore a lambskin vest, two layers of flannel, an extra pair of thick woollen socks, a pair of quilted cotton overalls, a long-sleeved sheepskin topcoat known as a poshteen and a pair of knee-length felt boots known as Gilgit boots – the two last, fruits of the Indian Army's long experience of the North-West Frontier. On his hands he wore two pairs of gloves, one woollen, the other more in the nature of a fur-lined bag. Either a balaclava helmet or a large turban tied under the chin with a woollen scarf covered his head and much of his face. A pair of goggles with small blue or green lenses shielded his eyes.

Despite this padding, the men who made up the military column were of recognisably different types: 'There is no mistaking the tall, stolid, bearded Sikh, the squat little snub-nosed Tatar Goorkha, the dark-skinned, lank Madrassi Sapper, and the British "Tommy Atkins".' Of this last category a number advanced on foot and, unusually, walked as muleteers beside the animals carrying their heavy weaponry. Seventeen were gunners drawn from No. 7 British Mountain Battery, with their two new-pattern breech-loading ten-pounders. Another seventeen were infantrymen from the 1st Battalion of the Norfolk Regiment with two of Sir Hiram Maxim's improved machine-guns, weighing only forty pounds each and capable of firing two thousand rounds in three minutes. Both these parties were accompanied by their camp-followers – in the Norfolks' case, one cook, one *bheesti* or water-carrier, and a sweeper who did the menial jobs that the other two refused to touch.

The riders in the column were the officers, each with his small retinue of followers. One such mounted officer, Lieutenant Mark

Synge, had with him his military orderly, his bearer and his *syce* or groom. 'I think they all died in imagination many times before they reached the top of the pass,' he later wrote. 'They turned wild eyes of anguish and reproach towards me whenever I waited to see how they were getting on.'

For every soldier in the column there were several camp-followers, mostly of the category known as 'coolies', porters inducted into a support force known as the Coolie Corps. Some were drawn from as far afield as Kashmir and Garhwal, others from much closer at hand: Lepchas, Bhotias and Tibetans from Sikkim and Bhutan. All had the immense advantage of being hillmen, but not all were willing volunteers: the largest group were little more than serfs, some five thousand porters from neighbouring Nepal rounded up and despatched on the orders of the governing Durbar in Kathmandu as part of its contribution to this adventure. Yet despite heavy loads, hostile terrain and lack of hot food, these coolies appeared the least unhappy members of the expedition. 'For a cheery family party it would be hard to beat that cooli [*sic*] corps,' noted Mark Synge, whose duties as a transport officer allowed him to observe them at close hand. 'The cooli . . . was as merry a soul as you meet on a day's march. Some were quite boys, not more than sixteen, yet the way they shouldered their loads was wonderful. The regulation load was eighty pounds, but I have often seen quite a youngster with a hundred pounds on his back, taking it steadily up thousands of feet, and taking it as a matter of course, and giving you a grinning greeting as you passed him.'

The porters were not the only load-carriers, for at every stage of its journey from the rail-head at Siliguri into the mountains the little army was bolstered by an enormous assembly of transport animals, ranging from the camel to the yak. From Siliguri to the Himalayan foothills the force's food and supplies were carried on carts drawn chiefly by pairs of bullocks. Two hundred buffaloes and seven camels were also employed, but briefly, for the camels were more trouble than they were worth and all but three of the buffaloes perished 'by way of protest'. Then, at the point where the *pukka* road gave way to a *kutcha* or rough track, the loads were shifted onto the backs of mules. To begin with only two of the Indian Army's Mule Corps had been involved, but by December the number had risen to five, employing more than ten thousand mules and almost three thousand drivers. To Lieutenant Synge's less than impartial eyes, this combination of man and beast made up the backbone of the Indian Army: 'The average Indian transport pack mule, aged probably fifteen to eighteen years old, is the finest old soldier we have got. If, like Lord Roberts's grey arab, he were allowed to record his services round his neck, he would display a fine collection of medals and clasps . . . His is a rough lot but he takes it kindly, and with good grain and fodder is not unhappy.'

The original plan was for these campaign-hardened regulars to be replaced by yaks as soon as the higher altitudes were reached. On paper the yak was just the job; in practice it turned out to be a disaster. 'The yak', wrote the journalist Edmund Candler after he joined the expedition, 'is the most extraordinary animal Nature has provided the transport officer in his need. He carries 160 pounds, and consumes nothing. He subsists solely on stray blades of grass, tamarisk, and tufts of lichen, that he picks up on the road. He moves slowly, and wears a look of ineffable resignation. He is the most melancholy disillusioned beast I have ever seen, and dies on the least provocation. If only he were dependable, our transport difficulties would be reduced to a minimum. But he is not.' No fewer than 8,500 of the creatures had been rounded up and despatched from neighbouring Nepal, but a thousand succumbed to anthrax before they even crossed the border and the rest were now quarantined in 'segregation camps' in an effort to contain the disease.

Even Synge's hardy mules were proving to be dangerously vulnerable. Some paused to nibble the aconite plants that lined the track-side and, despite the best efforts of the veterinarians, succumbed to their poison. But many more were simply being worked to death, forced to carry ever-heavier loads and to travel over greater distances as the numbers of transport animals diminished. According to Edmund Candler, half the first draft of mules employed on the trail through Sikkim were dead within weeks, and the remainder were only saved by a fresh draft of army mules from the North-West Frontier.

As for the men who now clambered up the trail, the contrast between their present conditions and those experienced at the start of their march could hardly have been greater. A day after leaving the rail-head at Siliguri they had entered sub-tropical jungle, following the course upstream of the river Teesta. 'Even for troops marching along a road running through its midst it has a certain fascination,' wrote Mark Synge of the lush forests through which they marched for seven days:

> The incessant call of the jungle-fowl on either side of you, the constant shade, so unusual in India, the bright orchids in the tree-tops, the heavy luxuriance of vegetation that loads the air with scents that are generally sweet, the gorgeous butterflies, the steamy hothouse atmosphere – all combine to form a kind of sedative, suggestive of the lotus flower, of pleasant physical enervation, and perpetual afternoon. One could enjoy this feeling as one sat idly on one's pony, till it was dispelled by the rain. It rained very heavily all those days. Even when it did not rain the air was so laden with moisture that the very clothes you wore were always wet on the outside.

After the seventh day they had begun to ascend, following a side-tributary of the Teesta before climbing up and along a ridge, then entering a rain-forest dominated by teak, kapok and bamboo. But this soon gave way to a third level of vegetation dominated by rhododendron and tree fern which, in its turn, led on to pine forest. At each stage the track grew worse. 'From here to Gnatong', recorded Mark Synge, 'we were to climb continuously, and at as steep a gradient as laden mule with straining breast-piece could hope to tackle.' He was surprised to see, even in these early days, that the track was already littered with discarded horse-shoes. Then, as they reached and passed 11,000 feet above sea-level, the first symptoms of altitude sickness began to make themselves felt: 'Giddiness, nausea, headache, loss of appetite, insomnia, difficulty in breathing, and, saddest of all in some cases, an utter inability to enjoy either your drink or your tobacco.'

A chance to rest and recover came at Gnatong, two days short of the Tibetan border, where a forward supply base had been established at 11,700 feet. It had served briefly as a frontier outpost for British troops during an earlier dispute with Tibet in 1888, and its dilapidated barracks were now brought back into service to

accommodate a new influx of troops: 'The Gnatong post was plac-
arded everywhere on the inside with the names of its tiny streets. It
appeared that we were occupying what was on the whole a straggling but quite fashionable part of London. I myself lived at "Hyde
Park Corner". The post commandant, if I remember right, occupied a mansion in "Carlton Mansions". We went for constitution-
als up and down "Rotten Row", and found "Buckingham Palace"
used as a supply depot.' A bazaar soon sprang up, including a small
store run by an enterprising Parsi merchant which did a brisk trade
in phenacetin and Stearne's 'headache cure'.

Here at Gnatong came the first intimation of what a Tibetan
winter had in store for the troops. What limited supplies of firewood
had been carried up were for cooking-fires only, so they had to rely
increasingly on body-heat and clothing for warmth. Personal
hygiene soon went by default: chins were left unshaved, washing
was abandoned and underwear went unchanged. Within days the
men began to look and smell different. 'I have papered my room
with Pioneers,' wrote Major William Beynon to his wife Norah at
home in England, referring to copies of British India's *Pioneer* newspaper, 'and the wind no longer whistles through my whiskers as I lie
in bed. We all here are growing beards. Genl Macdonald says he is
going to give a prize for the best beard at Christmas . . . We all look
fearful ruffians.' As the days passed it became increasingly difficult to
tell one officer from another, each service beard making its wearer
'resemble any such normal being as a naval officer, a parson, or
respectable middle-aged civilian of everyday life'. Some beards
acquired a distinction of their own. According to Mark Synge,

the glamour of royalty suddenly attached to old friends who
were found to be 'the veritable double of the Prince of Wales'.
Other beards were the 'Infant prodigy', a monstrosity adorning
the chin of a quite youthful officer who was taken to be at least a
colonel, and the 'British workman' beard, allowed to grow in its
own sweet way. I remember a certain stalwart major whose
beard grew in two inverted horns that splayed outward on his
chest, and who was the very image of my father's old gardener. I
once very nearly addressed him as 'Horton' by mistake, for that
happened to have been the gardener's name.

As November gave way to December, so the winter conditions became increasingly severe. The little army experienced its first blizzard, leaving its members 'benumbed and blue', and its first cases of frostbite. Then, as they prepared to move forward once more, from Gnatong to the Tibetan frontier at the Jelep La, the skies cleared, allowing the sun to burn away all but the deepest snowdrifts.

As the army climbed ever higher the pine forests gave way to straggling birch and alpine flora. 'Birch-trees alone survive among the frozen rocks of the upper snows,' was how the journalist Perceval Landon described this sparse but still colourful vegetation. 'At their roots, or from the hillside above their tops, round their stems, or springing from their wood is almost every flower known to man, here wasting its luxuriance along the loneliest and loveliest two hundred miles on earth. Pepper ferns, with their dark green glossy foliage, vines and bind-weeds, begonias and asphodel tangle themselves about the undergrowth of gorgeous shrubs, or stumps gay with scarlet fungus and dripping moss.'

Now the path itself became their greatest obstacle, for this forward section had yet to receive the attentions of the road-builders and was too steep and too narrow to allow more than one man or one animal to pass at a time: 'Our column winding like a snake up the steep zigzag track to the pass, was over four miles long, and seemed to crawl along up amongst the bleak black rocks almost at a snail's pace.' Long delays occurred as transport animals slipped or shed their loads: 'It was impossible to take the mule aside to adjust the load, for there was no room at the side, and the mule had to be halted where he was until the adjustment was completed. This involved the halting of say five hundred mules, who happened to be behind the mule who had first halted. And when the latter at last moved off, it of course took an appreciable interval of time before the next mule followed suit. Multiply that appreciable interval by the number of mules in the rear, say five hundred, and you find it takes perhaps a full half hour before the five hundredth is at last on the move again.'

As they advanced up the mountain side altitude once more began to take its toll, forcing the marchers to halt every few yards to regain their breath. Even among those who had acclimatised at Gnatong, the sudden gain of 2,500 feet was enough to leave them sick and dizzy: 'Scarcely anyone, even those who rode most of the way, escaped having aching temples and eyeballs; many suffered from actual mountain sickness, and several of the transport animals succumbed on the roadside.'

Yet it was still only mid morning on that twelfth day of December when the head of the column reached the summit of the pass – 'a knife edge in a narrow cleft . . . swept by a merciless icy blast, which cut painfully like a knife'. So biting was this wind that, according to Lieutenant Synge, it 'snatched away our breath' and 'pierced through our thickest garments as if they were mere gauze'. There was no sign of an enemy, which was just as well. Captain Arthur Hadow's two Maxim guns had water-filled cooling jackets, which he had been forced to empty 'lest they should emulate a bursting water-pipe'. Only later was fire-power restored by the addition of rum to the water – together with a dash of kerosene (paraffin) 'to prevent anyone from wanting to drink it'. But there was also the problem of freezing gun oil. As one of Captain Hadow's men advanced up the slope he thought to test his Lee-Enfield .303, only very recently introduced to British infantry regiments. He cocked his rifle and pulled the trigger on an empty chamber – to find, to his surprise, that there was over a second's delay before he heard the faintest of clicks. Hadow then checked the other rifles in his unit and found them similarly affected. 'I informed the General,' he later wrote. 'The whole force was halted and everybody proceeded to inspect his rifle, but of course we could do little to rectify it, and I believe if the enemy had appeared on the scene we should have been somewhat unpleasantly surprised to find that none of the rifles, or very few of them, would go off . . . Altogether it would have been an excellent opportunity for a regrettable incident.'

At the cairn that marked the crossing-point of the Jelep La, and thus the border between Sikkim and Tibet, the advance guard was joined by two groups of officers. Muffled in their goggles, bala-clavas and scarves and the sheepskin poshteens that reached below their knees, both parties looked much the same, but an observant onlooker might have noticed that one group was luxuriantly bearded while the other was generously moustached in the prevailing fashion, but with chins and cheeks covered by lesser growths.

The full-bearded ones were predominantly politicals, men who carried military rank but whose first loyalties lay with the Viceroy of India in the person of Lord Curzon, by way of the Foreign and Political Department of the Government of India. The moustachioed party was entirely military, a mixture of British officers from the Indian Army and officers from British Army regiments currently serving in India. They too owed loyalty to the Viceroy, but by way of his new Commander-in-Chief, Lord Kitchener.

Each group had its leader. The most senior political was, in the unguarded words of one diarist, 'a little stiff man with a bushy black beard'. Dominating that black beard was a moustache so long, thick and walrusy that even by itself it entirely concealed its owner's mouth. The eyebrows, too, were decidedly bushy and in marked contrast to the high forehead and receding hair-line above. But it was not the moustache or eyebrows or bald pate that most men remembered, for the most striking feature about Colonel Francis Younghusband was what his biographers have called variously his 'penetrating blue eyes' and his 'watery blue eyes', and what one of his many ardent lieutenants remembered as his 'two big, brown spaniel eyes'. Sir William Quiller Richardson's oil portrait, painted a year after his return to England, shows a man with what are undeniably dark – but blue – eyes. Whatever their hue, they were 'kindly', deep-set, and separated by a fine aquiline nose. After those hypnotic eyes it was the demeanour of the man that most impressed. He was, by almost every account, a man of few words and, to all outward appearances, unflappable and dignified, compensating for his short stature by projecting an almost palpable air of gravitas and stillness – the kind of man, in fact, who inspired hero-worship among his subordinates to an extraordinary degree. To his closest aide, Captain Frederick O'Connor, the Colonel was

one of the few specimens of the typical 'strong silent man' whom I have ever met. Very quiet, very laconic, sturdily built, with aquiline features and bushy eyebrows, he is at once a philosopher and a man of action . . . I never once saw him for a moment even ruffled, far less discomposed or perturbed, by any circumstance or crisis which we had to encounter. An imperturbable exterior covered a strong and steadfast character and a most equable temperament. His decisions were deliberately made, but once made they were absolute, and his 'yes' or 'no' were more convincing and reassuring than half a dozen speeches from a more voluble man.

Now in his fortieth year and still in his physical prime, Francis Younghusband was already the undoubted star of the expedition, a living legend renowned throughout British India for his exploits as a major player in that dangerous high-altitude contest of bluff and counter-bluff that had come to be known as the Great Game, the long-range struggle between Britain and Russia for the political control of the great open spaces of Central Asia.

In 1884, as a twenty-year-old subaltern 'holding' with a smart British cavalry regiment before joining the Indian Army, Younghusband had taken two months' leave to go exploring across the Rhotang Pass into Lahaul in the Western Himalayas – and had there vowed 'to make a great name for myself, and to be known ever after as a famous explorer'. Over the next years he had worked hard to ingratiate himself with the Quartermaster-General's Intelligence Department, and quickly became its most high-profile intelligence-gatherer as he explored known and unknown passes along British India's northern frontier. In 1887, returning to India from an expedition in Manchuria, he had pioneered a new route over the high Mustagh Pass in the Karakoram which involved hacking steps down a treacherous ice precipice. This coup and the best-seller that came out of it made him a public figure. Further high adventures followed, the details of some of which could only be guessed at since they remained hidden from the public gaze in the secret files of the Government of India's Foreign and Political Department.

These journeys brought Younghusband into contact with numerous pieces in the Great Game, not only Russian knights but also some of the kings and bishops of his own side, most notably the Parliamentarian, Central Asian traveller and man of undis-guised ambition, George Nathaniel Curzon. More than a decade before Curzon achieved his long-held aim of becoming Viceroy of India (as a stepping-stone to a Cabinet appointment leading in turn to the premiership of Great Britain) the two had formed a mutual admiration society of 'fellow-travellers' with a shared view of the Russian peril, albeit one with a well-defined pecking order. 'Ld Curzon . . . talked away about the mission saying he was convinced the Russians were up to some harm & he was determined to forestall them and that there was no man in India he could trust better than me to carry out his plans,' Younghusband had written after being named by Curzon as his choice for the man to lead the Tibet Frontier Commission. But before that happy moment there had been a dangerous foray into South African politics – a bad case of misjudgement on Younghusband's part since his involvement in the Jameson Raid might have ruined him had it come out – followed by six years in political backwaters, first in Rajputana as a junior Political Agent, then in the princely state of Indore in central India as the British Resident. He had also married unwisely, to a hypochondriac given to 'nerves' who more or less demanded a no-sex clause to their marriage, though a daughter was born to Helen Younghusband in January1902.

The years of stagnation ended for Younghusband on the morning in early May 1903 when he received a puzzling letter from a friend in the Foreign Department up at Simla, begging to be allowed to come with him on his journey. A few days later a summons to confer with Curzon in Simla ended both the mystery and Younghusband's sense of isolation. 'I am to go to Tibet in charge of a very important mission,' he wrote to his father as he journeyed by train to the British hill station. 'Very strictly in confidence, Lord Curzon <u>had</u> intended to send me to Lhassa with an armed force capable of putting down all resistance. The Home Govt would not however agree to this. But they have agreed to a mission being sent to Tibet to meet Chinese & Tibetan representatives & I have been nominated British Commissioner.'

Over the teacups at a gymkhana at Annandale, Simla's sole piece of flat ground, the Viceroy told him the whole story and explained what he wanted of his lieutenant. Again, it was to his father – an old Indian Police officer, long retired, and his closest confidant – that Francis Younghusband told all: 'This is a really magnificent business that I have dropped in for,' he wrote on 21 May.

What has brought matters to this head is that the Russians have concluded, or tried to conclude, a Secret Treaty with Tibet

– though their ambassador in London has sworn to Ld Lansdowne that such a thing is the very last thing in the world that his Govt wd. dream of doing. However, from India, Peking, Paris, & St Petersburg identical reports arrive so evidently an <u>attempt</u> at least has been made by the Russians to get hold of Tibet: and so I am being sent to forestal[l] them and to put our relations with Tibet on such a footing that we will be able to prevent any other power gaining a predominant influence there.

As Tibet Commissioner, Francis Younghusband was to be promoted to full colonel and accorded an armed escort. What was less welcome was that a joint Tibet Commissioner was to accompany him, 'a Mr White at present Political Officer Sikkim, and who, poor beggar, has been there for fourteen years and always looked upon this job as the project of his life. He is very sore at not getting the charge of the Mission but he seems a good chap for [from] what I have seen of him here and of course I will make it as easy for him as I can.'

Claude White was a big, hefty man – 'tall and grey and very well made', according to a late-comer to the mission escort – with an imposing manner and an even more imposing white moustache, more handle-bar than walrus. Eleven years older, White had every right to consider himself, if not Younghusband's senior, then at least his equal, by virtue of his long experience in Sikkim. But although he was very much the *burra sahib* in Sikkim – a 'big man' in the political as well as physical sense – White was not quite the *pukka sahib*, for in Anglo-India's strict order of precedence an engineering background in the Public Works Department (PWD) placed him several rungs socially below the military, or the Indian Civil Service. After training at the Royal Engineering College at Cooper's Hill, White had begun his PWD career with several years as an engineer on the Behar–Assam Railway before being posted in 1888 to Sikkim, where he had supervised the building of roads for an expeditionary force despatched to settle a border dispute between the Tibetans and the Sikkimese. He had then been asked to double the role of engineer with that of a Political Officer in this remote outpost, and had notched up fifteen years there by the time he and Younghusband first met at Simla. As early as 1898 White had made it clear where he stood on the question of Tibet: 'I believe the time has come now to take up a strong position such as would lead to Great Britain becoming paramount in Lhasa . . . The Russians are making progress in the north, and have already, I am informed, tried to make their progress felt in Tibet. We should certainly be there before them.' Here, then, was another man after Lord Curzon's heart.

As sole representative of the British Raj in Sikkim, White exercised a great deal of power in what was theoretically a sovereign Buddhist kingdom ruled by a hereditary monarch, but was in practice administered like any other frontier state within India's borders. A contemporary speaks of him as 'much beloved by all the primitive folk of Sikkim, to whom he was a second father', going on to describe him as 'a tall, handsome man, very simple in his habits . . . just the man to open up the country.' Although upset at having a stranger encroach upon his territory, White took it like a sahib, and Francis Younghusband, initially at least, had only kind words to say about him: 'White', he wrote to his father, 'is quite a good chap and I think we shall get on all right. He is an excellent "local" man & is very patriarchal with these people . . . He must feel it hard having me come over his head like this & I have no doubt Mrs White feels it even more than he does. However they have both been most kind to me and it certainly has been a great boon to me having him.'

As well as the two commissioners, the Tibet Frontier Commission was to have a British representative from the Chinese Consular Service, together with an intelligence, a survey and a medical officer. Initially, Francis Younghusband entertained hopes of bagging the key intelligence post – 'the only billet for a military officer' – for his younger brother Leslie, whose Indian Army career had fallen into the doldrums. However, he very soon learned that the post had already been filled: 'I should like to have got the Small Boy in somehow or other,' he had written, 'but there is a chap in Sikkim now who speaks Tibetan fluently and knows the whole question & I am afraid he will have to come as Intelligence Officer.'

This fluent Tibetan-speaker was a young Anglo-Irishman named Captain Frederick 'Frank' O'Connor, a protégé of Claude

White. The two had first met in 1895 when O'Connor went out to Darjeeling to join a Mountain Battery as a 24-year-old junior subaltern in the Royal Artillery. O'Connor had had the good fortune to be billeted in a little bungalow 'perched on the very summit of the Darjeeling spur', an eyrie that gave him uninterrupted views to the north and south: in one direction the endless plains of India streaked with the silver threads of rivers; in the other, the forested ravines of the Ranjit and Teesta river basins and, beyond, the Kanchenjunga massif and the line of snow peaks that defined the Sikkim–Tibet frontier. 'From the moment of my arrival at Darjeeling and the first view of the snows,' O'Connor wrote many years later, 'I became obsessed and fascinated with the romance and beauty of the whole of this frontier . . . I set to work to learn all I could about Tibet. I devoured every book on the subject that I could lay my hands on and I set resolutely to work to learn the language.' With the help of a Tibetan servant 'of very doubtful honesty but always good tempered and chatty' he had learned spoken Tibetan, and by the end of his first year had acquired 'a pretty fluent flow' of the vernacular.

His interest in Tibetan affairs soon led O'Connor to the Whites' large and comfortably- appointed bungalow at Gangtok, the little township that served as Sikkim's capital. Despite nearly twenty years' difference in their ages the two men hit it off and O'Connor was invited to join White on a tour of Sikkim's northern frontier. Although orders forbade British officers to set foot on Tibetan territory, there was an unwritten understanding that Government turned a blind eye on those who chanced to stray while on *shikar* or hunting expeditions in the Himalayas – provided there was no fuss. White's official position made it impossible for him to contemplate such risk-taking, but O'Connor was not bound by any such constraints. He twice made forays into Tibet, but on the second occasion was spotted by Tibetan border-guards near the Tibetan fortress of Khamba Jong and chased back into India after a brisk fight with 'fists, sticks and stones'. Word of this exploit got out, and he was summoned to Simla to explain himself to the military authorities. He was reprimanded – but then ordered to report to the Intelligence Branch of the Quartermaster General's Department at Army Headquarters, where he was immediately put to work compiling a Sikkim Route Book under Colonel Hamilton Bower of the Survey of India.

O'Connor had now entered the shadowy world of *Kim* and the Great Game. In 1897, with the North-West Frontier ablaze, he was sent to Malakand as the official correspondent of the *Pioneer*, India's most influential English-language newspaper, and then to Tirah, where he witnessed the bloody taking of the Dargai Heights by the Gordon Highlanders. The next years found O'Connor at various postings on the North-West Frontier, one of which took him into Chinese Turkestan for an abortive rendez-vous with some Russian scientists. Then a hawkish Secret Memorandum by O'Connor, arguing the case for a mission to Lhasa to stop the advance of Russia, caught the eye of the 'forward policy' men in the Government of India and brought him back to the Sikkim border in 1902, where he did some more map-making while his friend Claude White settled another grazing dispute with the Tibetans.

A year later, in December 1903, O'Connor again ran across his older mentor at the great tented encampment outside the walls of Delhi that was the scene of the Coronation Durbar, devised and orchestrated by Lord Curzon to celebrate the accession of King Edward VII. Here O'Connor first heard from White of Lord Curzon's scheme to end Tibet's isolation by sending a political mission into the country. He at once sought out Louis Dane, the head of Curzon's Foreign Department, and a week later was back in Darjeeling on secret duty with orders to prepare 'a detailed campaign for a force advancing through Sikkim, either by the Chumbi valley or via Khamba Jong', as well as 'data regarding roads and supplies and other details necessary for military opera-tions'. In Darjeeling O'Connor had a further stroke of luck, acquiring as his assistant an exiled Tibetan named Shabdung Lama, 'a monk who had held high and influential position as secretary to one of the great incarnate Lamas, and had travelled extensively in Tibet, but he had got into political trouble and had been obliged to fly the country. Like many monks of the better class, he was a remarkably intelligent man . . . and he was thoroughly au fait with all the details of the administration, politics, and personalities of his own country . . . He was, in fact, the very man I wanted.'

From Shabdung Lama O'Connor learned that the Dalai Lama was not the supreme ruler of Tibet, as had been generally assumed. Over recent decades a succession of juvenile Dalai Lamas had died in mysterious circumstances without reaching maturity, and all political power had been concentrated in the hands of the Regents who had governed in their names. The present Dalai Lama had somehow managed to avoid the early death his previous incarnations had suffered and was now in his mid twenties, but he was still largely a figure-head. Real power resided with the Kashag, a four-man cabinet of ministers made up of clerics and laymen known as Shapés, who had the right of access to the Dalai Lama. They in turn took advice from a larger body known as the Tsongdu, or national assembly, which was dominated by representatives of the three most powerful monasteries in the land. Then there was the Amban, who represented China in much the same way as British Residents represented the British Government in India's Princely and Native States, but whose degree of influence over Tibetan affairs depended very much on the strength of the grip of the Manchu government on China. Shabdung Lama also proved invaluable in teaching O'Connor the finer points of Tibetan, in particular the *she-sa* or honorific language spoken by Tibet's nobility and higher officials, together with all the diplomatic phrases and courtesies that went with it. He became O'Connor's right-hand man and chief intelligence-gatherer: as the shadowy figure referred to by O'Connor's colleagues as his 'tame lama', he had an important but largely hidden role to play in the months of negotiations to come.

When Francis Younghusband reached the summit of the Jelep La that December morning in 1903, Frank O'Connor was at his side. So too was Younghusband's Bengali clerk, Mr Mitter, probably on foot rather than in the saddle. Claude White was not with the party, however; he had lost his fight for equal status with Younghusband, been demoted to the role of Assistant Tibet Commissioner, and ordered by Younghusband to stay behind to sort out the coolies in Gangtok.

Since their first meeting in Simla in May that year, relations between the two had deteriorated to the point where Younghusband had lost all confidence in the man he now dubbed 'Old

White'. Like many men of slight stature and, indeed, like many of his fellow officers in the Indian Political Service, Younghusband was obsessed with status, a constantly recurring theme in his private letters and despatches. In early July White and O'Connor had been sent by Younghusband across the border to Khamba Jong to set up talks with the Tibetans prior to his arrival. They had been ordered to impress upon the two delegates from Lhasa how important a dignitary Colonel Younghusband was, and to put on a great display of salutes and guards of honour to greet his first appearance – efforts that greatly amused the youngest officer present, Lieutenant F. M. Bailey of the 32nd Sikh Pioneers, who noted in a letter to his parents that 'Colonel Younghusband is trying to make out what a big man he is'.

But the two Tibetan delegates who subsequently met Young-husband at Khamba Jong had signally failed to be impressed. They had been polite and good-humoured – but implacable in their refusal to hold talks until the British had gone back to their side of the border. After railing at the two Tibetan officials for imagining themselves to be 'infinitely bigger men than I am', Younghusband had then directed his wrath at Claude White, who, as he pointed out in a letter to Helen, was 'whole streets below me'. White, in Younghusband's opinion, had made a 'terrible hash' of the opening negotiations. 'He is absolutely useless & even worse than useless in dealing with high officials of an independent nation,' Young-husband wrote to his father from Khamba Jong on 19 July. 'I do not intend to let on about this to the Simla people but am taking up the direct dealing myself now & bitterly regret I ever let him come on alone.' Subsequently Younghusband *had* 'let on' to Simla, and seen to it that White was demoted to Assistant Tibet Commissioner and confined to a supporting role in Sikkim.

With White out of the way Younghusband turned for support to his intelligence officer and translator. 'Frank' O'Connor soon transferred his allegiance from his old mentor, becoming the Colonel's most devoted follower. 'I knew from the moment I set eyes on him, that he was a man whom one could trust implicitly and follow with confidence,' O'Connor later wrote. 'He is an ideal leader of men and no better choice could have been made.'

Over three months of fruitless impasse at Khamba Jong,

Younghusband, O'Connor and the handful of Indian Army officers who had accompanied them as part of the Commissioner's armed escort become a close-knit band. All of them were, in the parlance of the day, 'thrusters', and they took to calling themselves the 'old firm'. In September their numbers were doubled and they were also joined by some civilians, yet they continued to live together under the shadow of the fortress of Khamba Jong in great harmony – and very much to Francis Younghusband's satisfaction. 'Now we have a Geologist & a Botanist on special official visits and a Naturalist doctor Captain Walton who has joined the Mission permanently to do all the Natural History,' he told his father. 'I am in a perfect paradise & enjoy nothing more than wandering through the mountains with the Geologist one day, the Botanist another, then bird & butterfly men.' After years of being stuck in dreary diplomatic posts in the Indian plains, Francis Younghusband had once more come into his own, doing what he loved best and surrounded by a group of like-minded admirers. 'Up till now I have got on swimmingly with everybody,' he boasted in early October. 'The Bengal Govt is doing everything I want: Though I am nominally only in charge of the Mission practically everybody looks to me to run the whole of this bit of frontier.'

During their five months at Khamba Jong the members of the Tibet Frontier Commission were guarded by Sikh and Gurkha infantrymen drawn from three regiments of the Indian Army: the 23rd Sikh Pioneers, two companies of which supplied the main garrison, supported by units of the 32nd Sikh Pioneers and the 8th Gurkha Rifles. Like all Indian Army regiments, these three were each commanded by a handful of British officers, supported by what were known as Native Officers who more or less did the jobs of senior warrant officers and non-commissioned officers in the British Army.

The two Sikh Pioneer regiments were not 'smart' – not the sort that young gentlemen with connections aspired to join – but they were as tough as they came, and well known to Francis Younghusband from his earlier days on India's North-West Frontier. Indeed, it was rumoured that he had asked specifically for their services. Both units were veterans of frontier warfare but unusual in that they fought with a pick-axe in one hand and a rifle in the other, having been raised to take on a dual role combining the duties of a pioneer regiment with that of fighting infantry. The 32nd Pioneers had made a great name for themselves in 1895 at the lifting of the siege of Chitral, when they forced a path through five feet of snow and over the Shandur Pass to bring the guns through, a business in which Younghusband had contrived to get himself involved as a freelance correspondent for *The Times*. The 23rd Pioneers were no less distinguished, having involved themselves in recent frontier operations against the Utman Khel, the Afridis, the Waziris and the Mahsuds. Thus both regiments had come to Sikkim with officers and men who were battle-hardened and eager to test themselves on a new and untried foe.

The 8th Gurkhas were less tried than the Sikhs, having been raised specifically for duties on India's less volatile North-East Frontier. It was ten years since they had seen action, but over the last five months they had proved themselves quite as professional as the Sikhs, and better adapted to working at altitude.

The officers of these three battalions were no less eager to prove themselves, and even the most junior present at Khamba Jong knew of and shared the Colonel's overriding ambition to get to Lhasa. One day towards the end of July the young subaltern F. M. Bailey entered Younghusband's tent at his invitation so that they could compare their collections of Tibetan butterflies. 'He hadn't any that I hadn't got,' Bailey wrote cheerfully to his parents, adding that 'all his room is covered with maps of Tibet with various routes to Lassa marked in coloured chalks so I rather think he may be going on.'

Lhasa was the goal of every ambitious explorer in the West. Only one Englishman had ever reached it, the eccentric Thomas Manning, in 1811. After Manning only two other Westerners had repeated his success, a pair of French priests named Huc and Gabet, in 1845. Thereafter Tibet's natural inaccessibility had been compounded by the xenophobia of the Manchu emperors, who had declared Tibet out of bounds to the rest of the world, thus providing a tantalising lure to every self-respecting Victorian traveller. Once the sources of the Nile had been discovered, Tibet's 'forbidden' holy city became the Blue Riband of exploration. Since 1845 almost a score of daring travellers from the West

– Russians such as Prjevalsky, Szechenyi, Ruborovsky and Kosloff; the American Littledales and Rockhill; the French explorers Bonvalot, Grenard, d'Orléans and the ill-fated Dutreuil de Rhins; Englishmen such as Deasy, Carey, Wellby and Bower; and, most recently, the Swedish explorer Sven Hedin – had set out for Lhasa, but none had got within ten days' march of the holy city. All had been bested by an English spinster and missionary named Miss Annie Taylor, who had got within a week's march before being discovered and briefly imprisoned. Younghusband himself had had a plan to journey to Lhasa in disguise in 1889 foiled by his commanding officer's demand that he do some soldiering instead.

None of this was of particular interest to Bailey. Always addressed by his parents as 'Eric' (to avoid confusion, since both father and son were named Frederick) but known to his brother officers as 'Hatter' on account of his mad-as-a-hatter interest in *shikar*, at this early stage of his adult life young Bailey showed no interest in politics. Like Younghusband, he had been born in India. Their fathers had both served in the Punjab, and after retirement Bailey *père* had come to know and admire young Francis Younghusband through his work as honorary secretary of the Royal Scottish Geographical Society. However, the younger Bailey's presence on the Tibetan frontier was more an accident of regimental posting than the result of any fixing. *Shikar* or shooting for sport was Hatter Bailey's main pleasure in life and he found plenty of it at Khamba Jong, riding into the hills surrounding the camp to stalk *goa* (Tibetan antelope), *bhurrel* (blue sheep) and *Ovis ammon* – the last especially prized among sportsmen for its great curving horns. Bailey's unguarded letters show how from August 1903 onwards Colonel Younghusband and his escort commander at Khamba Jong, Lieutenant-Colonel Herbert Brander of the 32nd Pioneers, did everything they could to provoke the Tibetans into a confrontation. On 12 August Bailey was ordered to take out a section of Sikh sepoys mounted on ponies to a village thought to be hostile. 'We want to start a row & are going to send patrols round like this,' he told his parents. As they approached the village, a group of Tibetans came forward and one raised a hand to seize his bridle: 'I pointed to the handle of my revolver and said I would shoot him if he did. Then they all came round us & begged us not to go [on] as if we did they would all have their heads cut off. We rode on like this for about ¼ of an hour the men begging me not to go on and sticking out their tongues, which is the way they say how do you do. Then as it was raining & beastly cold and I knew they would do nothing else I turned back.'

In a subsequent foray Bailey and his men seized several Tibetans and brought them back to camp as prisoners, yet neither this nor further provocations could stir the Tibetans into retaliation. However, a casual line added to one of his letters in early August read simply, 'Two of our spies in Shigatze have been caught.'

Hitherto, the brake on any advance had not been the Tibetans' refusal to negotiate so much as the continuing reluctance of the Liberal Government in Britain to sanction such a step. Younghusband argued that no progress could be made with the Tibetans 'until we move forward'. His view was shared by Lord Curzon but had failed to impress St John Brodrick, the new Secretary of State for India. Brodrick was an old friend of Lord Curzon but had no illusions about his ambitions. 'I know that George intends ultimately to go to Lhasa,' he declared gloomily to a friend. But he had made it plain to Curzon that there was 'no appetite' among the Cabinet for an entanglement in Tibet.

Younghusband persisted in his efforts to sway the British Government, plying Simla with a succession of rumours of Russian Cossacks advancing on Lhasa or Russia supplying modern rifles to the Dalai Lama, but to no avail. As autumn approached and with it a growing risk that the Tibet Frontier Commission would be snowed in and cut off on the wrong side of the Himalayan passes, the British Government proposed pulling the Commission out of Khamba Jong and occupying the more accessible Chumbi Valley instead. Against this Younghusband protested vigorously: any sign of withdrawal would 'elate the Tibetans, would cause the Nepalese to waver and decide the Bhutanese to rise against us'. Besides, he 'knew the style of country' and there was no cause for alarm. If military campaigns could be waged in India in the height of summer, then there was no reason why they could not be mounted in Tibet in winter: 'I had had as much experience as most people of Himalayan passes, and I knew that passes which are closed for single men or small parties, are not necessarily closed for large parties, which can organise regular shelters and trample down paths in the snow.' It was a risk, of course, but one well worth the taking.

None of these arguments cut any ice in London, and it began to look as if all Younghusband's efforts had been for nothing when the matter of the two spies came suddenly to the fore – initially, in the form of a report from Claude White in Sikkim that two Sikkimese yak-herds had been captured and imprisoned in Shigatse. This was exactly the sort of incident Lord Curzon and Colonel Younghusband had been praying for. White was ordered to lodge an immediate protest to Lhasa, while Younghusband fired off a telegram urging the Government of India to take note of this 'unfriendly act'. Lord Curzon followed up by cabling the Secretary of State for India, and a diplomatic protest was duly made to Peking about the Tibetans' unwarranted seizure of two British subjects who had been going peaceably about their business as traders.

Six weeks later Younghusband was summoned to Simla for urgent talks with the Viceroy and the new Commander-in-Chief. There he was thrilled to find himself on intimate terms with the two most powerful men in the land. With the Viceroy in the chair he argued his case in Council, then sat down with Lord Kitchener and his military staff to draw up operational plans for an advance on Gyantse, the fortress-city that guarded the southern approaches to the Tsangpo valley and Lhasa. His advice was sought at every stage, even to the strength and composition of the enlarged military escort that was to accompany him. 'I said that politically we ought to have some white faces to show up there,' Younghusband wrote to his father directly afterwards:

Kitchener said 'All right you should have a section of a <u>British</u> mountain battery and the maxim gun detachments all of British soldiers and I will give orders that not a single man is to be under six feet.' I thanked him & said that I wd. tell the Tibetans that we only send <u>small</u> men with our guns. The whole interview was very informal & cheery and at the end he told me to write to him privately from up there to tell him how things were going & to ask him for anything I wanted . . . it is much to be in private correspondence with both Ld Curzon & Ld Kitchener.

The outcome of Younghusband's meeting with Kitchener was a beefing-up of the existing Tibet Frontier Commission escort and the appointment of a senior officer with the rank of brigadier-general to command it – a post Francis Younghusband thought just the ticket for his older brother 'Jack', Lieutenant-Colonel George Younghusband, then kicking his heels in Bellary as commandant of the 27th Light Cavalry. Indeed, he thought there might even be a civilian billet going for his wife's younger brother, Vernon Magniac, perhaps as his private secretary.

However, the Home Government had still not come into line, for the Prime Minister, Arthur Balfour, was making it clear to Curzon that his Cabinet still showed 'a strong and unanimous feeling against any permanent entanglement in Tibet'. Some sort of 'rupture' had to take place before the British Government could sanction the sought-for advance. To this 'inveterate flabbiness' Curzon responded with a fierce despatch, dated 4 November, arguing that rupture had *already* taken place, and the seizing of the two Sikkimese was merely the last straw. No sooner had this telegram been sent than fate delivered Lord Curzon further proof of Tibetan belligerence. 'An overt act of hostility has taken place,' he telegraphed in a postscript, 'Tibetan troops having, as we are now informed, attacked Nepalese yaks on the frontier and carried off many of them.'

It was afterwards established by the British Resident in Nepal that this act of Tibetan hostility was nothing worse than the herding of some trespassing Nepalese yaks and their drovers back across the border. But the bazaar rumour served its purpose. This final provocation swayed the collective judgement of a bemused British Prime Minister, his Secretary of State for India and the British Cabinet, and they gave way. On 6 November St John Brodrick sent a telegram to the Viceroy authorising 'the advance of the Mission to Gyantse . . . for the sole purpose of obtaining satisfaction, and as soon as reparation is obtained a withdrawal should be effected'.

That was all Lord Curzon needed. Orders were at once issued for what was now the Tibet Mission to proceed to Gyantse by way of the Chumbi Valley – together with an enlarged escort that had taken on all the characteristics of an invading force. Its fighting arm now comprised six companies of the 23rd Sikh Pioneers and four companies of the 8th Gurkhas, leaving the 32nd Pioneers and two companies of the 8th Gurkhas in reserve at Gnatong in Sikkim, as well as another two Gurkha companies guarding the British camp at Khamba Jong. To the 8th Gurkhas' two antique seven-pound mountain guns 'Bubble' and 'Squeak' were added two ten-pound screw guns from No. 7 British Mountain Battery, and Captain Hadow's two Maxims – the records remain silent as to whether the men who manned this heavy weaponry were indeed six-footers, as Kitchener proposed.

Delighted though he was to get the go-ahead, Francis Young-husband's immediate response was to urge a two-pronged assault, based on a plan drawn up by Frank O'Connor: let the main body advance northwards up the Chumbi Valley under its new commander, while he led a lightning advance from Khamba Jong eastwards across an unexplored mountain range to strike directly at the great fortress of Gyantse. It was a gamble, certainly, but one based on the Nelsonian philosophy that 'the boldest measures are the safest'.

This plan was put to the new escort commander and at once rejected. The success of the advance depended on a secure supply route, which meant proceeding by carefully executed stages from the south by way of the Jelep La and the Chumbi Valley. A dramatic dash across unknown country might well succeed, but even in the best of circumstances it would take weeks for supplies to reach this strike force, months if the passes were closed by snow or the main column opposed by force. There was no question of living off the land, as Colonel Younghusband seemed to think, so that the advance force risked being cut off and starved into surrender – or worse. It took three days of polite argument before Younghusband would concede that his escort commander was probably right.

A month later, as the little army stood poised to begin the climb up and over the Jelep La, Francis Younghusband sent off a last-minute telegram to the Viceroy intended to strengthen the British

Cabinet's resolve. 'Information', he declared, 'that the Tibetans are relying on Russian support, and that Russian arms have entered Tibet, has now been received from several independent sources. It may be assumed as certain that Dorjieff . . . is at present in Lhasa; that a promise of Russian support has been given by him to the Tibetans; and that the Tibetans believe that this promised support will be given to them.' This squib earned him a private rebuke from Lord Curzon and a warning to be more diplomatic: 'Remember that in the eyes of HMG we are advancing not because of Dorjieff', he cautioned, 'or the Russian rifles in Lhasa, but because of our Convention shamelessly violated, our frontier trespassed upon, our subjects arrested, our mission flouted, our representations ignored.'

2

The View from the Jelep La

THE SECOND knot of officers gathered on the saddle of the Jelep La was led by a taciturn Aberdonian named James Ronald Leslie Macdonald. A month earlier Macdonald had been a colonel in command of the large force of sappers and pioneers constructing the new road that would run from Siliguri up through the Teesta Valley as far as Rangpo, and then eastwards to the Tibet frontier at Jelep La. Now he was a brigadier-general and Commander of the Escort to the Tibet Mission.

At this stage Macdonald was known to one and all simply as 'the General': a nondescript, elderly-looking 41-year-old, bald-pated and with a far from luxuriant grey moustache, gloomy and morose by all accounts and in almost constant poor health – but also a thoroughly professional sapper with an excellent service record and, in Colonel Younghusband's early estimation, 'an excellent, sound, solid fellow'. In the months to come a story came to be put about of a plodder, stuck in a third-rate job in the backwoods, accidentally elevated to the command of the Tibet Mission escort due an oversight on the part of General Headquarters because he just 'happened to be the only officer of suitable seniority in Sikkim at the time'. It was a story that stuck.

The truth is that James Macdonald was a very able engineer

officer, described by an obituarist more than twenty years later as 'one of the most brilliant officers of the corps'. Nevertheless, he lacked means and connections, and in those circumstances had done extremely well for himself by the time his name was put before Lord Kitchener as Mission Escort Commander. Macdonald was a fellow sapper, which Kitchener certainly approved of, but his service record also indicated that he was ideally qualified for the role.

A grammar school boy, the son of a military surgeon of modest means, Macdonald had passed out of 'the Shop' – as the Royal Military Academy at Woolwich was known among gunners and sappers – as the outstanding student of his year, winner of the Pollock Medal and Sword of Merit. After two years of engineer training at Chatham he had sailed to India in 1884 as a 22-year-old lieutenant in the Royal Engineers. Most of his early years in India had been spent building railways in Baluchistan and forts on the North-West Frontier, but had included a campaign in which he was mentioned in despatches. After a spell of home leave the promising young captain was offered a plum post in East Africa, as chief engineer and leader of the preliminary survey for a railway to be built between Mombasa and Lake Victoria Nyanza. The survey had been completed and Macdonald was on his way back to the coast when civil war broke out in Uganda. After playing a leading role in the subsequent military operations, which became known as the Christian War of 1892, he arrived in Kampala in May 1892 with a detachment of Indian troops and orders to escort a certain Captain Frederick Lugard, DSO, and party through hostile country to the coast.

During the course of the next three months these two men quarrelled. According to Lugard – another little man with an exaggerated sense of status – this was chiefly over the issue of who gave the military orders, the political officer or the escort commander. According to Macdonald, their differences had more to do with Lugard's intemperate behaviour. 'Lugard was at once for war,' Macdonald wrote in his published account of these years, and 'Lugard had raised a spirit that he could not now control'. Ironically, considering what was to follow a decade later in Tibet, Macdonald at one critical point overruled Lugard to insist on pushing on for the coast with only limited transport and supplies, rather than sending supplies on ahead. 'Events proved I was right,' he had declared, although this was not how Lugard or his later biographers saw it.

This feuding might have been forgotten had Major Macdonald not subsequently been made Acting Commissioner for the Uganda Protectorate and appointed to head a commission of enquiry into charges that Captain Lugard had provoked the war in Uganda by his high-handed actions. Macdonald's subsequent report was a damning indictment of Lugard's bias in favouring Protestant Ugandan converts over the Catholic majority. It would have wrecked the career of a lesser man, but the budding empire-builder was not the sort to take such charges lying down. He had powerful friends and he fought back so effectively that the Colonial Office not only buried Macdonald's report but circulated a list of counter-charges made against him by Lugard.

Yet the fact is that the Colonial Office still thought highly enough of Macdonald to ask for him when in 1897 an experienced officer was required to lead a secret military expedition from Uganda to the Upper Nile to forestall the French advance into the Sudan. In the event, the Juba Mission was aborted and Macdonald found himself instead commanding operations against Muslim rebels that ended with the pacification of the Uganda Protectorate. This was no minor skirmish in the bush. 'For close on nine months,' wrote a fellow sapper, 'the Macdonald Expedition was employed on active operations against the Sudanese Mutineers and Waganda Mahommedans over a wide stretch of country. It was largely due to his outstanding personality that Uganda was later extricated from one of the most grave crises of its history . . . which threatened at one time to drive the British out of the Protectorate.'

It was while Macdonald was engaged in these operations that Frederick Lugard struck back. As Macdonald's brother officer put it, 'while he was bringing his great brain, energy, local influence and resource to bear on combating the serious situation with which Uganda was faced, certain cowardly attacks were made on him in England. Their author, without knowledge of the actual facts, ascribed responsibility for the Mutiny to Macdonald's previous handling of Sudanese malcontents, when acting as Commissioner some years earlier. This despicable accusation has long since been demolished; but a man of Macdonald's sensitive nature felt these unwarranted attacks bitterly.'

Macdonald's response was to set down his own side of the story in a manuscript he intended to publish under the title of 'Uganda in Revolt'. Most unwisely, he also included his own highly critical views of the buccaneering and partisan attitudes of British empire-builders in East Africa. On his return to England in the summer of 1899 he duly submitted his manuscript for clearance, only to be accused by an affronted Foreign Office of a 'breach of confidence' in disclosing the real objective of the Juba Mission, which was to occupy the Upper Nile. His manuscript was subsequently either destroyed, or interred in the deeper recesses of the Foreign Office. Shaken by the FO's hostility, he never again sought to put his views into print. But it is worth noting that in 1900 he was appointed a Companion of the Order of the Bath and gazetted brevet lieutenant-colonel for his services; and that in Uganda at least he won the loyalty of those he commanded. His second-in-command, a Major Herbert Austin, regarded Macdonald as the ideal military leader: a man of courage and good humour who inspired officers and men alike.

Africa was followed by a brief respite in England, where Lieutenant-Colonel Macdonald was placed in charge of the balloon factory at Aldershot. In 1900 the outbreak of the Boxer Rebellion led to Macdonald being sent to Peking as Director of Balloons, a post at which his later detractors sneered while overlooking the fact that he was very soon made Director of Railways for the expeditionary force. A second mention in despatches and the brevet-rank of full colonel followed. Macdonald then returned to India and was employed in military works in Quetta until 1903, when he was posted to north Bengal to command the road-building operations into Sikkim. So when in September of that year a commander was being sought for the escort to the Tibet Mission, Colonel J. R. L. Macdonald was not only in the right place and of the right rank: he was also, to all appearances, the right man. He found himself commanding a group of predominantly infantry officers who were, socially, a distinct cut above him – one, for example, pleased to find himself among fourteen Old Marlburians on the expedition, set about organising an Old Boys' dinner.

We may imagine the General at about mid morning on 12 December dismounting from his pony on the saddle of the Jelep La, holding out his hand for the large telescope and tripod carried by the orderly who was always positioned two paces to the rear of his right shoulder, and then scouring the country spread out before him: the ground falling away below until it met the black pine forests blanketing the lower slopes of the Chumbi Valley, directly ahead the winding side-valley that led up to an open plain dominated by the fortress of Phari Jong, and in the far distance the final mountain range that stood between them and the Tibetan tableland. Although still sixty miles away, the lowering white dome of Chomulhari shone in the sun 'like burnished gold'.

Before ordering the advance the General conferred with the senior members of his staff: his second-in-command and chief staff officer, Major Iggulden of the Sherwood Foresters; Major Bretherton, his 'capable and affable' chief transport officer; Captain Elliott, who now commanded the engineers and road builders; and his ADC, Lieutenant Bignell. On the periphery of this group were other military personnel, among them Colonel and Doctor Laurence Austine Waddell of the Indian Medical Service (IMS), a fellow Scot who had served with James Macdonald in Peking three years earlier and whose local expertise was now particularly useful to him.

Dr Waddell was officially the Principal Medical Officer of the Mission, but he was also British India's leading Tibetologist. Early in his medical career Waddell had been posted as a sanitary officer to Darjeeling, where he became an expert on venomous snakes and the birds of the Himalayas, collecting no fewer than sixteen hundred specimens of birds which he presented to Glasgow University's Hunterian Museum in 1893. More significantly, he had also developed an interest in Tibet, and in Darjeeling had come to know four remarkable Indians who in their younger days were part of that cadre of explorer-spies known as the 'Pundits': in Waddell's own words, 'brave men who, carrying their lives in their hands, are engaged in what Kipling calls the "Great Game", the exploration of the most savage and least known parts of the Trans-Himalayan valleys, and I heard from their lips the stirring narratives of their adventures.' By quite remarkable coincidence these four

Indians had each in their time penetrated Tibet in disguise to reach Lhasa: first the Bhotia Nain Singh Rawat, code-named 'No. 1', who with his sextant back in 1866 had, quite literally, put Lhasa on the map; then his cousin Kishen Singh Rawat, code-name 'Krishna' or 'A-K'; after him the Bengali scholar Sarat Chandra Das, the model for Hurree Chunder Mookerjee in Rudyard Kipling's recently published *Kim*; and lastly an illiterate Sikkimese named Kinthup, the 'Almighty One', code-name 'K-P'.

Austine Waddell first met Kinthup a decade after the Sikkimese completed his pioneering solo trek along the Tsangpo River into India in the early 1880s, an extraordinary journey in the course of which he endured a year as the slave of two Tibetan lamas.* Since then this doughty hillman, described by Waddell as 'a thick-set, active man with a look of dogged determination on his rugged, weather-beaten features . . . and, with the strength of a lion, a host in himself', had accompanied Waddell on a number of private and sometimes illicit expeditions in the Himalayas. With a cook named Achum, they had 'tramped many hundreds of miles along the mountain tracks of the Tibetan frontier, at various points from Garhwal and Nepal in the west, to Assam in the east . . . often at great altitudes, sometimes sleeping in caves to evade the frontier guards, and on several occasions penetrating some days' journey into the territory of the Lhasa Government.'

Waddell was no less keen than Younghusband to reach the *ultima Thule* of Lhasa. In 1892 he, Kinthup and Achum had together, tried to reach the 'mystic citadel' in disguise, complete with surveying instruments secreted in prayer-wheels, hollow walking-sticks and baskets with false bottoms. However, Dr Waddell's blue eyes had proved their undoing, and they had soon been turned back. 'During those years of preparation,' he later wrote, 'I had accumulated such accurate pictures of the land that my ultimate entry into its capital, when it came, seemed but the realisation of a vivid and long cherished dream.' One curious outcome of those years of apprenticeship in the Himalayas was that Waddell gained an extraordinary reputation among the Buddhist lamas in Darjeeling and Sikkim, some of whom came to believe that he was an emana-

---

* Charles Allen, *A Mountain in Tibet*

tion of the Amitabh Buddha, the Buddha of Infinite Light, whose Paradise was said to be in the far West and whose reincarnation was said to be prophesied in their scriptures. This did him no harm as he pursued the studies that culminated in the publication in 1897 of *The Buddhism of Tibet or Lamaism*, a ground-breaking study but one that put forward an image of Tibetan Buddhism as a perversion of the original teachings of Gautama Buddha, and of the priest-monks of Tibet as a debased body of devil-worshippers exercising a malign influence over the country. It was widely read, and the negative image of Tibet it created greatly strengthened the hands of those who argued that the Tibetan people were being held in thrall by a corrupt priesthood.

As an officer in the IMS Dr Waddell had always found it difficult to balance his private interests with his official duties,* but in 1895 his attachment to the Chitral Relief Force on India's North-West Frontier gave him a magnificent opportunity to collect for the Government of India 'those several hundreds of beautiful Greco-Buddhist sculptures, which now adorn the Calcutta and Peshawar Museums'. In 1900, as the principal medical officer of the Peking Relief Force, he tried to repeat this coup, only to find that looters from the Japanese and other international forces present had beaten him to it. Other military expeditions followed, the Mahsud–Waziri blockade in 1901 and the Malakand campaign in 1902. It was while serving on the latter that Dr Waddell first got wind of Francis Younghusband's proposed Tibet Mission. He at once fired off a telegram to the Government of India representing 'the unique opportunity offered by the Mission for procuring from that closed land those manuscripts and books so greatly required by Western scholars'. He also lobbied to secure Colonel Younghusband's 'active support', so that he now came to Tibet with a dual role: as chief of the Mission's medical team and as its 'archaeologist', with a brief to collect objects of antiquarian interest. One sees here the hands not only of that most cultured of pro-consuls, Lord Curzon, but also of Lord Kitchener, for Dr Waddell was given a confidential order to acquire for that ardent collector of ceramics whatever he could find in Tibet in the way of Chinese porcelain.

---

* Charles Allen, *The Buddha and the Sahibs*

When Dr Waddell joined the Tibet Mission he was 49, two years younger than Claude White but the oldest Briton actually attached to the Mission. Like James Macdonald, the doctor had little social polish about him, and to those under him he appeared aloof and uncaring. With him he brought his two 'faithful companions', the lion-hearted Kinthup and his Sikkimese cook Achum. They were later joined by a young Anglo-Sikkimese from Kalimpong named David Macdonald, who proved invaluable as Waddell's assistant and Tibetan interpreter.

Although its members were as yet unaware of it, the invading army had already begun to divide into two camps; not along political and military lines, as might have been expected, but into 'old' hands and 'new'. The former were those who had already spent several months at Khamba Jong and considered themselves to be seasoned frontiersmen. Colonel Younghusband was their chief and Frank O'Connor their cheerleader. They included Lieutenant-Colonel Herbert Brander, the pugnacious commandant of the 32nd Sikh Pioneers, the no less doughty Lieutenant-Colonel Arthur Hogge, commanding the 23rd, together with officers from these two regiments and the 8th Gurkhas who had taken turns of escort duty up at Khamba Jong – among them young Hatter Bailey.

The other camp, led by Brigadier-General James Macdonald, was made up predominantly of staff, transport, supply and medical officers. Not only were they less familiar with conditions in Tibet, but they had priorities very different from those of the front-line fighting soldiers or the political officers. Their prime task was to ensure that Younghusband and the men who guarded him were at all times able to carry out their duties, which meant keeping them fed and clothed, in good health, armed and supplied, and in open communication with their headquarters. Given the hostile terrain, the even more hostile climate and the fact that the Tibetan winter was now upon them, this was no easy task. Nothing quite like it had been attempted before by the Indian Army, but there were a number of dreadful precedents involving frontier operations lodged firmly at the back of every military commander's mind. Two, by coincidence, had occurred in the winter of 1841–2: one in Afghanistan, where an entire British army and its Indian camp-followers had been cut off and destroyed; the other in western

Tibet, where a force of invading Sikhs and Dogras from Kashmir had been similarly isolated and wiped out. In both cases a combination of mountains, cold, over-extended lines of communication and complacency had proved quite as fatal as a belligerent native population. Then there were the two more recent and no less relevant catastrophes that had taken place in James Macdonald's own youth: in 1879 at Isandhlwana, when Lord Chelmsford fatally divided his forces and so allowed spear-wielding Zulus to overwhelm a British infantry battalion by sheer weight of numbers; and in 1885 at Khartoum, when General Gordon was hacked to death by a mob on the steps of his own mission. More recently still, and much closer at hand, were Manipur in 1891 and Chitral in 1895, when British political agents and their escorts were isolated and besieged in hostile Indian states. At Chitral it ended happily and memorably, but few cared to remember the murder of the Chief Commissioner and his staff at Manipur, or the losses among the 4th Gurkha Rifles as they fought their way back to the safety of British India.

By the exercise of due care and deliberation James Macdonald had come out of tight corners in Africa with little or no loss to his troops, and a very similar approach had worked extraordinarily well for his Commander-in-Chief, Lord Kitchener, the hero of Omdurman. So Macdonald had every reason to apply the same military philosophy in Tibet. Furthermore, he was no 'forward policy' man; like his master, he had no overriding concerns about Russia in Asia, and he had no personal ambition to reach Lhasa. He followed orders to the letter, and he expected those under him to do the same. This position put him almost from the start at odds with practically every other British infantry and political officer present.

Even the latest arrivals had caught the urge to push on to Lhasa. Captain Arthur Hadow of the Royal Norfolks was stationed with his regiment at Bareilly in the Indian plains when word came through that Simla had called for a Maxim gun detachment to join Younghusband's escort. 'I believe we shall march right over the Himalayas into Thibet, and possibly to Lhasa, the city of Thibet, in which no white man is allowed to set foot,' he had written enthusiastically to his clergyman father on hearing the news. 'They do not call it an expedition but the "Sikkim Thibet Mission" so I suppose I am a missionary of a sort! The first one in the family after all! though my means of persuasion consists of maxim guns & 12,000 rounds of ammunition. I am delighted with the whole thing.'

It was thus all but inevitable that the political leader of the Tibet Mission and the commander of his escort should not get along. Only a year in age separated the two men but they might almost have come from different planets, so disparate were they in appearance, personality, attitude and approach to a task that required them to work together in almost as close harness as a pair of yoked oxen.

After nearly six months of running the show his own way, Francis Younghusband had to adjust to working with a man who, in his opinion, knew a great deal about road-building and nothing about frontier operations. The job of Mission Escort Commander ought to have gone to brother Jack, who for a start would never have overruled his scheme to strike out from Khamba Jong, as James Macdonald had. But Francis Younghusband had swallowed his disappointment and accepted the military logic of the new arrangement, which was that his Escort Commander was the senior man, with the first and last word in all military matters. Indeed, he had written graciously to Macdonald to say as much, asking that he, Younghusband, should be regarded 'simply as a precious parcel of goods to be carted from one place to another & taken the greatest possible care of on the way'; only once they reached Gyantse would he resume his role as negotiator. This was the sort of jocular remark one man might make to put another at his ease, but Macdonald was not the sort who read between the lines. He took Younghusband at his word, and acted accordingly.

Not everything went smoothly. The makeshift road Macdonald's sappers and pioneers had cut from the Teesta valley up to Gnatong proved unequal to the heavy burden of hooves and boots placed upon it. Much of the track rested on loose shale which rain and landslides washed away in entire sections, causing a series of supply bottlenecks. Yet despite these irritations and delays Colonel Younghusband felt able to tell his father, in a letter dated 24 November, that he had every confidence in his Escort Commander. 'Macdonald', he wrote, 'is an exceedingly cautious methodical Scotchman' but 'an exceptionally pleasant man to work with.' Three weeks later, as the column headed for the Jelep La, he was still of this opinion: 'Macdonald is a good methodical hardworking man & as good a man for this particular job as we wd be likely to find.'

Fourteen-and-a-half-thousand-foot Himalayan passes are not places to linger, and the windswept saddle of the Jelep La was no exception. As soon as the scouts had confirmed the absence of any opposing force, the General gave the order to enter Tibet. Preceded by an advance guard of Gurkha riflemen and two mounted orderlies carrying British flags, Brigadier-General Macdonald and Colonel Younghusband guided their ponies down the steep mountain side.

The rest of the army followed on behind. 'From our feet,' wrote Dr Waddell, 'a stony track sank rapidly down into a deep ravine of dark pine-trees far below us, in which the Kargyu monastery seemed a mere white speck. Diving and then sliding and slipping down the loose shoot of frost-splintered rocks which here formed our track, along which the heavily-laden coolies stumbled footsore and weary and bruised by the rocks, we passed a small frozen lake of green ice; thence descended some 2,000 feet more, and across frozen side-torrents, now solid ice, till we reached the black pine-forest.'

Others in the column may have had their doubts, but not Francis Younghusband: 'It was no ignoble little raid, as ignoble Little Englanders were saying, that we were embarking on. It was an undertaking with every moral justification behind it. And it was a feat which, if successfully performed, would add one more to the triumphs of man over Nature, and bring added glory to the Indian army by whom it was accomplished.' Glory too to the man who had conceived the undertaking and at whose behest the army advanced.

As the main force descended into Tibet a number of late-comers were struggling to catch up, among them Captain William Ottley of the 23rd Pioneers, who had seen six companies of his regiment march off without him, leaving him stuck at Gnatong. A flame-haired Irishman with a powerful streak of derring-do about him, Ottley was the only officer of his regiment to have attended the Mounted Infantry course at Sialkot, and it was this that had kept him back.

The idea of putting infantrymen on ponies in mountain country and employing them not as cavalry but as scouts and skirmishers had been tested on the North-West Frontier and in Burma with some success. Up at Khamba Jong, Hatter Bailey and another officer had tried mounting some of their Sikhs and Gurkhas on Tibetan ponies, and the experiment had worked well enough for the General to order Ottley to raise a Mounted Infantry unit from volunteers drawn from the two Sikh and the one Gurkha regiments. Seventy men had come forward, but there had been no time to find proper mounts before the main column's departure from Gnatong for the Jelep La. Desperate to be part of the advance, Ottley had paraded his volunteers and a number of pack mules on the evening of 10 December – with predictable results. Given the order to mount, several sepoys arrived in the saddle to find themselves facing the tails of their mounts, while those who had failed to tighten the girths sufficiently slid, with their saddles, under their mules' stomachs. Further disasters had followed. 'Mules', wrote Ottley later, 'have a way of herding together like sheep, and pushing and shoving against one another in seemingly aimless manner until they get rid of their loads. The sepoys had not bargained for this manoeuvre, and several dropped to mother earth. Other mules, being of an enterprising spirit, took charge of their riders, and galloped off wildly.'

Although ponies had been found for them next day, only thirty of the men had been considered sufficiently experienced to join the column when it left Gnatong, while Ottley and the rest had no alternative but to grind their teeth and continue their training.

No less frustrated were the newspaper correspondents, each desperate to out-scoop his rivals and all three outmanoeuvred by the authorities in Simla. The first to catch a whiff of something in the air had been Henry Newman, assistant editor of the Calcutta *Englishman*. Newman had come out to India in 1893 to join the staff of the *Civil and Military Gazette* in Lahore, the same newspaper on which Rudyard Kipling had cut his journalistic teeth a decade earlier. Sitting at the same desk, filling precisely the same role, he had sought to model himself on his now very distinguished predecessor – by attempting, as he put it, 'to solve the mysteries of Indian life'. His big break came in 1900 when he was sent to Peking to cover the Boxer Rebellion for a rival paper, the

Englishman, in the course of which he observed that the best transport organisation present was that run by the Indian Army – in which a certain Director of Railways named Colonel Macdonald played an important role.

In the early summer of 1903 Henry Newman began to pick up bazaar rumours that the Government of India intended to invade Tibet and annexe it – rumours which the authorities were quick to deny. But he made enquiries among a small colony of Tibetans living on the outskirts of Calcutta and learned that one of them had received a letter from a relative reporting talk of war in Lhasa. Then came a letter from a friendly tea-planter in Darjeeling hinting that 'something was certainly afoot' up there. Acting on a hunch, Newman caught the train to Siliguri, hired a pony and did a bit of scouting around. He met large numbers of Sikh Pioneers engaged in road-building and was fobbed off with a throughly implausible story about a general coming up for a tiger shoot. His own paper had lost interest by this point, but a friend pulled strings to get him a temporary post as a representative of Reuters International news agency.

Early in December Newman again took the train from Calcutta to Siliguri, this time accompanied by two servants and several boxes of kit each labelled with his name and that of Reuters. Sharing his compartment was a young Englishman who eyed his baggage with interest and introduced himself as Edmund Candler. The two men got talking, and Newman learned that Candler had come out to India to teach at St Paul's School in Darjeeling but later became tutor to a minor Indian princeling, spending his leaves travelling in south-east Asia. Before they arrived at Siliguri, Candler asked Newman about his travel plans – which were to hire a pony and then ride north as far as he could – while remaining rather vague about his own. On arrival, he shook hands and jumped into the little narrow-gauge train which climbed the hill up to Darjeeling.

As Newman enquired about pony hire from the station-master he learned that the stranger on the train was a rival newspaper man, a correspondent for the *Daily Mail*. Furious at being outwitted, he at once paid over the odds for a stout pony 'which served me well and gallantly all through the campaign', and trotted off down the

Sikkim road – without food or bedding, and leaving his servants to catch up as best they could. As he himself later put it, 'the one thing that I had to do was to beat Candler and not allow the *Daily Mail* to get ahead in news . . . But I had not reckoned with the fact that if I had a mad idea, Candler was also wild and reckless.'

Edmund Candler was not a journalist, but he had contributed a number of articles to the Allahabad *Pioneer*, and if he was 'wild and reckless' it may have been because a year earlier he had married a Miss Tooth in Calcutta and now found himself with a wife and baby girl to maintain – and no means of support. He, too, had heard the rumours, and although the *Pioneer* had not offered him a post its proprietor had put in a word with the *Daily Mail* in London. The role of special correspondent now presented him with a wonderful opportunity to make a name for himself, one he was determined to exploit by any means. Having, as he hoped, misled his rival by going to Darjeeling, he procured his own transport and set off for Sikkim without delay. Taking nothing with him other than a poshteen and a sleeping-bag tied to his saddle, he rode all through the day and late into the night. At eleven he stopped at one of the roadside travellers' rest houses known as *dak* bungalows, where he slept for six hours before again climbing into the saddle.

Newman was following the same punishing schedule but, having set off earlier by a more direct route, was now a full day ahead of Candler. However, at the end of the second day Candler learned that his rival was only five hours ahead of him. He set spurs to his pony and by mid morning on the third day had gained another two hours, at which point the exhausted beast died on him. But he had discovered that Newman was intending to stop at the next *dak* bungalow, twelve miles further on, so 'I made up my mind to steal a march on him'. He bought a mule, rode it through the night and passed Newman as he slept, reaching Gnatong 'in time to breakfast with the 8th Gurkhas'. Grubby as he was, Candler was led into the regimental mess by a kind-hearted subaltern and there 'enjoyed a ram [that is, mutton] breakfast and a good deal of chafe about correspondents who "were in such a devil of a hurry to get to a God-Forsaken hole where there wasn't going to be the ghost of a show"'. Not everyone was impressed.

Major William Beynon, commanding one of the five coolie corps based at Gnatong, retailed to his wife how 'a fearful bounder of a man came through who said he was the correspondent of the "Daily Mail". I am sorry for the readers of the "Daily Mail". Colonel Kerr asked me to lend the cad a pony to go on with – anything to get rid of him, so I did.' Having eaten his fill, Candler mounted the borrowed pony and rode on, over the Jelep La to where the mission and its escort were now encamped.

Newman arrived at Gnatong to discover that he had been out-foxed and outridden. But he too pressed on, crossing the Jelep La three days after Candler and now taking the time to enjoy scenery that made him almost believe 'that one is no longer on earth but on the moon. Everything is so hard and bare. Then from the top of the pass one looks down upon serried rows of gigantic firs, stretch-ing far away on each side; very gloomy and impressive they look, rank on rank. I remember thinking to myself as I looked on these stiff and lonely giants that there must be some magnificent shoot-ing in this part of the world.' Although it took him another two days to catch up with his rival, Newman had the last laugh, for while Candler in his inexperience simply waited for a story to break, the professional immediately sat down to file four imagina-tive reports which the Post and Telegraph clerks very obligingly wired down the newly-erected telegraph line.

Two months later Candler and Newman were joined by a third special correspondent, Perceval Landon, representing *The Times*. Landon had connections. He knew Lord Curzon well enough to bandy his name about, had been up at Oxford with Lord Ampthill, soon to deputise as Acting Viceroy when Lord Curzon went on home leave for the summer, and was an intimate of Rudyard Kipling, then approaching the height of his fame as the British Empire's poet laureate. Indeed, with his thick glasses and scrubby moustache he even looked like Kipling, with whom he had worked closely in South Africa during the war against the Boers. He had a private income and saw himself as a gentleman-traveller and man of letters rather than a newspaperman. Nevertheless, he had represented *The Times* as a special correspondent in the recent war in South Africa, and had offered to do so again in Tibet for a handsome fee. But as he settled himself in Landon was unwise enough to remark that he proposed to write a 'big book' about the opening of Tibet – which was precisely what the other two were planning. Although relations remained outwardly cordial, a fierce rivalry developed between the three which mirrored that at higher levels. Here too, there was no disguising the motives which coloured their reports. As Henry Newman put it, 'We wanted to get to Lhasa, and if the Tibetans caved in and made a treaty there would be no hope of getting to that romantic city.'

3

The View from the Potala

A s THE invaders began their descent into Tibetan territory, five hundred miles away to the north-east water was seen to drip from the mouth of one of the bronze dragon-heads that guard the four corners of the gilded roof of the Jokhang, Lhasa's oldest and most sacred temple. There had been no rain, so this was judged to be an omen. Messengers were immediately sent to the nearby state oracle at Nechung Chok, revered by Tibetans as the demon fortress of the Oracle King and Dharma Protector Pehar, to determine what it foretold. The monk-medium at Nechung duly went into a state of trance and became possessed by the spirit of the protector-deity Dorje Drakden. The question was put and, once it had been determined which of the four dragon-heads had dripped, the oracle whispered the ill tidings: an enemy was approaching from the green country to the south.

This enemy could only be the 'powerful elephant of the south', the name used by Tibetans in referring to the British Raj in India. For almost as long as anyone could remember this pachyderm had been constrained by a personification of the most powerful female incarnation in Tibet and its guardian deity, the fierce sow-faced goddess Palden or Dorje Lhamo, whose home was the great scorpion-shaped lake known as Yamdok Tso or Heaven Lake, the waters of which made up the life-essence of the Tibetan state. That personification was Queen Victoria, and it had long been believed that so long as she remained on the throne of England there could be no threat to Tibet. But when the Queen-Empress-goddess entered a state of higher bliss two years before, that protection had ended.

Furthermore, the Nechung Chok oracle's prediction seemed to confirm what had been foretold in a prophecy set out in an almanac for the coming year, designated, in accordance with the sixty-year cycle of the Tibetan calender, the Year of the Wood-Dragon: that there would be 'a great coming forward of robbers, quarrelling and fighting, full of many enemies'. War was proph-esied, and 'troublous grief by weapons'. It would involve the two most important spiritual and temporal leaders in the land, the Dalai Lama, 27-year-old Nawang Lobsang Thubten Gyatso, and his fellow incarnate and political rival, the younger Panchen Lama.

Since being found and identified at the age of five as the thir-teenth incarnation of Chenresig, patron deity of Tibet, the present Dalai Lama had lived a life of monastic seclusion while a regent governed in his name. He had assumed his full powers at the age of twenty in 1895, and had been fortunate to reach that age, since five of his previous incarnations had died in mysterious circumstances before reaching their majorities, and he himself had been the subject of an attempted assassination for which his regent had been condemned and executed by drowning. But the idea of a Dalai Lama thinking and acting for himself had all but fallen into abey-ance, and Nawang Lobsang Thubten Gyatso had, in consequence, spent the first eight years of his majority as little more than a figure-head in matters temporal, devoting his waking hours to religious studies. For generations the Manchus had exercised in-direct control over Tibet through the person of a Resident in Lhasa, known as the Amban. Ever since the Emperor Chien Lung had sent an army to Tibet's aid in 1792 to drive out an invading Nepali army, China had refused to countenance any foreign influence other than her own. So when news reached Lhasa in the late summer of 1900 that a letter was on its way from the Protectress-Queen's Viceroy in India, the Dalai Lama meekly fol-lowed Chinese orders to have it returned unread. A second letter sent a year later in the care of a Bhutanese envoy was again refused, with the Dalai Lama's explanation that an agreement made by his predecessors with the Chinese forbade him receiving or sending any letters. And when, two years on, a small band of British officials and escorting soldiers trespassed and made for the frontier fort of Khamba Jong, the advice given to the Dalai Lama was that this provocation must also be ignored. Besides, he was about to enter a three-year period of intense meditation that could not be interrupted save for the gravest matters of state.

But the hairy-faced *peling* barbarians at Khamba Jong refused to go away. They dug trenches, threw up breastworks, and surrounded their camp with wire barbed with spikes. They had a device that trapped and threw the sun's rays, another that captured and repeated the sound of a man's voice, and there was one man among them whose sole function was to attack the rocks surrounding the camp with a hammer, with no regard to the sanctity of the earth. On the orders of the Tsongdu, the Dalai Lama's chief secretary and a senior military commander, Depon (General) Tsarong Wangchuk Gyalpo, were sent from Lhasa with instructions to order the intruders to withdraw to their own side of the border so that talks might take place. Their requests were ignored. Two Chinese officials representing the Amban came and went, also without any appreciable effect. So too did a high abbot from Tashilumpo, sent by order of the Panchen Lama from his great monastery at Tibet's second city, Shigatse. But the little man with the black beard and bushy eyebrows they knew as Kushab Sahib – Colonel Younghusband – still refused to budge, saying he could talk only with the Dalai Lama or his highest representative. An impasse had been reached, with the Tibetans refusing to negotiate before withdrawal and the intruders refusing to withdraw.

The Nechung Oracle's new pronouncement changed everything, alarming the Dalai Lama no less than his advisers and forcing him to postpone his meditation. A second messenger was sent to seek the oracle's advice on what might be done to avert the impending disaster. The medium's whispers produced no coherent answer, so the attendant monks were forced to clarify for themselves the Nechung Oracle's reply. They trailed their fingers over a slate dusted with powdered lime, and from the patterns deduced that through a combination of spells and the force of Tibetan arms the devil-masked invaders could be repelled.

Tibet's cabinet of four wise men, the Kashag, met in urgent council. One of the four Shapés or Lotus Feet who constituted the Kashag had lived in Darjeeling and knew something of British India, and after they had heard him out the other three members concluded that armed resistance to a British military force was futile, and that they would do well to negotiate. Such pusillanimity was immediately opposed by the assembly of the Tsongdu, dominated by monks with no experience of the outside world and no understanding of modern fire-power. They let it be known that there was a traitor in the Kashag, and when the Nechung Oracle failed to identify the culprit they acted in the name of the Dalai Lama to arrest all four Shapés and place them under house arrest in the Norbulinka, the Dalai Lama's summer palace below the Potala. Four new Shapés were then appointed to the Kashag, one of them Depon Tsarong Wangchuk Gyalpo, the military commander who had negotiated with Kushab Sahib and White Sahib at Khamba Jong. This time the Kashag fell into line and declared that the invaders must be opposed, in accordance with the oracle's advice.

With sealed orders bound to their chests, and halting only to change ponies, messengers rode to all the district capitals in the southern regions of Tsang. At the fort of Phari Jong, which lies thirty miles due north of the Jelep La as the alpine chough might fly, the two local jongpons, or district governors, were told to stand firm and refuse to negotiate. Other district officials were ordered to call up their local militias and send them on to Gyantse, the regional capital. The country's equivalent of a standing army of regulars was put on a war footing, and a regiment consisting of four battalions, approximately one thousand armed men, was despatched from Lhasa under the command of Depon Lhadang with instructions to march to Gyantse. A regiment of approximately similar strength was already based at Gyantse and another at Shigatse, with smaller local units of fifty to a hundred men quartered at district forts such as Khamba Jong and Phari Jong. These units were supported by bodies of cavalry irregulars and militiamen made up of unwilling conscripts, selected by their liege lords in much the same way as knights in early medieval England provided quotas of rustic soldiery for their local baron. The core of the army was made up of Khampa mercenaries from eastern Tibet: tall, well-built men with a swagger who had a high estimation of themselves as a warrior people and were greatly feared by the more peaceable elements of the population because of their predisposition to banditry.

As for arms, the majority carried *mendah* or 'fire-arrows' as their main weapon, together with side-arms in the shape of long, straight swords with heavy, one-edged blades. The *mendah* were matchlocks similar in form but greatly inferior to what the Indian Army knew from its years on the North-West Frontier as jezails. They came with two curved wooden prongs attached by a hinge to the muzzle so as to provide a rest to steady the gun, and they were best used in close-quarter ambush against unsuspecting prey, when there was time to steady and aim the gun while applying a fuse. In battle they were only really effective when fired in a volley, but musketry drill even of the kind employed by Cromwell's New Model Army was a military concept as yet unknown in Tibet. Only a very few Tibetans possessed breech-loading rifles of modern pattern, some brought in from India by traders but the bulk – as Younghusband's Mission discovered – originating in a small firearms factory in Lhasa run by a pair of renegade gun-makers from India's North-West Frontier who turned out replicas based on the Martini rifle. Although not on a par with the Indian Army's Lee-Metford rifle, let alone the British Army's more advanced Lee-Enfields, these were still capable of accurate fire at 500 yards.

At the same time, Tibet's more traditional mechanisms for the expulsion of foreign devils were also brought into play. The Tibetans had come to regard their religion as a far more effective bulwark against an invader than their fighting forces. Three great monasteries surrounding Lhasa, known as the Three Seats and all belonging to the dominant Gelugpa sect, had for centuries played a controlling role in the politics and government of the country. At Sera, Drepung and Gongkar the monks came out in force to chant special prayers that invoked the protection not only of Chenresig and Palde Lhamo but also of the Eight Dolmas Who Protect from Fear, the Guardian King of the South and many other deities in their wrathful aspects. Teams of masked dancers gyrated in the

The Tibetans cast spells against the invaders of the Tibet Mission:
drawing by 11-year-old Ts'an-chih Chen, the son of a Chinese
merchant living in Lhasa

monastic courtyards to the sound of trumpets, conch shells, cymbals
and drums. Crowned sorcerers moulded images in wheaten dough
and cursed them in a series of rituals which involved the drawing of
mystical symbols and the use of such powerful articles of magic as
eagles' wings, snakes' tails, crows' and owls' feathers and three-
headed axes. Spells of entrapment were cast by the weaving of intri-
cate cat's-cradles of string. Arrows were fired and imprecations
hurled at life-size effigies of white-faced men in solar topees, which
were then immersed in cauldrons of boiling oil.

Had Tibet's military commanders been given a greater say in the
many fruitless negotiations that took place with the intruders,
events might have taken a different course, but it is abundantly
clear from the accounts of Younghusband, O'Connor and others
in the British camp that it was the lamas and not the generals who
called the shots – and that these religious figures were tragically

incapable of grasping the true state of affairs. Once the Dalai Lama's more experienced ministers had been arrested and the hot-heads from Sera, Drepung and Gongkar had taken charge, armed conflict became all but inevitable. The Tibetan clergy's lack of worldliness was encapsulated in an exchange that took place at the British camp at Khamba Jong between Colonel Younghusband and the abbot of Tashi Lunpo. 'I inadvertently let slip some obser-vation that the earth was round,' wrote Younghusband afterwards. To this the abbot, who had attained his high office at Tashi Lunpo monastery only after decades of religious study, replied that when Younghusband had lived longer in Tibet and had found time to study, he would learn that the earth 'was not round, but flat, and not circular, but triangular, like the bone of a shoulder of mutton'.

The lives of the abbot and his countrymen followed social pat-terns that from those few Westerners who caught a glimpse of them evoked comparisons with very early medieval Europe, and there was indeed a certain superficial resemblance between Tibet in 1903 and the England of King John in 1203, allowing for the advantages that England enjoyed in terms of climate and geography. Tibetan society had been fashioned by what its people termed Chos, the application of the Buddhist Law as introduced into Tibet by Indian gurus in the tenth and eleventh centuries and reinterpreted over the following centuries to become Vajrayana, the 'Thunderbolt Vehicle' or 'Diamond Path'. But King John's subordination to the Pope in Rome had been in name only. In the nation-states of Western Christendom church and state had long since cleaved in two, whereas in Tibet spiritual and temporal power had fused together to become the closest approximation to theocratic government to be found anywhere in the world.

There were Westerners such as Madame Blavatsky, co-founder in 1875 of the Theosophical Movement, who believed that this theocracy was based on a form of Buddhism that had become cor-rupted over the ages. Among those who agreed with her was Dr Austine Waddell, who took the view that Buddhism had been introduced into Tibet from India in an already debased form and had then become further adulterated into Lamaism – 'a priestly mixture of Sivaite mysticism, magic and Indo-Tibetan idolatry, overlaid by a thin varnish of Mahayana Buddhism'. He believed it to be 'a cloak to the worst forms of devil-worship, by which the poor Tibetan was placed in constant fear of his life from the attacks of malignant devils both in this life and in the world to come'. In Dr Waddell's mind, and in the minds of most of the Britons who accompanied him to Tibet in December 1903, it was these lamas (by which Waddell and others meant the monk-priests of Tibet in general, rather than those who were truly religious teachers) who were chiefly responsible for the mess in which Tibet now found itself: 'The Lamas ruled the country entirely in their own interests. They were not even ecclesiastics; they never preached or educated the laity, but kept the latter in ignorance and servitude, with the result that the Tibetans have become the most priest ridden in the world.' These lamas had 'thrust down the throats of the peasantry that Buddhism consists in sacrifice to idols. They have thus induced the people to lavish all their wealth upon building and beautifying scores of temples, and filling them with idols; and through their power over the latter, the priests, as the sole mediators between God and man, are supposed to be able to drive away the hordes of evil spirits that are ever on the outlook to inflict on the poor Tibetan and his family disease, accident, or other misfortune.'

This thoroughly Presbyterian view of Vajrayana Buddhism and its malign influence on Tibetan society was unjust, but it was perhaps no less distorted a view than the Tibetans' perception of themselves as a uniquely privileged people, inhabitants of a pristine land wherein a primordial wisdom had been preserved from all the corruptions of the outside world.

The Tibetan world-view had taken shape in the wake of the Mongol invasion early in the thirteenth century, at a time when Tibet was a country divided into warring factions and rival schools, each promoting its particular interpretation of Chos. The Mongols had soon withdrawn, but not before adopting Tibet's Vajrayana Buddhism as their national religion and establishing themselves as temporal protectors of the Buddhist faith in Tibet. This 'Elder Brother' patronage led to Mongol intervention in 1635 in a civil war between Lhasa and Shigatse, when Gushri Khan threw his weight behind Nawang Lobsang Gyatso, the so-called 'Great' 5th Dalai Lama, leader of the Gelugpa school of Buddhism, popularly known as the Yellow Hats. His protection enabled the

Dalai Lama, and subsequently his successors, to become unchallenged rulers of a centralised Tibetan theocracy based in Lhasa. It also enabled the Gelugpa monastic order to become all-powerful in central and southern Tibet. A century later the Mongols gave way to the Manchus of China, who became the new Elder Brothers and continued to control both Tibet's external relations and, through Chinese Ambans and Chinese-appointed regents, her internal affairs. Manchu xenophobia effectively closed off Tibet from the outside world.

By the start of the nineteenth century Tibet was trapped in a cycle of social and economic stagnation from which there seemed no escape. Nearly every acre of cultivable land, pasture land and forest, as well as most of the livestock, was in the hands of Tibet's thirty or so aristocratic families and the monastic orders. Each noble family had allied itself to one or more of the larger monasteries, and both parties became ever more interlocked, powerful and wealthy. The administration of the country was theoretically shared between the clergy and the nobility; but in practice the former held the reins, since the latter were entirely beholden to the Dalai Lama and the order of which he was the religious head. The aristocracy acknowledged him as their overlord, held their great estates only by his permission, and were required to provide a regular cadre of civil servants as well as militiamen when required. The failure of a succession of Dalai Lama minors to reach maturity and so acquire full ruling powers led to the Gelugpa monasteries gaining greatly in strength, authority, and the ability to resist any changes that threatened their ascendancy or the loss of the many privileges they had gained for themselves over the years. At the time of the Younghusband Mission, Drepung Gompa was the mightiest of Tibet's two and a half thousand monasteries, and, with a population of monks rumoured to approach ten thousand, probably the largest monastery in the world. Not for nothing was it called the Rice Heap: it owned one hundred and eighty-five manors and three hundred pasture-lands, together with a workforce of more than twenty thousand peasants and sixteen thousand herdsmen. These were all serfs, who made up the bulk of Tibet's population, at that time amounting to anywhere between one and two million souls. The serfs possessed little or no land or livestock of their own, provided unpaid corvée labour to the landowners, and were taxed on whatever they managed to produce for themselves. An unknown but significant number of the peasantry were bonded slaves and, according to the harsh legal codes of the time, their lives were valued at the price of a straw rope; they could be sold or punished at will by their owners, and they had to pay hefty redemption fees if they wished to marry or secure their freedom. For this oppressed under-class mere existence was harsh in the extreme, with high rates of infant mortality and a short life expectancy.

Only Chos offered an escape. Many families chose to give their second and subsequent sons to the monasteries at an early age and (to a lesser extent, since there were fewer of them) their daughters to nunneries. Here they were housed and fed, were given an intensive religious education and the opportunity to develop their talents as painters, clay-modellers or wood-carvers, and in general lived longer and easier lives. For the peasantry quite as much as for the clergy, the Buddhist faith, coupled with an unshakeable belief in the power of the spirit-forces of nature, was their great consolation. Their devotion to Chos was absolute: it gave them hope, brought meaning to their lives, even helped to shape the national character of a people who were in general cheerful, good-humoured, patient, tolerant and fatalistic, with no great desire to challenge or improve their lot. Whatever their present situation, it was of their own making, for every being on earth was trapped by its particular weaknesses and delusions in an endless cycle of birth, death and rebirth. Only by attaining perfect understanding could one escape from this cycle of suffering. In the monastic orders, the Perfect Way might be followed through the study of the ancient *sutras* and in the esoteric meditative practices of the *tantras*. But even those who lived outside the monastery walls could shorten the cycle by their own efforts: through the constant recitation of mantras, the turning of hand-held prayer-wheels, the performance of charitable deeds, and the undertaking of rigorous acts of religious piety such as pilgrimage.

Religious devotion was also a national duty, for even the most ignorant serf knew that Tibet was the 'inner land', the very heart of true Buddhism. Their devotions helped to keep that true Buddhism alive and safe. The enemies of Chos had triumphed in the south, the west and the east, but so long as they devoted themselves to its cause Tibet itself would remain inviolate. To this end, a family of nomadic yak-herders would far sooner burn its surplus yak-butter at the altars of the nearest monastery or temple than sell it at market. Thus Chos pervaded every aspect of social life in Tibet, to the extent that the two were to all intents indivisible.

Some countries devote all their resources to nation-building and military expansion; Tibet chose the diametrically opposite path. Awesome as this national piety was, it was greatly to the detriment of the Tibetan economy and very much to the advantage of its religious houses. This might not have mattered if the country's resources had been considerable, or if its population of providers had expanded to keep pace with its main consumers, the celibate monastic orders. But when a nation's gross domestic product is expressed largely in terms of prayer, meditation, study, pilgrimage and religious art, and its productive population is small, scattered and static, the final outcome can never be in doubt. In other Asian countries where Buddhism flourished, monastic communities had always depended on the patronage of a wealthy mercantile community. But in Tibet there was no such community of any significance. A point of no return was reached probably at the start of the nineteenth century, just as the climate of the Tibetan plateau entered something approaching a minor ice age. The country's agricultural and diary yields fell, its population went into decline, and year by year less revenue was available for Tibet's administrators to spend on maintaining the state. Half-hearted attempts to impose taxes on the nobility and the monastic orders failed, as did more serious attempts to place heavier tax burdens on the peasantry. Forts, bridges and roads fell into disrepair, internal and external communications began to break down, and outside Lhasa and Shigatse the provinces became increasingly isolated. Tibet slipped into a state of semi-paralysis, having entered that fatal state of non-viability that had brought about the downfall of every great Buddhist theocracy in the past, from Ashoka's Mauryan empire in India to Ankor Wat in Cambodia – a condition that only outside intervention could change.

News of the advance of the great elephant of the south failed to rouse Tibet from this torpor. There was concern in Lhasa, for it was believed that the British were among the enemies of Buddhism, but there was no great alarm, because it was known that the prayers of the people were more than enough to keep Tibet inviolate, with or without the intervention of Tibet's protector-deities. The idea that the invaders might reach Gyantse, let alone Lhasa, was too fanciful to be taken seriously. The generals and their armies were sent south, but with the Dalai Lama's prohibition against attacking the invaders ringing in their ears, for in accordance with Buddhist precepts against violence they were given orders to 'check them but not fight them'.

4

The Advance on Tuna

THE DESCENT from the Jelep La into Tibet proved quite as difficult as the climb. Whereas on the southern side of the pass the snow had melted away, here it had frozen into hard ice. The track, 'as steep as the side of a house, became a regular slide, as slippery as glass', sending men and horses sliding and tumbling down the slope. After descending some two and a half thousand feet the army reached the tree-line, when the General gave the order to make camp in the shelter of the pines. 'Here', wrote Austine Waddell, 'on the banks of a half-frozen rivulet we encamped on a springy bed of pine-needles amongst fallen pine-trunks, which latter were soon converted into welcome log-fires, and afforded us a hot cup of tea until our baggage animals came up and were unloaded and tents pitched.'

As the officers stood drinking their tea a party of Chinese officials in colourful silk robes rode up from below, each with an umbrella of honour held over his head and accompanied by foot-soldiers armed with halberds and spears. Among the party were a smiling young Tibetan who wore in his left ear a four-inch-long gold earring studded with pearls, and Captain Parr, a British officer employed by the Chinese Government as their Customs Commissioner and based at the Tibetan frontier post of Yatung, two miles below the British camp. Through Captain Parr, the Tibetan introduced himself as the Depon or military governor of Phari, and thus the administrator of the Chumbi Valley. He requested that Younghusband retire across the frontier so that talks could take place. The Tibet Commissioner declined to do so; he had waited long enough and now intended to go on into Tibet – and if his passage were opposed, General Macdonald had orders to overcome the opposition by whatever means necessary. With this, the Chinese and the Tibetan governor mounted their ponies and rode away in silence.

Long after dark, weary and footsore coolies continued to stumble into camp, and as the officers sat down to their supper they learned that an entire corps of five hundred coolies had refused to carry their loads up to the pass, while further down the road scores of conscripted Nepali porters had deserted. Fed by bazaar rumours of massed Tibetan armies waiting for them up ahead, they believed the Anglo-Indian force to be advancing to its doom. The officers of the coolie corps were mostly drawn from the Gurkha regiments, able to speak Gurkhali and used to hand-ling hillmen, but they now found that the only way to impose dis-cipline was by taking harsh measures. Major William Beynon, DSO, of the 3rd Gurkhas was an ambitious man and so determined to be in on the Tibet show that he had agreed to a temporary posting as a 'coolie-driver' as a means to this end. His response to the strike was to round up the mutinous coolies and have them flogged. 'I had the beggars tied up across some gram [parched grain] bags,' he wrote to his wife Norah, 'and well flogged in front of all the coolies & then put in guard – I then gave the coolies ½ an hour to collect their kit & get started with loads & they went off like lambs. I have told them that henceforth I would treat them like dogs and I am. If a man is at all slow in obeying an order I knock him flat. I think they understand that the time for fooling is past. I expect a good many of them will bolt but it can't be helped.' Despite such harsh measures coolies and other camp-followers continued to desert, making it increasingly difficult for Major Bretherton, the chief transport officer, to maintain the steady stream of supplies that the advancing column required.

Before the soldiers retired to their tents every infantryman was ordered to wipe as much oil from the bolt of his rifle as possible. Tired, depressed and with pounding headaches, the men then crawled into their sleeping-bags – the wise ones taking their boots with them – believing that the moment of confrontation was fast approaching

Though the temperature dropped sharply during the night, the men rose next morning to find their headaches gone and the air crisp and dry. The column moved forward in good spirits, descending 'through a forest of silver firs, crossing many frozen hill torrents which were now sloping sheets of solid ice, which, filling up the hollows, formed literal "death-slides" where the mules and baggage animals slid at every step'. Soon they reached a clearing in a narrow defile that marked the trading mart of Yatung, defended by a stone wall stretching across the valley and up both sides. There was a gate at the centre which had been left open, and this Colonel Younghusband took to be a good sign, but as he urged his pony through a Chinese soldier stepped forward to seize his reins. The Colonel brushed him aside and continued.

What ought to have been a moment of high drama was marred by the noisy intervention of 'Ani Memsahib', a middle-aged white woman dressed in Tibetan costume who turned out to be Miss Annie Taylor, a formidable Scots spinster who had made it her mission in life to convert the Tibetans to Christianity, the same Miss Taylor who had probably got closer to Lhasa than any other Westerner in the last half-century. Although discovered and sent back to the Chinese border she had subsequently browbeaten the Tibetans into allowing her to establish herself at the trade-mart at Yatung – largely, it was said, because her first name was the same as the Tibetan word for 'nun'. Since then Ani Memsahib had made only one convert and, according to Captain Parr, had become an 'intolerable nuisance'. According to another observer, she had also become worryingly 'native', adopting Tibetan dress and habits. Even her Christianity seemed doubtful to this same observer, who noted that throughout their brief meeting Miss Taylor 'kept up a running low chant almost below her breath of "Mani Pad-me Hum", the well-known formula of Tibetan Buddhism'.

Miss Taylor's loyalties were by this time deeply divided. She believed the expedition would open friendly relations between

Britain and Tibet, thus making missionary work easier, but she was also greatly concerned that there would be violence – so much so that she had fed Colonel Younghusband a succession of tall tales of Tibetan armies poised to attack and of Russian soldiers massing in Lhasa that the Colonel was happy to pass on to Simla. She also wrote to the newspapers, pleading for a better understanding of the Tibetan position. In a letter published in the *Morning Post* at around this time she argued that they faced an irreconcilable dilemma: 'They have to chose between death and dishonour at the hand of a Chinese executioner if they offer no resistance to the advance of the mission, or death with honour by resisting the advance, and like brave men they choose the latter.'

Now, as Colonel Younghusband advanced through the gate, Miss Taylor descended on the party, shouting for the Colonel to identify himself and, once she had located him, deluging him with questions about his religious beliefs. Only after she had professed herself satisfied was Younghusband able to speak to the most senior Tibetan, the Depon whom he had met the previous evening. Seating himself on a boulder, he listened to what the military governor had to say: 'A large crowd gathered round while I let him repeat at any length he liked – for his own satisfaction & the benefit of the crowd – his protests against our advance. Then I told them all our reasons for it & the meeting broke up in great good humour & I patted the Tibetan general on the back telling him he had done what was wisest, and then we adjourned to Parr's house where Parr first gave us an enormous lunch & then the Chinese and Tibetan official sent in a meal and themselves came and sat down with us to eat it.'

As all parties tucked in to an array of dubious Chinese delicacies – 'sharks' fins, birds' nest soup, putrid black eggs etc.' – healths were proposed, glasses were clinked and it was smiles all round. 'An excellent beginning,' noted Younghusband, as his troops streamed through the gate and on down into the valley below.

The column soon emerged onto the open floor of the Chumbi Valley, which evoked comparisons with the finest scenery to be found in the alpine valleys of upper Kashmir: 'Craggy mountains rise on either side into jagged snow-streaked peaks banded by dark pines, and between, the clear green waters of the Mo [Amo] river wind noisily in their shingly bed through grassy meadows and fields.' These meadows were sprinkled with the remains of the previous summer's wild flowers – 'primulas, anemones, wood-sorrel, celandines, wild strawberries' – and dotted with small settlements whose houses looked remarkably like Swiss chalets, two and three storeys high with projecting eaves and carved wooden balconies. Instead of the hostile army they had been led to expect, a bemused male population stared 'in open-mouthed astonishment at our invasion of their valley'. Once it was clear that they were not to be massacred on the spot, the men were joined by their womenfolk and children, and were soon occupied in supplying the British camp with corn, meat and fodder. For some of the late arrivals this was their first opportunity to observe Tibetans at close hand. 'They are a curious looking people,' mused Arthur Hadow in a letter to his parents. 'They are rather like a cross between a Chinaman & an Esquimau!'

The column's advance now took it up the main valley to the village of Chumbi, following the fast-flowing Amo Chu. Every turn revealed glimpses of snowy peaks beyond variegated clumps of willow, birch and pine and, closer at hand, bare fields divided by low stone walls. 'Flocks of finches and red-legged crows were foraging,' wrote Dr Waddell of this ornithothologist's paradise, 'with larks overhead whose joyous notes awoke memories of home; flights of snow-pigeons shot swiftly by; whilst the bark of a silver fox on the hillside suggested pheasants and other game in the uplands.' Others shared his enthusiasm for this delightful country. To transport officer Lieutenant Mark Synge, the Chumbi Valley resembled 'a sheer Garden of Eden . . . a place to dally in, in which to wander about accompanied by your best girl, picking wild flowers for her, and listening with her to the humming of the bees, and the bubbling of laughing brooks, rather than a place to concentrate an army for an advance into the enemy's country.'

They passed their first Tibetan monastery, perched high on a cliff against the skyline, and closer at hand Dr Waddell observed other manifestations of the Buddhist faith, in the form of white-washed stone monuments called chortens and prayer walls faced by carved slabs of stone 'bearing the mystic legend of the Grand Lama, "*Om*! *Ma-ni pad-me Hung*!", each syllable painted in a different colour, and bordered by the tall poles of the "Prayer-flags", which are the favourite perches of redstarts and hoopoes.'

The original plan had been to set up a forward headquarters at Chumbi village, but General Macdonald declared the position to be unsuitable for defence so scouts were sent out and one more secure was found a mile and a half further up. This new site proved to be uncomfortably exposed to the north winds, but by then 'New Chumbi' had become too well-established to be abandoned.

The General's next objective was the great fortress at Phari, Phari Jong, 28 miles further up the valley. Two of Frank O'Connor's network of intelligence-gatherers had brought news that they should expect armed resistance there, so a flying column of eight hundred fighting men was put together to march on ahead and, if necessary, take the Jong by force. This led to a second mass desertion of camp-followers, mostly of Lepcha and Bhutanese coolies, convinced that disaster was about to strike them. Nevertheless, on the morning of 18 December General Macdonald led his eight hundred men northwards through a narrow gorge known as Gab Jong or the Vulture's Fort, across which a second stone wall had been built. A handful of determined riflemen could have held off an army here but, unaccountably, the Tibetans had chosen not to defend it – and, again, the gate in the stone wall had been left open. Among the porters and ponymen who remained with the flying column there was now talk of their being drawn into a trap from which there could be no escape.

From Gab Jong the path zigzagged across a vast landslip which had blocked the valley some centuries earlier to create a long, narrow lake that had then silted up into a magnificent grassy meadow flat as a billiard table, half a mile wide and about three miles from end to end. It formed a natural encampment, and there was exited talk among the officers of turning what they named Lingmathang Plain into a hill-station. Dr Waddell took the lead in extolling its advantages over Darjeeling as the future sanitorium for Bengal: 'In this belief I went around and selected sites for hotels and hydropathic establishments, with graduated exercises in walking and climbing through the woods above the golf links in this delicious alpine air.'

By riding late into the night with his squadron of newly trained mounted infantrymen Captain William Ottley had caught up with Macdonald's force, and he now took his place at the head of the flying column. The next morning with fifty of his men he went forward to scout the trail, which led them through 'great masses of sharp-cornered rocks which bruised the feet and bodies of both men and the struggling beasts'. Their surroundings grew increasingly rugged, with 'great overhanging naked cliffs of blackened granite' closing in on all sides. Soon the pines gave way to silver birch and then at 14,000 feet Ottley and his men emerged onto 'open, bare, wind-swept uplands, furrowed into bright red and ochrey yellow and purple streaks from the shaley formation of the Tibetan plateau'. It was their first intimation that they were approaching the fabled Chang Tang or Northern Plain, the so-called 'roof' of Tibet.

A mile-long trudge over undulating grassy slopes brought them just before sunset to a patch of open ground named Do-tak, the Rocky Stones, where the flying column camped below a hundred-foot-high frozen waterfall of ethereal beauty. Here there were no trees to give them shelter or fuel, and as night fell the temperature plummeted to minus eleven degrees Fahrenheit and falling. Again, officers and men had to wait for the mules and porters to arrive with their baggage and tents. An icy wind sprang up, chilling them still further, and it soon became apparent that every scrap of clothing was going to be needed to get them through the night: 'Before creeping into the sleeping-bag and strapping the canvas cover of the valise over the whole, we put extra clothing on to our already thick day wear. The sleeper lay on his back, since a sideways turn would open a leak of air into the bag.' But even then there was no escape. 'The terrible intensity and penetration of the cold of this wind was excruciating,' wrote William Ottley:

> it seemed as bitter in our tents as outside; our felt boots gave no warmth to our benumbed feet, and none of us, shivering as we were in our sheepskins, could sleep during that awful night. The poor chilled troops and followers, huddled cowering together in their tents, kept up around us a chorus of coughs and sneezes till day broke. It was a marvel that no one died, except a few of the

mules, and that there were so few cases of frostbite. At last the day dawned in the arctic region, the wind died down, and we began to venture out in the sunlight. A comical sight we were, as, wrapped up in our furs with livid blue faces, we stamped about for warmth, our breath falling in snowflakes, or frozen into long icicles on our moustaches and beards.

One officer had unthinkingly placed his false teeth in a tumbler of water, only to find it frozen solid, 'his dentures in the midst like a quail in aspic'. However, the miseries of the night were soon forgotten as the sun flooded the valley. They struck camp and continued their advance, and within three miles found themselves upon the 'bare waste' of the Phari plateau, an open plain so constantly swept by bitter winds as to have given rise to a popular expression, 'When rice grows on Phari Jong', the Tibetan equivalent of 'When pigs fly'. Here the long winding thread of the column was reordered into an extended front, with sections of the Mounted Infantry riding a mile off on either flank: 'In this order our little army advanced across the plain, bounded on either side by round-topped bare hills, above which towered, only about twelve miles away, the snow-capped chaste Chumolhari . . . On the plain, several gazelles (*Ga-wa*) were quietly grazing within shooting distance, but were safe from us, as no shooting was allowed on the march; and on the hills a glimpse was got of the wild blue sheep (*Barhal*, or, as the Tibetans call them, *Na-wa*).'

They crossed several broad streams of frozen water, the ice of which was thick enough to bear the weight of men and beasts. Then, quite suddenly, they rounded a low bluff and Phari fort came into view, a cluster of low stone houses at its base.

Although dwarfed by the backdrop of the great white peak of Chumolhari, the fortress of Phari Jong, the Keep of the Hill Made Glorious, was nevertheless an imposing sight, towering over the bare, windswept plain like a castle from a fairytale, its stone bastions and central keep giving the appearance of 'great massiveness and strength'. Ottley's Mounted Infantry were ordered on and as they trotted forward they could see a great commotion taking place, the Tibetans 'buzzing about like bees'. Expecting at any moment to be fired upon, Ottley gave the order to spread out and ride hard: 'But no! We were again received with open arms and open doors.' A deputation of townsmen came out to meet them, their tongues stuck out to signify their submission and to make it plain they offered no resistance. Although Ottley found it hard to believe – 'we thought it impossible that the Tibetans would be such fools as not to hold this place' – it soon became evident that the Depon with the golden earring had abandoned the fort.

Sending one of his mounted infantrymen back to the General with the good news, Ottley skirted the fortress and pushed on to scout out the next obstacle on their path: the ridge that made up the last link of the Central Himalayan Range. Unlike the earlier pass, the Jelep La, which had steep approaches on both sides, this second barrier was less dramatic and the climb to its summit more gradual. The crossing point was the 15,200-foot Tang La, the Clear Pass – so named because its exposure to the winds meant it was usually clear of snow – which they reached after a gruelling seven-mile ride. The slower slopes of Mt Chumulhari now towered above them 'like a perpendicular wall of snow'.

These were early days for the Mounted Infantry, but Ottley was determined to prove their worth. He was the kind of young officer whose leadership from the front brought out the best in his men and they responded by giving him their all. Their ponies, however, were utterly exhausted. 'Mine lay down under me and began to eat grass,' recorded Ottley. 'They were greatly in need of water also, for all the streams we had passed were frozen solid, and, much as the ponies tried to break the ice with their forefeet, they could not get a drop to drink.' From the summit of the pass they could see far across the Chang Tang, and in the rarefied air could even make out a cluster of three stone buildings nine miles distant and beyond them the waters of a lake: the Tibetan summer settlement of Tuna and the waters of Bam Tso. Of Tibetans there was not a sign.

It was too cold to linger so they turned back, walking to spare the weakened ponies. Ottley spotted his first Tibetan gazelle, a buck which he stalked and shot: 'His horns were 13¼ inches, which is a little above the average.' They arrived back at Phari Jong long after dark, having covered during the day a distance of thirty-five miles. Only now did Ottley discover that the loose serge trousers worn by his men for want of regulation riding breeches had chafed their inner thighs so horribly that many were bleeding and barely able to walk. To cap it all, his exhausted ponies refused to settle and fights broke out periodically throughout the night: 'The ground was frozen so hard that what pegs there were, both iron and timber, could not be driven into it; so we tied the ponies in rings, and if they had not been such bad-tempered little brutes they would have been safe enough. They spent most of the night careering through the General's camp, and I was hauled over the coals next morning.'

To the indignation of some of the troops, Phari Jong had fallen into British hands without a shot being fired. Two companies of Gurkhas were now in possession of the citadel, having ousted scores of Tibetan women in the process. These turned out to be the wives and dependents of the fort's military garrison, which had not fled as had been thought but had been transferred north in a bid to stop an anticipated British advance from Khamba Jong. What was no more than a stroke of luck was trumpeted by the special correspondents as a great coup for Brigadier-General Macdonald: 'By a swift and secret swoop he was able to seize this great mobilisation centre of the Tibetan troops, with its tons of gunpowder and bullets, without firing a single shot . . . We had now got possession of that fortress which dominates the great trade route to India, and had obtained peaceful possession also of the almost invincible lower ravines, which, if held by the Tibetans against us, could not have been captured without very much bloodshed on both sides.'

Phari Jong turned out to be far less imposing within than without. Its courtyards were strewn with 'old lumber, chain-armour, iron helmets, spears, matchlocks, and miscellaneous rubbish' and its interiors found to be a warren of narrow passages and cave-like, malodorous and dingy cells. In a small chapel Dr Waddell discovered and appropriated his first cultural trophy: a set of religious texts known collectively as the Kanjur, 'the Tibetan version of the Buddhist Scriptures in 100 volumes'.

The best rooms were to be found on the top floor of the citadel, the quarters of the fort's joint magistrates, the Jongpons. After

many basketfuls of dirt had been removed these became the headquarters and officers' mess of the new garrison. Fires of dried yak-
dung were lit to warm them up, but seemed to produce little heat
and a great deal of acrid smoke. 'The thawed ink froze on our pen,'
recorded Dr Waddell, 'boiled eggs crunched in ice-spangles in our
teeth, and some kerosene oil which I had brought froze solid and
had to be thawed before it could be poured into my lantern.'

It very quickly became apparent to its new occupants that the
outstanding quality of 'Phari-the-Foul' was its dirt. There was
general agreement that the huddle of houses in front of the fort
constituted 'the filthiest and foulest town on the earth'. According
to Dr Waddell, 'Its benumbed villagers for generations have been
throwing all their refuse immediately outside their doors into their
streets, where this accumulated dirt of ages has raised the level of
the streets so high that the dingy rooms now seem subterranean
cellars, entry to which is got by digging steps down through the
layers of this garbage. It is indeed a vast barrow in a muck-heap,
with an all-pervading foul stench everywhere.' Phari's townspeople
Waddell judged to be at one with this squalor, being 'sunk in
almost the lowest depths of savagery', and 'more like hideous
gnomes than human beings'. Clothed in 'greasy rags and sheep-
skins, their ugly flat features scourged by the cold and seared by the
frost, begrimed and blackened like a chimney-sweep's with the
deeply ingrained dirt and smoke of years, they were repulsively
hideous'. Perceval Landon shared his opinion but did find one
redeeming feature:

Ingrained dirt to an extent that it is impossible to describe
reduces what would otherwise be a clear, sallow-skinned, but
good-complexioned race to a collection of foul and grotesque
negroes. It is, of course, difficult to say what the effect would
be if some of them were thoroughly washed . . . [but] one thing
in common fairness must be said, and that is that nowhere in
the world will you find such exquisite teeth in men, women,
and children alike as in Tibet, though it is beyond dispute
certain that no tooth brush or any form of cleansing them has
been practised, or indeed known, from one end of the country
to the other.

What no European yet understood was that Tibetan women smeared their faces with a red paste that blackened as it oxidised. This was done not to improve their looks but to protect their skins from the damaging effects of the sun at high altitude. And if they smeared their bodies with butter, it was not because they liked the rancid odour but because it provided a protective coating against the cold. Furthermore, as anyone who has wintered at 14,000 feet or above knows all too well, frozen water and frozen soil make sanitation a problem for the fastidious. As Dr Waddell and his companions were only just beginning to discover for themselves, to survive on the Chang Tang in winter one had to make many sacrifices. Within a matter of days they too began to take on 'an almost Tibetan aspect and condition'. No one cared to set down in writing the more intimate details of these sacrifices but, as Lieutenant Leonard Bethell's jocular account makes plain, they were extensive:

Personal cleanliness went by default. Had there been fuel to spare for hot water, the bath would have suffered the same fault as the teacup. There was no shaving, and a most atrocious beard disguised everybody. A change of underclothing became a risky adventure, rarely to be indulged in; and since going to bed involved only the addition of more clothing to that of the day, the matter was steadily overlooked. The writer remembers two pairs of thick socks, pulled one on top of the other at the beginning of November, the start, and removed on Leap Year's Day. The legs and feet were normal, but the soles had been compacted into a kind of hard felt which resisted separation and, force being used, snapped like a biscuit.

Because supplies of food and fuel were limited, the bulk of the flying column had soon to return to New Chumbi, leaving a garrison of two hundred Gurkhas behind in the fort with just enough food to see them through until fresh supplies could come up. The issue of how, with the limited means at their disposal, they could keep the men and animals at the sharp end of the advance supplied, as well as extend that advance, now became a logistical nightmare that General Macdonald and Major Bretherton had

somehow to solve. Their main problem was that the further the
coolies and transport animals travelled, the more they consumed of
what they carried. Or, as Dr Austine Waddell put it: 'A coolie on a
single stage would eat up by himself a whole load in a month; so
that thirty coolies carrying their loads up one stage would deliver
only twenty-nine loads to be passed on; and so the loads go on
rapidly dwindling at every stage of the journey until there is comparatively little left to deliver at Chumbi to keep the garrison there
in food, let alone the storing of any for our advance. Mules are
even worse offenders than coolies in this respect, for a mule eats
four times the weight of grain that a coolie does, and only carries
twice the load of a coolie.'

Other sacrifices besides hygiene had now to be made. 'Our diet
is pretty plain,' wrote Arthur Hadow to his parents from New
Chumbi two days before Christmas 1903, 'porridge, mutton stew,
biscuits (similar to dog biscuits), jam and a limited amount of
butter, and chupatis. The latter are made of flour and water, and
look something like a mustard plaster. However, when one is
hungry one is not too particular.' It soon got worse. For the Sikh
Pioneers the army's increased reliance on hard grains for flour
came as no great hardship, but for the Gurkha troops and others
whose staple food had always been rice, this change of diet caused
considerable hardship and a great many stomach upsets, which
they took 'bitter bad'. Yet by the British officers, at least,
Christmas Day was celebrated in style, for special supplies had
been laid in. At the Pioneers' Mess in New Chumbi nineteen
officers sat down to a spread of turkey, ham, plum pudding,
mincemeat, cakes and Champagne: 'The only thing that fell flat
was the Champagne, which was so cold that nobody could drink
it, and we wished we had ordered beer instead.' Almost ten
months passed before any of those present enjoyed another meal
even half as good.

A second supply route was opened, which cut ten miles off the
one between Gangtok and Chumbi and raised the amount of food
carried in to an average of forty thousand pounds a day, which
took the edge off the crisis, further eased as the inhabitants of the
Chumbi Valley began to bring in fodder, buckwheat and potatoes
to sell to the force. The General had planned to winter in Chumbi

while the roads were strengthened and sufficient supplies were built up at Phari to allow it to serve as the springboard for their advance on Gyantse in the spring. This was the sensible thing to do, but Colonel Younghusband would have none of it, and at the start of the New Year made it plain to the General that it was time to move on: 'Just over the Tang-la we knew there was a small place called Tuna, and there I wished the Mission established with a good escort and plenty of ammunition and supplies, while all arrangements were being completed for the further advance on Gyantse. There was a certain amount of risk in this; but to be among the Tibetans proper, and to compensate for the withdrawal from Khamba Jong, I thought it necessary to run it.' By 4 January he had secured from the General a reluctant admission that enough supplies had now reached Phari to allow a second flying column to advance over the Tang La and set up the Tibet Commissioner and a small escort at Tuna.

The first cracks began to appear. 'We are starting off in a couple of days now to move a little further forward,' Younghusband wrote to his father:

> Good old Macdonald is the most cautious & methodical of people. He is going to plant me down with half a battalion, two maxim guns & a 7 pounder & some sappers, & any amount of ammunitions & two months supplies – in a fortified position in a open plain & he thinks nothing so desperate was ever done before though he with his force will be only four marches off & we shall be within signalling distance. He asked me very solemnly if I thought it was safe . . . Caution is all very well to a certain point, but meanwhile we are losing many advantages thro. advancing so slowly.

On 6 January the flying column once more set out from Chumbi, but up a track now much improved by the combined road-building of the Sikh Pioneers and the sappers. Hard on its heels came a small contingent of telegraph engineers with rolls of wire and telegraph poles. Within a day Phari was in direct contact with Simla and the outside world – but only briefly, for the line was soon cut. The General's response was to impose a collective fine of fifteen tons of yak-fuel on Phari and its inhabitants. To everyone's surprise, the Tibetans asked to be allowed to pay half the fine in Indian rupees rather than part with what was to them a vital commodity. Harsh as it was, the fine had the required effect and no further attempts to sabotage the telegraph line were made.

At Phari the flying column loaded up with as much in the way of supplies as its transport animals could bear. But before it could continue there arrived from Lhasa a delegation made up of three monks from the three great monasteries and a senior commander in the Tibetan army, Depon Lhadang —'a man of stocky but imposing appearance who became known to Younghusband and his officers as the 'Lhasa General'. These four were in fact the representatives of the Kashag and the most senior delegation yet mustered by the Tibetans, but this fact escaped Colonel Younghusband and he was content to let Frank O'Connor deal with them. The delegates had nothing new to say, beyond demanding that the invaders return to Yatung in order that negotiations might begin, but O'Connor was struck by the level of hostility shown by the three lamas, who in contrast to the always courteous Lhasa General were 'especially rude in their snarling and snappish refusal, and used disrespectful language'. His concerns grew when he was waylaid by a 'wild-looking Lama' from Sikkim who some days earlier had agreed to take a personal message from Colonel Younghusband to the Dalai Lama. Now the lama was back and in a state of great agitation, claiming that he had news of vital importance: 'Looking furtively about to see that he was not over-heard, he whispered hoarsely, "War! War! They mean War!"' After being calmed down, he explained that just a few miles north of Tuna he had come across a large armed force made up of two thousand five hundred Tibetan warriors who were preparing to halt the *pelings'* advance.

On 7 January the Tang La was crossed without incident and the tiny settlement at Tuna occupied with no sign of opposition, the only alarm being the appearance of 'hundreds of large wild asses, the *kyang* of the Tibetans, in troops of tens and twenties and more. At first we mistook them for detachments of Tibetan cavalry, the wild horsemen of the Chang-t'ang, as they came galloping along in a whirlwind of dust, then executed a perfect wheel-round, then extended out in line at regular intervals, and advanced again; and as if at the word of command reformed into close order and came to an instant halt.' Although the Tibetans considered them untameable, Dr Waddell found himself wondering if 'here, in the home of these large wild asses, we have a great field for breeding mules for the Indian army, the supply for which never can meet the demand'. Of much greater concern to the other officers was the continuing problem of the Maxims and rifles freezing: on the General's orders every man's weapon was tested, and half were found to be unworkable. Fortunately, a number of rolls of the barbed wire that had recently proved its worth against the Boers in South Africa had been included in the supplies brought up to Tuna, and these now provided the camp's main defence against sudden attack until such time as proper entrenchments could be dug out of the frozen soil.

Tuna turned out to be, in William Ottley's words, 'one of the most miserable and uninviting spots on the face of the globe'. It was made up of no more than three stone buildings set in the midst of an empty plain, a profoundly depressing place according to Dr Waddell: 'With nothing to relieve the dullness but these herds of roving kyang and the encircling hills beyond, the eye wearies of the stretches of loose gravel with its stunted tufts of withered grass, and the monotony of it all oppresses the spirits. The wind, which we had all fortunately escaped on the pass by getting over it so early, now began, and even at midday pierced through our clothes.' Francis Younghusband, however, was delighted, writing almost ecstatically to his wife (then moving restlessly from one temporary home to another with their infant daughter and an entourage of servants) of his pride at having accomplished 'a feat which will be historic & increase our prestige both in Europe & Asia for it is no small thing to have been able to take Indian troops into Tibet in the coldest season of the year & across a pass 15,200 feet high – only a few hundred feet lower than Mont Blanc.' Before turning in that first evening, Younghusband took a few moments to enjoy the sunset: 'My dear mountains took on every shade of purple & blue & delicate pink on the snows. Then the wind eased as the light faded away & a calm still night set in with the stars shining out more brilliantly than you could ever imagine them.'

As soon as the Tibet Commissioner had been settled in at Tuna, the General and his flying column returned to Phari, leaving Younghusband with an escort of four companies of the 23rd Sikh Pioneers under Lieutenant-Colonel Arthur Hogge, a section of Mounted Infantry under Captain Ottley, Captain Hadow's Maxim gun detachment, and a squad of British gunners with one of the seven-pounder mountain guns. Two days later Francis Young-husband wrote his father a letter full of enthusiasm and optimism:

> The idea of crossing into Tibet in midwinter of course seemed horrible at first & had never been dreamed of till I put it before Govt. But I knew Tibetan passes were extremely easy. I knew too that the sun so far down south as this is very much more powerful than further north. And I knew above all that though cold is very horrible to think of yet as a matter of fact does not really knock over so many men as heavy rains & malaria will . . . It is cold though by Jove, minus 20° the coldest & bitter winds nearly all day. But it is beautifully firm always & if you shelter yourself from the wind the sun is always so strong you can make yourself perfectly warm.

But Younghusband was putting a brave face on it, for he had placed himself and his three-hundred-strong escort in an extremely vulnerable position. What was more, he and General Macdonald were now at loggerheads, for soon after the flying column had arrived at Tuna the General had made an assessment of their position and concluded it to be untenable. Captain Ottley had sent out three mounted scouting parties, one of which had almost ridden into a two-thousand-strong force of armed Tibetans concealed behind piles of brushwood fuel some twelve miles distant. A second group of Tibetans had been found encamped even nearer, at some hot springs beside the Bam Tso lake near a small hamlet called Guru. Here, as the transport officer Leonard Bethell later put it, 'These Tibetan built them a wall where the open plain was narrowest by a large frozen lake and an outlying spur of one of the ranges. From the edge of the lake to the bottom of the cliff they built it, thus barring the track by which we would advance . . . It was their equivalent for "full stop". Reconnoitred, it was a wall right enough; and the area beyond was a brown and buzzing beehive.'

Having seen for himself how precarious was the Mission's intended post at Tuna, the General had exercised his right as Escort Commander to order an immediate withdrawal to the safety of Phari Jong – and Colonel Younghusband had refused. 'I will now tell you a thing which neither you nor Emmie [Younghusband's sister] must mention to any one,' wrote Francis Younghusband to his father of what had then transpired:

Two hours after we arrived here on Jan. 8th Macdonald came up to me & said we could not stay here & would have to retire the next day as there was no fuel & grass & the men would not be able to stand the cold. I told him I would never agree to retire, that I knew the style of country and would consider it abounding in fuel & grass compared with the Pamirs & that as to the cold if fifty men died of it that would be better than retir-ing. He appeared to give way. But the next morning he came again to me & said that he found we had only seven days rations & so we must retire. I told him I would absolutely refuse to move. He said I must give him that in writing & assume all responsibility. I said I would gladly do so. So it was decided to stay. Later in the day he came to me & said he had not been well in the morning & not his proper self & said he would not ask me to give it in writing. So I have made no mention of the matter officially but only told Dane [Louis Dane, Secretary of the Government of India's Foreign Department] & the Viceroy about it privately – not to be placed on official record & they have said I was 'entirely right'. But it was a close shave.

In fact, Younghusband and Macdonald had had a blazing row – as the former later revealed to his wife: 'I pitched into him harder than I have ever pitched into anybody. You would have been astonished & I was indeed surprised myself. But somehow I felt with a rigid man like that I had to lay into him like I would into a donkey.' Quite apart from the General's wish to withdraw from Tuna, other issues had been building up: Macdonald's habit of pitching his tent to the right of Younghusband's while on the march, implying that he and not the Tibet Commissioner was the senior man; his refusal to allow two members of the 'old firm' – Hayden the geologist and Ryder the Survey of India's map-maker – permission to proceed to Phari without an escort; and, most especially, Macdonald's insistence on occupying Phari Jong with a military garrison after he, Younghusband, had given the Phari Jongpons an assurance that the British troops would take no hostile action so long as the Tibetans took none. These and other grievances, long pent up, were now forcefully aired: 'He became quite pale and speechless,' continued Francis Younghusband in his letter to Helen, 'and I almost laughed as I thought I was talking just like Barrett [perhaps a reference to the tyrannical father of the poetess Elizabeth Barrett Browning, the publication of whose letters in 1899 had aroused great public interest]. But he was a good enough chap to take it very well and he has had no doubt since who is boss up here.'

Younghusband knew he had taken a huge gamble in advancing the Mission to Tuna, and for some time it must have seemed to him that it was not going to come off. General Macdonald and the bulk of the flying column left Tuna on 10 January and ran into the worst gale of the winter as they struggled back across the Tang La. 'Several of our transport followers,' wrote Dr Waddell, who was returning with the column, 'buffeted by the pitiless icy wind, lay down, and would have died in the frozen clutches of the Goddess Lady, had they not been roused up and helped along, staggering like drunken men. All of us had the skin peeled off our faces by the biting wind, and nearly all suffered from loss of voice for some days.' On reaching Phari they learned that the first hostile acts of the expedition had occurred: Lieutenant John Grant of the 8th Gurkhas had been felled by a stone as he tried to prevent Depon Lhadang and the three senior lamas from leaving the fort, losing his rifle in the ensuing scuffle. In retaliation the garrison commander, Captain Ross, had 'seized a dozen of the chief men of the village – cut off their pigtails and gave them 20 lashes apiece'.

Two days later what amounted to a third force of Tibetans was seen advancing on Tuna. It was said to have come from Lhasa and appeared to be led by a number of tall men whose maroon togas and yellow vestments showed them to be monks. 'They sent a messenger', reported Arthur Hadow in a letter to his parents, 'to say that the lamas were afraid to come in for fear of being ill-treated & would Colonel Younghusband come out half way to meet them. This he naturally declined to do, and eventually a junior member of his staff [Captain O'Connor] went out & met them, and I covered them with one of my guns in case of treachery. However, they returned in safety, and the lamas departed. It seems they cannot quite make up their minds to attack us.'

O'Connor's spies then reported that the Tibetans planned to mount a night attack, which meant the posting of double sentries and every man standing to for an hour after dusk and again for an hour before dawn. Younghusband wrote to reassure his wife that he was 'perfectly safe against the attack of thousands shd they be foolish enough to make one . . . The whole place has been barricaded, the walls loop-holed and barbed wire laid down outside.' Besides, the commander of his present escort, Lieutenant-Colonel Arthur Hogge, was 'a much more experienced officer than Macdonald & his regiment is splendid'. But the truth of the matter was that they were at grave risk. The men slept with their boots on and with their rifles at their sides, bayonets fixed and magazines charged – but knowing that they would probably fail to fire if the triggers were pulled. 'They never had a better chance of wiping us out,' wrote William Ottley of this period. 'The cold was so great (57 degrees of frost) that the bolts of the rifles froze, and the Maxims would not work, in spite of the oil having been carefully wiped off both previously. The men were exhausted, and it was very hard to get them to wake up. The sentries were visited every half-hour throughout the night by British and native officers, so these did not get much sleep. The ground was frozen so hard that a shelter trench could not be dug. Everything was in favour of the Tibetans if they attacked.' Some men took the bolts of their rifles with them into their sleeping bags, considering the risk of replacing them in the dark to be smaller than having a rifle that might not fire at all. Arthur Hadow, the Maxim gun commander, did the same with the locks of his two Maxims, giving orders to his men that during the daytime these locks were to be kept in inner pockets next to the skin except when actually needed on the guns. To add to his worries, Hadow had discovered that it was not just the oil that was causing problems: the intense cold was affecting the metal springs of his Maxims and even the cordite in the rounds, causing frequent stoppages.

Had the Tibetans launched a night attack on the Mission at Tuna the garrison would almost certainly have been overwhelmed – and Colonel Younghusband would no doubt have found a place in the same pantheon of lost military heroes as Generals Custer and Gordon. But the attack never came. It was later learned that the Tibetans had gone so far as to begin a night attack – only for it to fall apart as the men refused to advance. The British view was that they had lost heart, but it is more likely that it was halted because it went against the Dalai Lama's order that no violence be shown to the intruders. Whatever the reason, it cost the Tibetans dear, for here at Tuna they lost their best chance of removing Young-husband and his Mission from Tibet.

The British were also fortunate in the weather, for by local standards the winter was exceptionally mild that year, so much so that the Tibetans in the Chumbi Valley attributed the lack of snow to the flashing of the General's heliographs and sent a deputation begging him to desist and allow more snow to fall, so as to feed the springs and save the crops of the coming summer. Nevertheless, week by week the weather grew colder and the winds sweeping off the mountains more icy – and up at Tuna conditions began to deteriorate. The entire garrison had initially squeezed into the three stone-walled houses, but the acrid smoke from the yak-dung fires proved unbearable and the majority moved out into tents. 'It was certainly warmer inside but one could not sleep,' explained Hadow, 'and when one did, one very soon woke with a sense of suffocation owing to the smoke & the altitude. I have now had my tent pitched outside. The cold at night is great. About 4° below zero even in one's tent. All the day time a gale of wind blows laden with dust, so that everything inside one's tent is smothered, so that altogether this is one of the most uncomfortable spots I have ever been in!'

Several stormy and sleepless nights with the wind tearing at their flysheets were followed by a blizzard. 'Snow on the pass will increase the difficulties tremendously of sending up supplies,' Hadow noted with just a trace of concern, while back at Gnatong

Major Beynon's coolie corps was forced to suspend operations. 'I have had to stop working my coolies for the last two days,' he reported to his wife in a letter written on 21 January, 'as they are about 200 of them suffering from snow blindness – and the goggles which I asked for in November & have written & wired for constantly have never been issued to me . . . Another corps of coolies under other officers have been sent up without boots. Three of them are reported to have died on the road – and a good many will lose their toes from frostbite – all from miserable economy.' But here too the force was in luck, for the skies cleared and the snow melted, freeing the way for fresh supplies to be brought up to Chumbi and on to Tuna.

By mid January Colonel Younghusband and most of his escort were suffering from a range of illnesses. Dyspepsia and flatulence, regular if unwelcome bedfellows of high-altitude expeditions, could be lived with. Much more serious were the bronchial complaints that now began to wear the men down. Writing to Mrs Younghusband on her husband's behalf, Frank O'Connor took the opportunity to blame Dr Waddell and his medical staff for their condition: 'The Col I am sorry to say is not himself at all. It is nothing serious but a nasty cough & cold & subsequent weakness. Would you believe it the Doctors & field hospitals have come up to these windy conditions unprovided with medicines for coughs & colds of any sort, kind or description! One just coughs until one gets well – or doesn't! They can find literally nothing – except quinine.' But it was the combination of altitude, cold and wind-blown dust that was the real cause of their troubles, not the lack of cough medicine. To this day, arguments continue to rage in mountaineering circles over the best way to treat Acute Mountain Sickness, the one point of agreement being that only immediate evacuation to lower altitude will prevent death occurring once fluid has begun to accumulate in either the lungs or the brain. Dr Waddell took the quite reasonable view that oxygen was the answer, and ordered tubes of it to be sent up from India. However, he also believed that the root of the problem was bad cooking, due to a combination of insufficient fuel and the lowered boiling-point of water at altitude: 'Mountain sickness is undoubtedly induced by indigestion, hence probably the custom for hill-men to chew cloves or ginger when crossing high passes. The remedies we found most efficacious were phenacetin with brandy and purgatives, and to get down to a lower altitude in the more obstinate cases.' The cause was incorrectly diagnosed, but at least the treatment was on the right lines.

Although the British officers and the BORs remained relatively healthy, the Sikh sepoys of the Pioneers begun to go down like flies. 'Another sepoy died yesterday from pneumonia,' wrote Hadow on 3 February. 'The Sikhs cremate their dead like all Hindus and it rather uses up our precious stock of firewood.' Three weeks later he was reporting more Sikh deaths – 'and the Assistant Post Master is having most of his feet taken off today from frostbite!' Writing to an 'Uncle George' three days later he noted: 'About 13 natives have died up here to date, and there are a good many cases of frostbite.' Two weeks on he reported the death of their Eurasian Assistant Post Master: 'As he was a volunteer, we gave him a military funeral.' Recounting this first non-Indian fatality in a letter to his father, Francis Younghusband remarked rather brutally that he was 'much too delicate a youth to send up here'. Coincidentally, at this same period a second Post Master died at Gnatong, this time of cerebral oedema followed by heart failure. According to William Beynon, the man was found dead at his desk 'holding a pencil in one hand and an official letter in the other'.

What was equally disheartening for the officers at Tuna was the knowledge that the Sikkimese, Nepalis and Tibetans who made up the bulk of their porters, drovers and camp-followers continued to regard them as doomed. 'The local people and even the Chinese think that advancing into Tibet we are advancing to our destruction,' fulminated Younghusband in a letter to Louis Dane. 'They are not impressed by our troops; they know how few they are; they know of thousands of Tibetan troops on this side of the pass . . . Numbers of our camp followers deserted, and local men in our employ all brought in stories of the numbers and prowess of the Tibetans, and how they intended to attack us in the night and swamp us. We have, in fact, as I have so often remarked, not one ounce of prestige on this frontier.'

It was against this background of ever-worsening conditions that

Francis Younghusband now took a second gamble. As he himself put it some time later, 'I was heartily tired of this fencing about at a distance . . . and I thought that if we could meet and could tell them in an uncontentious and unceremonious manner what all the pother was about, we might at any rate get a start . . . even if a very considerable risk was incurred in the process.' He had taken to wrapping himself up in his thick Jaeger coat after breakfast and walking out from the camp to the shelter of a pile of rocks to read and to contemplate nature in solitude. His seeming indifference to the cold and his air of detachment, as though his mind dwelt constantly on higher things, greatly impressed his subordinates – as, indeed, did his composure when Captain Hadow tested his Maxim guns, unaware that the Tibet Commissioner was sheltering behind the boulders that were his target. However, on the morning of 13 January, instead up picking up a book and heading for his rocks, Colonel Younghusband summoned Frank O'Connor. The day before he had despatched to the Government of India a strongly-worded message – subsequently removed from official records – urging it to 'throw aside the idea of advancing as a purely peaceful mission and definitely assume a militant attitude'. Now he informed O'Connor that he had woken with the 'strong conviction' that he must speak to the Tibetans man to man. He therefore intended to ride over to the Tibetan camp, directly and unescorted. He would, of course, need an interpreter.

O'Connor had no doubts about how hazardous this proposal was, but he also knew his *burra sahib* too well to remonstrate:

> I merely remarked that it was a bit risky, and declared myself ready to accompany him. The Officer Commanding our small escort, Colonel Hogge, of the 23rd Pioneers, was naturally rather perturbed at the danger which the Commissioner proposed to run, as he was responsible for his safety. But Colonel Younghusband absolved him from all responsibility, and said that he alone was responsible for what he was about to do. Captain Sawyer, a young officer of the 23rd, begged to be allowed to accompany us, and Colonel Younghusband consented, so we three set out alone and rode north across the plain towards the Tibetan camp.

After a ninety-minute ride the three officers reached the Tibetan encampment, which was about half a mile short of the hamlet of Guru at a point where a low ridge extended out into the plain and towards edge of the lake of Bam Tso. Here beside a hot-spring called Chumik Shenko they had built a wall and pitched their tents. The Lhasa General had made his headquarters in one of the houses in Guru. 'As we drew near,' wrote O'Connor,

> we saw that there were a good many so-called soldiers, just or-
> dinary peasants armed with matchlocks, swords, etc., who
> swarmed out of their tents as we approached, but otherwise
> manifested little excitement or interest. We found that the dele-
> gates were living in a rather superior stone house, whither we
> proceeded, and were civilly greeted by one of the generals, who
> conducted us to an upper room, where we found all the dele-
> gates, including the representative monks of the three great
> Lhasa monasteries, in solemn conclave.

There now began a three-cornered debate between Francis Younghusband, the three lamas and a group of military com-manders led by the man the British knew as the Lhasa General, Depon Lhadang – with Frank O'Connor acting as go-between in the middle. From the start the military men were friendly, the monks barely civil. According to Younghusband, the latter became increasingly hostile after he challenged them about Russian influence and the role of the envoy Dorjieff: 'The monks brusquely intimated that they disliked them just as much as they did us. They protested that they had nothing to do with the Russians; that there was no Russian near Lhasa at the present time; that Dorjieff was a Mongolian, and the custom of the Mongolians was to make large presents to the monasteries, and they asked me not to be so suspicious.' Both Younghusband and O'Connor published dramatic accounts of the sudden change of mood that took place when the Colonel got up to take his leave; how the atmosphere suddenly became 'electric' after the monks refused to allow them to leave the room without naming a date for their withdrawal from Tuna. Both men also wrote private accounts of what happened in letters addressed to the same person: Helen Younghusband. Francis Younghusband's was written two days after the event:

> The generals were most polite & affable. The lamas were under-bred, rude, cunning & bigoted to the last degree. The visit lasted two hours & I strove hard for a peaceful settlement of the business – especially warning them against relying on Russia for support. But the worst of it is they are so appallingly ignorant of their true position in the Universe & so overweaningly superior that the more you argue with them the more convinced they are that you are afraid of them . . . They demanded that I shd retire to Yatung and the Lamas kept shouting for me to fix a date for my withdrawal from here.

Frank O'Connor's version of the encounter followed a week later and was altogether more dramatic:

> Did the Colonel tell you of our visit to the Tibetan camp? It was most interesting & not devoid of excitement. No one but he would have thought of or done it. I was horrified when he suggested it. He & I & a young officer rode down almost into their camp & had a 2 hrs interview with their officials, & towards the end the bunch got very nasty & we all thought we would certainly be collared. But his perfect coolness & sang-froid saved the situation & we got away all right. I will tell you all about it some day.

Both accounts demonstrate how close the visit came to disaster. It achieved nothing, and the upshot was a severe ticking-off for Younghusband from Lord Curzon for taking a quite unnecessary risk, and a reprimand for Lieutenant-Colonel Arthur Hogge from the General for not insisting that Younghusband take a proper escort with him. Younghusband's reaction to Curzon's rebuke is revealing, for he wrote back to the Viceroy implying that he had ridden into the Tibetan camp almost as if to force the issue: 'If the Tibetans had seized me, it would have been the most signal proof Your Excellency's policy of coming to a settlement with them was justified.' He also grovelled, adding that 'there is nothing I would not do for you; and if you asked me to eat dirt before the Tibetans for the next six years . . . I would do it'.

But others were less critical. In the officers' messes in New Chumbi and Gnatong, Colonel Younghusband's adventure added a further chapter to his legend. Some years later, former transport officer Leonard Bethell wrote a glowing account of how 'our leader' rode out to Guru alone but for one orderly, and continued:

We may imagine Younghusband – as we saw him often afterwards – well-versed in the punctilio of Mongolian debate, seated on a spread carpet facing the three big hats; legs crossed, hands up sleeves, sliding and slipping along in the singsong monosyllables; each fresh sentence prefaced by the sizzling intake of breath through closed teeth, the hallmark of ceremony, and the slight bowing forward from the waist in rhythm with the points of his argument; the 's's' all most ceremoniously flattened to 'z's'; the right hand only removed from within the left sleeve to raise it, palm outwards, forefinger and thumb joined, and the least little side-to-side waggle of the finger-tips till, the point made, the hand slid back up the other sleeve and the body half-bowed again at the waist; the little uplift of the bushy eyebrows, and the flattening of the deep-rift between the two, big, brown spaniel-eyes; the halt on the rising voice, and the silence which marked the close of one more period in his argument. Then the patience – the 'La-lo' interjection at the proper places and the slight bow, as each of the points in the opposing argument were made . . . no point of ceremony omitted, even though his legs must have passed from pins and needles to numbness and on to an almost complete absence of feeling . . . even though his very life hung, as it must have hung in that campful of puzzled hostility, hour after hour by a single steadily fraying thread.

In word, in voice, manner and gesture, in play of features and in the instinctive tact of generations of good blood behind him, he, sitting alone on the roof of the world, must have come near to convincing the mediaevalism which faced him . . . And now do you understand me when I say that that man's smallest wish, unexpressed or half-divined, was both law and stimulus to us?

Never was there a leader in whom his following had blinder or more affectionate trust.

Bethell was fantasising in his portrayal of Younghusband riding out alone but for an orderly and being 'well-versed in the punctilio of Mongolian debate', but such fantasies had become part and parcel of the Younghusband image, one that O'Connor and most of the officers of the escort were happy to foster – just as they were now happy to regard Brigadier-General Macdonald as the main obstacle to the advance on Lhasa. Word of his row with Younghusband at Tuna had spread through the force, and to many he was no longer 'the General' but 'Retiring Mac'. The phrase was deliberately offensive, for it was a play on 'Fighting Mac', the nickname given to General Sir Hector Macdonald, the most celebrated ranker ever to rise so high in the British Army. In 1904 it carried an additional overtone, because only the year before Hector Macdonald had shot himself in a French hotel room after learning that he was to be tried by court martial in Ceylon – for alleged sexual offences said to have been committed against some English schoolboys in a railway carriage.

The encounter at Guru did wonders for Younghusband's self-esteem. Two weeks later he was writing to Helen from his frozen eyrie of having found a strong sense of mission: 'I am so absolutely in God's hands fulfilling some hidden purpose of His. I must just go on carrying out the work He places before me from time to time.' And he was in the care of the group of officers devoted to him and his cause: 'I could not possibly be in safer hands. They are all very nice to me too. Even their Colonel never sees me without saluting & at the same time they will come into my tent & chat away & chaff. It is rather a relief old Macdonald & Iggulden are away for two such gloomy wet blanketers I never came across.'

In mid February the new moon signalled the ending of the Water-Hare year and the start of the new, which in accordance with the Tibet sixty-year cycle was to be the Year of the Wood-Dragon. The first day of the new year was known to Tibetans as Lama Losar, and at dawn the Dalai Lama emerged from his private quarters in the highest corner of the Potala Palace to take his place at the head of a procession consisting of the abbots of the three great monasteries, other senior lamas, members of the Kashag and Tsongdu and other dignitaries. To the sound of trumpets, conches and drums the procession wound its way through the dark recesses of the Potala and then up a succession of ladder-like staircases on to the open roof. Here the monks of the Dalai Lama's own monastery of Namgyal offered a sacrificial cake to the glorious goddess Palden Lhamo, the supreme hierarch of the protectors of Chos, and invoked her blessing. When the ceremonies had been completed the participants retired to the great inner hall on the ground floor of the Dalai Lama's Red Palace, where the pontiff took his place on the central throne to exchange New Year greetings with his flock and to receive pills of roasted barley dough representing good health and long life. Dances were performed while the assembly sat cross-legged drinking salt-butter tea and eating sweets and cakes, followed by a series of religious debates. Over the next two days more ceremonies followed, religious and secular, including one in which a number of sportsmen slid at speed down a rope from the highest roof of the Potala to the open ground in front of the palace – a sometimes fatal ceremony commemorating the descent of the first Tibetan kings of legend on a rope linking the earth to the heavens.

Elsewhere in Tibet the new year was marked with ten days of celebrations, carefully charted by Austine Waddell. In the Chumbi Valley these took the form of 'great rejoicing and a carnival of bright colours and dissipation, which attracted the villagers from all the hamlets, and, dressed in their best, they indulged in a revelry of dance and song, and a saturnalia of drinking. Some of the women actually washed their faces at this season, when it was discovered that most had rosy cheeks. New prayer-flags for good luck were erected on their poles tipped by tufts of fir-tops, crimson-dyed yaks' tails and wool. Amongst games, shooting with the long bow at targets 50 to 80 yards distant was practised with considerable skill.'

The new year festival marked the official end of winter: 'Almost immediately this festival ceased the weather became milder and spring-like, and the people commenced to plough and sow their fields in the Chumbi Valley.' Higher up, however, the long-delayed snows finally arrived with a vengeance, accompanied by violent thunderstorms and lightning that killed two porters as they laboured over the Jelep La. Here and on the Tang La the snow lay several feet thick, covering the remains of the scores of transport animals that had fallen by the wayside and closing both passes.

5

The Advance on Guru

EVERY EFFORT was now being made to build up a stockpile of rations and supplies at Phari. After each snowfall relays of coolies were sent out to shovel the snow off the track and to tread it down. It proved well-nigh impossible to keep the path clear over the Tang La – yet somehow the supplies still got through. 'The drivers arrived at Tuna frozen to the waist,' recorded Edmund Candler of one convoy that took thirty-six hours to cover the eighteen mules between Phari and Tuna. 'Twenty men of the 12th Mule Corps were frost-bitten, and thirty men of the 23rd Pioneers were so incapacitated that they had to be carried in on mules. On the same day there were seventy cases of snow-blindness among the 8th Gurkhas.'

Captain William Ottley's Mounted Infantry had been enlarged to a hundred men and took on the role of escorting the supply columns sent over the Tang La to restock the little outpost at Guru. On 8 February he arrived to find Colonel Younghusband 'as cheerful as ever notwithstanding the miserable existence he and the other officers were leading . . . nearly everybody had a severe cough.' On the following day he and most of his men returned to New Chumbi, but leaving behind young F. M. Bailey and a small section of Mounted Infantry to act as Lieutenant-Colonel Hogge's eyes and ears.

One of Hatter Bailey's first duties was to deliver a letter from Colonel Younghusband to the camp at Guru, which gave him an excellent opportunity to reconnoitre the Tibetan defences:

> I sent the man with the letter on with 2 sepoys & the rest I dismounted about 400 yds off so as to be able to help if anything happened. When I was waiting there the whole army came round out of curiosity. I didn't want them too near as if they were my men could not have done anything to help the munshi [interpreter; that is, the man with the letter] – so I drove them all back & then pointed to a furrow at the edge of a field & made signs that they were not to cross it & they were very amused and all laughed & toed the line – Then 2 men came over the line to show that they could do what they liked & I knocked them both down & some of the crowd picked up stones to throw at me but I got out my revolver & showed it to them & the men who were going to throw stones put them down & all the others laughed at them. Then some officers came and ordered them all back.

Bailey returned with the news that the Depon Lhadang, the Tibetan known to Colonel Younghusband as the Lhasa General, had refused to accept his letter and wished only to know the date on which they proposed to retire. He had also done a careful count of numbers, reporting that behind the wall at the hot-springs of Chumik Shenko there were '24 large white tents evidently belonging to the officers & 167 yak hair tents belonging to the men & a pile of arms outside each'. This suggested that the Tibetan force gathered at Guru amounted to somewhere in the region of eight to nine hundred men, rather more than Colonel Younghusband's estimate made a month earlier, when he had written to reassure Helen that 'The soldiers – 600 in number – were mere country yokels, grinning & affable. They had no military precautions & were armed with matchlocks & spears only – no breechloaders.'

Two weeks later Bailey assisted the two doctors at Tuna as they operated on the unfortunate Assistant Post Master, holding him down as they removed his frostbitten legs. His own complaint at this time was of the lack of *shikar*, because it was now considered too risky to go out alone to stalk mountain sheep or antelope. On 29 February he sent his parents an account of a second reconnaissance of the Tibetan camp at Guru, this time accompanied by Captain O'Connor. As before, they halted some distance off but were jeered at by the Tibetans and told that 'if we wanted to talk we were welcome to go into the camp but that it was rude to ride up & look at them & then ride away'. They returned to Tuna with two pieces of doubtful intelligence: one that 'All the Tibetan soldiers have been made to sign a paper to say they will not run away and the officers the same'; the other that they were to be attacked on the following Wednesday night when there was a full moon: 'We have heard this so often that it is most likely untrue but it is the most hopeful rumour we have had.' The Mission and Escort duly stood to with their arms for much of the night, but there was no attack.

Cheerful though he had appeared to Captain Ottley, Colonel Younghusband was becoming increasingly troubled and restless. For all that his fellow officers admired him, his position as Mission leader quite as much as his own nature kept him aloof and at a certain distance. His reading and his solitary ruminations continued to be his great solace. 'I spend nearly all the day on the mountain side under the shelter of a rock reading & writing,' he wrote to Helen on 27 January. 'I began today the outline of a book I am going to write to be called "The Religion of a Traveller" giving the results of all my experiences and studies. It will be a most fascinating book.' Some idea of its philosophy and of the thoughts passing through his mind at this time can be gleaned from several surviving pages of notes. One passage, dated 16 February, reads as a meditation on the great mountain that dominated their eastern skyline, Mt Chumolhari:

Today it emerges calm & strong and [indecipherable] from out of a mass of cloud tossing wildly & frantically around it. Its base is hidden in dark storm clouds from which the sharp needles of the secondary ridge from time to time emerge. But against the snowy peak itself these clouds are tossing themselves in very fury – wildly beating round it. Yet above them it rises serene & majestic & loftier than ever. And above it lies the calm blue sky.

Below it seems chaos. It is difficult to stand against the driving wind. The dust & the snow battle furiously against one. The birds are blown hither & thither. But the mountain stands firm & indifferent. Yet its time must come. These little flakes of snow seem but altogether feeble weapons to employ against it. However furiously the wind may blow it can hardly affect the granite mountain!

It needs no psychoanalyst to interpret the metaphor of Francis Younghusband as a calm, strong mountain that stands firm and serene; however wild the storm clouds and furious the wind, his time would come. Another note, written in early March, speaks of sunshine and clear skies after a storm, heralding the start of spring:

From the river course and the lake in the lower part of the valley a soft mist is rising, adding to the dreamy haze & the bare brown of the base of the mountains is turned into purples and pinks; while the snowy summit becomes the most ethereal blue shading into the cerulean blue of the sky above. On the plain plump little larks and finches are scurrying about – in short rapid turns – in search of food. Now and then a little vole is seen basking in the sun at the mouth of his hole. Over all there is a sense of peace & quiet & coming joy and it is hard to think that for the last five days some of the highest lamas from Lhasa have been cursing us at the Tibetan camp only six miles off.

Younghusband had been forced to abandon any thoughts of advancing on Gyantse from Tuna in late February. His sense of frustration grew with every passing week, and in his irritation he looked for someone to blame. To the man who was at his side throughout this period, Frank O'Connor, it was quite clear that Brigadier-General Macdonald and his transport staff were doing their best in appalling circumstances: 'It was all the GOC [general officer commanding] could do to keep his troops supplied with the necessary fodder and provisions . . . It was a herculean task to keep the road open and working all through the bitter cold and snow of those winter months, and no better work was done during the whole course of the Mission.'

But this was not how Francis Younghusband saw it. He became increasingly convinced that James Macdonald and his chief staff officer, Major Iggulden, were together to blame for the delay. His private letters over this period are peppered with tirades against 'old Macdonald', his 'wanting to treat everybody like a drill sergeant' and, above all, his desperate slowness that 'would have turned Cecil Rhodes' hair grey'. They could easily have been in Gyantse by now if 'that old stick in the mud Macdonald had risen to the occasion a bit', he wrote to Helen on 5 March, following up two days later with a longer analysis of the General's faults: 'I am beginning to lose patience with him. All that solemn manner is very impressive at first & you think he is a very sound sensible man. As a matter of fact he has not shown himself even that, so has nothing to make up for his want of energy. He does nothing but make elaborate paper calculations. You don't know how I sigh for Jack.'

Younghusband's patience finally snapped on 7 March after his escort commander at Tuna, Arthur Hogge, showed him a letter from the General threatening him with a court martial 'for criminal misappropriation'. Hogge had used the opportunity of a brief visit to New Chumbi to bring back to Tuna a number of sacks of charcoal as well as some personal belongings. The General had got to hear of it – and now accused him of misappropriation because he had used regimental mules to carry the charcoal and other items. Younghusband's response was to write Macdonald what he termed a 'stiff letter', making no mention of his threat to charge Hogge but criticising his insistence on sending military escorts to accompany the Tuna convoys. The Tibetans 'would not have the nerve' to attack, so why did Macdonald 'suck in every yarn the Tibetans tell him' and waste precious supplies on these large escorts?

This was an unwise move on Younghusband's part. Not only was the issue a military one and thus outside his sphere, but he was also in the wrong. The danger of advancing deep into hostile country without a proper supply system was succinctly put by Edmund Candler when he wrote of the Mission and Escort having been 'practically launched into the unknown. As far as we knew, no local food or forage could be obtained. It was too early in the season for spring pasturage. We could not live on the country. The ever-lengthening line of communication behind us was an artery, the severing of which would be fatal to our advance.' No sensible military commander could have taken the risk of allowing a supply convoy to cross the Tang La unescorted, and there is no question but that the General and his staff were working valiantly to keep supplies moving – to say nothing of the labours of Claude White and the officers of the various coolie, mule and yak corps. Threatening Lieutenant-Colonel Hogge with a court martial was an act of pettiness on Macdonald's part, but it also demonstrated how far he was prepared to go to ensure that the best use was made of the supply route to Tuna. By contrast, not a line can be found in Younghusband's voluminous correspondence to show that he had grasped the true situation facing the General and his staff at New Chumbi – which was that the supply line was on the verge of collapse because so many transport animals were being lost.

Scores of mules and ponies had died by the wayside through accidents or overwork, and in the plains rinderpest had devastated the bullocks, but it was the yaks that had suffered worst. Of the original 8,500 gathered from Nepal the previous autumn, at least a third died of anthrax before the disease could be brought under control. The survivors were then struck by the rinderpest, and by distemper brought in by the transport animals coming up from the Indian plains. The subsequent calamity was not something that transport officers like Mark Synge felt free to write about so it was left to a journalist, Edmund Candler, to set down the facts about what he likened to 'the flight of the Kalmuck Tartars'. The unfortunate yaks had lived all their lives above 12,000 feet but were now put to work in the Teesta and Chumbi valleys at altitudes as low as 5,000 feet. 'No real yak survived the heat of the Sikkim valleys,' wrote Candler. 'All that were now left were the zooms, or halfbreeds from the bull-yaks and the cow, and the cross from the bull and female yaks. In Sikkim, which is always a hotbed of contagious cattle diseases, the wretched survivors were infected by foot and mouth disease. The epidemic is not often fatal, but visiting an exhausted herd, fever-stricken, and weakened by every vicissitude of climate, it carried off scores. Again segregation camps were formed, and the dead cattle were burnt, twenty and thirty at a time. Every day there was a holocaust.' Yet even this was not quite the end of the disaster: 'Then followed the ascent into high altitudes, where a more insidious evil awaited the luckless corps. The few survivors were exterminated by pleuro-pneumonia . . . On 21 March eighty exhausted beasts struggled into Chumbi.' Thus it was that just as the invading army entered the altitudes to which the yak was best suited, it found itself with less than a tenth of the original 8,500 beasts that had originally set out from Nepal.

Desperate measures were called for. In mid March Captain Ottley was summoned by General Macdonald and told to round up as many Tibetan yaks and their yak-drivers as he could find in the Phari area. The local Tibetans had been ordered by their own authorities not to co-operate with the invaders and threatened with dire punishments if they did so. Now they were given no option as Ottley and his mounted infantrymen conducted a 'yak drive' that, despite being conducted in a raging snowstorm, netted more than 1,700 beasts. Of these the strongest 750 were purchased and the rest returned to their owners. The Mounted Infantry then searched Phari village, house by house and byre by byre, turning out 130 good mules and ponies hidden by their owners. According to Ottley, the villagers were more than happy at this turn of events: 'In their hearts they were uncommonly glad that the village was being raided, as they had seen the large prices paid to the yak drivers for their yaks, so they all turned up smiling to be paid. They had saved their faces also with regard to their own country-men, and they had no reluctance in asking three times the value of a mule or pony.'

Another part-solution to the crisis was supplied by the General himself, who had observed that from Phari onwards there seemed to be no insurmountable obstacles to wheeled traffic, even if the Tibetans themselves ignored the wheel as an aid to transport. He came up with the yak-drawn *ekka*, which combined the light one-horse carriage of the Indian plains with the pulling power of the yak or the yak–cow crossbreed. Hundreds of *ekka* parts were duly constructed in the plains, carried up in pieces to be assembled on the edge of the Phari plain by a team of carpenters, and then passed on to the yak corps. The *ekka*'s carrying capacity turned out to be four and a half maunds or four hundred pounds, which was two and a half times what a yak or mule could carry on its back – and when the savings in fodder and the weight of fodder were added, the yak *ekka* turned out to be over three times as efficient as a single animal. Together, the commandeered yaks and the yak-*ekkas* saved the day.

By the end of the second week of March over fifteen thousand maunds of rations and supplies, amounting to approximately six hundred tons, had been piled up at Phari – representing in sum about seven and a half thousand mule, pony or yak-loads, or thirty thousand coolie-loads. This was judged sufficient to allow what General Macdonald now insisted on calling a 'reconnaissance in force' to proceed over the mountains to Tuna – and on to Gyantse. And it was precisely at this juncture that the Tibet Commissioner suddenly and dramatically upped the stakes.

What set Younghusband off was a telegram from Macdonald saying that since armed opposition from the Tibetans was expected, the advance on Gyantse should be considered a 'purely military move'. Would Colonel Younghusband therefore give him 'an absolutely free hand'? The telegraph-line extension from New Chumbi to Tuna was now in full operation, and just days earlier Younghusband had received a copy of a telegram from the C-in-C India, Lord Kitchener, to Brigadier-General Macdonald giving him the order to move as soon as Younghusband was satisfied with the arrangements. The implication was clear: he and not the General was in charge, and giving Macdonald a free hand would be tantamount to relinquishing political control. He at once tele-graphed the Government of India for a ruling on who had ulti-mate authority – only to be told bluntly and unequivocally to toe the line: 'As it seems likely that resistance will be encountered when Mission leaves Tuna, General Macdonald should have full control during the move to Gyantse.'

This was a bitter pill to swallow. 'I am trying to play the game but am terribly afraid of Macdonald in the coming move to Gyantse,' he complained to his father on 25 March. 'He has got a head like a donkey's and I cannot drill into it that I <u>cannot</u> give him a free hand & that it is not a military move. Of course he thinks he is fettered by these d——d politicals and if anything goes wrong I shall be blamed for not allowing him to do as he wished.'

Younghusband spent the next two days brooding over his posi-tion and then on 28 March – the very day that General Macdonald's two-thousand-strong 'reconnaissance in force', together with some six thousand transport yaks, mules and ponies, set out from Phari Jong – he sent Louis Dane, Secretary to the Government of India's Foreign Department, a telegram subsequently published only in part in the Blue Books and omitted entirely from his own later account of the Mission. In it he made a formal disclosure of Macdonald's threat to pull out of Tuna eight weeks earlier, asked the Government of India to reconsider its decision to give Macdonald military control – and threatened to resign if it did not. As he put it to his father, 'I telegraphed back to Govt. that there was just as much political risk in giving Macdonald full control as there was military risk in leaving me the chief control & I instanced the orders he had given to withdraw from here in January . . . I asked therefore to be relieved of the responsibility for the conduct of our relations with Tibet and, if they could not alter their orders, to put Macdonald in both military and political charge with my staff as political advisers and allow me to return to India.'

If Younghusband was expecting a Government climb-down, he did not get it. Instead, he was urged to think again and to accept that in the eyes of the military authorities this was indeed a military operation. The General's reconnaissance in force had now arrived at Tuna, having crossed the Tang La the previous afternoon along with a vast herd of yaks and mules. Its tents were laid out in orderly lines about his Mission headquarters. Younghusband capitulated, replying to Dane that he would 'loyally accept' the Government's decision and carry on. To his father, however, he presented a face-saving interpretation of Dane's latest telegram: 'The military control must be in Macdonald's hands but otherwise I was to have the same control & position as I have up till now held and Macdonald was to be emphatically ordered to carry out my wishes unless they involved "serious danger" to the troops . . . As a matter of fact the decision of Govt gives me more power than I had before – or at any rate assumed I had for nothing had up till now been laid down.'

Although outwardly cordial, relations between the Tibet Commissioner and the Mission Escort Commander remained strained for the next few days. They give only one side of the story, but from Francis Younghusband's letters and the letters Frank O'Connor wrote to Helen Younghusband in the weeks that followed it is clear that James Macdonald took every opportunity to demonstrate his military control, while Younghusband became offended whenever a chance arose – ably seconded by his lieutenant. 'In what way he imagines he [Macdonald] will benefit himself by this extraordinary conduct is more than I can think,' reads part of one of Frank O'Connor's letters to Helen Younghusband:

> Colonel Younghusband has never of course interfered in the smallest particular with regard to military matters & details, & has never wished to do so even when in entire control. But when the General has been put at the head of affairs temporarily he immediately seizes the opportunity to interfere in the most discourteous manner with matters connected with the mission. He will not I think benefit by his action in the long run. Even in military matters his troops have no confidence in him. Hardly a day passes when some officer does not say to me – 'Oh if only Colonel Y. were in military as well as civil command.'

As a consequence of the military process of reinforcement and rotation of duties, Colonel Younghusband now lost all but the fittest of the sepoys of the 23rd Sikh Pioneers who had guarded the Mission at Guru, as well as their commander. And as they prepared to return to warmth and civilisation Lieutenant-Colonel Arthur Hogge's parting words to Francis Younghusband can have been of little comfort: 'I fear there is trouble brewing between you and Macdonald.' Their place was now taken by four companies of the 32nd Sikh Pioneers and four of the 8th Gurkhas, together with the second of the British Mountain Battery's ten-pounders, and two squadrons of Mounted Infantry, now enlarged by the formation of a second mounted unit made up of Pathans under the command of Captain Peterson of the 46th Punjabis. Captain William Ottley's original unit now became the 1st Mounted Infantry and Peterson's the 2nd Mounted Infantry. With Arthur Hadow and his Maxim gunners and the remaining companies of the 23rd Pioneers already at Tuna, this put the fighting numbers of Macdonald's 'reconnaissance in force' at between 1,250 and 1,300 men.

The Mission had also been joined by the gentlemen of the press – and they too were in no mood to look kindly upon the General.

Not only had his chief staff officer, Major Iggulden, kept them kicking their heels down at New Chumbi for nearly three months but he had also subjected their telegrams to what they regarded as quite unnecessary military censorship. 'Much of my writing was cut about,' complained Henry Newman the Reuters correspondent, who was offended by the General's indifference to the requirements of the press. 'I remember going out one day with the General and his staff to have a look at the Tibetan position,' he wrote many years later in his autobiography. 'The General had a big telescope on a stand and he and the staff had a thorough inspection. Then began a staff talk. I was listening to this rather eagerly, but presently the General saw me and I heard him say to a staff officer, "Tell Newman to withdraw out of earshot." After that I always kept clear of the General and his staff.'

At New Chumbi Newman had passed the time building himself a small house that he named the Emerald Bower. His rival Edmund Candler did rather better, having made friends with the military to such effect that he was invited to move in to the officers' mess of the 32nd Sikh Pioneers. Shortly before the advance to Tuna these two had been joined by a third special correspondent, Perceval Landon of *The Times* – so recent an arrival that he was the only Englishman in Tuna without a full beard.

Having had little time to acclimatise at New Chumbi, Perceval Landon found the long haul up and over the Tang La a harrowing experience: 'For the sufferer himself I do not suppose that there can well be condensed into three or four hours such an agony of aching,' he wrote feelingly of his own introduction to mountain sickness.

> The brain seems cleft in two, and the wedge, all blunt and splintery, is hammered into it by mallet strokes at every pulsation of the heart. Partial relief is secured by a violent fit of sickness, and through all this you have still to go on, to go on, to go on . . . The lungs seem foolishly inadequate to the task imposed upon them; the pluckiness of one's own heart is an unmistakable, but somewhat terrifying, symptom, for it goes on beating with increasing strokes till it shakes the walls of the body; and not the written testimony of the leading heart expert in London will convince you that it is not on the point of bursting its envelope.

Equally distressing was the experience of crossing a high Himalayan pass in a blizzard: 'The frozen mist, laced with stinging splinters of ice, was blown horizontally into our faces by the wind that never sleeps over this terrible pass. Men and animals alike were stiff with an armour of ice, and beards and even eyelashes were powdered and hoary with the fine particles of frozen mist. It was difficult to see fifty yards . . . Slowly creeping on against the blizzard, the long line of animals and men moved into and out of the narrow radius of one's sight, demi-cloaked with ice.'

Making what was his third crossing of the Tang La in company with Landon was Dr Austine Waddell but he, having no newspaper despatch to write, chose to describe the blizzard as a heavy mist, albeit one 'so thick that the four columns, marching abreast about 100 yards apart, were entirely hidden from one another until we reached the summit and entered the great plain, when the mist rolled itself up around the majestic Chumolhari and hung there.' What did impress him, however, was the line of telegraph poles that now 'stretched away across the many miles of plain in a bee-line, straight as an arrow, and serving as a good guide to the village of Tuna'.

Perceval Landon lost no time presenting himself to the Tibet Commissioner. He bore a message of goodwill from the Viceroy, and immediately impressed himself on the Mission staff as a sophisticated man of letters. 'To us Indian officials who so seldom came across anyone outside our walk of life,' wrote Frank O'Connor, 'it was especially enlightening to meet someone from the outside world whose experiences and viewpoints were so entirely fresh from ours . . . His curiosity and interest in everything were (as befits a real journalist) insatiable.' Landon was at once invited to become a member of 'our little Mission mess', even though Francis Younghusband thought him 'a common feller', albeit not as common as Henry Newman, who was 'a very rough diamond'. Only the Old Reptonian Edmund Candler passed social muster.

As the reconnaissance in force prepared to advance on Guru, Younghusband wrote to explain to Helen who was really in charge:

Macdonald is to be most emphatically ordered to carry out my wishes unless a serious danger to the troops is in his judgement thereby incurred. This is a very different thing to giving him 'full control' as in the previous telegram. Poor Macdonald I must say has been extremely friendly since he has arrived and of course it must be very galling to him to have to do all the grind while I remain boss. Tomorrow we move out in force to the first Tibetan position. I do trust for the poor Tibetans' sake there will be no fighting. The signal for or against has to be given by me.

At 8 a.m. on the following morning, 31 March, Macdonald's army paraded in six inches of snow. Owing to the scarcity of ammunition each infantryman was issued with no more than thirteen rounds. At 8.20 it moved out from Tuna towards Guru in the same four-column formation in which it had advanced over the pass. According to Henry Newman it was one of those mornings 'the Tibetans call "golden". There was a clear, bright sun and no wind at all. Everybody marched proudly and full of elation, hoping that there would be a good fight.' Whatever was said later, every man in the army was certain he was marching into action. After writing a letter to his father the evening before, Arthur Hadow added a short postscript giving details of the battle plan: 'The Tibetans have been building walls or sangars on the hills forming their position and we are going to advance straight on their position. 3 coys of the 23rd Pioneers will be on the right, my guns in the centre, & 2 coys of the 8th Gurkhas on the left, so if there is any fighting I ought to get my share.'

As Newman rode alongside Dr Waddell behind the main force he learned from him that the place where the Tibetans had chosen to make their stand was of special significance to them because of a hot spring known as Chumik Shenko, the Waters of the Crystal Eye, issuing at the foot of a spur. The water that bubbled from this hot spring then meandered as a rivulet across the plain for a mile or so before entering the broad lake known as Bam Tso: 'Colonel Waddell told me the Tibetans believed that no enemy could cross that stream and that they had put a charm on the stream in addition. Anybody who tried to cross it would simply disappear.'

Whether the Tibetans believed in the spring's magical properties or not, the site did indeed have special significance, for historically this was the point at which all invasions from the south had been halted. This was, in effect, Tibet's Thermopylae. But whereas in the past the waters of the lake had extended almost up to the spur, so creating an easily defensible bottle-neck, its geography was now very different. The desiccation of the Tibetan plateau that had taken place in recent centuries had caused the waters of the Bam Tso lake to retreat by almost a mile. The hot spring of Chumik Shenko on the last day of March 1904 was not merely indefensible but in many respects a perfect killing-field for a modern army. The only thing defensible about it was a newly erected wall, between five and six feet high and approximately a hundred yards in length, running out from the foot of the spur as far as a single, roofless stone hut.

They had been marching for about an hour when a Tibetan messenger rode up to tell Colonel Younghusband that he was to go no further. Through O'Connor, Younghusband replied that since the Tibetan envoys would not come to him, he was going to them. The advance continued without a pause. The messenger trotted away, only to return minutes later with a companion, who asked them to wait there for the Tibetan envoys. Again Younghusband declined. When they were some three miles short of the stone wall and the Tibetan camp beyond it, a deputation rode out to meet them with the familiar figure of Depon Lhadang, the Lhasa General, at its head. He was accompanied by a lama whom Younghusband recognised as one of the monks who had threatened him in January, and two laymen: the Phari Depon with the gold earring first met at Yatung, and a Depon from Shigatse named Namseling,

General Macdonald gave the order for the troops to halt and stand easy as he, Younghusband and O'Connor, with a small escort of Sikhs, went forward to parley with the Tibetans. A carpet was produced and spread on the ground for the Tibetans and two over-coats for the Britons, on and about which the leading protagonists of either side sat with their legs crossed, O'Connor on one knee between them. Onlookers from both sides soon began to crowd around, including the three special correspondents and Dr Waddell – who observed that three of the soldiers who formed part of the Tibetan retinue's escort carried 'Russian-made rifles' bearing the Czarist eagle. According to Francis Younghusband, he made a final effort to reason with the Tibetans:

I reiterated the same old statement – that we had no wish or intention of fighting if we were not opposed, but that we must advance on Gyantse. If they did not obstruct our progress or did not attack us, we would not attack them. But advance we must . . . They replied with the request – or, indeed, almost order – that we must go back to Yatung, and they would negotiate there. They said these were their instructions from Lhasa. They also did not wish to fight, but they had orders to send us back to Yatung . . . I urged that for eight months now I had patiently tried to negotiate, but no one with authority came to see me, my letters were returned, and even messages were refused . . . the time for further parleying here was gone. The moment for advance had arrived. I would give them a quarter of an hour after their return to their lines within which to make up their minds. After that interval General Macdonald would advance, and if the Tibetans had not already left their positions blocking our line of advance, he would expel them by force.

As he watched these proceedings, Perceval Landon was struck by the contrast between their own dun-coloured khaki uniforms and the exotic costumes of the Tibetans: 'the gay yellow and green coats of the generals from Lhasa and Shigatse; the various head-dresses; the purple and blue of the robes; the strange forked guns embossed with turquoise and coral; the richly-worked sword-hilts; the little grey and bay ponies, saddle-clothed with swastika-patterned stuffs and gay with filigree brass headbands and wide molded iron stirrups.' He observed O'Connor's composure and Younghusband's impassiveness in the face of the heated declamations of the Tibetans. Henry Newman, slightly better placed, noticed how Younghusband's initial poise turned to irritation as the Tibetans reiterated their demands that he retire. He overheard Younghusband say angrily that, 'although his instructions were to avoid bloodshed, bloodshed could not be avoided if the Tibetan troops did not move out of the way.' He then saw Younghusband move his hand in a gesture 'implying "so be it"', which brought proceedings to a close.

When the designated fifteen minutes were up, General Macdonald gave the order to resume the advance. The three companies of the 23rd Sikh Pioneers and the two companies of the 8th Gurkhas now wheeled into extended line and fixed their bayonets, flanked on the left and right by Peterson's and Ottley's Mounted Infantry. The General and Colonel Younghusband, together with their respective staffs, followed in a small group in the centre, their two British flags fluttering in the light breeze. Behind them in reserve came the men of the 32nd Sikh Pioneers, together with the two ten-pounders of the British Mountain Battery, the two antique guns of the Gurkhas, the medical officers, medical orderlies and stretcher-bearers, the engineers and ancillaries.

Virtually every account of what followed, published and unpublished, refers to the General's order not to fire until fired upon. Arthur Hadow wrote to his father of 'orders being issued that not a shot was to be fired until the Tibetans opened fire'. F. M. Bailey similarly states: 'We were told not to fire until fired upon.' In his published account Younghusband explained why such an order was given: 'I wished still to give them just one last chance, in the hope that at the eleventh hour, and in the fifty-ninth minute of the eleventh hour, they might change their minds. I therefore asked General Macdonald to order his men not to fire upon the Tibetans until the Tibetans first fired on them. In making this request I knew the responsibility I was incurring. We were but a handful of men – about 100 Englishmen and 1,200 Indians – in the face of superior numbers of Tibetans.'

Much was subsequently made of this quixotic order and the risks that Macdonald's troops took in obeying it. 'It was such a policy as has probably no parallel since the days of the Old Guard at Fontenoy,' declared Landon, adding that 'not a man, Gurkha or Sikh, disobeyed the order all the day'. Advancing at marching pace, their Lee-Metfords loaded with a round 'up the spout' and raised at the 'on guard' position, the Sikhs and Gurkhas came on in extended line until they were within a stone's throw – and thus fully within musket range – of the Tibetans crowded along the wall and on the spur to their left. 'On we went,' wrote William Ottley, 'getting closer and closer and wondering when the Tibetans would fire the first shot and take advantage of the splendid opportunity we gave them.'

Gallant as this advance was, it was not quite the risk that it was presented as being. In the first place, it was known that the Lhasa General had his orders to resist but not to fight, so that it was a case of two armies closing, both under orders not to initiate hostilities. And secondly, General Macdonald had ordered the 23rd Sikh Pioneers to thin out at the centre where they were most in danger of being fired upon, but where the wall – about six feet high in the middle and five feet high at each end – rendered it impossible for the Tibetans to make a sudden rush. Indeed, so thin was the line of Sikhs at this point that Henry Newman, following on behind, got the distinct impression that the General and Colonel Young-husband and their combined staffs in the centre were advancing 'without any troops in front of them'. Long before they closed on the wall the Pioneers and Gurkhas in front had began to extend to right and left, both to thin out at the centre and to outflank the Tibetan position on either side.

On the extreme right of the line Captain Ottley's men of the 1st Mounted Infantry, together with one company of the 23rd Pioneers, moved round between the end of the wall and the lake, while on the left Captain Peterson led the Pathans of the 2nd Mounted Infantry up onto the spur. Here the Tibetans had erected a series of stone embrasures, known to the Indian Army as sangars, which they occupied in strength. The mounted Pathans were closely followed by the two companies of Gurkhas, who continued to clamber up past them and along the spur until they were extended right across the high ground overlooking the rear of the main Tibetan position behind the wall. Arthur Hadow and his seventeen-man squad of Maxim gunners had also shifted their positions, doubling with their mules behind Ottley's men on the right of the Tibetan position until they were some six or seven hundred yards beyond the stone wall and facing the rear slope of the spur. 'I was given a free hand as to the position I was to take,' Hadow wrote afterwards to his father, 'so I decided to get round the enemy's left flank & catch them when they bolted . . . I moved round by the plain and got on the flank & in rear of the enemy's position until I was within 200 yards of a sangar in which was a large number of Tibetans at the foot of the spur.' Here the Norfolks had enough time to unload, assemble and mount their two Maxims. They were now positioned between Ottley's

Mounted Infantry dismounted on their left and one company of 23rd Pioneers spread out to their right, so that between them they covered the Tibetans' only line of retreat. Hadow's orders from General Macdonald were unequivocal: he was to 'make as big a bag as possible'.

Nowhere is this virtual encirclement of the Tibetan position more clearly illustrated than in a drawing from a sketch made by Captain Sawyer directly after the action (see page 118).

Much has been made by Francis Younghusband's advocates of two statements included in letters to his father of 1 and 4 April. In the first he wrote: 'Twice Macdonald asked me to be allowed to commence firing; but each time I refused partly out of sympathy for the poor people whom I knew would simply be massacred once we began firing; & partly because I knew how very import-ant it would be to Govt to show that up till the very last moment – till the Tibetans had actually forced us to fight – we had refrained from firing.' This and a subsequent reference – 'I am glad I twice restrained Macdonald from commencing firing' – have been taken to mean that Younghusband twice refused Macdonald at this junc-ture: that is to say, with the Tibetans to all intents surrounded.

The General had indeed proposed firing on the Tibetans, but long before he and his men were closing on the wall. The first occa-sion was on the day before the advance, when Macdonald wanted to drive the Tibetans out of their position by shelling them with his field guns. The second took place immediately after the initial parley with the Tibetan generals broke up and the fifteen minutes' grace ended. As military commander, Macdonald evidently consid-ered himself quite within his rights to order such an assault, because the two Tibetan armies – one blocking his advance at Guru and the other preventing him from bypassing Guru by positioning itself on the far, eastern side of the lake of Bam Tso – clearly constituted a 'serious danger' to his troops. As it was, he deferred to Colonel Younghusband, who refused to accept his argument of serious danger and withheld his permission to open fire.

Yet Younghusband knew the chance of securing a bloodless victory at Chumik Shenko was an outside one. Did he really imagine that he could march his troops up to the Tibetan position and force them to disperse without a shot being fired – or is it possible that he deliberately set out to repeat what he had tried before at Guru, which was to offer himself as a political sacrifice by exposing himself (together with the General and their respective staffs) very obviously behind the thin khaki line at the centre? Did he, in fact, want the Tibetans to open fire, knowing what the political consequences would be? What is harder to dispute is that Francis Younghusband, by refusing to allow Macdonald to clear the way for the advance to Gyantse by conventional military means, made the subsequent massacre all but inevitable.

6

The Massacre at Chumik Shenko

THE TIBETANS held their fire. Just before the single line of
sepoys closed on the wall two Tibetans – Younghusband refers
to them as 'the Lhasa Majors', but they were Depon Lhadang's
fellow depons from Phari and Shigatse – pushed through and again
asked Younghusband not to proceed further. They again told
Younghusband that they had been ordered not to fire, and begged
him to stop the troops from advancing. He replied that the
advance must continue, and that he could not allow any Tibetan
troops to remain on the road.

Depon Lhadang and his escort now came forward through a gap
at the extreme end of the stone wall, where stood the remains of a
ruined stone house. The Sikh sepoys moved round them until they
stood with their rifles resting on the wall. General confusion now
reigned in the Tibetan camp. Some of the Tibetan troops began to
disperse, but were called back by their officers. Some ran up to
reinforce the sangars on the spur, passing others who were running
down to take shelter behind the wall.

Meanwhile, up on the spur itself the Gurkhas and Peterson's
Pathans had moved in to oust the Tibetans from their stone
defences. Hatter Bailey had been temporarily attached to Peterson's mounted infantry unit, and these two officers approached the

nearest sangar together and told the Tibetans to go:

> They refused but did not fire, so we did not know what to do, and Peterson sent me off to ask the General. I could only find the Goorkhas, who were taking the Sangars on the right. Major Murray, in command, said the Tibetans had all gone from his Sangars, so I went back and told Peterson. We then told the Tibetans to lay down their arms. They refused, and we had a bit of a scuffle in which a man threw a stone and hit Peterson on the head. A Pathan immediately bayoneted him, and they then all ran down the hill. We all followed these men, about 200 yards behind them.

On the right flank opposite them Bailey's colleagues in the 1st Mounted Infantry had also begun to dislodge the Tibetans from their defensive positions. They disarmed a group gathered behind a large rock some six hundred yards behind the wall, securing a 'very fine jingal' in the process. They then relaxed and, according to William Ottley, stood talking to the Tibetans out in the open beside the track leading north to the village of Guru.

Perceval Landon watched this clearance from a safe distance, at the back of the force. 'There was a hush of suspense among the two staffs out in the plain who were watching with straining eyes the slow progress of the khaki dots on the hillside,' he later wrote. 'It was not till the last of the hundreds of gray-coated figures had slowly come down to the wall that the officers shut up their field-glasses . . . The sense of an insecurely leashed anger which might break out at any moment was suddenly replaced by an exaggerated sense of security and congratulation. The incident was regarded as practically over. The Commissioner and the General rode in together to the wall.'

According to Younghusband's official account, he too believed the affair to be 'practically over', and that the Tibetans were dispersing – until 'a change' came over them, which he thought was the result of a new order being issued, either by the Lhasa General or the lamas present. He was once again informed that the Tibetans would not fight – but nor would they vacate their position behind the wall. He and the General conferred, and agreed that 'the only thing to do was to disarm them and let them go'.

That was the official version: Younghusband and Macdonald met, and decided that the Tibetans must now be disarmed. Yet the evidence suggests that what they actually agreed on was one last effort to provoke the Tibetans into opening fire. In a letter written by Younghusband to his father a month after the event, he referred to an 'incident' taking place *after* the Tibetan troops had been dislodged from their sangars and surrounded behind their wall: 'After the Tibetans had been outflanked by the guns, maxims, mounted infantry and a company of Inf. on each side, *another company was told to charge straight up to the wall. They charged with fixed bayonets shouting loudly* but the Tibetans remained stolid behind this & our sepoys brought up against it as you see in the photo. It was that as the Tibetans neither got out of the way, nor fought that I said they must be disarmed & sent off.'

As the words highlighted in italics show, this was no 'incident' but a clear order given for a company of Sikhs to make a dummy attack. It is hard to see the purpose of this if it was not a deliberate effort to provoke the Tibetans into opening fire. No published account makes reference to this charge with fixed bayonets, yet it undoubtedly occurred, because it was seen by Arthur Hadow from his vantage-point out on the plain on the right and he spoke of it in one of his letters to his father: 'One company charged their sangars, with fixed bayonets, in the hope that the Tibetans would bolt, but they took no notice.'

Once this dummy attack had failed, Frank O'Connor went forward to tell Depon Lhadang of Brigadier-General Macdonald's order to disarm his men. The Lhasa General and his two fellow depons were seated in a huddle close to the gap in the wall: 'I rode up close to where the Tibetan officers were sitting and dismounted from my pony and went and gave them the General's message, speaking as gently and politely as I could, and using of course the honorific language. But their demeanour was sulky and reserved. They barely replied to me, and sat still on the ground, occasionally muttering to one another.'

While this was going on Macdonald, a number of his officers and all three special correspondents dismounted and gathered in the lee of the ruined house at the end of the wall. 'On its inner side,' recorded Dr Waddell, 'the armed Tibetan warriors formed a dense packed mass, glaring with anger at the white-faced intruders only a few yards from them, and at our soldiers, who now enclosed them on three sides; whilst we stood by, alert but unsuspicious of the tragedy which was impending, some of us photographing or sketching whilst others were munching sandwiches.' Each side now examined the other with curiosity; the Tibetans, in Henry Newman's view, 'looking at us almost as one might look at animals in a cage'. He watched Dr Waddell stretch out and take a rifle from one of the Tibetans: 'The man surrendered it quite willingly, because he realised that Waddell only wanted to examine it.' Francis Younghusband, curiously enough, was not with them. As he later assured his wife, he stayed on his pony and kept well clear: 'As a matter of fact I was further off than anybody & was mounted. Your Dodo is a very careful man.'

If the peaceful disarming and dispersal of the Tibetan army was indeed what Younghusband intended, then for a few moments it seemed as if this extraordinary gamble was about to come off. 'No one', wrote Edmund Candler, 'dreamed of the sanguinary action that was impending.' Seeing Colonel Younghusband's despatch rider preparing to mount up, he hurried off to his own pony and rested his notepad on the saddle to scribble a short note 'to the effect that the Tibetan position had been taken without a shot being fired'.

O'Connor now reported back to Macdonald that Depon Lhadang had refused to listen to him: 'The General gave the necessary orders, and a few Sikhs were marched up, and seizing hold of some of the Tibetans' muskets they began to disarm them by force.' As Edmund Candler made his way back to the wall after writing his despatch he saw scuffles break out between the Sikhs and the guards grouped round the Tibetan generals. 'It was a ridiculous position,' he recorded, 'Sikh and Mongol swaying backwards and forwards as they wrestled for the possession of swords and match-locks. Perhaps the humour of it made one careless of the under-lying danger. Accounts differ as to how this wrestling match developed into war, how, to the delight of the troops, the toy show became the "real thing".'

His fellow journalist Perceval Landon was in no doubt that the man who set off what he termed 'the slumbering mine' was the Lhasa General, Depon Lhadang: 'He shouted hysterically to his men to resist. They replied by stoning the Sikhs. Even then, though, the whole affair hung in a slippery balance, the latter held themselves in check. One of them advanced to the head of the Depon's pony as the Lhasa General tried to move up towards the wall. In an evil moment for himself and his countrymen, the head of the great house of Lheding drew his pistol and fired, smashing the Sikh's jaw. There was an awful pause, that lasted for perhaps three seconds.'

It was widely reported afterwards that this firing of the pistol by Depon Lhadang was the signal for a general attack by the Tibetans. Even Francis Younghusband subscribed to this view: 'He threw himself upon a sepoy, drew a revolver, and shot the sepoy in the jaw. Not, as I think, with any deliberate intention, but from sheer inanity, the signal had now been given. Other Tibetan shots immediately followed.'

But of all those who wrote about this first shot, only Henry Newman described himself as an actual eye-witness to the opening moments of the tragedy:

I saw a Sikh orderly put out his hand and push back a man who was holding a pony, the very pony that the Depon had ridden out upon to meet us. This Tibetan had pushed himself and his pony forward into a break in the Tibetan walls. The Depon was standing close by when this incident took place, and he was carrying a Winchester rifle. When the man holding the horse was pushed back, the rifle the Depon was holding went off. The shot wounded the Sikh in the jaw. Now I do not know whether the shot went off by accident or whether it was a signal, but immediately it did go off the mass of Tibetans in front of us surged forward . . . The people standing in front of the break in the wall were the General himself, Major Wallace Dunlop of the Sikhs, and Candler, and of the Tibetans who first came through the break in the wall all were swordsmen. Candler, I think, was the foremost man.

Newman's version of events is partly corroborated by a second-hand account provided by a Chinese named Ts'an-Chih Chen, who was living in Lhasa at this time. He was told that the firing began after an Englishman approached a horse owned by one of the Tibetan generals: 'When the foreigner placed his hand in admiration on the horse's saddle a superstitious Tibetan lost his temper . . . Needless to say, both parties accused each other of starting the fighting.'

Dr Waddell had been examining some Tibetan tents but got back to the wall just as the first shot was fired. Turning towards the direction of the shot he saw 'the infuriated Lhasa Depon and some of his men scuffling with some Sikh sepoys on our side of the wall about 15 yards off'. He then heard a 'wild war shout' as a number of Tibetans 'rushed out at us with their great swords already unsheathed'.

These swordsmen who rushed forward through the gap in the wall were probably the Lhasa General's guards. Edmund Candler became their first victim: 'The first man was on me before I had time to draw my revolver. He came at me with his sword lifted in both hands over his head. He had a clear run of ten yards, and if I had not ducked and caught him by the knees he must have smashed my skull open. I threw him, and he dragged me to the ground. Trying to rise, I was struck on the temple by a second swordsman, and the blade glanced off my skull. I received the rest of my wounds, save one or two, on my hands – as I lay on my face I used them to protect my head.'

The second man to go down was Major Wallace Dunlop of the 23rd Pioneers, who was similarly hacked to the ground. General Macdonald and his ADC, Lieutenant Bignell, were the next two in line. 'The General would have fallen next,' recorded Newman, 'but for the fact that his orderly thrust into his hand a shotgun which the General fired from his hip. That killed the leading Tibetan and I think wounded others. A Sikh soldier was the next man to fall. But by that time both the Gurkhas on the left and the Sikhs on the right had realised what had happened and were firing into the mass of Tibetans.'

Within seconds fire was being brought to bear from three sides on the Tibetans crowded behind the wall. 'Under cover of the wall,' wrote Austine Waddell, they poured a withering fire into the enemy, which, with the quick-firing Maxims, mowed down the Tibetans in a few minutes with terrific slaughter. Those who had rushed out were soon all killed; and the remainder were so huddled together that they could neither use their swords nor guns. This mob in a few seconds, unable to stand against the concentrated hot fire of our men, surged to the rear, and throwing away their arms, broke and ran, as fast as they could, which in such an altitude was not swiftly. Most of them as they fled through this zone of fire sank quietly down, riddled by the hail of our bullets and shattered by the shrapnel of the mountain batteries bursting over them, and perished almost to a man . . . It was all over in about ten minutes, but in that time the flower of the Lhasa army had perished!

Away on the right Ottley had heard the first single shot fired, which he could tell was not from an Indian Army Lee-Metford. Soon afterwards he found himself being fired upon by his own side: 'As we were straight in the line of fire, their bullets came right among us. It can be imagined with what agility we got under the shelter of that solitary rock; but the Tibetans also thought it was a good place to make for, and tried to drive us out, whereupon arose what is called in Ireland "an argument" of which they got the worst.' Now Ottley and his men found themselves being fired upon by the force's ten-pounders: 'When the gunners opened fire, the first thing that caught their eye was this rock and the Tibetans surrounding it: they had not noticed that a small party of us were behind it also, and they loosed off at and over the rock, which made us all the fonder of it . . . we had one native officer and two men wounded, two ponies killed and two wounded.'

After initially finding his line of fire blocked by some Sikh Pioneers, Arthur Hadow soon had an opportunity to put his two Maxim guns to work, manning and firing one himself. In a lecture on the machine-gun delivered afterwards to a military audience in England he spoke of his guns not working well, 'all sorts of failure occurring'. The true explanation for these failures may well be found in his first letter to his father after the battle, which begins with a warning that he had a 'horrible story' to tell.

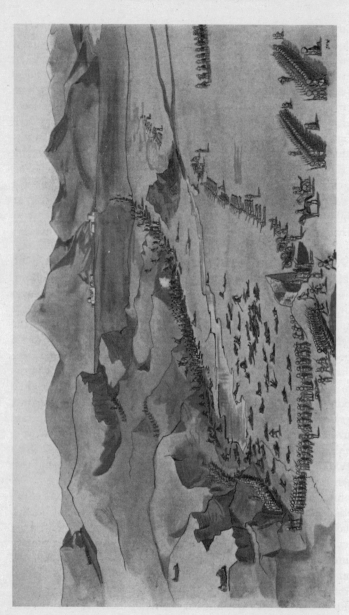

The Massacre at Chumik Shenko: a sketch by Captain Sawyer

Of his own part, Hadow wrote: 'As soon as my front was clear I opened fire with both guns, one of which I fired myself. The Tibetans broke out of the enclosure & and moved at a fast <u>walk</u> along the foot of the hills straight across my front. As soon as my guns got to work the slaughter was terrible, as the Tibetans fell in heaps where the maxims struck them. I got so sick of the slaughter I ceased fire.'

This walking rather than running away horrified all who saw it. 'It was an awful sight,' wrote Perceval Landon, yet he found himself unable to turn his eyes away: 'One watched it with the curious sense of fascination which the display of unchecked power over life and death always exerts when exercised. Men dropped at every yard. Here and there an ugly heap of dead and wounded was concentrated, but not a space of twenty yards was without its stricken and shapeless burden . . . the slowness of their escape was horrible and loathsome to us.' Even Edmund Candler had to watch, despite the severity of his injuries:

As my wounds were being dressed I peered over the mound at the rout. They were walking away! Why, in the name of all the Bodhisats and Munis, did they not run? There was cover behind a bend in the hill a few hundred yards distant, and they were exposed to a devastating hail of bullets from the Maxims and rifles, that seemed to mow down every third or fourth man. Yet they walked! It was the most extraordinary procession I have ever seen. My friends have tried to explain the phenomenon as due to obstinacy or ignorance, or Spartan contempt for life. But I think I have the solution. They were bewildered. The impossible had happened. Prayers, and charms, and mantras, and the holiest of their holy men, had failed them. I believe they were obsessed with that one thought. They walked with bowed heads, as if they had been disillusioned with their gods.

Among the Tibetans gathered behind the wall at Guru was a Dingpon or 'Middlemaster' (the nearest Tibetan equivalent to a British Army lieutenant) named Tseten Wangchuk, commanding twenty-five soldiers from Lhasa. He survived the massacre and later set down a deposition that provided the only Tibetan eye-witness account of what took place. It was his impression that the firing began without warning:

> A hail of bullets came down on us from the surrounding hills. We had no time in which to draw our swords. I lay down beside a dead body and pretended I had been killed. The sound of firing continued for the time it would take for six successive cups of hot tea to cool. When the firing ceased, the British troops came into the camp to examine the dead and wounded. They prodded me with a bayonet, but I remained quiet and held my breath. Later a sore developed where I was pricked by the bayonet . . . Though afraid, I lay in the company of the dead until it grew dark, and then, at night, I ran to Guru. All the Tibetan officials had left, so I proceeded to Dochen.

Two other accounts of the battle from the Tibetan perspective, both second-hand, have been published in recent years. Both claim that the British opened fire without warning, and one goes so far as to suggest that the Tibetans were tricked by Macdonald and Younghusband into extinguishing the fuses for their match-locks as a gesture of good faith. Since the only way these fuses could be relit was by the laborious process of striking flints, this would have effectively disabled the Tibetans' main weapon. No first-hand evidence exists to show that any such trickery took place, while there is considerable testimony indicating that match-locks were fired. Dr Waddell, for example, noted as he wandered among the Tibetans that 'the fuses of their matchlocks were already burning', and moments later he either saw or heard them fire their muskets 'point-blank at us'. The fact that no British, Sikh or Gurkha soldiers were killed had nothing do with extin-guished fuses, and everything to do with the circumstances in which these absurdly unwieldy weapons were used and the fact that those troops closest to the Tibetans were nearly all protected by a high wall.

Before the firing had ended Dr Waddell and the five other doctors present had set up a dressing-station at the house at the end of the wall. It soon became clear that their own side had suffered no fatalities whatsoever and only twelve men wounded, Edmund Candler and the Sikh injured by the first shot being the most serious cases. The doctors then went forward with their medical orderlies to do what they could for the Tibetans left alive on the battlefield. 'It was a ghastly sight and all the more so in such sublime surroundings,' recorded Waddell. 'The dead and dying lay in heaps one over the other amidst their weapons, while a long trail of piles of bodies marked the line of retreat for half a mile or more; and cringing under every rock lay gory, wounded men, who had dragged themselves there to hide.' Among the dead he found 'the poor Lhasa General, who paid the penalty for his rashness, the Shigatse Depon and that truculent mischief-making yellow-robed Lama. Our old acquaintance of Yatung, the Phari Depon, I was sorry to see amongst the wounded, and had him carried to a tent.'

The dying were given water or brandy and had their pain eased by morphia, the Indian troops using their own field-dressings on the Tibetans' wounds. 'It was especially pathetic', noted Dr Waddell, 'to see the wounded Tibetans expecting us to kill them outright, as they frankly said they would have done to us, kowtowing with out-thrust tongues, holding up their thumbs in mute appeal for mercy, and grovelling in the dust to the humblest of our coolies.' Among those treating the wounded was Captain Mainprise of the Royal Army Medical Corps, who was disgusted to find that most of the Tibetans employed as stretcher-bearers had scattered – and not out of fear. 'I found my Tibetan Doolie bearers had run off and were looting the Tents, and houses and corpses,' he afterwards wrote in a letter to his brother Bertie. 'It took me about an hour before I could collect my Hospital and proceed along the bloodstained road – strewn with about 150 bodies.' Nearly two hundred of the more severely wounded were eventually carried either in the dhoolies – ambulance litters – or on the backs of prisoners to Tuna, where a field hospital was set up.

Dr Waddell interrogated many of the prisoners. He wanted to learn more about the structure of Tibet's government and its army, but he also questioned the men about their religious beliefs, concluding that they had been deluded by their lamas into believing that the charms they were given would render them impervious to bullets: 'Thus every one of the warriors who opposed us at Guru had one of these charms hung round their neck in amulet-boxes.' What struck him as 'a bitter irony of fate' was that, as he himself found on the battlefield, 'many at Guru received their death-wounds through their charm-boxes'.

Lieutenant Gurdon of the 32nd Pioneers was ordered to count the Tibetan casualties. He found 'in the immediate vicinity of Hot Springs 340 killed, 150 wounded'. Most sepoys and riflemen were found to have expended their allotted thirteen rounds per man. The two ten-pounders had fired fifty rounds of shrapnel between them, the two Maxims fourteen hundred rounds, which averaged out as each machine-gun firing for just over one minute's duration.

Excluded from this body-count were those Tibetans who died or were wounded in the subsequent pursuit, which continued for a distance of twelve miles. At the village of Guru, two miles north of the wall, some braver than the rest attempted to make a stand, firing on Peterson's 2nd Mounted Infantry as soon as they came within range. Hatter Bailey was with them and was forced to take cover behind a wall where, to his great irritation, he was joined by his pet whippet Jane – who unaccountably chose to sit on the wrong side of the wall, drawing fire onto their position. 'A lot of bullets went just over my head, but all were high and none short,' he wrote to his father. 'I hadn't got enough men to rush my Village, but soon the Goorkhas came up, and we all rushed together. When we rushed, they stopped firing or we should have lost a lot of men.' In the event three sepoys were killed, including Lieutenant Bailey's orderly Mela Singh. The Tibetans had stored large quantities of gunpowder in some of the houses which, according to official accounts, exploded during the storming of the village, killing the three men. Only weeks later did Bailey learn that they had in fact died while looking for booty. They had found a large box and were trying to break the lock by hitting it with a stone 'when it struck a spark & it turned out to be powder'. Perhaps this explains why these three fatalities were omitted from the casualty lists.

Whatever the cause of the original explosion, much of Guru village was in flames by the time Dr Austine Waddell got there.

Hearing that there were sacred texts in the home of the headman, he dashed from house to house looking for them: 'I found some books, which I brought out hastily as the adjoining house was afire, and I had to run the gauntlet of explosions, which were occurring all round, and the house in which I had been blew up a short time afterwards.'

It was still only eleven o'clock in the morning. At this point Henry Newman realised that, with Candler now *hors de combat*, he had every chance of beating Landon to a scoop. He hurried back through the battlefield and rode to the camp at Tuna, where he sat down and wrote furiously for an hour. He then hurried over to the Mission's tent to get his copy cleared and was surprised to find Colonel Younghusband there, already working on an official despatch. To Newman's further surprise, Younghusband was quite happy for him to send his report first. 'The telegraphists,' wrote Newman,

> were as keen as everybody else on the news. They wanted to know what had happened. They received the message eagerly, and a signaller said that the line had been specially kept clear to allow news to get through quickly and mine was the first news that had come. With the hastily written sheets in his hand he said: 'This will be in London quicker than you can imagine.' And so it happened. The newsboys in the Strand were bellow-ing through the fog with news of ''orrible slaughter' long before Whitehall had heard of it.

The General's telegram to the Adjutant-General in Calcutta, sent late in the evening, was the first to give details of how the firing had begun: 'Pioneers began to disarm Tibetan troops . . . At this point without any previous warning the Tibetans behind the wall opened a hot fire point blank on our men 15 or 20 yards off which they maintained for some minutes, several men also rushing out with swords.' There was no mention of the General's own close shave or of his part in the fight, which according to Newman included the shooting of several assailants with his revolver. Macdonald's despatch also gave the first official account of the losses on both sides: 'Our casualties are – Major Wallace Dunlop slightly wounded; Mr Candler, 'Daily Mail' correspondent, severely wounded, and seven sepoys wounded. The enemy's loss is nearly 500 killed and wounded, and 200 prisoners . . . Among the Tibetans killed was the chief Lhasa Depon and the Lama representative of the Ganden monastery; also one Shigatse Depon, whilst the Phari Depon was captured, severely wounded.'

Tibetan records state that more than five hundred Tibetans died at Chumik Shenko. Taking the further casualties sustained in the retreat and stand at Guru village into account, that figure was probably as accurate as any.

Macdonald's despatch also listed what had been seized on the battlefield: 'All their camp and baggage, about 60 yaks and 30 mules, with 2 gingalls [jingals] and a large number of matchlocks and swords, together with a few breechloaders, two of which were of Russian make.'

The issue of Russian rifles was a crucial one, for if significant numbers had been discovered at Guru it would have gone a long way towards justifying Lord Curzon's intervention. Rumours later began to circulate of several box-loads of Russian rifles found abandoned on the battlefield, the weapons still unpacked, but it is clear from every account that only a handful were recovered. As he toured the battlefield with the medical orderlies Dr Waddell saw plenty of swords and matchlocks and 'several rifles, mostly of Lhasa manufacture, but a few Russian'. Arthur Hadow went looking for trophies which, he told his clergyman father, he hoped 'to see in the Vicarage at Sutton some day'. He found no modern rifles but reported that a 'few' Russian weapons had been picked up. Later in the day Hatter Bailey had a chance to go over the same ground. He noticed cooking fires still smouldering in many of the Tibetan tents: 'They left everything just as it was; in one tent I found a game of dominoes unfinished, and in another they had been playing with dice and apricot stones.' But he saw no Russian guns, only 'some Russian cartridges'. The official figure for Russian rifles taken at Guru was later put at three, one of which was secured by Perceval Landon and sent down in the next convoy with orders for it to be delivered directly to Lord Curzon.

Once Guru village had been cleared the General ordered his infantry and guns to retire to Tuna. Arthur Hadow called in at the makeshift hospital to see Edmund Candler, who had left Hadow's old school, Repton, a year after he himself arrived. Candler had just had his left hand amputated at the wrist, by Captain Mainprise, the chief surgeon, and was expected to lose the other, but was doing 'as well as possible'. Mainprise had set up an operating theatre in a cowshed where he and his assistant surgeon, Lieutenant Davys, worked late into the night and throughout the following day. Despite his own wounds, Edmund Candler was able to marvel at the courage and endurance shown by the Tibetans: 'The patients showed extraordinary hardihood and stoicism. They were consistently cheerful, and always ready to appreciate a joke. One man who lost both legs said: "In my next battle I must be a hero, as I cannot run away" . . . They never hesitated to undergo operations, did not flinch at pain, and took chloroform without fear. Their recuperative power was marvellous.'

By Candler's account, only twenty of the Tibetan wounded brought into the field hospital died, the remainder recovering sufficiently to be sent to their homes on hired yaks. 'Everyone who visited the hospital,' he noted, 'left it with an increased respect for the Tibetans.' The Tibetans, for their part, were astonished by the humanity shown the British doctors – 'and looked upon Davys as some incarnation of a medicine Buddha'. To their great surprise all but the most senior Tibetan prisoners were released, among them a relative of the battlefield survivor Tseten Wangchuk, who later reported to him that the *pelings* had shown the most surprising kindness. All the Tibetans had been well fed and had their wounds treated. Each man was asked if he knew what foreign powers were providing assistance to Tibet, then photographed, given five rupees and a packet of cigarettes and told he could go – but with the warning that if he took up arms again he would be killed, and that 'the British army was such, that if it lost one hundred soldiers today it could replace them with a thousand tomorrow'.

The last to get back to camp were the Mounted Infantry, who did not return till late at night. Henry Newman, woken by the sounds of their return, was struck by how the men remained awake for most of the night, talking excitedly in their tents. 'Sometimes their voices rose so high I wondered whether they were not on the point of coming to blows,' he wrote later.

Breakfast next morning was marred by 'furious arguments developing among the officers and among the members of the mission. Disputes arose as to the exact sequence of the events which had taken place the day before and even about their nature.' Newman failed to set down why exactly the officers were arguing so furiously, but the central issue was clear: 'The disputes which were taking place in the camp at Tuna were, later on, I was told, revived in military circles all over the world . . . What they did not explain was how so many Tibetans had been killed with such a slight loss on our part.'

No one was more shaken by the turn of events than Francis Younghusband. 'I have had an absolutely miserable day,' he wrote to his wife Helen on the night after the massacre. 'It was a horrible sight, but I feel I did every single thing I could to prevent this.' As always, he was more forthcoming in his letters to his father, the first written next morning, 1 April, at Tuna. The Tibetans, he declared, were entirely to blame for what happened: 'I did what I could to prevent it and the troops behaved splendidly up to the last moment when they <u>had</u> to open fire. But it was a wretched affair – a pure massacre – brought on by the crass stupidity and childishness of the Tibetan general. They <u>will</u> not believe in our power and poor things have to suffer terribly in consequence. I am fearfully disappointed for I had so wanted to get through without this – as I have known all along how worthless these Tibetans were both in their generalship & military organisation all round.' This was followed three days later by a second letter in which he expanded on the theme of Tibetan irresponsibility:

> It was all the Tibetans' own fault and I am glad I twice restrained Macdonald from commencing firing but of course it was nothing but pure butchery – the poor things were penned up in a hollow within a few yards & even feet of our rifles. I did give them every chance up to the time the silly Lhasa general threw himself upon one of our sepoys & so commenced the fray. Then of course there was nothing for it but to begin firing . . . I don't think that we shall have any more fighting . . . Iggulden, Macdonald's Chief Staff Officer, was always croaking about 30 or 40,000 Tibetans meeting us at Gyantse. As a matter of fact

even the Tibetans do not claim more than 5,000 to have been here & at Gyantse the other day & these have now all bolted.

Scarcely less important than how the fighting started or how many Russian rifles were found was the issue of how many Tibetans had opposed Macdonald's army at Chumik Shenko. The General's estimate was two thousand men, half regulars and the rest militia. As already stated, in his own account of the engagement Colonel Younghusband wrote of 'a handful of men – about 100 Englishmen and 1,200 Indians – in the face of superior numbers of Tibetans'. Yet patrols had been observing the comings and goings of the Tibetans at Guru almost on a daily basis and all the officers had a good idea of the numbers involved. So, indeed, did Francis Younghusband, who had written to his father on 28 February belittling the exaggerated press reports and setting out what he believed to be the true figures: 'I visited the camp myself & carefully took stock of the numbers – wh. do not exceed 600 there . . . We reconnoitre it constantly & it has been increased to 1000 at most & none armed with rifles . . . Today however for the first time reports have really come in that the camp is being reinforced.' But in fact, there were no further reinforcements. Believing that the British would take the shortest route from Tuna to Lhasa, the Lhasa General had concentrated the bulk of his forces not at Guru but on the other, eastern side of Bam Tso.

Two days after the massacre Hatter Bailey set down what were probably the most accurate figures of Tibetan troops engaged at Guru. While reconnoitring the road beyond Guru village he had found two wounded Tibetans and brought them back on his ponies for treatment. In the field hospital he recognised one Tibetan as having been among the officers he had encountered during the clearing of the sangars: 'I had him in to tea yesterday,' Bailey wrote to tell his father, 'when he told me that they had only 900 Lhassa soldiers here, and that the 2000 Militia had gone the other side of the lake to stop us if we went that way.' Thus in all probability the Tibetans at the hot springs of Chumik Shenko were not only outgunned but also outnumbered.

Convinced the Tibetans had had the stuffing knocked out of them, Francis Younghusband now gave it as his considered opinion that there would be no more opposition. 'I was very low about that fight at first,' he wrote to his wife on 3 April, 'but I think it will prove good in the end & ought certainly to bring this Mission's work to an end sooner . . . It is very unlikely we shall have any fighting.'

7

On to Gyantse

T HE DISASTER at Guru and the loss of two of their senior generals threw the Tibetan military leadership into disarray. The
main force encamped on the eastern shore of Bam Tso was immediately pulled back over the mountains to defend the approach to
the great lake of Yamdok Tso and the southern road to Lhasa,
leaving the remnant of Depon Lhadang's army to fend for itself as
it retreated northwards to Gyantse. Yet small groups of Tibetan
warriors continued to resist, giving their comrades time to regroup
at the point where the upper waters of the Nyang Chu, the River
of Joy, cut through the mountains to form a narrow, deep and
winding gorge.

For his part, Brigadier-General Macdonald was determined to
exploit the military advantage won at Guru by pressing on to
Gyantse before the Tibetans could recover. Although his scouts
had reported the withdrawal of the main Tibetan force, he had no
idea at this stage that they were retiring to defend Lhasa rather than
Gyantse. On 5 April, a 'lovely spring morning', Macdonald's
reconnaissance in force marched away from the inhospitable plain
of Guru, along the Bam Tso shore, its still-frozen verges abounding in wildfowl, and over a battlefield littered with corpses. For the
next seven miles the route was strewn with 'heaps of gory dead

where our mounted infantry had crashed down upon the retreating enemy'. Then they came to their first green meadow, where their transport yaks and mules at last found something upon which to graze. Here they were met by a fat and smiling representative of the Chinese Amban, referred to by the British as General Ma, who urged them to wait there for the arrival of his master, who would soon be setting out from Lhasa to meet them. Given short shrift, he returned with his escort to Gyantse while Macdonald's army made camp on the meadows beside Bam Tso.

A second day's march took them down a narrow defile to the edge of a smaller lake, Kala Tso, which now became the northern terminus of the extended telegraph line. The lake was found to be full of fish and 'swarmed with the waterfowl preying on them – thousands of geese, ducks, teal, all very wild, also sheldrakes, terns, gulls, lapwings, red-shanks, snippets, etc.' Both fish and fowl became prey to the army's sportsmen and fishermen, who dined well that night. On the following day they reached the headwaters of the Nyang Chu, the 'pale bluish waters' of which were welcomed as the first clear evidence that they had actually crossed the great water-parting of the Himalayas: 'for we now knew that these rushing waters we were looking down on were hastening past Gyantse and Shigatse to meet the great central river of Tibet, the Tsang Po.' Villagers came out to meet them, kowtowing and showing signs of surprise but little fear. Here they saw the first signs of trees, in the form of low shrubs of dwarf red juniper – but also more high mountains ahead. 'We have discovered a magnificent range of snow mountains with peaks up to 25,000 feet,' wrote Younghusband to his wife. 'Everybody is in much better spirits & I am not so cross with Macdonald as I was! I walk along with different officers of the force & have great talks. Landon too is always interesting.' Since arriving at Tuna the special correspondent of *The Times* had worked hard to charm the Tibet Commissioner and his efforts were beginning to bear fruit: 'Old Macdonald does bore us to death & is incessantly about here in camp – such a bore. I try when I can to get away with Landon & talk about something else than mules, & rations & Tibetans.'

It was during the 70-mile advance on Gyantse that the Mounted Infantry showed their true worth, the 1st and 2nd taking it in turns

The 'old firm' reunited. Officers of the Mission staff and Mission Escort at Changlo Manor. Seated at the centre is Col. Younghusband (with bald head), flanked by Col. Brander on his right and Dr Waddell on his left. Seated in the row behind them are (from left) Mr Mitter, Capt. Walton, Capt. Hadow, Capt. O'Connor, Capt. Peterson and Mr Landon (wearing the sola topee). Standing next to Landon is Capt. Ottley.

The 'enemy'. The General, James Macdonald (seated centre), flanked by members of his staff at his New Chumbi headquarters. Col. Austine Waddell is seated on his right, Major Iggulden on his left. The popular Major Bretherton, drowned at the crossing of the Tsangpo, stands on the far right.

Above 'The first wheeled transport in Tibet. Ekkas entering Phari Jong': Phari with Mt Chomolhari in background. Pen and ink drawing by Lt. Norman Rybot.

Below Mounted Infantry soldiers and their ponies break the ice on the saddle of the Tang La, photographed by Lt. F. M. 'Hatter' Bailey, whose dog Jane/Gin also appears in the frame.

Above Brig.-Gen. Macdonald's 'reconnaissance in force' camped at Tuna prior to marching on Guru, 30 March 1904.

Right Capt. Arthur Hadow outside his tent at Tuna.

The enemy: a Tibetan nomad firing his matchlock.

The parley before the wall: the Lhasa General (seated centre) speaks to Col. Younghusband (wearing topee) with Frank O'Connor (kneeling, back to camera) interpreting. The General is hidden behind Younghusband. Edmund Candler watches on extreme left.

'Eric's men trying to peaceably disarm the Tibetans at the sangar.' Photo taken by Hatter Bailey just before the massacre at Chumik Shenko.

The massacre at the wall, with Sikh sepoys firing into the massed Tibetans, from a sketch by Lt. Norman Rybot.

Three Tibetan dead beside the wall at Chumik Shenko, said to be the Lhasa General and the two swordsmen who attacked Edmund Candler.

Dying Tibetan, photographed by Lt. G. I. Davys, and captioned by him: 'The Tibetan major who commanded the left sangar at Hot Springs. He is dying, his left hand shot away and his right leg torn to pieces by a shell.'

Frank O'Connor and his 'tame Lama' interrogate Tibetan prisoners guarded by Sikh Pioneers after the battle of the Red Idol Gorge.

Part of the Mission building at Changlo Manor, with Younghusband's and White's tents and Hadow's Maxim gun position on the roof all identified in pencil. The Tibetan cannon beside Younghusband's tent was found in Gyantse Jong.

Panorama of Gyantse, with Palkor Chode monastic complex in the left foreground, the town in the middle distance and the Jong behind, seen from the north.

to scout in front of the advancing army and to guard its flanks. At the village of Samunda, 18 miles north of Kala Tso, Peterson's 2nd Mounted Infantry squadron encountered its first opposition since leaving Tuna. According to Hatter Bailey, he, Captain Peterson and an officer from the Royal Engineers all but walked into a trap when they dismounted to talk to a group of monks who were waving them forward. At a distance of a hundred yards they were met by a volley of fire: 'The bullets buzzed all round us, and struck the ground, mostly beyond us, and I can't think why they did not hit some of us.' Their Pathan sepoys, who had been rather less trusting, returned fire with a volley of their own that allowed the officers to run for cover. The Mounted Infantry then withdrew and circled round to the back of the village, which was taken with the loss of six Tibetan lives and no losses to itself. This attempt to lure them into an ambush was seen as evidence of lama-inspired 'treachery', confirming the beliefs of Younghusband, Waddell and others on the expedition that it was the lamas who were orchestrating the fighting.

The army followed the Nyang Chu northwards as it descended into an ever more hospitable landscape marked by small fields of barley, planted wherever there was flat ground, and stunted willow trees that caused great excitement when first seen. Manifestations of Tibet's religion also began to appear, in the form of chortens, prayer-walls and, as Dr Waddell put it, 'parasitic' monasteries with their 'lazy priests'. On the hillsides above the monasteries were to be seen 'texts in gigantic letters written . . . by means of white quartz stones. Each letter was 15 or 20 feet long and could be seen several miles off.' Most bore the invocation '*Om Mane Padme Hom*' associated with the Indian sage Padmasambhava, known to Tibetans as Guru Rinpoche, the Blessed Teacher, and believed to have introduced Buddhist teachings to Tibet in the eighth century. That afternoon, as the lines of white tents began to spring up, Frank O'Connor learned from a village headman that Tibetan forces were gathering in strength at the village of Kangmar, just at the point where the Nyang river entered a fifteen-mile gorge that ended at the plain of Gyantse. This was presently confirmed by the Mounted Infantry, who sent back a messenger with news that they had come under fire. The

Tibetans had again taken up a position behind a wall, but a wall that was an altogether tougher proposition than that encountered at Chumik Shenko: it was loopholed, it extended right across the mouth of the gorge, and it continued up the mountain on both sides of the river for about a thousand feet.

The following day, 8 April, the General advanced his forces cautiously – too cautiously, for some – to within sight of Kangmar, the village of the Red Foot, which took its name from the surrounding spurs of red sandstone that projected into the valley like giant toes. They made camp early while the scouts probed the heights on either side of the wall. Early next morning a party of Gurkhas accompanied by signallers with a heliograph began to climb up the mountain side to a high point from which they could overlook the wall. Very soon they were signalling that the wall appeared to be unmanned. It was soon confirmed that the Tibetans had abandoned their positions in the night, leaving behind the bodies of six of their number, apparently killed during the Mounted Infantry's skirmish two days earlier. The Sikh Pioneers spent the rest of the day pulling the wall to pieces.

However, it soon became clear that, far from fleeing, the Tibetans had merely retired to a stronger position at the throat of the gorge, at a point where it was at its narrowest, for Brigadier-General Macdonald's telescope and the officers' field glasses were able to pick out lines of sangars high on both sides of the defile, together with the exposed barrels of up to a score of jingals, the Tibetan's heaviest small arms – a jingal being defined by Lieutenant-Colonel Brander as 'a magnified musket weighing anything up to 120 lbs and throwing a leaden or copper ball up to 1 lb weight'.

Reveille was sounded at 5 a.m. on the morning of 10 April, and three hours later the army advanced in battle formation. While William Ottley and his men clattered forward on their ponies into the defile and down the narrow trail that ran alongside the river, the mountain guns were dragged by gangs of coolies up the hillside on the right to a point of high ground from which they could bring fire to bear on the nearest sangars. The Tibetan jingals soon started to bang out, spewing large tell-tale clouds of grey smoke and sending lumps of shot whizzing among Ottley's men. They dismounted and took cover behind boulders while Ottley made a quick sketch of the enemy positions ahead and above before ordering a retreat. He had gone deep enough into the defile to see that the main defences were concentrated some distance further in: 'The road and valley seemed blocked in front by a spur extending towards the right about 1,500 feet high. The road along the bottom of the defile bears to the right also for about a mile. Here the valley widens out to about 150 yards, with a length of some 800 yards. On the left the cliffs are perpendicular, solid walls of rock, on the right the rocky slopes could be climbed by infantry with great difficulty – a regular scramble.' But this was only the Tibetans' first line of defence: 'The defile, road, and stream take a sharp turn to the left round the foot of the precipitous spur, and this cannot be seen till one arrives actually at the corner. It was at this corner the Tibetans hoped to stop us, and they were quite right in their choice of position, as they had a good line of retreat, and the strongest of positions to hold. The road round the corner through the boulders was only six feet wide for about 500 yards.'

When it came to scaling heights the Gurkhas were acknowledged masters, and it was they who were now set to scramble up the cliff on the left-hand side of the gorge, covered by shrapnel thrown by the ten-pounders. The rest of the army stood at rest and 'with our field-glasses glued to our eyes watched them laboriously climbing up amongst the rocks to dizzy heights' – until a sudden snowstorm swept down and blotted the Gurkhas from view. The waiting troops were soon numb with cold, so William Ottley and his men were pleased to be ordered to make a second dash down into the defile. 'Down we went in single file, about fifteen yards between the men, at a smart trot,' wrote Ottley. 'No enemy was discovered, and we began to think what fools the Tibetans were. Then we came to where the defile opened out to about 150 yards, with the front blocked by a precipitous hill covered with boulders. On we gaily went, and the leading man was just at the corner where the road and valley turn sharp to the left, when the whole of the hitherto silent, unanimated hillsides burst forth into flashes of fire and puffs of smoke.' They had ridden into an ambush: 'The Tibetans had concealed themselves splendidly, and had waited till we were within 150 yards of them, and could have allowed us to get within twenty if one of their men had not become excited and let his gun off too soon, which set them all going in front and both flanks and rear. There was nothing for it but to blow a whistle and signal the retire at the gallop, and off we went *ventre à terre*.' Quite unexpectedly, the Tibetans failed to inflict a single casualty: bullets fell all round them yet 'not a man nor a pony was hit'.

Believing the retiring horsemen to be in retreat, the Tibetan musketeers jumped up from their concealed positions on the hillsides to reload their cumbersome weapons and give chase. Seeing them so exposed, Ottley once more blew his whistle to signal a halt and dismount. His men took cover and returned fire. Now the Tibetans, in Ottley's words, received 'a taste of their own bullets . . . They sat down again in quick time when they found our Lee-Metford bullets buzzing in amongst them.' At the height of this uneven firefight a solitary female *Ovis ammon* – the great wild sheep of Central Asia – suddenly broke cover to appear on a prominent rock midway between the two sides. Trapped between two walls of fire, it remained exposed on its rock platform, wheeling first one way and then the other until the firing had died down.

Platoons of the 32nd Pioneers now came jogging up the track, and hard on their heels a group of Gurkhas and Nepali coolies carrying the parts that made up the Gurkhas' two ancient artillery pieces, Bubble and Squeak. It struck Ottley that the coolies seemed just as eager as the Gurkha riflemen to join in the assault, which began with the Sikhs skirmishing forward and up the lower slopes, kneeling and firing as they went. The return fire from the hillsides above suddenly diminished in volume and quality, leading Ottley to believe that those Tibetans who bore modern rifles had withdrawn, leaving only the men armed with antique matchlocks to fight on. This rearguard fought as best it could: 'It was not till Captain Bethune's men had got within fifty yards of them and had fixed bayonets that they began to move off. Thanks to the splendid cover they had, I don't think more than twenty of them were killed amongst the rocks, but they were driven out of a magnificently strong natural position, with only one man wounded on our side.'

As the retreating Tibetans scrambled across the hillside and back along the track, Captain Peterson and his mounted Pathans took up the chase on their ponies. 'They came clattering down the defile round the corner and after the fugitives,' wrote Ottley. 'As soon as we could get hold of our ponies and mount, we joined up with Captain Peterson.' Far above their heads to the left, the Gurkhas had reached a position from which they could bring a sharp fusillade of rifle fire down on the Tibetans manning the jingals, forcing them to abandon their weapons and join what soon became a general retreat. At its middle section the gorge contracted into a narrow cleft with great cliffs towering almost perpendicularly on either side. Here half a dozen sharpshooters armed with modern rifles could have halted the British force, but panic had now set in among the Tibetan soldiery, so that far from providing a defence this cleft, which continued for over a mile, its floor a jumble of rocks and boulders and fast-flowing water, became a death-trap. It now filled with terrified men, those in front scrambling over the obstacles as best they could while being jostled and shoved by those behind – who made easy targets for the pursuing sepoys.

On the right-hand bank of the river at the point where the cleft at last began to open out, two Buddhist images had been carved in semi-relief on a large boulder and painted in bright scarlet and gold leaf. One of these figures gave its name to what the British later called the fight at Red Idol Gorge. 'It is a crude, repellant image of the wizard priest who founded the order of Lamas,' declared Austine Waddell, 'and by his side is an equally large red-painted likeness of the Buddhist god who is supposed to be incarnate in the Grand Lama of Tashilhumpo.' The first of these figures was a representation of Guru Rinpoche, revered throughout Tibet as much as anything for his taming of the fierce demons and spirits held to inhabit such dangerous places as river crossings, mountain passes and, of course, gorges. The second was of Amitabh, one of the five peaceful meditational buddhas who together formed a body known as the Five Families. The red colour in which he was always depicted represented purity of perception.

Just beyond this spot two side valleys came in from left and right to create a patch of open ground strewn with giant boulders. Here the leaders of the Tibetan troops tried to regroup their forces, but before they could reimpose order the Mounted Infantry were upon them. 'The Tibetans', wrote Ottley, 'tried to make a stand

and stop us; but what could they do, although there were about 1,500 of them? They were broken and flying, and we were advancing – about 150 Mounted Infantry – at full gallop, with the men making excellent practice, shooting from their ponies.' The Tibetans now had several avenues of escape, but many chose to flee up the side valley to the left – only to find their way blocked by the Gurkhas as they descended from the ridge they had earlier climbed and crossed. Fortunately for them, the Gurkhas had had enough target practice, and began to round them up like so many sheep.

By the time Francis Younghusband and the other politicals emerged from the Red Idol Gorge, the fighting was over. He found time to scribble his wife in Darjeeling a brief note that was telegraphed back down the line from the newly-established telegraph post at Kala Tso. It read simply: 'Tibetans bolting like rabbits.' A subsequent letter gave the full story and a possible explanation for the Tibetans' seeming inability to shoot straight: 'We hear today that when the Tibetan generals were advised by the Chinese not to fight the tears streamed down their faces as they said they had to fight for if they did not their families wd be seized. So they pretended to fight & about a hundred of them were killed.'

More than a hundred prisoners were taken, a 'truculent savage rabble' that put Dr Waddell in mind of the 'new-caught sullen peoples, half devil and half child' of Rudyard Kipling's already famous celebration of imperial law and order published five years earlier as *The White Man's Burden*. Among the prisoners were a number of monks in red robes, who were judged to have played a pivotal role in the fighting by urging the soldiers to stand and fight. Hundreds of crude weapons were gathered up but, as at Guru, only a handful of rifles that could be described as Russian in origin. The prisoners were put to work breaking them to pieces, which, according to Austine Waddell, they did with 'evident delight, jumping on the splinters most cordially. They said that they were only peasantry who had been forced by the Lamas to fight under the threat of having their homes burned down and their families taken from them.'

The official figure for Tibetan casualties at Red Idol Gorge was 150 killed and wounded. This was an estimate and almost certainly well short of the true figure, for no search was made of the mountain sides. The Mission Escort's casualties were three: one of William Ottley's Sikh Native Officers and two of his sepoys wounded in the pursuit. Francis Younghusband was able to declare in writing to his father from Gyantse that 'we have got here without the loss of a single man . . . Literally, our only loss between India and here has been two fingers and an arm.' The arm – more accurately, hand – had been Edmund Candler's and the two fingers had belonged to Major Wallace Dunlop. No mention of the two amputated legs of the Eurasian Post Master and his subsequent death, the three Sikh sepoys killed in the explosion at Guru village, the fourteen Sikhs dead of pneumonia and pulmonary oedema at Tuna, or the more than twenty deaths from exposure and other unnatural causes among the coolies, yak-drivers and muleteers.

The town of Gyantse, the Dominating Peak, was reached on 11 April. Early that morning Brigadier-General Macdonald's army marched past a solid, fort-like building whose walls were painted in vertical bands of red, white and blue. This was Naini Gompa, the Monastery of the Ancient Year that guarded the southern end of the Gyantse Valley. Since its occupants showed no signs of hostility and the General was anxious to reach Gyantse by nightfall the monastery was bypassed without a second thought.

'We were now', wrote Dr Waddell of this final leg, 'in an open bay of the rich plain of the Gyantse Valley, which we could see stretching up and down on either side about two miles ahead of us . . . On turning the corner of a spur on our left the broad plain-like expanse of the fertile valley of Gyantse shot fully into view, dotted over with neat white-washed farmhouses and villas clustered in groves of trees amongst well-cultivated fields, and high over all near the middle of the plain the glistening white fort on its dark rock towered up boldly and apparently impregnable.'

This citadel caught and held every eye as the army marched towards its foot, for it was planted on the summit of a rock eminence that seemed to rise directly out of the plain, its sides rearing four hundred feet sheer into the sky. To Waddell it recalled Edinburgh Castle 'to some extent' but also St Michael's Mount. Viewed from the south it appeared to all intents impregnable. But as the army drew closer it could be seen that the fortress was actually perched on the southern extremity of a crescent-shaped,

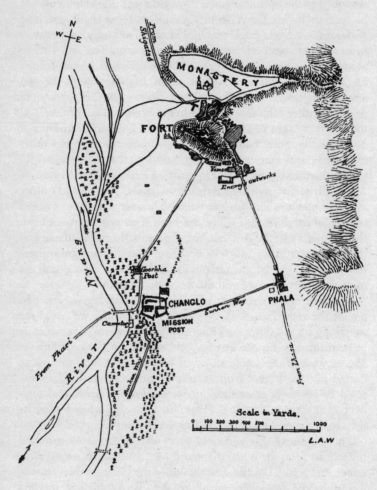

Gyantse and the Mission post at Changlo Manor

steep-sided ridge that ran north and south down the centre of the plain for about a mile and a half, with a protective wall of towers and battlements that followed the spine of this ridge before climbing up to a high point at the southern end, where it wrapped itself around the rock buttress in a series of tiered defences. Shielded within the curve of the crescent by wall and fortress, but initially out of sight of the advancing army, was the town itself and its monastery, the latter known and revered throughout Tibet as Palkor Chode, the Illustrious Circle of the Religious Residence.

After following the river until they were close to what the General judged to be cannon range of the fortress, the army forded the stream and camped in the fields two miles south of the town. Gyantse stood at an altitude of 13,000 feet above sea level, but the difference between Tuna and here was remarkable. The air was soft and mild, and even though the fields were still bare, spring seemed just around the corner. 'Here we are & a lovely place it is,' wrote Francis Younghusband to his father. They had pricked the Tibetan bubble and Gyantse was about to fall to them without a shot being fired. 'Dear old Macdonald is making a solemn attack on the fort as I write this but all the Tibetan soldiers bolted last night & the fort commander only wants an excuse for chucking it. He was in my camp yday. & said he dared not give it up until we compelled because if he did all his family & belongings wd. be seized. This is the secret of all the Tibetan fighting. They don't want to fight but they are afraid of their own people . . . As I have always said, the Tibetans are nothing but sheep.'

The General's 'solemn attack' had been prompted by the appearance in camp the day before of the governor of the fort, Depon Tailing, described by Perceval Landon as 'a kindly heavy old man like a saddened Falstaff'. The Depon had declared himself unable to hand over the fort since, regrettably, he was under orders from Lhasa not to do so. This had resulted in an ultimatum: surrender the fort by 8 a.m. the following morning or face an assault. Though his garrison had already fled, the Depon kept up the pretence of holding his fort until the very last minute, forcing Macdonald to bring up his heavy guns, before finally flinging open the gates. The occupation of the empty jong by two companies of the 32nd Sikh Pioneers was then achieved without further incident, and the

British flag was hoisted on its highest battlement to cheers from those watching down below. 'Thus', wrote Ottley, 'the strongest fortress in Tibet, and the one to which the Tibetans attach most sentiment and reliance, fell into the hands of the British without a shot being fired.' There was grumbling among the sepoys and Gurkha riflemen, 'because we had not had a decent hammer-and-tongs fight yet'.

James Macdonald was now chain-smoking forty cigarettes a day and suffering from fever, but he was well enough to pay a courtesy call on the abbot of the Palkor Chode monastery. Among those who accompanied him as he rode through the town on horseback was Dr Waddell, who was surprised to find the town's populace going about its business without signs of fear or hostility: 'We met people going to or from the market, men in flowing cherry-coloured coats riding lean ponies, which they flicked with their dog-whips; lines of donkeys plodding in single file with loads of grain or fodder; chattering women, slatternly dressed, carrying baskets or children slung on their backs.' Their ride took them along the main street of Gyantse, consisting of about a thousand tightly packed stone houses built in the shelter of the curved ridge, and on to a market-place sited directly in front of the main entrance to the monastery:

> The traders displayed their wares in booths or on the pavement by the roadside, where they sat beside their piles of goods, waiting to sell or barter their commodities, which consisted, among other things, of tea, tobacco, sugar, cotton cloth, brown and yellow broadcloth, and dark corduroy, cotton thread – red and white – matches, pipes, enamelled iron tumblers, kerosene oil – bearing the Russian mark, but which came by way of Darjeeling – and a host of Tibetan nicknacks, drugs, fresh vegetables, meat, including pork, and the barley beer of the country. The most attractive exhibits for us were the carpets and saddle-rugs of local manufacture, for which this town is famous.

Dismounting from their ponies, the officers pushed their way through a crowd of 'clamorous beggars' to reach the main gate. They passed through a wooden portico on either side of which were ranged the 'colossal leering figures of the four mythological guardian kings of the four quarters . . . clad in mail armour of Chinese pattern, each bearing a special emblem and having a different colour'. Awaiting them in the main courtyard was the abbot – 'of dignified mien and fair intelligence' – and a bevy of shaven-headed monks who struck Waddell as being 'anything but ascetic or intellectual in looks. All were visibly unfamiliar with ablution, as if purity of soul was not compatible with cleanliness of body.' Yet much as the Presbyterian doctor despised these 'sleek Lama-priests' for inducing the laity of Tibet to lavish their all on temples and idols, he had to accept that here at Palkor Chode the consequences were far more impressive than anything he had yet seen: 'Its cluster of buildings rise up in several tiers like a huge amphitheatre, and encircle at their base a great pagoda standing on the edge of the plain below a celebrated place of pilgrimage whose minaret-like top, of massive plates of burnished gold, towers up nearly 100 feet high, a glittering landmark for all the country round.'

While Brigadier-General Macdonald was rebuking the abbot for allowing his monks to take part in the fighting at the Red Idol Gorge and imposing a hefty fine to be paid in the form of 36 tons of barley, Dr Waddell explored the extraordinary pagoda-like structure that formed the central feature of the monastic complex of Palkor Chode. Known to Tibetans as the Kumbum, or Temple of One Hundred Thousand Deities, this was a giant nine-storey stupa incorporating seventy-five small chapels, each with its own statues of greater and lesser deities. In the ascent from one stage to the next, so the chapels grew fewer and the deities more elevated, culminating in a single chapel on the ninth and highest storey. Dr Waddell was delighted to learn from its attendants that the structure was modelled on a building in India that he was familiar with through his own archaeological explorations: the Mahabhodi temple at Bodhgaya, marking the spot where Gautama Buddha first achieved enlightenment under a bodhi tree. However, when it came to describing or even making sense of the complex iconography represented in the building – a three-dimensional meditational mandala encapsulating in architecture and art the entire spiritual path to enlightenment as interpreted in the Buddhist tantric tradition – Dr Waddell found himself at a loss. It was left to one of the force's transport officers, Lieutenant Mark Synge, to supply the first proper, if highly subjective, description by a European of this gem:

> The centre of it consists of one huge Buddha reaching from the ground to the height of, I should say, one hundred and fifty feet. Round this are built tiers upon tiers of small shrines; each tier contains one less shrine than the tier below it. The shrines are of equal size, so that the general effect of the whole edifice is that of a pyramid. You rise from tier to tier by a narrow hidden staircase. Each shrine contains one idol. If you start at a certain point on any of the tiers, and go round that tier, you will first enter the shrine of a perfect Buddha, for whom you will feel at least some reverence. The next shrine will contain an idol that impresses you less, and has about it some taint of the world. The next is a thoroughly worldly idol, the next is ugly, the next is obviously wicked, and the next a demon. The demons grow in demoniacal qualities till suddenly you arrive again at the Buddha from whom you started. The tiers above are all arranged on the same principle, except that, the number of shrines decreasing by one in each case, the gradation from Buddha to demon grows more abrupt as you ascend.

Like so many Westerners at this time, Synge was troubled by the apparent contradictions in Tibet's Buddhism. He was happy with the benign but oversimplified image of Tibetan Buddhism as represented by the old lama in Rudyard Kipling's recently published masterpiece *Kim*, but not with what he saw on the road to Lhasa: the portrayal in paintings and sculptures not just of demons but of all sorts of ugly beasts engaging in the most frightful activities, such as dancing or feeding on bloody corpses and, worst of all, in cross-legged sexual embrace with attractive female deities. 'Such strange excrescences on the external face of a religion that ranks so high in regard to the spirituality of its essential tenets, and the extent and depth of its influence on human life,' Synge lamented. 'One of the noblest and purest of religions tainted – at any rate as regards the art which is ancillary to it – with those twin poisons of demon-worship and priapism.'

His views were totally in accord with those of Britain's leading authority on Tibet's religions, Dr Austine Waddell, whose scholarship was blinkered by his own strongly held religious convictions and a detestation of popery and anything that resembled it. At Palkor Chode he chose to focus his enquiries on the largest of the temples, the Tsuklakhang, where he found plenty to shock him, such as the inordinate amounts of butter wasted in keeping the lamps burning on the altars, but also much to marvel at. He arrived in the main hall just as a service was getting under way in which a hundred claret-robed monks participated, seated in rows along either side of the nave:

> When all was ready they began a chant, which distinctly recalled that of a High Church service at home. The deep, organ-like bass of the singers, the swell and fall, the intoning, the silvery-tonged bells, accentuated at times by the muffled roll of the drums in the second row, gave altogether a majestic and sacred character to the service, while the flickering lights and the figures of the priests, looming out of the darkness and through the thin clouds of incense fumes, like shadows, vivid yet veiled, made up a most impressive spectacle.

Dr Waddell was both moved and sickened, for he was constantly put in mind of the rituals against which his own church had rebelled several centuries earlier. It was a relief when at the back of the main chapel and in one side chapel he discovered tiers of pigeon-holes containing bundles of sacred texts. These were what he had come to Tibet for, particularly the hundred volumes that made up the Tibetan canon, the Kanjur, translated from Sanskrit a thousand years earlier, and the companion commentaries, the Tanjur, comprising two hundred and fifty volumes. 'These musty volumes in their faded wrappings are believed by the Lamas to contain all knowledge, everything worth knowing, as were once the voluminous works of scholastic philosophy which still encumber the libraries of Europe.' These were not books as the West knew them, for each folio had either been written by hand as a manuscript or hand-printed by the laborious process of carving the text in reverse onto a wooden board: 'Each volume forms a cumbrous, unwieldy, heavy package about 2½ feet long and 8 inches broad, weighing 10 to 30 pounds, and containing several hundred loose leaves wrapped in cloth and strapped between heavy wooden boards.'

To Dr Waddell's disappointment, but perhaps unsurprisingly in the circumstances, he came away from Gyantse's great temple with nothing more than a promise from the abbot to provide him with a catalogue of all the books in his library. He left with his prejudices intact, professing dismay at the ignorance displayed in this supposed grand temple of learning: 'On the contrary, it trains chiefly in incantations and silly mystical gestures and puerilities, and has little that is intellectual about it. The monks are of a low type of intelligence . . . and their discipline is rather lax; for during the intervals of the service they gabbled away and joked among themselves indecorously, and several refused to obey the order of their superior when he asked them to come out to be photographed by me.'

From Palkor Chode the General's party rode back through the town to inspect the Jong itself, entering through an impressive gateway from which hung the stuffed carcasses of four wild yaks, 'with artificial eyes and tongues protruding in a fearsome way'. These were evidently intended to overawe any visitor, but to Perceval Landon they seemed decidedly unimpressive: 'The beasts were falling to pieces from age, and rather resembled badly stitched leather bags than anything else. Everything that could fall from them – hair, horns, hoofs – had already fallen, and handfuls of the straw stuffing bulged out from every seam.'

From here a path overlooked by inner walls and towers climbed diagonally upwards to a number of dilapidated houses and a large store-house in which were found 'thousands of pounds of powder, tons and tons of supplies, and tens of miles of matchlock fuse'. The supplies consisted of a hundred tons of barley, flour and dried peas, as well as large stores of dried mutton and yak meat, all of which was soon brought down to camp on the backs of mules and coolies. The accident at Guru had demonstrated the volatility of Tibetan gunpowder, so the order was given that the several tons found in the fort were to be carried down to the river and thrown into the water. According to Hatter Bailey, the officer in charge of this operation took it into his head to set fire to one box, which exploded, setting off a chain of further explosions among the remaining boxes. Either this or a second accident during the clearing of gunpowder from the Jong killed at least two soldiers and injured 'many more men than the Tibetans themselves had done'. The General had the officer court-martialled and 'sent down'.

As the fort was being searched a number of curious discoveries were made. One was a chamber 'full of decapitated heads of men, women and children'. Austine Waddell examined them, and gave his opinion as a medical man that their 'gory necks' showed they had been executed – 'which disposes of the idea that the Buddhism of the lamas stops short of the atrocious crime of murder'. Another room housed what Hatter Bailey termed an 'idol factory', stacked with small religious images. These were declared legitimate booty under the rules of war and shared out between the officers by a prize committee, with Dr Waddell, in his official capacity as expedition archaeologist and collector, getting the first pick. According to William Beynon, 'A selection for the British and other museums was first made and then a dozen each for Genl Macdonald and Col Younghusband. After that the remainder were divided amongst the officers of the force, each getting two or three pieces.' Elsewhere in the citadel, some chests were found containing 'some fine painted scrolls', which were distributed 'in the same way as the images were'. In addition to these statuettes and scrolls, Austine Waddell also acquired 'a finely inscribed stone reciting the virtues of a chief who restored the fort'. All this was also deemed to be legitimate spoil, on the grounds that troops from Gyantse Jong had initially resisted the advance of Macdonald's reconnaissance in force.

The doctor's visit to the Jong ended with a climb to the crest of the fort where 'the British flag flapped noisily in the wind'. From here a magnificent panoramic view could be obtained of the valley and the surrounding hills, causing the doctor to reflect on how, centuries earlier, the warrior king who built the fort 'must often have looked down with pride on his prosperous town and the far-reaching fields, studded over with the trim white farms and dark garden groves of the nobles and rich merchants of the town'. He also observed the tents of the British camp to the south 'within easy rifle range', and in the middle distance to the north-west the 'dark hill of Tse-chen, dotted with the while cells of its monks, a town itself'. Tsechen was only the largest of a number of hilltop monasteries that ringed the valley, none of which would be easy to assault if they turned hostile.

It had always been planned that as soon the Tibet Mission and Escort had been securely established at Gyantse, the General would take the rest of the force and the supply train back down to Chumbi, establishing a couple of staging-posts along the way. Despite threats from the lamas, traders had been quick to set up a large bazaar outside the camp, and were starting to bring in quantities of fresh vegetables, grain and meat, for which they were well paid. But these local supplies were never going to be enough to meet all the needs of the Mission and Escort, let alone those of the main force. A brief survey of the Jong showed that to hold it would require a considerable garrison, and also that it lacked a proper water supply. On Macdonald's orders the outer wall was dismantled and the great gate blown up – sending stones, beams and stuffed yaks flying into the air in a most satisfying explosion.

A more suitable residence for Younghusband's Mission staff and Escort was found just north of the existing camp, at the point where the river was crossed by a stone bridge. Here in a grove of willow trees stood a grand country mansion and farmstead owned by a well-known Tibetan noble family named Changlo. Outhouses were knocked down, trees felled and lines of sharpened stakes known as abattis set into the ground as the site was speedily converted by the Pioneers and sappers into a defensive post encircled by a loopholed wall some three hundred yards in circumference. Changlo Manor now became the Mission headquarters, deemed eminently suitable since its main building had a large audience hall where Colonel Younghusband could hold his durbars or formal audiences with representatives of the Dalai Lama. He chose to sleep outside in his tent in the garden, but most officers found rooms for themselves in one or other of the main buildings. One even found a comfortable home inside a room that housed a giant water-driven prayer wheel, converting the five-foot-high prayer wheel into 'a useful dumb-waiter by fixing on it a few nails and a bracket or two'. Austine Waddell did even better,

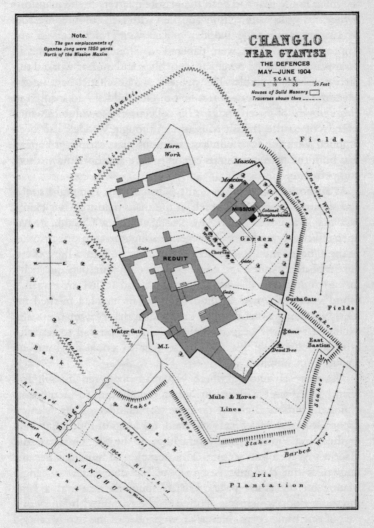

Note.
The gun emplacements of
Gyantse Jong were 1350 yards
North of the Mission Maxim

CHANGLO
NEAR GYANTSE
THE DEFENCES
MAY—JUNE 1904
SCALE
0   5   10   20   30 Feet
Houses of Solid Masonry
Traverses shown thus _____

Abattis

Fields

Horn
Work

Maxim

Maxim

Barbed Wire

Stakes

MISSION

Colonel
Younghusband's
Tent

Garden

Gate

Chorten

REDUIT

Gate

Gate

Abattis

Gurha Gate

Fields

Gate

Stakes

N.

W.   E.

S.

Water Gate

Guns

M.I.

Dead Tree

East
Bastion

Bank

Abattis

Riverbed

Stakes

Bank

Stakes

Bridge

Flood level

August 1904

Mule & Horse

Lines

Barbed Wire

R.

Low Water

NYANCHU

Riverbed

Low Water

Bank

Stakes

Iris
Plantation

The Tibet Mission at Changlo Manor: the defences, May–June 1904 securing an upper room in a double-storeyed building adjoining the main house that had been the private quarters of the mansion's owner: 'Its walls were lavishly adorned with rich coloured frescoes of Lamaist saints, the wooden pillars were finely carved and painted, the windows were papered in Chinese fashion, and its floor was a tessellated pavement of pebbles and mortar worked to a high polish like marble.' The owner's private chapel became the Mission's mess – although not before Dr Waddell had secured its entire library of sacred texts for his collection: 450 volumes which later went to the British Museum. Although Waddell had been supplied with funds to purchase religious manuscripts, it appears that both the mansion and its contents were appropriated without compensation.

As an honorary member of the Mission mess Perceval Landon also secured a room for himself in the main mansion, but Henry Newman was not so lucky. At Gnatong and New Chumbi he had been effectively snubbed whenever he sought to join one or other of the officers' messes, and here at Changlo he found the experience repeated: 'When I asked whether I could join such and such a mess, I found that all were full up. So I had to live by myself. I found a sort of corner in the farmhouse in which I pitched my tent.' Not being a member of a mess meant that Newman was also excluded from the officers' dining rooms, so he had to fend for himself, relying on his Gurkha servant to cook for him and scrounge for supplies.

The large farmhouse where Newman quartered himself had been handed over with its surrounding outhouses to Lieutenant-Colonel Herbert Brander, the new commander of the Mission Escort, to house his officers and men, made up of four companies of the 32nd Pioneers, two companies of the 8th Gurkhas, and Hadow's Maxim gun section. This complex of buildings became known as the Redoubt (see map of the defences of Changlo Manor on preceding page). On its southern side was a large threshing floor which was allotted to the Mounted Infantry and part of one mule corps. Neither commander of the two Mounted Infantry squadrons had wanted to leave Gyantse but William Ottley won the toss, staying on with twenty of his mounted infantrymen. Excluding the politicals and such non-combatants as a section of an Indian Field Hospital, the Changlo Manor garrison amounted to about 550 fighting men. The site's one military drawback was that it was not much more than 1300 yards from the Jong and well within range if any jingals or heavier guns were ever reinstalled. Given the fort's obvious disadvantages, Brigadier-General Macdonald was probably right not to occupy it. What was less excusable was his decision to take the ten-pounders back to New Chumbi with him, leaving the Mission's defenders no serious weaponry with which to hit back at the fort other than the two Maxims and the Gurkhas' antique Bubble and Squeak.

Five days after he arrived at Gyantse the defences of Changlo Manor were deemed secure and James Macdonald gave the order for the main force to begin the long march back to New Chumbi, leaving behind three weeks' supply of rations. The two remaining special correspondents, Perceval Landon and Henry Newman, were asked if they wished to return to Chumbi but declined, having heard from Colonel Younghusband that the Tibetans were refusing to negotiate. 'Of course, we were all delighted to hear of these messages,' wrote Newman, 'for we wanted to get to Lhasa, and if the Tibetans caved in and made a treaty there would be no hope of getting to that romantic city.' Hatter Bailey was given no such choice, and when he heard that he was to march with the main force he at once appealed to Colonel Younghusband, who interceded with the General on his behalf. But Macdonald was not a man who did favours. As 'H.H.A.', an old sapper chum of Macdonald's, put it many years later (in writing his obituary for the *Royal Engineers Journal*), Macdonald saw himself as a man of the highest principles 'and expected these virtues in others with whom his work brought him into contact. Sometimes it was his misfortune to be deceived in this respect; and he then made no secret of his contempt for those who played him false, and seldom forgave these lapses from the paths of rectitude.' He declined to change his orders, angering Younghusband and making an enemy of Bailey in the process.

With the General, his staff and the main force gone, the 'old firm' began to reassert itself: Francis Younghusband was once more in moral as well as political command, and spirits rose. 'Such a relief old Macdonald having gone,' he declared to his wife. 'We have a very cheery mess of ten now. Wilton (Chinese expert), O'Connor, Ryder and his assistant Cowrie (both REs), Haydn (geologist), Waddell, Hadow (escort), Walton (doctor), Landon, & play bridge every evening. I have just enough work now to keep me going.' Even the Indian members of the Mission staff were in high spirits, none more so than Younghusband's Bengali chief babu or head-clerk, Mr S. Mitter, who had long been a figure of fun among the officers because of his insistence on always wearing a wing collar and tie in the most hostile surroundings: 'Mr Mitter is quite exuberant,' wrote Younghusband. 'He goes about beaming and says this place quite compensates him for all he has gone through. But he says that not going on to Lhasa would be like leaving out Hamlet in playing Hamlet.' If there was one drawback to their present situation it was that the Mission mess had run out of whisky and liqueurs, and was having to make do with commissariat rum as issued to the troops, tasting 'more like furniture polish than anything else'.

The Mission and its garrison now entered a halcyon period. The sun shone, the snow began to melt on the surrounding hillsides, and beards, poshteens and Gilgit boots were no longer de rigueur. Inside the walls of Changlo Manor a small unoccupied plot was converted into a garden and planted with vegetable seeds, a member of the Mission having had the foresight to bring up a box of Sutton's best. A trio of gardeners was engaged: 'a buxom Tibetan dame' who became known to the officers as 'Mrs Wiggs', after the chief protagonist of a popular Edwardian book on gardening, and her two husbands. 'Mrs Wiggs' was the 'moving spirit in her own domestic circle' and quickly had her 'pair of semi-imbecile husbands' hard at work carting in soil from the nearby woods to create a series of vegetable beds. 'We soon', wrote Waddell, 'had croppings of young cress salad, with which and with our mutton and a dairy of half-bred yak cows, abundant eggs, fowls, potatoes, turnips, dried apricots, and other fresh supplies from the town, we were able to live in luxury after our meagre fare and hardships of the long winter and the march.'

What Dr Waddell termed 'the mighty rupee' began to work wonders in the valley, with townspeople, villagers and even monks flocking in to offer goods for sale at the Changlo bazaar: 'There was nothing the people were not willing to sell in exchange for rupees. They would take off their turquoise earrings and other ornaments, also their treasured amulet charm-boxes, and press you to buy them. Even the sleek Lamas brought out their sacred scrolls and books and images and bargained them for cash, and everybody seemed supremely pleased, never having had so much money in their lives before.'

The tradition of street ballads flourished in Tibet, as it still does today. Verses from two of the many songs sung in the streets of Gyantse at this time have survived, and chart the change of attitude among the local population. One lamented the loss of freedom:

> Gyantse the turquoise valley
> Is filled with marauding outsiders.
> Oh! When I see such things happen
> I wonder what is the use of gathering riches.

The second ballad was still being sung a decade later when a young political officer named Charles Bell arrived in Gyantse as British Trade Agent:

> At first, they speak of 'Foes of our true Faith',
> And next the cry is of 'Foreign Devildom'.
> But when they see the foreign money bags,
> We hear of 'Honourable Englishmen'.

A more altruistic contribution to good relations came after Captain Walton, surgeon and natural history expert to the Mission, set up a small surgery just outside the perimeter and invited the Tibetans to make 'the fullest use of his own skill and the medical equipment of the Mission'. He soon had patients queuing at the door: 'By preference he selected cases requiring surgical treatment, and many unfortunate wretches disabled by cataract or by a particularly hideous form of hare-lip, which is common in Tibet, were relieved by him.'

It was soon considered safe enough for the officers to explore the town unescorted, and to venture further afield in small parties. Some went fishing or shooting, others shopped or went sightseeing in the town and its surrounding hamlets. 'I was able to satisfy my curiosity more and more about Tibetans and the manners and customs,' wrote Henry Newman. 'No Tibetan suggested I was an intruder when I wandered into courtyards or even into houses. They were all friendly . . . I could write a book about what I learned in Gyantse.' A few ventured as far as a day's riding allowed, particularly O'Connor and Ottley and the other officers of the Mounted Infantry, for whom this was more scouting combined with a spot of *shikar* than sightseeing. Dr Waddell accompanied them on several excursions, visiting the monasteries in the surrounding hills, and towards the end of April rode some fourteen miles north to a place known as the Cave of Happy Musings on Misery to inspect a colony of what he termed 'entombed hermits'. They set out on a perfect spring morning. 'All Nature was vibrating with the joy of new-found life,' wrote Waddell:

> The frost-bitten land had thawed under the few weeks' genial sun, and through the soft soil by the roadside and on the borders of the fields, fresh green shoots were pushing themselves up alongside deep olive-beds of exquisite pale-blue iris-lilies, and pink clumps of dwarf primulas and gay saxifrage which already begemmed the ground amongst the golden gorse bushes. From every hamlet the cottagers had swarmed out into their fields and were busy ploughing and sowing in the glorious sunshine, forming pleasing bits of bright colour. The men were ploughing with oxen gaudily bedecked with plumes of wool dyed glowing scarlet and blue, with long throat-tassels of dyed yaks'-tails, and harness of jingling bells, whilst close behind the ploughers came the gaily dressed women as the sowers, scattering broadcast the seed from their baskets. Most of them, men and women, were humming snatches of song in lightheartedness.

From this 'genial valley, pulsating with life', their guide led Waddell and his three companions up a bare, rock-strewn side valley and finally into a dark ravine, the upper cliff of which was dotted with the cave-dwellings of 'buried anchorites', ascetics who had chosen to immure themselves in their caves in a stage-by-stage process that ended with them being walled in and entombed for life. Attendants led them from one such bricked-up cave to another. The first cell was occupied by an old hermit who 'had not seen the light, nor had been seen or spoken to by anyone, for over twenty-one years'. His only link with the outside world was a tiny sliding door outside which food was left, the signal for its arrival being three taps on the wood. They watched as an attendant gave the signal and then waited for the cave's occupant to respond:

> Whilst we held our breath expectantly, in a silence like that of the tomb, the tiny rabbit-hutch door in front of us trembled, then began to move and was jerkily pushed ajar about three inches or so, and from the deep gloom came slowly faltering forth A GLOVED HAND! This was all! Only a gloved hand! It protruded about four inches onto the stone-slabbed sill and slowly fumbled there for two or three seconds, and finding nothing, it returned slowly, trembling as in a palsy, and the door closed up like a snail retreating into its shell, and nothing broke the agonized silence save, as I fancied, a suppressed moan. The whole action was muffled like a dream, so slow, so stealthy, so silent and creepy. In the daylight it was unearthly and horrible to a degree.

Dr Waddell found the whole business fascinating but 'sickening', and later speculated on what it was that drove these wretches to give up 'their liberty, their home, and all that enriches life, and sacrifice themselves in this horrible way?' It seemed to him but one more example of 'the mistaken and mechanical way in which the semi-savage Tibetans, sunk in the depths of ignorance, try to imitate the rites and practices of Indian Buddhism'. Being incapable of understanding the rationale behind a particular practice, they had seized on the externals. This 'superficial mimicry' had led them into 'absurd perversions of the original'. It would, he concluded, 'be humorous were it not so pathetic', and he was thoroughly relieved to get away from these 'melancholy captives entombed and inarticulate' and back into the sunshine.

For the majority of the occupants of Changlo Manor these were carefree days. There was 'not a cloud on the horizon,' wrote Perceval Landon. 'The dak [post] ran through from the Chumbi Valley without interruption, day after day . . . The afternoon weather, but for clouds of dust that blew eastwards from Dongtse, was perfect; and though the trees were long in showing the first sign of spring, the lot of the Mission seemed cast in a fair ground indeed.'

Indeed, everyone at Changlo Manor seemed content but the man upon whose shoulders political cares again began to weigh heavily. Though all resistance on the part of the Tibetans had ended, they were still refusing to negotiate. General Ma reported that the Chinese Amban in Lhasa was endeavouring to come out to Gyantse but was being prevented from doing so by the Tibetans. The Amban himself wrote to say that he was experiencing difficulties with transport, and could offer no hope of a senior representative of the Dalai Lama joining him. To Colonel Younghusband there appeared only one way out of this impasse. On 22 April he telegraphed London to say that 'the most effectual and the only permanent way of clinching matters' was to move the Mission to Lhasa without further delay. 'Our prestige is now at its height; Nepal and Bhutan are with us; the people are not against us; the soldiers do not want to fight; the Lamas are stunned.'

Younghusband got no reply. The reaction in Britain to the massacre at Chumik Shenko had been one of shock coupled with growing disquiet. As far as the general public was concerned the Tibet Mission was just one more in a long line of frontier expeditions, but there was that extra twist of 'Tibet the mysterious', and the news that several hundred 'half-armed and very brave men' had, as *The Spectator* put it, been crushed 'with the irresistible weapons of science' struck at British notions of fair play. 'We are sorry to learn,' announced *Punch*, 'that the recent sudden and treacherous attack by the Tibetans on our men at Guru seriously injured the photographs that the men were taking.' The subject was debated in the House of Commons and a number of Conservative MPs made it clear to their whips that they would vote against the Government unless it stuck to its proclaimed policy of non-intervention and abandoned all thoughts of a permanent mission in Tibet. In Whitehall, the Cabinet kept its collective head down and waited for the storm to blow over. In India, Younghusband's patron and ally Lord Curzon was busy completing the temporary handover of the Viceroyalty of India to his deputy, Lord Ampthill, and all he could offer was a case of Champagne to raise Younghusband's spirits. As the days passed and still no answer came, the Tibet Commissioner grew increasingly dejected. Guru continued to prey on his mind, even if he absolved himself of any personal responsibility. At Helen's request he had asked that her younger brother, Vernon Magniac, be allowed to join him in Tibet as his private secretary – 'I could say to Govt that Macdonald had an orderly officer so why shd not I have a Private Secretary' – and had also written to a contact linked to the *Daily Mail* suggesting that 'Vernie' should act as that paper's special correspondent in Edmund Candler's place. But both these schemes had gone awry: his brother-in-law was now stuck in Darjeeling, because the General had refused to allow him to proceed further until he received written authority from the Government of India; and the *Daily Mail* had appointed someone else as Candler's replacement.

If a letter written to his doting older sister Emmie is anything to go by, Younghusband was venting his frustrations in bullying the Tibetans: 'I have been engaged today in keeping monks in order,' he boasted heartlessly on the evening of 25 April. A deputation of senior monks from Palkor Chode had come to beg for the fines imposed on the monastery to be reduced, and he had gone out of his way to humiliate them:

A more cringing lot I never came across. They are not worth powder & shot. I have them in great awe of me though . . . They came bowing low before me. I remained seated in my chair very stern & dignified. I silently motion them to seats and ask what they want. They rise to their feet but not presuming to start upright before me or look me in the face remain bending low and with eyes cast down. I rebuke them sternly for fighting against us. They say those who presumed have been well beaten with sticks and none will ever fight us again. I tell them it is too serious a matter to be passed by unnoticed and unless the fine is paid within the next five days troops will occupy their monastery. They make regular whinnies of pain & say they are all as poor as church mice; but, knowing that they are as rich as Croesuses and are really laughing in their sleeves at my moderation, I remain obdurate – and they retire still bowing profoundly and stepping backwards like they do before the King. It is great sport.

But this sport ended that same evening when Frank O'Connor came in with a report, from a trusted source, of Tibetan troops converging on the 16,000-foot Karo La, the Wide-Mouthed Pass, situated at the point where the road between Gyantse and Lhasa crossed a high mountain range some forty-five miles due east of Gyantse. This was confirmed a week later, on 1 May, when a Mounted Infantry rider carrying an urgent despatch interrupted a lecture on astronomy being given by Lieutenant-Colonel Brander. Captain Hodgson had taken a scouting party up and over the Karo La, and just beyond the saddle had spotted another of those walls the Tibetans were so fond of building at strategic points. It appeared to be undefended, so Hodgson had advanced on foot with half a dozen of his men until they were within two hundred yards of the wall. At this point they had, in the words of Brander's later account, been 'ambuscaded. A burst of fire greeted [Hodgson] from the entire length of the wall, while on his flank an avalanche of stones was loosed on his head. With great coolness he successfully extricated himself from this hot corner, without the loss of a man.' Hodgson believed the wall to be defended by at least 1,500 Tibetan troops, effectively blocking the road to Lhasa.

8

Alarms and Excursions

LIEUTENANT-COLONEL Herbert Brander was, in hunting parlance, a 'thruster' – one who likes to ride up with the hounds –
or 'eager-hearted', as an old military friend later described him.
He had always been keen to get at the Pathan while serving with
the Sikh Pioneers on the Afghan border, and had been no less
enthusiastic while commanding the earlier Mission Escort at
Khamba Jong. There he had formed an allegiance to Francis
Younghusband that was as firm as that between the Tibet
Commissioner and his Intelligence Officer, Frank O'Connor. The
two men were of an age and of a type. In seniority Brander
deferred to Younghusband but, as Commander of the Mission
Escort at Changlo Manor, he took his orders from his military
superior, Brigadier-General James Macdonald. Those orders were
to defend the Mission and keep open its line of communications.

As soon as Herbert Brander got the news of the Tibetan build-
up at Karo La he decided to strike against it without delay. An
assault such as he contemplated, by a small and lightly armed force
against a larger one in a strong defensive position three days'
march away, hardly seemed in line with the General's orders – but
Macdonald was now at the far end of a very long telegraph link
and two days' hard riding. So Brander consulted not with the

General but with the Tibet Commissioner. Or, as Francis Young-husband later put it, 'Colonel Brander now came to me and asked for leave to go out and attack the Tibetans before these gatherings could come to a head.' Both men recognised this to be a highly dangerous move that must place both Brander's attacking force and the Mission at Changlo Manor at risk. 'I said', wrote Younghusband, 'that if he, on his side, did not mind taking this risk, I, on my side, did not mind it, and, as far as my military opinion was worth anything, was quite in favour of the opera-tion.' In fact, he was much more than 'quite in favour': as he put it to his father, 'I was entirely in accord with him. The way to prevent mischief is to knock such gatherings on the head at the start.' This was, after all, how Younghusband's and Brandon's heroes of earlier days on the North-West Frontier had acted – strong-armed men such as John Nicholson, Harry Lumsden and William Hodson.*

Lieutenant-Colonel Brander's telegram announcing his inten-tion to march on the Karo La and clear the Tibetans off the wall was dated 1 May, but it had then to be carried by Mounted Infantry despatch rider sixty miles south to the telegraph station at Kala Tso before it could be sent on down the line. With it went Colonel Younghusband's message to Simla saying that he had no political objection to Brander going out to attack the Tibetans 'before they could attack our line of communication'. This was to be their defence for a course of action they knew would be seen by Macdonald as an act of insubordination on Brander's part. That the venture was thought ill-judged by at least some of those in the know at Changlo can be deduced from the reaction of one of Younghusband's most vocal admirers, Perceval Landon, who on the night before Brander's departure wrote privately to Lord Ampthill in Simla expressing his concerns. He had, rather remark-ably, sat in on Brander's and Younghusband's discussions, and had even been asked whether he was going to condemn the operation in his press report. His reply is not recorded, but he told Ampthill that he thought it 'injudicious' to attack the Tibetans 'during the period of time which was to elapse before the Amban's visit' and,

---

* Charles Allen, *Soldier Sahibs: the Men Who Made the North-West Frontier*

furthermore, 'quite out of keeping with the studious way in which we have hitherto kept ourselves in the right'.

That very same evening, as Henry Newman went for his evening constitutional through Gyantse town he noticed several 'malevolent' faces peering down at him from upper windows. It was the first time he had experienced any hostility since coming to the valley, and it struck him that these must be newcomers. He thought no more of it.

Brander's telegram reached New Chumbi on 3 May and provoked the anticipated response. Macdonald immediately ordered the telegraph line to be cleared of signal traffic and fired off a short and terse order to Brander:

> The Moveable Column should not have gone as far as the Karo La without reference to me. If you are not committed return at once to Gyantse. Fear your action will be considered as attempt to force the hand of Government. Younghusband's concurrence does not relieve you of responsibility. You may clear out any Tibetans threatening communications between Ralung and Kangma [the area directly east of the road between Gyantse and Tuna] and this piece of road should be reconnoitred. Please acknowledge.

But of course, he was too late. Brander had ridden off at first light that same morning, with Frank O'Connor at his side and at his back three companies of the 32nd Sikh Pioneers, one company of the 8th Gurkhas plus Bubble and Squeak, Arthur Hadow and his sixteen Maxim-gunners. With them had gone the two special correspondents, Landon and Newman. Because of shortages of supplies at Changlo Manor and because he wanted to move fast, Brander's column took only limited amounts of ammunition.

Brander's departure left behind at Changlo Manor a garrison reduced to one company each of Sikhs and Gurkhas, both under strength, a number of sepoys convalescing in the field hospital and, of course, Colonel Younghusband, Mission staff, and the non-combatants. By Dr Waddell's calculation, this amounted to 125 armed men, which in Younghusband's view was quite sufficient to maintain the safety of his Mission against 'sheep' and 'rabbits'.

At around midday on 4 May Captain Walton noticed that even

the sickest of the patients in his Tibetan hospital, sited just outside the Mission perimeter, were making themselves scarce. Within the Mission compound itself, Mrs Wiggs and her two husbands also disappeared, as did other locally recruited Tibetan servants – but not before one of them had confided to a fellow Tibetan from Sikkim that they were leaving to escape being massacred. In response to this warning a patrol was sent out, but reported no signs of unusual activity in the surrounding area. However, Francis Younghusband considered the portents serious enough to send for Gyantse's governor, the plump and careworn Jongpon, and detain him in the camp overnight as a hostage. As Dr Waddell returned from a walk to the nearby country mansion of Palla just before dusk that evening, he noticed how vulnerable the Mission post appeared and 'how it seemed almost to invite attack'. This was about the same time that a despatch rider and escort rode in from the telegraph office at Kala Tso with the General's order.

In Brander's absence the telegram from Macdonald was delivered to Major Murray of the 8th Gurkhas, in temporary command of the garrison at Changlo. He immediately handed it over to Younghusband – who applied the Nelson touch by sitting on it. His reasons he afterwards made clear in another of those unconstrained letters written to his father:

If I had sent that message on at once Brander wd have got it a march before he reached the Karo la & before he was actually committed. But I knew the effect of his returning without fighting, when all the Tibetans knew that he had gone out to fight, would have been absolutely disastrous. So as it had been left with me to procure a messenger I took my time about it and I told the messenger he was to go along very cautiously & not hurry and I hoped he wd reach Brander <u>after</u> his fight. But in case he shd reach Brander <u>before</u> the fight I wrote him a note saying I had the strongest objection on political grounds to his retiring without fight unless the enemy were so considerably strengthened that the result of a conflict was doubtful.

Younghusband's covering note to Brander was explicit and scarcely called for any reading between the lines: 'I am sending you an urgent letter, which Murray has handed me to send on to you. My Jemadar will take it, but he is rather nervous of the Tibetans, and his pony is slow, so perhaps he will not reach [you] very quickly . . . I need hardly assure you that we are perfectly safe here, or that any turning back now on your part would have a disastrous effect.'

Younghusband's Jemadar was not a junior Native Officer, as the title suggested, but an old Ladakhi Muslim named Mahmood Isa, a Buddhist convert to Islam who had acted as his caravan leader on his earlier expeditions in the Western Himalayas. He had joined Younghusband the month before in hopes of filling the same position, only to find himself relegated to a servant's role, which had prompted him to name himself the Colonel's Jemadar. Now Mahmood Isa was handed the two messages and instructed to get a good night's sleep before setting off in pursuit of Brander's column in the morning. He was further instructed to travel with the greatest caution, however long it might take.

Before retiring to his room in the outer building which housed the Mission staff Dr Waddell spoke to the sentry posted outside its entrance, warning him to be vigilant. Just before daybreak, about half-past four on the morning of 5 May, he was woken abruptly by an unearthly sound: 'the shrill barking yell of "*Ki-hu-hu-u-u! Ki-hu-hu-u-u!*" which burst forth from several hundred hoarse Tibetan throats . . . followed almost immediately by the crack of hundreds of muskets and the whizz of their bullets from every side.' Before Dr Waddell had time even to reach for the loaded revolver he kept under his pillow, several bullets had come through the paper panes of his window. He grabbed his rifle, a bag of cartridges and a haversack that he kept packed with surgical dressings, and ran out onto the landing – straight into a crowd of servants who had just run upstairs and now huddled together shouting that the Tibetans were over the wall and were about to break into the building. Waddell was joined by Captain Ryder, the Royal Engineer surveyor, and a Sikh sepoy, and the three of them braced themselves for what they believed would be a last stand, 'for we knew that capture meant for all of us death by cruel torture'.

A minute crept by, it dawned on them that after all their last hour had not come, and they cautiously opened the lesser of the two gates of their building. General Macdonald's orders were that in case of an attack officers were to assemble at the Redoubt (shown on the map on page 147 as 'Reduit'), the complex of farm buildings next to the mansion housing the Mission Escort, so Waddell, Ryder and the sepoy now ran across the thirty yards of intervening open ground to find a number of other officers gathered there, armed with rifles. They all ran up to the flat roof. 'It was now broad daylight,' recorded Waddell, 'and we saw several hundreds of armed Tibetans firing along the outside of the wall, and blazing from behind all the trees in the neighbourhood.'

The garrison had been taken completely by surprise. The sentries on duty had either been asleep at their posts or culpably lax, allowing the Tibetans to creep right up to the walls at several points. 'We were as nearly as possible let in [down] through the quite appalling slackness of the Gurkha sentries,' was Colonel Younghusband's view. 'Heaven knows what the sentries were doing but at any rate on a moon light night and after the break of dawn when you could see a man at least half a mile away, they let the Tibetans right up under our wall . . . If they hadn't fired or begun boo-ing but simply climbed silently over the wall we should have had a precious nasty time.'

The attack was fiercest on the north side of the perimeter, where the Tibetans reached the wall enclosing three sides of the Mission building and were able to fire through the loopholes on Younghusband's and the other tents erected in its garden. They also succeeded in breaking through what was known as the Gurkha Gate on the eastern side of the perimeter wall (misspelled 'Gurha Gate' on the map) and then pushing open the gate into the compound of the Mission building, where some fierce hand-to-hand fighting took place before the Tibetans were beaten back. Elsewhere the attack failed. Very few assailants succeeded in mounting the walls, most being content to fire through the loopholes, but since these had been built for defenders firing from a raised firestep, they were too high for the Tibetans outside to be able to do little more than push their matchlocks through and fire blindly. This failure to press home the attack gave those members of the garrison not already engaged time to get up into positions from which they could bring fire down on the several hundred men now crouched behind and beyond the wall. From that moment there could only be one outcome. 'Our sharp-shooters', wrote Dr Waddell, 'from the roof of our "citadel" soon laid most of these [the Tibetans] low; and after about twenty minutes the remainder broke and ran off to the town and fort, whereupon Major Murray and some of his Goorkhas, having thus flung back our assailants, rushed out and pursued the fugitives for about half a mile, in a slight snowstorm, killing many of them, until forced to return by a brisk rifle-fire from the fort, which the enemy now held in force.'

Francis Younghusband's role in all this was minimal. Asleep in his tent, erected in front of the Mission building but within thirty feet of the north perimeter wall, he had woken to find the Tibetans firing through the loopholes just yards above his head. It was widely reported later that he played a gallant role in defence of the Mission, and the Younghusband legend was thus further embellished. The most extravagant account came from Lieutenant Leonard Bethell, who was miles away in New Chumbi at the time of the attack. 'A merry night for Younghusband,' he wrote, 'who, with a borrowed rifle and bayonet, took an hour's holiday from thinking and planning, and, in the forefront of it all, fought as part of a group of elated little Gurkhas who knew not in the darkness and little cared, who might be the berserk sahib among them who was making of it a battle so debonair.'

By his own account, however, Francis Younghusband did not behave well. 'I ought', he later admitted, 'to have made straight for the wall with whatever weapon came to hand, and joined in repelling the attack during the few crucial moments.' In the event, he too remembered the General's orders and ran – 'in my pajamas and only half awake' – to the Redoubt, where he remained under cover, listening to the firing for 'about half an hour. Then the report went round that the enemy were bolting so I went on the roof & saw the Tibetans flying across the plain and half our garrison – including Pestonjee, with a revolver! – after them.' Pestonjee was the junior of the Mission's two Indian clerks and both he and his superior, Mr Mitter, behaved with great courage during the attack – the latter grabbed a double-barrelled shotgun and engaged the Tibetans face to face as they broke down the gate into the Mission building.

Instead of commending the behaviour of these men, Young-husband mocked them. His letter to Helen about the attack ends with a description of Mr Mitter and the other Indian members of the Mission staff gathered on the roof of the Redoubt: 'Mitter walked about in a superior way. Pestonjee rushed about with a revolver stuck out straight in front of him. I told him I hoped it was not loaded. Wilton's Chinaman and a Sikkim munshi were in tears. My Darjiling bearer armed himself with a walking stick . . . and my syce [groom] flourished a gigantic Tibetan sword he had looted on some former occasion.'

One hundred and thirty-four Tibetan dead were counted outside the Mission's perimeter wall and a few more inside. Forty wounded men were carried in to Captain Walton's little hospital for medical attention and ten men, found shamming death, were also picked up and brought in for questioning. This time the garrison had not got off so lightly: three men killed, one of whom had been mortally wounded by a bullet from a high-velocity rifle fired from the Jong – 'which was now bristling with the black-headed Tibetan soldiery, who began to bombard us with missiles weighing 3 ozs. to 1 lb fired from small cannon, the so-called "jingals" of the Indians, which were now set in position against us'.

The Tibetan prisoners were expecting to be tortured to death, so when they learned their lives were to be spared they were happy to talk. They had come from Shigatse as part of a force of 1,600 regular soldiers from the Shigatse and Gyantse garrisons. Led by a lama from Lhàsa, half their number had advanced by forced marches, crept up on the Mission post at midnight and then lain in wait until dawn, with orders to attack when the war-cry was given. The other half had headed straight for the Jong and were now busy digging themselves in: 'Under cover of a dropping fire they were to be seen actively building fresh defences and repairing the old broken ones . . . The red-robed lamas stood by in clusters to see the effect of the Tibetan shots, and they could be seen inciting their men to further bloodshed.' The building operations would have made excellent targets for the Maxims and the Gurkhas' light mountain guns but, as Dr Waddell later pointed out without comment, 'these had all been carried off by the Karo party'. Thus, overnight, the tables had been turned: the Tibetans had regained the fort and the Mission was not only under fire but, to all intents, under siege.

It cannot have been a comfortable moment when Colonel Younghusband realised that the only way to get Mahmood Isa and his messages through forty-five miles of what must now be considered hostile country to Lieutenant-Colonel Brander was with the support of a large escort – and that such an escort could no longer be spared. The road south to the telegraph station at Kala Tso was probably still open, provided he acted swiftly, so he did, despatching a messenger and light escort with orders to ride south hard and fast. A short message informed Macdonald of the attack on the Mission and the reoccupation of the Jong, and there was another and equally pithy communication intended for Simla and Whitehall, the tone of which suggested that the Tibet Commissioner was mortally offended: 'Attack confirms impression I had formed that Lhasa government are irreconcilable, and I trust His Majesty's Government, in deciding future attitude towards them, will remember that I have now been ten months in Tibet, that I have met with nothing but insults the whole time in spite of the extreme forbearance I have shown, and that I have now been deliberately attacked.' The Tibetans had now 'thrown down the gauntlet', and he trusted that Government would now 'take such action as will prevent the Tibetans ever again treating a British representative as I have been treated'.

Every able-bodied soldier at Changlo Manor, and even some of the invalids, was now needed to defend it from the further attacks that must surely come. Yet Younghusband was nothing if not resourceful. His solution, never officially acknowledged, was to summon the Jongpon from the room in which he had been detained overnight and demand that he arrange for the message to Lieutenant-Colonel Brander to be delivered safely – on pain of the Jongpon forfeiting his own life if his messenger did not return to Changlo, mission accomplished, within a set time.

A servant who had accompanied the Jongpon into captivity was detailed to ride with all speed, for the safety of the Mission depended on Brander's force getting back to Gyantse as soon as possible. Younghusband's covering letter now carried a scribbled postscript giving brief details of the attack on the Mission – but also reaffirming that he still wished Brander's attack on the Karo La to proceed. The departure of his servant was followed by the Jongpon's immediate collapse, for he supposed that his country-men would never allow the messenger to leave the valley – and this could only mean that he would soon lose his head. 'The poor Jongpon', wrote Waddell, 'was demented with fear, and sat cring-ing comically in a corner with his head inside a large iron cooking-pot for protection, and would not be persuaded to lay aside this ridiculous head-piece for days.'

After a good breakfast the garrison set to under Captain Ryder's directions to strengthen their defences. By abandoning the weakest corner and concentrating on the main Redoubt and the Mission building, the perimeter was reduced to almost half its original size. Bags of earth and stones were used to build improvised breastworks on the roof, small towers were added to the palisade to allow the outside walls to be enfiladed, and an outer ditch was dug. More trees were cut down outside the perimeter, leaving untouched only a small copse on the Gyantse side of the post which was found to give some cover against the steady bombardment that was now being directed on them from the Jong.

In the afternoon there was a brief lull in the firing, and a 'rather refined and well-featured woman of middle age' was seen approaching from Gyantse waving a flag on a stick. She turned out to be the wife of their hostage, the Jongpon. She brought food for her husband, and the news that more troops had arrived from Shigatse that morning and further numbers were expected within days. The new general was Depon Tailing, the commander of the fortress at Khamba Jong, whom Frank O'Connor and the veterans of the mission remembered as a talkative young man with good manners. The Jongpon's wife also provided an explanation for the many pieces of chopped flesh that had been found outside their walls that morning and which were now being fought over by the town's innumerable pariah dogs: they were the remains of a Gurkha orderly belonging to the Mission and three servants employed by the Chinese Customs Officer, Captain Parr. They had been captured in the town and hacked to death.

That night the sounding of the 'Last Post' by a Gurkha bugler from the roof of the Redoubt was the signal for a massed counterblast of conch shells and trumpets from the Jong, which was at first taken to be the signal for a new assault. The entire garrison remained at their posts all night, the hours passing with maddening slowness. 'Several times during the night,' recorded Austine Waddell,

> I climbed to the roof, and from behind a parapet scanned with straining eyes, in the starlight, the fields strewn with the dead of yesterday's battle and the black clumps of trees, and out towards the jong, which stood up dark and gaunt in tragic silence . . . As the ruddy glow in the east shot up the first streaks of dawn we stood to, listening still more expectantly, knowing that the Tibetans consider that time, the 'third cock-crow', especially lucky for attack, but the dark outlines of the hills loomed into distinctness, and the soft light of day stole over the land and penetrated the gloom without a disturbing war-yell or shot. Then in the broad light a solitary gun flashed out, and every one sprang into action, till it was realised that it was from the distant fort, and was merely the beginning of the day's bombardment.

It was afterwards learned that Depon Tailing had indeed attempted to launch a second attack, knowing that he had only a very few days at most before Colonel Brander returned with more soldiers – and the Maxims: at Khamba Jong a Maxim gun had been put through its fearsome paces for the Depon's instruction, so he had a good idea of its fire-power. But his soldiery also knew they had lost their most valuable weapon, which was surprise. They had mustered in the dark outside the gates of Gyantse Jong but had then refused to move forward towards Changlo Manor, forcing the attack to be abandoned. Their colleagues up at the fort made better use of the darkness, for when daylight came and the officers of the Mission garrison began scanning the slopes of Khamba Jong through their binoculars they saw that more defences had risen in the night: 'high loop-holed stone walls which screened them and their jingals almost entirely from our view'. This was one skill that even their severest critics could not deny the Tibetans: their remarkable ability to construct, almost overnight, defensive walls capable of withstanding all but the heaviest fire, complete with embrasures and loopholes and 'chambers' partitioned by stone slabs that gave screening from everything except reverse fire. With only 125 rifles at his disposal, no Maxims and no mountain guns, there was nothing Major Murray could do but wait for reinforcements.

To everyone's surprise, the Jongpon's servant was back at Changlo Manor before nightfall on 6 May. He had ridden the ninety miles to the Karo La and back in less than thirty-six hours, and had successfully delivered his messages to Lieutenant-Colonel Brander at 6 a.m. that very morning – just as the assault on the Tibetan wall was getting under way. He brought back the briefest of notes from Brander, thanking Younghusband for his 'strong and cheering letter' and confirming that he was pressing on with his attack. The messenger had not stayed to see the final outcome of the battle but his report was not encouraging: it seemed that the Tibetans had beaten back Brander's initial offensive.

The Mission and Escort now braced themselves for a long wait, but news of the outcome of the battle of Karo La came unexpectedly swiftly. Late at night on 7 May the pickets heard the sound of hooves, and in rode William Ottley and a section of his Mounted Infantry, together with Frank O'Connor and the indefatigable *Times* correspondent Perceval Landon. Their begrimed but grinning faces told the story: the Tibetans at Karo La had been dispersed – though at some cost.

Brander's men had covered the forty-five miles to the Karo La in three marches, which Arthur Hadow, for one, thought good going, given that it was uphill all the way from 13,00 to 16,500 feet, much of it done on foot and in single file – 'a tremendous exertion even walking, let alone climbing'. Their route had taken them up along the winding valley of a side tributary of the Nyang Chu to its highest source deep in the mountains, where it emerged from the base of a vast overhanging glacier, itself topped by a broad expanse of snow that formed the southern flank of a 24,000-foot peak. They had camped under the glacier just short of the Karo pass in a meadow known as the Field of Milk, laced with tiny rivulets whose banks were covered with the shoots of a flower which a decade later was identified and named by F. M. Bailey: *Meconopsis betonicifolia baileyi*. A more beautiful or awe-inspiring camp site could not have been imagined.

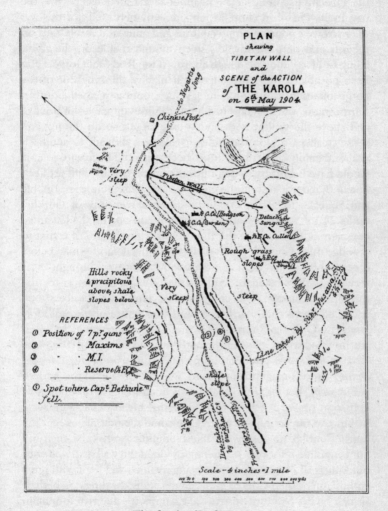

The first battle of Karo La

As Ottley's men had discovered from their earlier reconnaissance, the Tibetans had built their wall about a mile and a half beyond the pass itself. They had chosen their site extremely well, for this was the narrowest point, with precipitous and quite impassable cliffs on the left and only slightly less steep mountain-side on the right, rising to a large snowfield high above. At the Red Idol Gorge it had been possible to turn the enemy's flanks by climbing out of the gorge on each side, but here no such option seemed possible. Furthermore, the Tibetans had put up a series of sangars in front of and above the wall at both ends – one large one on the left and seven smaller ones on the right – making it difficult to approach without being fired upon from both flanks. The correct tactic would have been first to demolish these side sangars with artillery, but all Brander had were the Gurkhas' two museum pieces, Bubble and Squeak. To give them some cover, a company of Gurkhas under Major Row was sent up the mountain side on the left and a company of Sikhs up on the right, both with the aim of trying to dislodge the Tibetans from their forward sangars, while below them Bubble and Squeak and the two Maxims were brought as far forward as they could be without becoming easy targets for the men in the sangars. Two companies of 32nd Sikh Pioneers then advanced down the river bed towards the centre of the wall, followed by Ottley and forty of his mounted infantrymen. At about six hundred yards the wall erupted with smoke and fire. The Maxims and seven-pounders immediately came into play. 'The roar of firearms was magnificent,' noted William Ottley; 'in this narrow defile every shot was echoed and re-echoed scores of times over.'

It soon became obvious to Hadow that his machine-guns were making no impact on the wall. 'One could see nothing except the puffs of smoke,' he observed. 'Their loopholes were very small and quite invisible, although we afterwards found the wall spattered with our bullets all over.' And despite being manned and fired with great enthusiasm by their Gurkha gun-crews – under the direction of their British NCO, Sergeant-Instructor Champion – the two mountain guns were equally ineffective. The heavy ammunition brought up to Gyantse consisted entirely of shrapnel, which was useless against fortifications, so Champion employed his guns as mortars, aiming high so as to lob the shells over the Tibetan defences. 'The guns were extremely well handled,' noted Hadow, 'but one could never tell within a hundred yards or so where the next shell would fall, even at a range of 600 yards. Also many of the shells did not burst, as they did not always fall with the right end foremost.' Out of seventy rounds fired, only one hit its mark and exploded.

As the Sikhs advanced up the floor of the valley the Tibetans concentrated their fire on the foremost company, pinning the men down. Their commander, Captain Bethune − 'the most popular and, perhaps, the most capable of the junior regimental officers' − had no option but to give the order to retire. A hundred yards behind him, William Ottley saw Bethune motioning with his hand for Ottley to pull back his Mounted Infantry. 'This was the last time I saw that good soldier alive,' wrote Ottley. 'He commenced retiring after me, and was last of all himself, when I suppose, chaffing at not being able to breach the wall, and, indignant at retiring, he took a few men with him, climbed the steep bank on to the glacis [exposed slope] and made straight for the wall above, where he and his bugler and one sepoy, the first up, were all immediately killed.'

The rest of Bethune's company were now in serious trouble. 'The fire from the main wall never seemed to slacken in the least,' recalled their commanding officer, Herbert Brander, when he came to write the battalion's history. 'Our men lay, unable to move, on the fire-swept ground, unable, even, to raise their heads. Some were wounded more than once as they lay, but they still hung on, many of them with empty pouches. Urgent appeals began to come in for ammunition, which it was impossible to carry up into the firing line. The situation was gradually becoming uncomfortable and the tension great.' As the return fire from the Sikhs slackened, the Tibetans in the nearest sangars began to re-direct their weapons on Hadow's two Maxims: 'We found ourselves enfiladed from both flanks by the enemy's sangars . . . The more we fired, the more they fired, and as apparently we could make no impression, I had to cease fire with my guns, as the Infantry had run short of ammunition and wanted mine.' Meanwhile, the Sikhs who had been sent up the slopes on the south or right-hand side of the valley had found the vast screes of shale impossible to climb. Only Major Row's company of

Gurkhas, set to climb the cliffs on the left, had made any progress at all.

There was nothing for it but for Brander to order the Sikhs to pull back under cover. Besides Captain Bethune, four sepoys had been killed below the Tibetan wall and another thirteen wounded. Brander was, he told Younghusband afterwards, 'on the point of despair'. And at precisely this point in the action the Tibetan messenger arrived with his double dose of bad tidings.

Henry Newman, as he recalled later, was lying prone on some rising ground close to Lieutenant-Colonel Brander and saw him receive the messages 'that well might have turned a less resolute man pale' – although it was not until after the battle that Brander made known the news of the attack on the Mission. 'The only order he gave after receiving the message from Gyantse was that we were to be as sparing of ammunition as possible,' noted Newman. 'He showed no signs of perturbation . . . He made up his mind at once that it would be madness to break off the battle. We must win it.' Brander had to get back to Gyantse as soon as possible to relieve Younghusband and the garrison, but he also knew that if he withdrew his troops at this point in the engagement it would be interpreted by the Tibetans as a retreat. His force would then risk being harried all the way back through the mountains, with the real possibility, hampered as they would be by their mules and baggage, of being cut off or picked off one by one from the heights – just as General Sales's army had been on its retreat from Kabul in 1842.

'How long a time passed before anything else happened I cannot say,' wrote Newman. 'At one time, looking up on the left, I saw some Gurkhas seemed to be retiring, but I realised very quickly afterwards that they were only seeking a new way to outflank the Tibetans.' Finding it impossible to get any closer to the large sangar on his side of the valley Major Row had pulled back his company, but then asked half a dozen of his boldest men to attempt to scale the cliffs that rose directly above them. These climbers soon disappeared from sight, and to those waiting below it seemed as if nothing was happening. 'For two hours it was the guns only that answered the fire from the walls and the sangars,' wrote Perceval Landon, watching from the rear. 'There was a deadlock, and if no means could be found to drive the enemy from the advanced defences which they were holding so gallantly, there seemed little chance of doing anything more until nightfall. It was an anxious moment.'

But in fact, things *were* happening. Brander had gone up to where his Sikh Pioneers had taken cover, and called for volunteers – and a party of a dozen men led by a Native Officer, Subadar Wasawa Singh, had now begun to scale the 'almost perpendicular face of the 1,500-foot southern scarp'. A vertical cleft in the cliff wall now hid them from the Tibetans, and by climbing it to the top they hoped to reach a point where they could overlook the sangars guarding the wall on their side of the valley.

Everything now turned on whether these two small parties of climbers – Gurkhas on the left, Sikhs on the right – could reach the summits of their respective cliffs. Both disappeared from view, 'hidden behind the edge of the rock and ice above us'. Down below, the rest of the force could do nothing but wait anxiously and expectantly. Landon's attentions were focused on the top of the cliffs on his left: 'For upward of an hour the fight again languished . . . At last, however, one of the stones upon which our glasses had been fixed for so long seemed to move and, half-fainting over it, a tiny figure halted and unslung a miniature rifle into its right hand. He was joined in a moment by another, and his comrades in the valley below gave the first warning to the defenders of the sangar by raising a thin distant cheer.' These were the first two of Major Row's Gurkhas, who were soon bringing rifle-fire to bear down almost directly on the men behind the left sangar. From that moment the fortunes of the two sides began to change: 'The enemy did not wait; not more than four or five of the escalading force had reached their goal before the Tibetans bolted from their advanced post and ran back across the open coverless slopes of the mountainside to the protection of the great wall.' Arthur Hadow and the second gunner on the Maxims opened up, allowing not a single man to reach the safety of the wall.

Half an hour later the first of the Sikhs reached the top of the cliffs on the south side of the valley:

Pigmy figures appeared, silhouetted against the sky-line, on our right: through glasses it could be seen that these figures wore pagris [turbans], and must therefore be Subadar Wasawa Singh, and his gallant section. A fresh cheer rose from those below. Little could be seen in the nula [valley floor] of what was occurring above, but evidently Wasawa Singh's fire was beginning to tell on the right flank sangar, the occupants of which showed signs of uneasiness. Heads began to appear, where not a head had shown up to now. Presently two or three men made a bolt along the hillside, followed by two or three more, and, in a minute, the whole of the occupants of the sangar were in full flight, pursued by the relentless fire of the Maxims and Reserve Company.

As Perceval Landon watched, the Tibetan firing halted suddenly and dramatically: 'The day was won; for the Tibetans behind the wall, who cannot have lost more than two or three men throughout the entire day, and whose position was hardly weakened as yet, fled as one man back down the valley.' Lieutenant-Colonel Brander's bugler sounded the advance. 'Now was the chance of the Mounted Infantry,' wrote Ottley.

Down the sharp-stoned and frozen bed of the stream they rode at full gallop, till the wall stopped them. They dismounted and spent ten minutes in breaking a hole in the wall to get through. Riding through the Tibetan camp, we only found a few stragglers . . . but on reaching the top of the next ridge we saw the whole of the Tibetan army in one great mass in full retreat a mile and a half away, and carrying with them 500 men who were coming up to reinforce them . . . Down the steep incline went the men full pelt, and then along the open but hummocky valley at their best pace, till they got within 100 yards of the enemy, who tried to rally, but were scattered by the magazine fire delivered by these forty Mounted Infantry rifles. There were no horse-holders; every man, as he dismounted, putting the reins in his right arm, knelt and fired. The Tibetans scattered in all directions, and then the Mounted Infantry, remounting, continued the pursuit, firing from their ponies.

Dispersing the Tibetans wherever they tried to make a stand, Ottley's men rode on for some eight miles until they caught sight of a large party of mounted Tibetans ahead who, from their fine clothes, they judged to be officers who had left their men to fend for themselves at the wall. These were now harried for a mile or two until Ottley judged it was time to call a halt.

The two special correspondents followed hard on the heels of the infantry, together with the camp-followers, every man determined to secure whatever they could by way of spoils from the Tibetan camp. They found 'the tents still standing, the fires still alight, the water in the cooking vessels still boiling. Furs, blankets, horse furniture, spears, powder flasks, quick-match, bags of tsampa, skins of butter, tightly stuffed cushions, everything was there as the Tibetans had left it in their haste.' Following Henry Newman as he wandered through the camp was his Gurkha servant, leading his pony, and he also did his bit of looting: 'I saw my servant poking about inside a tent from which he suddenly emerged with a heavy scarlet gown in his arms. This garment must have certainly belonged to a very high Tibetan official.' Newman appropriated it, and finding it too heavy to walk about in, wore it as a sort of dressing-gown for the rest of the campaign, 'to the dissatisfaction of numbers of people'.

The range and severity of the fire from the sangars had convinced Lieutenant-Colonel Brander that the defenders there had been armed with breech-loading rifles. Here, perhaps, was the much-sought-after proof of Russian involvement. But when Brander's Sikhs cleared the sangars they found only large quantities of ammunition for the old-fashioned Lhasa-made Martini rifles.

Brander's only concern now was to get back to Changlo Manor with all speed. He ordered a halt to the pursuit and a return to their camp in the Field of Milk. There was no time to treat the Tibetan wounded or round up prisoners; the wall was left largely untouched, and the dead left uncounted where they had fallen. The Tibetans later put their casualties at six hundred. Had the Mounted Infantry not been ordered to go easy on the ammunition, the casualty figures would have been far higher.

Ottley's riders were the last to get back to camp, staggering in at 9.30 p.m., having walked their horses for some twelve miles in a blizzard of 'unequalled fierceness, driving straight into our faces'. They had collected a number of fine Tibetan ponies in the course of the chase, which was just as well since several of their own had died in the snow. A number of the men had also collapsed, and had had to be put on the fresh horses and held there by their companions. Yet all in all it had been 'a good fight', in Ottley's opinion, and once again they had come through almost unscathed: just three of his men wounded, and five ponies lost. No one had eaten since just after reveille that morning, but 'after a glass of rum all round and a glass from Colonel Younghusband's bottle of green chartreuse kindly kept for me by Colonel Brander, we began to think that life was still worth living'.

The Mounted Infantry's pursuit at Karo La, coming on top of its earlier successes on the road from Guru to Gyantse, gained them a reputation for ruthlessness that spread throughout central and southern Tibet. Whether deservedly or not, William Ottley was seen as the most remorseless of their number, becoming known to the Tibetans as 'the Nightmare'. To Edmund Candler, as to many others, he was held to be 'about the most dashing man on the show, steeped in gore for months, must have killed his hundred men, quite unscrupulous in war'. But of course, it was not the Mounted Infantry who won what was the first of the two battles of Karo La, but the half-dozen Gurkha riflemen of the 8th Gurkhas and the dozen sepoys of the 32nd Sikh Pioneers, together with their Native Officer, Subadar Wasawa Singh – later gazetted a member of the Indian Order of Merit, 2nd Class, for 'conspicuous gallantry'. In the course of the action these men had climbed to and fought at an altitude in excess of 18,500 feet, which Perceval Landon reckoned to be 'probably the highest point on the earth's surface at which an engagement has ever taken place'.

Brander's column returned to Changlo Manor two days after the battle, the Sikhs of the 32nd Pioneers bearing the bodies of Captain Bethune and their own dead with them on stretchers. 'The very best type of soldier,' recorded Francis Younghusband of Bethune, 'full of go and as bold as a lion . . . We all feel his loss terribly and I have put my flag at half-mast for him.' He was buried beside the river in a small patch of open ground carpeted with Tibetan irises, just beyond the Mounted Infantry lines; his Sikhs were cremated at the same site and their ashes scattered in the river. The 5th of May was thereafter celebrated in the regiment as

'Bethune Day', when the names of the fallen were solemnly read out on parade – a practice maintained until 1915, when the regiment began to suffer casualties on such a scale as to put the first battle of Karo La into a truer perspective.

The successful outcome of the Karo La engagement was as much a relief to Francis Younghusband as it was to his Mission Escort Commander. Only these two knew how close they had come to disaster. But the mood at Changlo Manor, despite their losses, was celebratory. 'All the officers are so grateful to me,' wrote Francis Younghusband to Helen, who had now taken a house in Darjeeling for the Hot Weather season in order to be as close to her husband as she could. 'The Native Officers too beam away and tell me of the wonderful things they have done. It is very jolly having everybody so cordial.' The unprovoked attack on the Mission and the Tibetans' reoccupation of the Jong had changed everything, coming as a shock to Younghusband and a blow to his pride. Their situation – under bombardment and all but under siege – presented continuing dangers, but it was equally clear that the Tibetans had also done him a great favour. To Lord Curzon, now in London, the Tibet Commissioner wrote privately and candidly, 'The Tibetans as usual have played into our hands.' To Lord Ampthill, deputising in Simla, he wrote that 'His Majesty's Government must see that the necessity for going to Lhasa has now been proved beyond all doubt.' To his more intimate friends he wrote of the need to 'break' or 'smash' those whom he believed responsible both for the impasse and for the violence directed against him: 'those selfish filthy lecherous lamas'.

Austine Waddell took an equally sanguine view. From what he gathered, more than eight thousand armed Tibetans were marching on Gyantse and the lamas were roaming the valleys 'preaching a "Holy War", like the fanatical Mullahs and Madhis of Mohammedanism . . . We heard of swarming horsemen from the steppes of Mongolia hurrying on to save the sacred city . . . The Grand Lama was obstinately bent upon opposing us tooth and nail, and it had at last to be acknowledged that we were "at war" with Tibet, and that the peaceful "Mission" had become transformed into a military expedition.'

9

The Entry of the Fusiliers

ON SATURDAY morning 14 May the British troops stationed in barracks at Lebong, a military depot five miles south of Darjeeling, woke as usual to the sound of reveille. However, shortly afterwards the normal routine of the 1st Battalion of the Royal Fusiliers was disturbed by buglers sounding for colour-sergeants to report to the adjutant at the double. By the time the men were at their ablutions rumours of mobilisation were flying – soon confirmed by the return of the colour-sergeants with the news that four companies were being sent on active service to Tibet. The attack on the Tibet Mission at Changlo Manor had galvanised the British and Indian Governments into action. It had provided conclusive proof of Tibetan 'intransigence'. An advance on Lhasa was to be made within a month, and what was now termed the Sikkim Tibet Field Force was to be augmented with more troops – including a British infantry regiment.

This was excellent news for the battalion, which had spent much of its Indian 'tour' in Burma without seeing any active service. Its officers and men considered themselves in fighting trim and cred-ited their selection to the GOC (General Officer Commanding) Northern Army, who had recently subjected them to a three-day inspection and had congratulated their commanding officer,

Lieutenant-Colonel Edward Cooper, DSO, on the best-trained and most efficient battalion in his sector. It has to be said that the battalion also happened to be the nearest British infantry available.

Private H. A. Sampson was a member of C Company, one of the four selected, and he noted in his diary that evening how swiftly things began to move: 'At 8.30 a.m. we were paraded and marched to the Station Hospital for Medical Inspection . . . After the men who were rejected by the doctor had been sorted out the Captain then rejected any man whom he considered in any way unfit. No 3rd class shots and no man who had been tried by court martial were to be taken on any account. These men being debarred caused much discontent because it separated many chums.' The next few days were taken up with drawing extra kit, sharpening bayonets and going out on long route marches through the surrounding hills dressed in full marching order and each man carrying a hundred rounds of ball ammunition. Out of the four companies only one man fell out, 'which showed how fit the men were – no doubt ambition spurred many on'.

Nine days later the battalion marched up to the military sanitarium of Jalapahar in Darjeeling, where the men made the most of what was to be their last night of freedom for months. Here they joined the other reinforcements: six companies of Indian troops from the 40th Pathans, known to the British troops as 'the Forty Thieves', an eight-man party from the 1st Battalion, The Royal Irish Rifles with two Maxim guns, a British Army Mountain Battery with four ten-pounder guns and the Murree Mountain Battery with two, and two Field Hospitals – one British Army and one Indian. The following morning the Fusiliers began their long march in earnest.

Among the four company commanders and eight company officers selected was Lieutenant Thomas Carey, a subaltern in A Company. He too kept a diary: 'Great concourse of people from Darjeeling to see us off,' he wrote that evening. 'A band of the "Kings Own" played us out, one man was too drunk to march & so was left behind. I hear more than half the men were "hors de combat" the night before but not a single man was placed in the Guard Room; that is the best of the RFs, they never get rowdy, although they drink as much as other regiments.'

At least two other 'rankers' or BORs (British Other Ranks) in the battalion besides Sampson kept diaries of the battalion's service in Tibet that have survived the passing years: Corporal Percy Coath of F Company and Lance-Corporal Alfred Dunning. Each was on a different rung of the strictly demarcated hierarchical ladder of the British Army as it was at the start of the twentieth century, so that together they provide a composite picture of the Tibetan adventure very different from that given by the more seasoned Indian Army officers and politicals who had gone ahead. As befitted his status as a section commander, Corporal Percy Coath went for the well-rounded sentence. 'The residents of this queen of hill stations', he wrote at the end of that first day's marching, 'had assembled in large numbers to give us a hearty send-off. They cheered again and again as we marched by them and wished us success in the mysterious country to which we were going. We have marched about sixteen miles today to a place called Pashok. The road was very narrow and anything but good to march upon. It has been rather a trying day, the thermometer going up all the time. I find we have descended 5,000 feet coming here, no wonder it is warmer.' Lance-Corporal Alfred Dunning's entry for that same day was pithy but graphic: 'March to Pashok, down, down, down. Toes are all raw. Never thought we should get to the bottom. Beautiful scenery . . . Our transport is the comicalest I have seen, poor old nags (ponies they are called). Our kits consist of 2 blankets, boots, change of linen and a few odds and ends and are tied on the back, each side of these horses . . . I don't require any rocking to sleep tonight and after eating my dinner and having a smoke I am soon in the land of dreams.'

The following day the battalion crossed the cable bridge over the Teesta river – reminding Lieutenant Carey of the Clifton suspension bridge back home – and began the long climb through thick jungle that would take them up through Sikkim and on to the Jelep La. 'I must say,' mused Thomas Carey, 'we are very lucky to have the men we have. They are not raw recruits but men whose average service is 9 to 10 years. They require no looking after, & give no trouble whatever, how unlike the Regts at home. We arrived at Mallighat, a very feverish place – as a preventative against fever I took 10 gr of quinine.' Lieutenant Carey's main duty on the march was to follow the four companies with a rear-guard 'to hurry up the transport & to pick up stragglers'. For the first four days he found the going 'heavy and hot', yet he was pleased to note that only one man fell out — 'and that was with fever'. Private Sampson, however, recorded that several men fell out at every stage, 'unable to stick it', although his main sympathies were reserved for the transport mules. On 29 May he noted in his diary that they had passed 'a lot of the mules with our kits on laying down, completely knocked up. The Transport Officer comes along, kicks the poor brutes and if they cannot get up he draws his revolver and shoots them, then has them rolled down the khud [hillside] to become food for the wild animals. The kits are left to be brought in by the rear-guard on the spare mules. There are hundreds of skeletons all along this march. All had been shot because they were unable to keep up with their load on.'

The oppressive heat soon gave way to thunderstorms and heavy downpours that soaked the men's uniforms by day and their bedding by night: 'every stitch we possess is soaked through'. In their diaries Sampson and Dunning gave full vent to their grumbles — and not without cause. When they arrived at a camping ground on the side of a steep hill named Jeluk the officers moved into a small hut while the men bivouaked wherever they could find a flat piece of ground. It rained all night. 'The cooks could not get a fire to burn to cook anything,' recorded Sampson. 'They gave us an issue of rum with which we retired shivering with the cold all night. Our transport animals have had nothing to eat and like us no prospect of getting any.' Dunning thought Jeluk 'the dirtiest hole I have ever seen. As you walked about you sank up over your boots in mud. Impossible to get a dry patch. Rain pouring. I lean my back against a tree and pull my knees up, first of all putting a blanket up on the tree to keep some of the rain off. But the wind shifted this in the night and I was like a drowned rat.' For breakfast next morning the men got 'a half Chuppatee not cooked'.

Corporal Percy Coath had anticipated difficulties in getting the mules going that morning and he was not wrong: 'We had awful trouble getting the baggage loaded, and started on the road, which was terrible steep and stony. It was quite a marvel the way in which the mules picked their way up the hill and struggled with the loads on their back. I did pity them. And the leeches are very trying to them. Some of the poor mules had their nostrils smothered in leeches and blood. These leeches are the curse of Sikkim.'

The next day the battalion reached the base at Gnatong, where the officers were given a 'tip-top lunch' at the officers' mess of the 4th Gurkhas. 'We have huts to sleep in, and the men mule lines, which they will appreciate,' noted Lieutenant Carey, apparently without irony. And indeed the men did appreciate them. 'Very dark and dirty but we imagine they are Palaces after our last camp,' wrote Alfred Dunning. Here the battalion rested for a day, dried out their clothes and blankets, and were issued with winter kit. 'To see me dressed you would think I was an esquimaux,' wrote Dunning. 'Coat made of a sheepskin, thick boots up to the knees, a cap to cover the head and face, finished up with a pair of blue spectacles.' They had now reached an altitude of 11,700 feet. 'No men sick up to date,' wrote Carey. 'All officers very fit except Alston, who complains of cold & a very bad head. I expect it is mountain sickness combined with a chill.' That same night Carey and the other officers learned of more fighting up at Gyantse: 'Position of Mission force at Gyansi is critical. Capt. Sawyer 23rd Pioneers & 9 sepoys killed. Telegram did not say how many were wounded, everybody says we shall get fighting, else why are we ordered up.'

The battalion now pushed on with greater determination, reaching the foot of the Jelep La pass on 31 May. 'Miles and miles of wild Rhododendrons which stretched as far as the eye could see,' wrote Private Sampson. 'We seemed to be walking on the tops of the Himalayas today,' wrote Corporal Coath. 'We could see nothing but numberless mountain peaks, which seemed to be on a level with us. The scenery was grand and awe-inspiring . . . The cold is intense and we are surrounded with snow.' The Jelep La was crossed on the following day, each company following the colonel's orders that it was to halt every hundred paces to allow the men to regain their breath: 'It was the thumping of our hearts which made it absolutely necessary to halt, if only for two or three minutes,' Coath noted. 'In this way we slowly gained the summit of the famous Jelap La Pass, which we crossed in a snow-storm.'

Perhaps it was this storm that prevented him from seeing that the saddle of the pass was now crowned with a signpost that read 'TO LONDON' on one arm and 'TO LHASSA' on the other.

The Fusiliers had next to negotiate the by now notorious icy descent to Yatung: 'It was with admiration,' continued Coath, 'that I watched the sure-footed pack-animals pick their way down with their 160-lb loads this way and that, stepping on the rocks with unerring instinct.' He closed that day's account with a late entry: 'I regret to write that towards dusk my Company Commander, Lieutenant Alston, was carried in on a stretcher, having had to give up before reaching the summit of the Jelap, owing to his heart. Poor fellow, he looked very blue in the face when I saw him and I fear he will not last long.'

The following day the battalion passed through the customs post at Yatung, where the men were pleased to see 'a little white woman dressed all in black . . . a very contented old lady', who was pointed out to them as the well-known missionary Miss Annie Taylor. 'What zeal and pluck, and devotion for the cause of Christ,' declared Percy Coath admiringly. 'I expect she was delighted to see so many of her countrymen swing by.' Not long afterwards they passed Chumbi village, and then the outskirts of the base depot of the Tibet Mission at New Chumbi:

> A little further and our own camping ground was reached. Here we found bell tents erected all ready for us to occupy . . . We will probably rest here for about nine days to allow the relieving force to be properly organised and fitted out for its march to Gyantse. I can hear the bagpipes of Gurkhas playing all day, and they sound very sweet amongst these gigantic hills. They are guarding Brigadier-General Macdonald's residence, about three-quarters of a mile from our Camp . . . We buried poor Lieut Alston who died this morning of pneumonia.

Alston and Carey had shared quarters: 'He was a very good chap,' mourned the latter. 'I have never known him to be ill before.' In accordance with Anglo-Indian custom, Alston was buried within hours of his death, with Carey commanding the party that fired a salute over his grave, and in the presence of the General and all his staff. This was Carey's first sight of Brigadier-General James Macdonald, who struck him as 'a very quiet man' who 'never worries one. There is little he does not know. He has seen a lot of service.' However, not every new officer joining the force was so impressed. Captain George Preston of the 40th Pathans reported to his wife the rumour that the General was said to be 'quite sick of the whole show & is determined to get it finished as soon as possible'.

Over the next few days the Fusiliers were joined in New Chumbi by Preston's Pathans and the mountain gunners. Then one morning, as the men of Alston's company were erecting a stone wall round his grave, they heard 'the blowing of innumerable trumpets and saw a long procession approaching'. It was the *de facto* (and soon to be *de jure*) ruler of neighbouring Bhutan, Ugyen Wangchuk, known as the Tongsa Penlop. Although the people of Bhutan were Buddhists of largely Tibetan stock, the Tongsa Penlop was astute enough to realise that it was in both his own and his country's interests to support the Government of India in its dealings with Tibet. He had made his position clear by doing what he could to mediate between the two countries and by urging the Tibetans to negotiate. From the point of view of the Government of India, the Tongsa Penlop was a valuable ally and friend, and the General made sure he was received as such. This was not quite how the troops saw him. 'A chap called Tongsa Penlop visited us,' wrote Alfred Dunning.

> He is some sort of a chief and friendly to us. He had a band with him. Oh the row. I shall never forget his band. It was composed of a long, shrill pipe, a couple of old cast off trombones and half a dozen drums, all dressed up in the colours of the rainbow, following one behind the other and making as much noise as possible. Then came Penlop on a mule, chewing Betle Nut. Everyone was roaring with laughter and the old man, thinking it was applause, was delighted, waving his hands in the air. He intends going to Llassa with us so I hope he will lose that band of his.

Corporal Coath was rather kinder: 'He looks a jolly old fellow, and was riding on a richly caparisoned pony, with something on his head which I suppose did duty for a crown. He put me in mind of the pictures I have seen of Bluff King Hal, of glorious memory.'

A guard of honour of a company of Fusiliers turned out to receive the Tongsa Penlop, followed by a parade of all the troops and a formal Durbar, all ordered, according to Percy Coath, 'that he might be impressed with our power, as he was shown the working of our big guns and maxims after the parade'. Private Sampson watched the Tongsa Penlop inspect the signalling equipment with growing bewilderment: 'He thought the flags a mystery but the Heliograph capped him altogether. He looked at the flash then at the helio, from the side & then the back. He then shook his head and gave it up for a bad job.'

The next major event in camp was more sobering: the arrival of a caravan of mules and dhoolie bearers bringing down forty-two wounded men from the fighting at Gyantse. 'They did look miserable,' recorded Percy Coath. 'I was sorry to see them, poor fellows. They have established a fine base hospital here, and I hear Miss Taylor, the lady missionary, is going to act as a nursing sister. She will be the only one.'

The wounded were followed on 10 June by an altogether more rousing arrival, and one that caused a great stir throughout the camp: the entry of a cavalcade of Mounted Infantry at the trot, 'in the midst of which rode a little stiff man with a bushy black beard'. Private Sampson watched them ride in: 'He turned out to be none other than Colonel F. Younghusband, the head of the Mission Party. The whole lot looked as if they had ridden far and fast, because their ponies were completely knocked up and smothered from the man's head to the ponies' heels with mud.'

Since the surprise attack on Changlo Manor in the early hours of 5 May, the Mission and its garrison had been living in what Frank O'Connor characterised as 'practically . . . a state of siege'. Although the post was never invested and its communications with India were maintained by the Mounted Infantry for all but a few days, it remained under constant fire from the Jong: 'The enemy's fire-arms were inefficient and primitive, consisting of old, smooth-bore brass cannon, about the size of our 7-pounders, and old muzzle-loading jingals, but they kept up a constant banging, and we had to keep under cover. And the scene at night was most picturesque when the garrison of the Jong got an attack of nerves or meditated an assault – the whole great fabric reverberated with the roar of all their noisy weapons and was illuminated like a Brock's firework display with hundreds of flashes from their black-powder cartridges.' Inadequate as these cannon and jingals were, they were still capable of inflicting lethal damage. They claimed their first fatality on 6 May and continued to take an irregular toll for the next seven weeks, killing another eleven members of the garrison and seriously wounding three.

The garrison responded aggressively, putting out snipers to disrupt the gangs of Tibetans rebuilding the Jong's defences and sending out patrols to harass the fort's supply lines. Arthur Hadow mounted one of his Maxims on the roof of the 'citadel' and directed short bursts of machine-gun fire whenever a promising target presented itself on the walls of the Jong. Initially, the Tibetans underestimated the garrison's capacity to hit back. On 8 May a party of colourfully-dressed Tibetan horsemen rode out from the fortress, unaware that Ottley and some of his Mounted Infantry had returned from the Karo La the previous evening. They were chased across the plain to the gates of the nearest monastery, whereupon a second and larger party of horsemen rode out of the Jong, apparently intent on rescuing the first. They were met by a fusillade of well-directed bullets from Ottley and his twenty men, who had just come into possession of the British Army's new standard issue rifle: 'It was the first time we put our new Lee-Enfield rifle to such a test, and we soon knew by the effect what a splendid weapon it is. The men opened fire at 1,000 yards on the enemy, which stopped them, killing or wounding ten of them and several of their ponies, and sending the remainder flying back into the jong.'

Over the following days the Mounted Infantry continued to harry the Tibetans in the vicinity of the Jong and in the surrounding hills, also gathering supplies in the form of grain or livestock whenever the opportunity arose. It soon became evident that Tsechen monastery, situated about two and a half miles to the north-west, was almost as strongly held as the Jong and in as strong a defensive location – 'built on another precipitous hill about 600

feet high, about one mile long, and rising abruptly out of the plain
. . . occupied by at least 1,000 of the enemy, who cheered vociferously when they saw us retire.'

Despite these sallies Tibetan reinforcements continued to arrive
at the Jong almost daily and their commander, Depon Tailing,
grew bolder, sending armed groups forward under cover of night
to occupy a number of houses scattered across the plain immediately to the north and east of Changlo Manor. The closest of these
was a rectangular building lying between the Jong and the Mission
post and less than two hundred yards away. From here Tibetan
marksmen with rifles were able to enfilade the new traverses and
bring fire to bear on anyone unwise enough to cross the open
ground between the Mission building and the Redoubt, which left
Lieutenant-Colonel Brander with no option but to seize and hold
it. The initial assault by the Gurkhas on the night of 18 May failed
when the riflemen were unable to gain an entrance. Lieutenant
Gurden, Royal Engineers, the explosives expert with the 32nd
Pioneers, then joined them on the following night with a box of
gun-cotton. A hole was blown in a gate and the Gurkhas charged
forward – to find the defenders crowded together in the centre of
the building's courtyard with drawn swords. Only Henry Newman
was candid enough to describe what followed: 'The Tibetans –
about fifty in number – herded themselves together as if to meet
a bayonet charge, but our troops, rushing through the door,
extended themselves along the edges of the courtyard, and
emptied their magazines into the mob. Within a minute all the
fifty were dead or mortally wounded.' The building was taken over
by a company of Gurkhas and became known thereafter as the
Gurkha House.

The following day the Tibetans struck back, ambushing the
Mounted Infantry regular mail train just north of the monastery of
Naini where the Nyang Chu debouched onto the Gyantse plain.
Alerted by the firing, the rest of the Mounted Infantry in Changlo
Manor saddled up and galloped to the rescue – only to find themselves assailed from three sides, which was clearly the Tibetan commander's intention. The men kept their nerve and went to ground,
returning fire for an hour before retreating under covering fire
from the Mission. 'This was quite the sharpest affair we had had so

far,' commented William Ottley. 'It also showed that the Tibetans had occupied all the villages for miles up the river, and that they intended to stop our daily mail and cut our communications.'

If the road to Guru was to be kept open then the Tibetans had to be removed from Naini, where the monastery together with a small fort overlooking it and the several small hamlets nearby were now occupied in strength. On the day following the ambush Brander led out the strongest force he could muster. A morning of grim house-to-house fighting followed as one village after another was rushed and cleared at the point of the bayonet. Just as the troops were poised to assault Naini monastery itself, the proceedings came to a sudden halt. Henry Newman, who had been following the action all day on foot, soon saw the reason why. 'The Pioneers had just extended and were advancing,' he wrote, 'when someone who happened to be looking at the jong [that is, Gyantse Jong] through his glasses suddenly uttered a loud exclamation.' Newman and those nearest to him turned about to see 'a dense stream of men, several thousands in number, forming up at the base of the rock, evidently with the intention of rushing the mission post while the majority of the garrison and the guns were engaged elsewhere.' Bugles were immediately sounded and whistles blown, and the entire force withdrew towards Changlo Manor at the double. A race now began between the Tibetans to the north and Brander's men to the south to see who could reach it first. It was won by Ottley's Mounted Infantry, who galloped ahead and swept across the front of the advancing Tibetans, all that was needed to halt them in their tracks and send them scurrying back to the safety of the Jong. It was, in Newman's opinion, a 'close shave'.

This was Depon Tailing's last serious attempt to take Changlo Manor but he continued to harry the garrison as best he could, keeping up a steady bombardment from the Jong by day and mounting a number of small-scale night attacks that soon began to take their toll on the defenders. After twenty days the garrison's casualties had amounted to fifty-six killed or wounded – one-sixth of the garrison – and the soldiers were exhausted. 'Our men', wrote Ottley, 'were beginning to feel the hard work, as the guard duties were very heavy, and all the defensive works which entailed fatiguing labour had to be carried out at night, so that the whole garrison had had only one or two nights in bed for the past fort-night.' However, relief was at hand, for on 24 May a company of the 32nd Sikh Pioneers spearheaded by Captain Peterson and twenty mounted infantrymen fought its way past Naini and arrived at Changlo. As well as doubling the numbers of Mounted Infantry at Changlo and adding another eighty rifles to the strength, this relief column brought further valuable reinforce-ments in the form of a half-company of Bengal Sappers and Miners and the two ten-pounders of the British Mountain Battery, together with a hundred rounds of 'common shell' capable of demolishing the sturdiest redoubt.

Commanding the sappers was a young officer, Captain Seymour Sheppard, DSO, who was already something of a legend in the Indian Army, where he was known (for reasons now seemingly lost to history) as 'the frontier Le Brocq'. Although primarily a demolitions expert (the author of *Demolitions in Savage Warfare*, published in 1904), Sheppard had made a great name for himself in half a dozen Frontier campaigns and was British India's champion racquet-player to boot. Francis Younghusband came to regard him as one of two outstanding officers of 'military genius' among his escort, the other being William Ottley. Sheppard's unheralded arrival with the relief column did wonders for morale.

It now became possible to send out more raiding and foraging parties – and to strike hard at the most threatening of the Tibetans' forward positions. A thousand yards east of Changlo Manor was a complex of buildings that made up Palla Manor, the country resi-dence of a Tibetan nobleman who had disgraced himself a decade before by giving shelter to the explorer-spy Sarat Chandra Das. Like Changlo Manor, it consisted of two large double-storeyed mansions surrounded by a series of lesser buildings, each with its own inner courtyard and outer wall. This complex was now heavily reinforced by the Tibetans, who had also begun to build a covered way that would link it to the Jong. At dawn on 28 May Captain Sheppard and his sappers crept up to the wall of the house closest to the Mission to lay their gun-cotton charges. With them was Frank O'Connor, who had been a cadet with Sheppard at Woolwich and now insisted on accompanying him. The explosion that followed blew in the side of the house but also roused every Tibetan in the Jong, bringing down on Palla a 'continuous storm of bullets . . . regardless whether friend or foe was hit'. As the sappers ran forward to the next building three of their number were killed. Under a hail of close-quarter fire Sheppard and his deputy, Lieutenant Garstin, laid and lit a second charge, but found that the breach only gave them access to an enclosed courtyard with high walls, and not to the main buildings. There was nothing for it but to blow their way through the intervening walls, charge by charge. 'Sheppard did not believe in small charges or half measures,' noted O'Connor. Nor did he believe in long fuses, almost blowing up himself, O'Connor and a party of Sikhs as they attempted to extricate themselves from an upper floor where they had just placed and lit an entire box of gun-cotton: 'We fell in a heap at the bottom of the ladder just as the gun-cotton exploded, blowing off the roof of the house and scattering its garrison in fragments all over the place.'

The Tibetans manning the defences of the two central buildings at Palla were Khampa warriors who fought, according to Newman, with 'extraordinary fury'. Watching through fieldglasses from Changlo Manor, he saw them 'exposing themselves boldly at the windows, calling to our men to come on'. Others on the roofs 'danced about thereon in what seemed frantic derision'. Some were armed with nothing more lethal than slings and stones, and made easy targets as they stood to whirl their slings above their heads, provoking Newman to comment that 'you cannot fight bullets with stones'. Many more, however, were armed with rifles and matchlocks, and were able to bring down concentrated fire on Sheppard's sappers, so that their progress from one block to the next became slower and slower and the gaps between explosions longer. After Sheppard had lost another three men killed there was a lull as he and Garstin pondered how they could break into the largest of the two central mansions without fatally exposing the remainder of their party. At this point O'Connor decided to climb onto a roof to get a closer look at their opponents:

I crawled to the edge and rashly popped my head up, and was immediately bowled over by a lump of lead from a muzzle-loading jingal and sent rolling head-over-heels down the slope of the debris. I distinctly remember, while I was still rolling, wondering whether any bones were broken and throwing out my arms to test it. I was soon satisfied. The bullet had passed through the fleshy part of my upper left arm, and then continued its course under the left shoulder blade till it stopped by the backbone. A great piece of luck. Not a bone injured, and very little loss of blood.

Hours passed, it seemed to Newman, without any further development. He heard the Tibetans defending the two central mansions shout in elation and the Tibetans in the Jong reply with answering cheers. But out of his sight two companies of Pioneers were approaching Palla from its far side, while a third force consisting of all four field guns and the two Maxims, protected by a company of Gurkhas, had taken up a position on a knoll to the north-east of Palla. The fire brought down by this heavy weaponry galvanised the Tibetan commander in the Jong into action, and a dozen riders on black mules and about forty infantry suddenly emerged from the end of the half-completed covered way and charged across the open ground towards Palla. 'No finer feat of personal bravery could be conceived,' thought Dr Waddell, for it was instantly apparent to all who watched that the men were doomed. They were directly below Hadow's two Maxims, which were now firing perfectly. 'In three minutes,' wrote Newman, 'every single man and mule was down, except one animal with a broken leg, gazing disconsolately at its master.'

This disaster also took place in full sight of the defenders at Palla, and it seemed to break their spirits. Shells from the two ten-pounders began to crash down on them. To the surprise of all who had seen them in action at the Karo La, Bubble and Squeak also performed perfectly, dropping their shells 'with the utmost precision on the tops of these two houses, and breaking through the roofs, setting them on fire'. The defenders' fire slackened, giving Captain Sheppard and his men the opportunity to run forward and place their final charges. At their first attempt the fuse attached to the gun-cotton went out. Lieutenant Garstin ran back to relight it and was shot through the head. Sheppard followed him and had better luck, the ensuing explosion allowing the troops crowding behind to enter and shoot down the remaining Tibetans in the central mansion as they made a last stand. Palla was declared taken at 2 p.m. 'The occupants,' observed William Ottley, 'to their ever-lasting credit, fought magnificently.' They had lost four hundred of their number killed or wounded. Another hundred and fifty were taken prisoner and put to work building a trench linking Changlo Manor with Palla, now taken over by a company of Pioneers.

The capture of Palla meant that all the open ground between the Gurkha House and the houses at the southern foot of Gyantse Jong was now a no-man's land, controlled by neither side. It took the pressure off the garrison and allowed Lieutenant-Colonel Brander to scale down his military operations to night patrols. The numbers of armed men now amassed in the Jong and the sur-rounding monasteries amounted to at least ten times his own, so there was no question of making any more major assaults until the General returned with more troops. Since this was unlikely to happen for at least three weeks, Brander concentrated his efforts on strengthening the three positions now held – Changlo Manor, the Gurkha House and Palla – and reopening their line of commu-nications with New Chumbi.

The Mission staff and garrison now settled down to make the best of their situation. Despite the dangers they very quickly grew accustomed to the early-morning and late-afternoon barrages, sometimes consisting of a 'ragged feu de joi' in which some fifteen or sixteen of the Tibetans' larger guns were fired as a volley. They learned never to show their heads above the parapets or beyond the network of covered ways that threaded their camp 'like a rabbit warren', and to duck instinctively whenever they heard a warning shout. They became experts at distinguishing the report of one gun from another, and at taking the appropriate measures. 'The fact', wrote Perceval Landon, 'that the report of a gun of an ancient pattern invariably precedes the ball was, we found, of the most invaluable assistance. There was always time to go four yards at least under cover of the nearest traverse before the ball crashed into the compound. There was one jingal, however, which was christened "Chota [Small] Billy", which only allowed three yards and in extreme cases of over-charge of powder only two.'

It was worked out that there were more than twenty guns mounted on the Jong capable of inflicting damage, with bores ranging from one inch to three and three-quarter inches. Initially they were considered relatively harmless, provided one kept under cover, and were termed 'silly billies', but as the days passed larger and more powerful weapons arrived, culminating in the arrival of 'William', whose appearance at the Jong was heralded by 'great shouting and blowing of trumpets and beating of drums'. While most shots from the guns tended to fall short of Changlo Manor into an area in front known as the 'football field', William and a later arrival, 'William the Second', both had a range in excess of 2,400 yards and were capable of doing serious damage. One of William's first shots all but penetrated the thick stone wall of Dr Waddell's room, damaging some of his precious manuscripts, 'the shot, almost as large as a cricket ball, burying itself 1½ feet down'. Brander's response was to put a number of his best marksmen on special duty to watch with binoculars the thick wooden door that had been built to protect William's porthole: 'At the word "William's open" everyone dipped behind a shelter, while the sharpshooters plugged at the opening and immediately ducked down till the thundering boom and the missile itself had passed or had smashed a bit of building or a tree nearby.'

For the two special correspondents, the aggravation of being bombarded by day was exceeded by the 'intolerable nuisance' of dogs howling and fighting by night. The Tibetans had been offered a ceasefire to take away their dead lying in the fields about the Mission but had declined to do so, with the result that scores of pi-dogs spent the nights 'disputing among themselves the possession of the disgusting spoils they had secured during the day'. At first they were shot, until it was realised that they provided a valuable early warning of Tibetan attempts to creep up to the post in the night. At the same time many of the defenders took in stray dogs as pets, some of which, such as a 'fearsome hound' named 'Major Wimberley' after its owner, became garrison characters, while others were best avoided – most particularly a 'bad-tempered, snarling little beast' known as 'the Lama'.

Exactly one calendar month after the start of the siege Francis Younghusband received a summons to go down to New Chumbi to confer with James Macdonald over future plans. As he himself later admitted in print, 'during all this Gyantse period I was not so steady and imperturbable as an Agent ought to be . . . I was very restive'. Simla's response to his call to regard the attack on the Mission as an act of war, to abandon negotiations and to head straight for Lhasa instead, had been to warn him that he was showing 'undue eagerness' and was causing the Cabinet in England 'some apprehension'. To his disgust, he had been ordered to reopen negotiations and try once more to communicate with the Dalai Lama. 'I should like people in England to know,' he had written privately to Helen in response to these orders, 'that I am thoroughly ashamed of my Government and that it is most distasteful to be serving men who have the honour of their country so little at heart.' The thought of negotiating with those whom he now regarded as his assailants was profoundly distasteful to him, and he did all he could to avoid reopening talks. 'I am replying that I have no means of communicating with the Amban as we are bombarded all day long and any messenger I sent to town wd be instantly murdered. This will give Govt time to think.' At the same time he sent off a stream of increasingly impassioned letters and telegrams claiming there was now overwhelming evidence that the Tibetans at Gyantse were 'relying most absolutely on Russian support and receiving a very substantial amount of it'.

The end result was a summons to report to New Chumbi, accompanied by a demand from Lord Ampthill as Acting Viceroy that he was not to leave Gyantse without delivering to the Tibetans an 'ultimatum' in the form of two letters, one addressed to the Dalai Lama and one to the Chinese Amban, demanding that the Tibetans negotiate or face the consequences. These letters had been duly delivered to the commander of Gyantse Jong – and, to Francis Younghusband's great satisfaction, immediately returned unopened. Depon Tailing then almost spoiled things by having second thoughts and requesting the letters' return – but was told that he had missed his chance. 'Luckily when they had once returned it I wd not have any more truck with them,' wrote Younghusband to his sister Emmie on 5 June. 'I was dead agst sending an ultimatum at all & thus giving them another chance of negotiating. My view was that once they had attacked the Mission we shd have declared war on them without any ultimatum. So when they returned the ultimatum I was not going to give them another chance.'

Younghusband knew he was sailing very close to the wind, and before he left Changlo Manor for New Chumbi he bowed to the Acting Viceroy's wishes and sent the returned ultimatum back to Depon Tailing. Then he gave the officers of the Mission and Escort the grandest dinner he could organise, almost as though it was a farewell:

> A dozen of champagne had arrived from Ld Curzon so I asked everybody to drink his health. We sat down 27 officers and two correspondents and really rigged up quite a decent dinner though everyone had to bring his own chair, table, knife, spoon, fork, plate, cups for soup, tumblers (there is only one real glass in the place), and though we brazened it out well with champagne at the beginning and with a bottle of chartreuse at 'dessert' we had to fall back on commissariat rum at the end for we had no whisky.

Younghusband set out for New Chumbi before dawn on 6 June, accompanied by forty men of the Mounted Infantry under Major Murray. Giving Naini monastery a wide berth, they arrived before nightfall at Kangmar, where a fortified post had been established, guarded by a hundred men of the 23rd Pioneers. Next day Younghusband rose early and had just finished dressing when he heard the now familiar howling that heralded a Tibetan attack – a sound that according to Herbert Brander resembled the cry of the Indian jackal: 'hya-hya-hya, uttered in a rising falsetto voice'. By his own account, set down in a letter to his father sent from Chumbi, Younghusband immediately took command:

> The officers of the post were still in bed but I told them it was an attack & I dashed out and saw about 300 coming along in a mob, waving their swords, shouting & pooping off their match locks. I shouted to the men to fall in. The officers immediately afterwards joined in but we had only just got the walls manned by the time the Tibetans were up to them. They then began

throwing stones over. We all of us took rifles and fired away and of course in a very few minutes most of the Tibetans had been shot down and the rest bolted. The mounted infantry and half the garrison then went off in pursuit and chased away two or three parties who had taken up positions one above & the other below Kangma ready to slay us when we ran away! I counted 106 dead bodies round our post. 68 were killed in the pursuit & about 30 more by long range fire on the hill side.

After breakfast Younghusband's party continued on to the telegraph post at Kala Tso, where two companies of the 23rd Pioneers under Lieutenant-Colonel Hogge — the same men who had made up his escort during his three cold months at Tuna — turned out in parade uniforms as a guard of honour to welcome him. From Kala Tso Younghusband sent two very undiplomatic telegrams to Simla. 'I was physically exhausted and depressed in spirit . . . and I was not in the mood to be respectful,' he later explained. He had just learned that Macdonald had given it as his opinion that keeping troops in Lhasa over the coming winter was impossible, and he was outraged. It was essential he spend the winter in Lhasa, Younghusband argued in his first telegram. If he was to conclude his negotiations satisfactorily, he *had* to stay on — and it was perfectly possible for a thousand men to winter in Lhasa without outside supplies. 'If it is really the case,' he concluded, 'that troops cannot be maintained in Lhasa next winter, I had better not go to Lhasa at all.' By way of a follow-up he telegraphed Louis Dane warning him that 'we are now fighting the Russians, not the Tibetans. Latter were easily knocked out on the way to Gyantse. Since Karo La we are dealing with Russia.' This was a claim utterly without foundation.

These two telegrams were not well received. Lord Ampthill had been making strenuous efforts to keep both Lhasa and Russia out of the frame, and had become increasingly perturbed by Younghusband's unsteady behaviour since the attack on the Mission. Meanwhile the C-in-C India, Lord Kitchener, had resolved in the wake of the Karo La affair to see to it that his man, Brigadier-General Macdonald, should henceforward be in charge of the Mission at all times, with Colonel Younghusband 'merely the political officer on the latter's staff'. It was at this juncture, with his fortunes at their lowest ebb, that Francis Younghusband and his escort of forty mud-bespattered riders arrived at New Chumbi.

The dramatic appearance of the Tibet Commissioner, combined with the news that his mounted escort had had to fight its way out, brought a renewed sense of urgency to the troops massed at New Chumbi. But in fact the General's preparations were complete, and what it was now politically safe to term a 'field force' was ready to march. There was a 'great confabulation' on 11 June as the two men met in Macdonald's quarters and tried to resolve their differences. Major William Beynon had at last managed to secure a transfer from the hated Coolie Corps on to the General's staff as a 'special service officer'. He was a witness as the two men stated their differences and, naturally enough, sided with the General: 'Younghusband wants to go to Lhasa and if necessary stay there all winter,' he explained to his wife. 'Genl Macdonald says that from a military point of view the idea of staying all the winter at Lhasa is very risky – as communications could not be kept up and the force left isolated for 6 months. He says we can go to Lhasa this year & if the Tibetans won't treat we can burn a monastery or two and then come back to Chumbi for the winter & tell the Tibetans we are going to Lhasa next year with a bigger army, and shall then play hades with the country if they are still obstinate . . . Of course this is the proper plan.'

On 12 June the Tibet Field Force marched out of New Chumbi, pausing briefly at Phari Jong for the rearmost column to catch up before crossing the Tang La. Lance-Corporal Alfred Dunning of the Royal Fusiliers was not impressed, writing on 14 June: 'If this is a sample of what Llassa is like I don't think much of it. Not a blade of grass or shrub or tree to be seen for miles. In the distance we can see the sacred hill of Llassa [Mt Chumolhari, perhaps confused with Mt Everest, 130 miles to the west] said to be 28,000 feet high. It looks like a huge snowball. Rations very bad.' Dunning's energies were now focused on supplementing his meagre diet: 'I bought some eggs yesterday. I don't know where they came from as I have seen no fowl, but they were all rotten. After paying 1 Rps [rupees] for 8, what luck. I have also bought about 7 lbs of rice – Rps 3 – and 4 lbs of sugar – Rps 2. I can pack it in my kit. This will keep me from starving anyway.'

Four days later the Fusiliers were over the Tang La and encamped on the Great Plateau some miles short of Tuna, shaken by the bitterness of the wind and finding it almost impossible to sleep at night. Next morning there was nothing more than half a chapatti and a mug of tea for each man, and as they pressed on to the Guru many of the men began to suffer from weakness and dysentery. 'I was very ill through drinking bad water,' wrote Private Sampson in his diary that night. 'Many men are complaining of sickness caused by the bad water. The Doctor says there must have been dead bodies higher up the stream.' Lance-Corporal Dunning was also in a bad way: 'We cross 2 rivers up to the knees and this is nice for marching. The sand gets in your boots and rubs the skin off heels and toes. I don't know how I got in today.' The following day they marched through the battlefield of Chumik Shenko. 'Three miles out we come across the scene of the recent fight. Two to three hundred bodies lying in our track, exposed to the sun, lying in all positions, some in the act of running away, others hiding behind rocks. I quite believe their losses were 500. Mr Candler of the Daily Mail lost his hand here. He is still with us. He evidently intends to see Llassa.'

In fact, it was not Edmund Candler whom Dunning saw at Guru but his replacement, a journalist who failed to last the course and soon retired. As for Candler, after his wounding at Guru he had been carried down to Darjeeling on a dhoolie, in a bad way. The stump of his amputated left hand had failed to heal well and a second operation had been necessary. Barely seven weeks later the Royal Fusiliers and the other reinforcements gathered in Darjeeling – and Candler learned that he had been replaced. This was a disaster for a man with a wife and infant to support, and no income. But it spurred him into action. Though his wounds were still far from healed, he set about rejoining the force. After more than a fortnight of 'arguing, and haggling, and hectoring' he was finally allowed to depart in pursuit of Macdonald, only to be beset by a series of mishaps – including the closure of the Jelep La due to an outbreak of cholera among the transport coolies – which meant that he arrived in New Chumbi a week after the General had left. Another week passed before he was at last able to cross the Tang La. Eighty-one days after the massacre there he was back at the springs of Chumik Shenko and wandering among the partially mummified corpses of the Tibetan dead:

> By the stream the bodies lay in heaps with parched skin, like mummies, rusty brown. A knot of coarse black hair, detached from a skull, was circling round in an eddy of wind. Everything had been stripped from the corpses save here and there a whisp of cloth, looking more grim than the nakedness it covered, or round the neck some inexpensive charm, which no one had thought worth taking for its occult powers. Nature, more kindly, had strewn around them beautiful spring flowers – primulas, buttercups, potentils. The stream 'bubbled oilily', and in the ruined house bees were swarming.

Burial parties had, in fact, done what they could to inter the victims of the Chumik Shenko massacre where they had fallen, only for the bodies to be disinterred after they moved on. This caused considerable revulsion among the troops, who were unaware that the Tibetans considered it an offence against the spirits of the earth to bury the remains of humans, preferring to leave them exposed to the elements.

It was another two days before Edmund Candler caught up with Macdonald's army in Gyantse. It is to him that the Younghusband Mission owes one of its most enduring images – that of two Fusiliers toiling up the slopes of the Tang La and overheard making the following exchange:

> FIRST TOMMY: I thought they told us Tibet was a ＊＊＊＊＊＊＊ table-land.
> SECOND TOMMY: So it ＊＊＊＊＊＊＊ well is, you silly ＊＊＊＊＊＊. This is one of the ＊＊＊＊＊＊＊ table-legs.

Since Candler was not actually with the Fusiliers at this point, it must be regretfully concluded that the exchange was apocryphal.

As the Tibet Field Force approached the start of the deep cut leading to the now well-known Red Idol Gorge, the Mounted Infantry scouts reported a large body of Tibetans shadowing their right flank. 'They could make it warm for us if they wished,' noted Alfred Dunning in his diary, but Private Sampson was more preoccupied by the sinister 'mottos' spelled out in white stones on the hillsides, said to be 'a warning to strangers to turn back'. An eagerly anticipated attack on a Tibetan position at Kangmar fizzled out in anti-climax when the occupants were found to have left in a hurry overnight. However, there was time for the troops to have, in Alfred Dunning's words, 'a bit of a holiday. Our camp is near a river so we get a wash and change. My whiskers are growing rather tangley. None of us have shaved since leaving Darjeeling.' Here George Preston of the 40th Pathans first came face to face with the enemy, in the form of a group of Tibetans recovering from their wounds in a makeshift field hospital. With the help of an interpreter he talked to two wounded men and was taken aback by their shifting loyalties: 'Both of them said they were quite willing to go on with our force and fight for us. They didn't know why they had been fighting against us except that one of the lamas had told them that the only way to get to heaven was to fight these white devils. All the Tibetans seem very friendly – and quite willing to join us – but they are all under the influence of these lamas.'

There was further disappointment for the troops when the Red Idol Gorge also turned out to be undefended, but as the men were making camp in the open valley at its northern end a party of Mounted Infantry rode in with one of their number shot through the thigh and dying from loss of blood, and the news that the Tibetans were preparing to make a stand at the village and monastery of Naini at the head of the Gyantse Valley. Here the Tibetans had fortified the main monastery on the valley floor, the nearby village, and two small forts built high on the steep slopes above the monastery. On the morning of 26 June these were subjected to bombardment by the field force's six field guns, firing 'common' shell that exploded on impact. Alfred Dunning was on guard duty that day, marching alongside the heavy guns and their ammunition: 'Start at 7 and march about 8 miles, then come in touch with the enemy, strongly entrenched at Naini. Our Mountain Battery opens fire and does extensive damage . . . The Battery keep pounding away at their Village until there is hardly a stick left standing. Hundreds must have been buried alive.'

After an hour and a half of this softening-up, the Gurkhas and 40th Pathans rushed and took the main monastery on the plain at the point of the bayonet. Once the monastery had been captured the guns of the field force were turned on the two forts, which now also came under fire from the hillside above: the garrison at Changlo Manor had been roused by the sound of gunfire and had come out to assist. 'This was a fine sight,' wrote Private Sampson, whose company was being kept in reserve, along with the other three Fusilier companies:

> Every shot found the mark, raising clouds of dust & knocking great holes in the walls. Then came shots from the top of the hill in rear of the Forts. These turned out to be the Mission Force which had come to help us get through. The Thibetans are now between two fires which prove too much for them. They are clearing out of their positions and do not seem to know where to go or what to do. Then our maxims had a turn at them, knocking them over like skittles. Another lot of Gurkhas came down on their left hemming them in altogether. This party of Gurkhas rush the Forts which they capture. When the losses are counted up there were 200 of the enemy killed. The wounded crawled away into caves & holes in the hills.

For those more closely involved, the fight seemed much less one-sided. Among them was Lieutenant Fred 'Hatter' Bailey, now returning to the fray in command of two troops of Mounted Infantry. He and his men were soon engaged in lethal hand-to-hand fighting as they cleared the villages house by house. 'I saw the muzzle of a matchlock sticking out of it, which went off just as I got out of the way' was how Bailey began an account of one such house clearance, in a letter that must have shaken his father to the core. After blowing in the doors with gun-cotton, he and his Sikhs charged into the smoke:

> We went in again & found nothing on the lower floor but a pony which we took. But some men above in the upper storey threw things down the trap door which led above & fired a few shots down. I climbed the ladder leading up very carefully

looking all round & with my revolver ready & just as my head was getting out I got an awful knock on it which almost stunned me & knocked me off the ladder. I don't quite know what had happened but found a man had hit me with a sword. Luckily I was wearing a [cork] helmet with a puggaree [cloth turban] & he hit me on the helmet just where the pugarree was thickest. The cut had gone though all the folds of cloth & through half the thickness of the helmet but no further.

After a second charge of gun-cotton had won them the first floor, Bailey and his men found themselves under another trap-door leading to the upper floor. They rushed it, killing all five defendants, then moved on to deal with the next house in similar fashion. Eventually all resistance ended – except at one strongly fortified house with thick stone walls that stood alone between the monastery and the river. Here the survivors fought on, despite being pounded at almost point-blank range by four field guns and a Maxim. 'The Tibetans in this house behaved splendidly,' recorded William Ottley, 'and although battered with seven-pounder shells from 250 yards, did not cease fire till the guns had knocked down most of the front face of the house.' To the disgust of officers and men, the General then refused permission for the 23rd Sikh Pioneers to rush the position and avenge the loss of several of their number. He ordered a ceasefire, believing that the Tibetans had suffered enough. As far as Bailey, O'Connor and other officers were concerned, this was sheer folly – and they were proved right when late that evening the baggage guard were fired upon as they passed the house, resulting in the death of a Gurkha rifleman. His enraged colleagues immediately stormed the build-ing, killed what they believed were its last living occupants and set fire to the place – only to find themselves again coming under fire from the burning house as they were marching away. By that time it was too dark to attempt another attack, and the Gurkhas left this last survivor to enjoy a rare if pyrrhic triumph.

Once the road past Naini had been cleared the four companies of the Royal Fusiliers continued their march towards Gyantse, halting only for a wash and a dip in the river. As they approached Changlo Manor they had their first taste of Tibetan artillery fire from the embrasures of Gyantse Jong – 'little damage being done except some mules being killed'. What did impress, however, was the fortress itself, 'for all the world like the rock of Gibraltar'. The sides of the great rock upon which it stood were so steep that it appeared insurmountable from every side except at its south-east corner, where the main gateway was protected by walls and earthworks to its front and one massive projecting bastion behind. A second and no less redoubtable inner ring of bastions was set some two hundred feet higher. 'It is a most formidable place,' Captain George Preston of the 40th Pathans wrote to his wife, 'and it will cost us dear before it is taken. It is an enormous place – how it is going to be taken beats me . . . If we do storm it and the Tibetans hold on we shall have a long list of casualties. Everyone is of opinion that the best thing to do would be to cut off their water supply and invest it [lay siege] – or else leave a small garrison here to look after it and go right on to Lhasa.'

The new arrivals set up camp in the fields just south of Changlo Manor and safely out of range of the guns of the Jong. Here they were soon enjoying the luxury of lighting camp fires with wood after three weeks of making do with yak dung, and conducting that all-important rite among British troops in the field – the brew-up. 'The river here is the colour of mud,' noted Percy Coath. 'Well, our tea which we soon made after arrival seemed as if heaps of condensed milk had been used with it, but it was simply the colour of the water. However, we were glad to get it, muddy or not.'

To Private Sampson's disgust, his company was immediately assigned to outpost duty, which meant putting pickets outside their camp and mounting sentries. His section was set to guard a small hamlet just east of the camp and here, to his horror, he almost shot an old Tibetan woman who appeared suddenly at a window. He remained on sentry duty until relieved at 3 a.m. and then turned in – only to be awoken an hour later by an appalling noise, 'the firing of guns from the Fort and ringing of hundreds of bells & banging of gongs & tom-toms. I looked at the time & found it was just 4. The daylight was just breaking.' Two hours later he and his company were falling-in on parade.

In typical army style, what had been announced as a day of

rest for the Fusiliers became instead extremely demanding as Sampson's company found itself participating in a major attack. Anxious not to waste a moment, 'Retiring Mac' had begun his campaign to reclaim Gyantse.

10

The Storming of Gyantse Jong

O N 26 June Francis Younghusband returned to Changlo
Manor in the company of Claude White, whose character he
thought 'much improved . . . though I know he has said some
nasty things about me', and two newcomers to the Mission staff:
his private secretary and brother-in-law, Vernon Magniac, and a
Tibetan interpreter named David Macdonald, a young Anglo-
Sikkimese who was supposed to be joining Dr Waddell as his
assistant but had been co-opted by the Tibet Commissioner to act
as his translator until Frank O'Connor was sufficiently recovered
from his wounds to resume his duties. As their ponies crossed the
wooden bridge over the Kyang Chu the Tibetans on the Jong fired
a salvo of round-shot at them, one missing Younghusband's head
'by a matter of inches only'. But for the Tibet Commissioner this
was only the latest in a series of near misses.

On the way up from New Chumbi Younghusband had received a
wire from the Acting Viceroy which he later described to his father
as 'a very God Almighty to a black beetle style of telegram'. It
reminded him that he was to act 'in conformity with the orders and
present policy of His Majesty's Government', and that he was to do
his utmost 'to carry out the present plans until there is unquestion-
able proof that they are impracticable'. In the circumstances it was a

remarkably mild reproof, but Younghusband's response was to offer his resignation. Yet for all his protestations about being deeply hurt and 'snubbed', this was a step he had been planning for some time. While cooped up in Changlo Manor he had become increasingly intimate with the *Times* correspondent Perceval Landon, who had somehow transformed himself from a 'common' type into someone with whom Younghusband had much in common. The idea of resignation came from Landon, who had suggested it 'as the only means of inducing Govt to make up their minds' and 'the only means of bringing Govt to their senses'. And the bluff worked. Only two weeks earlier Lord Ampthill had talked of pulling the Mission out of Tibet altogether or replacing Younghusband with a safer pair of hands; now he concluded that the Tibet Commissioner's resignation at this stage would cause a storm of 'undesirable speculation and comment' at home, in Parliament and in the national press. It would be better to let him stay on at least until the Tibetans had come back with an answer to the 'ultimatum' which Younghusband had had redelivered to the Tibetans at Gyantse Jong together with the deadline of 25 June for an answer. Ampthill informed Younghusband that he would not accept his resignation before that date.

What was more, Younghusband and Macdonald had begun to see eye to eye. The General's determination to settle their differences had won the Tibet Commissioner over, and on the march to Gyantse the two men had 'a good talk' during which each in turn spoke to the other of his difficulties. They resolved their differences to the extent that Younghusband agreed to give more time for negotiations to take place at Gyantse, even if that meant abandoning the dream of Lhasa. This was a remarkable turnaround on Younghusband's part. On 30 June he wrote to tell his wife that he might be coming back to Darjeeling sooner than expected: 'The Grand Lama has no attractions for me. So as the military say they cannot stay at Lhasa & the Home Govt say they don't want me to go there at all I am only too thankful to negotiate here . . . All that resignation business is settling itself.' Younghusband could even feel sorry for 'Old Macdonald', who was suffering from diarrhoea and vomiting and had to be carried over the Tang La in a dhoolie, finally arriving at Gyantse looking 'about

140 now and very Martha-like – caring for many things'. According to the new addition to his staff, William Beynon, the General was living on slops and hating it – but still insisting on smoking 'those beastly cigarettes'.

The Tibet Field Force arrived in Gyantse a day after the expiry of Younghusband's 25 June deadline for a response to his ultimatum, but he had let it be known through his new ally, the Tongsa Penlop of Bhutan, that he was extending it by another five days to 30 June. In the meantime, Brigadier-General Macdonald had concluded that Tsechen monastery, along with the village at its foot and the fortress that guarded its rear, would have be cleared before he could contemplate assaulting Gyantse Jong. On the morning of 28 June he initiated a complicated attack plan that had two companies of Gurkhas working their way along a steep ridge behind the monastery from the south-west while two waves of infantry – the Fusiliers and the 23rd Pioneers at the front, the 40th Pathans and the remainder of the Gurkhas following on behind – approached from the plain. For the men of the Fusiliers this was their first proper action and it turned out to be a great disappointment, since they spent most of the day clearing the villages on the lower slopes, whose only occupants seemed to be women, children and old men. 'We approach the doors with fixed bayonets,' noted Lance-Corporal Dunning in his diary, 'and 1 round in the chamber and burst open any doors that are fastened. We also break open a Monastery and kill 2 Tibetans found therein and secure some loot.' This was not the sort of fighting the men had hoped or trained for.

What was even more galling for the Fusiliers was that once the villages at the foot of the ridge had been secured the Pathans and Gurkhas jogged past, the combined fire-power of the ten-pounders came into play, and it dawned on them that only now was the real action beginning – in which they were to play no further part except as spectators. Yet there was much to admire. 'The marksmanship of our gunners was proved,' noted Private Sampson in his diary.

> They seemed to be able to place their shots within a foot. They put a round in one window, then one in a door and another in another window, which silenced their guns and made a lot of

them run out of the building. When our reserves came up the Gurkhas go to the left ridge the Pathans take the right to rush the position. We the Fusiliers & Pioneers get a rest. The whole lot of us are completely knocked up, having been wading through streams & rivers all day long without a blow. Several of our chaps have got chickens which they caught in the villages. I have two in my haversack.

Tsechen's seemingly impregnable fortress, perched above the monastery at the highest extremity at the end of the ridge, was stormed shortly before sunset. 'It was a beautifully executed manoeuvre,' observed Perceval Landon, watching through field-glasses from below. 'The Pathans reached the top almost at the same moment that the Gurkhas descended upon the jong, and the mingled figures of the lanky Pathans and the small Gurkhas were clearly distinguishable one from the other against the red glow of the dying sunset.' Private Sampson's company got back to camp at 11 p.m., tired and wet through. Nevertheless Sampson and his pal Bob got a fire going, and fried a chicken for their supper.

The next morning Sampson and Bob had the second chicken for breakfast, which was followed by a mass barbecue as the Fusiliers took full advantage of the fresh supplies rounded up from Tsechen village the previous day: 'The front of our lines is just like a cattle show. There are cows & yak all staked up. They were all killed by dinner time & at tea time cooked, the lads having a good fry of steaks & chupattis. The latter are made with barley-meal mixed with water & baked on a piece of tin placed over a fierce fire & are about the size of a small pancake. The men buy them off the Native troops at 4 for a Rupee or 4d [pence] each.'

Since Tsechen monastery had offered resistance it was consid-ered fair game by the troops, many of whom ignored Brigadier-General Macdonald's orders against looting, taking whatever they could lay their hands on. 'I at once made for the cellars,' wrote Athur Hadow to his mother, 'where we found some things hidden away. We only had time to visit a few of the buildings, so did not get very much, and we then had to divide the things between three of us. I got rather a nice gong which no doubt you will find useful when I am able to get it home.' Captain Mainprise of the RAMC wrote to his wife Delia to tell her that he had secured a 'few trifles' from the monastery, among them a number of Tibetan painted scrolls. He thought them 'very curious' and reckoned they would be 'very valuable at home – as they must indeed be very old'. These *thankas*, as they were properly called, were indeed old and valuable – and soon began to fetch high prices when the first of them came up for auction at Christie's later in the summer.

While the Fusiliers were still feasting a Tibetan was seen emerging from the Jong carrying a enormous white sheet on a pole, prompting Lance-Corporal Dunning to comment that 'they evidently know the use of this very useful article'. The outcome was a ceasefire and a twenty-four-hour extension of Younghusband's deadline to the afternoon of 1 July, in order to give time for an important official known as the Ta Lama, said to be one of the four councillors of the Kashag (he was, more correctly, a senior representative from the court of the Panchen Lama at Tashilumpo), to arrive in Gyantse. At three in the afternoon of 1 July a messenger from the Ta Lama appeared to say that his master would arrive very shortly and would attend the Tibet Commissioner on the following day, 2 July, after he had first called to pay his respects on the Tongsa Penlop. Francis Younghusband would have none of it, as he later recounted to his sister Emmie: 'I sent back to say that if they did not come to me by nine next morning military operations would commence. Dear old Macdonald when I told him of this begged me to show more patience as I might frighten them away! An odd state of affairs for a General to be begging a Political Officer to be patient!' Younghusband's headstrong nature had reasserted itself, and he and the General were once more at loggerheads.

Next morning nine o'clock came and went without any sign of the Tibetan dignitary. According to Hatter Bailey, now back with Ottley's 1st Mounted Infantry, Colonel Younghusband then 'asked the General to open fire but he refused as he is afraid of taking the fort'. Not a word of this refusal to commence hostilities subsequently appeared in print, the only other allusion to it being a conciliatory note from the General delivered apparently in answer to Younghusband's request that read simply: 'A little more patience and I think you have a fair chance of having the game in your hands and reaping the reward of your efforts.' In the event, the Ta Lama was shortly afterwards seen heading with his retinue towards the Tongsa Penlop's camp. On Younghusband's orders, he and his followers were immediately intercepted by a party of Mounted Infantry and brought to the Mission post: 'I simply sent out and brought them into my camp by force,' continued Younghusband in his letter to Emmie.

> I insisted upon their paying their respects to me first. I kept them waiting in a tent for two hours & then received them. I said we were ready to make war or we were ready to make a settlement, that personally after the way I had been treacherously attacked in the night I was in favour of war and we had an army here ready to march to Lhasa tomorrow, a second army in Chumbi ready to take this one's place, and a third in India ready to come up to Chumbi. But the Emperor [that is, King Edward VII] had issued his commands that I was to make one more chance of making a settlement here. They would however have to show me that they were thoroughly in earnest or I wd go on to Lhasa straight away.

The Ta Lama was then dismissed with orders to return to Changlo Manor at noon on the following day for a formal Durbar. In the British camp this conference was interpreted as 'a preliminary to peace'. According to Corporal Percy Coath's diary, all the Fusiliers were 'in a state of quiet excitement wondering what the outcome will be'. But there was also great disappointment that, having come so far and put up with so much discomfort, they were to be deprived of the chance to see the fabled city of Lhasa.

The audience hall of the Mission was now prepared, and at half-past eleven on 3 July a guard of honour made up of Arthur Hadow's Norfolk machine-gunners presented arms to the Tongsa Penlop, barefoot as always but on this occasion wearing a black Homburg in place of his usual gilded crown. He was welcomed by the Tibet Commissioner, dressed in his dark blue diplomatic uniform complete with cocked beaver hat. The ruler of Bhutan was then introduced in turn to the General, the senior Mission staff and some twenty officers. They all took their places in the durbar hall and

Above Reinforcements: the Royal Fusiliers begin their march from Darjeeling on 24 May 1904, their CO, Lt.-Col. Edward Cooper, mounted in front, the ill-fated Lt. Alston standing to his pony's rear.

Right Sapper reinforcements: the gallant demolitions expert Capt. Seymour Sheppard, DSO (centre), with fellow Royal Engineer officers from the Bengal Sappers and Miners, all wearing poshteens.

Above The taking of Tsechen monastery on 28 June 1904: the General (standing far right) watches with gunners of No. 7 British Mountain Battery as the infantry clear the village below the monastery and its fort.

Below The Royal Fusiliers hoist the Union Jack from the summit moments after the capture of Gyantse Jong on the afternoon of 6 July 1904.

Right Gyantse Jong, as seen from the roof of the Mission building at Changlo Manor, with the barrel of Capt. Hadow's Maxim gun in the foreground.

Below Panorama of the Field of Milk, with Macdonald's army encamped below the Karo La on the afternoon of 17 July.

: KARO-LA :

A = Gurkhas line of Adv.
B = Rocks occupied by enemy
finally dislodged by
Gurkhas
C = Distant rocky spur up wh.
majority of enemy retired
from Walls. It was up this
ridge that we[?] Pathans
eventually pushed.
D = Walls
E = Position line of Advance
F = 2 Coy Gurkhas.

Left above The second battle of Karo La, fought on 18 July 1904. Pen and ink drawing by Lt. Norman Rybot.

Left centre On the road to Lhasa: a group of mounted officers meet a mail *ekka* and transport.

Left below Crossing the Tsangpo: mules being loaded onto a Tibetan ferry-boat.

Right Lt. John Grant, VC, poses on his pony Jingal at the great western gate of Lhasa.

Below The nuns of Tatsang gompa, wearing their wigs, photographed by Claude White.

A deputation of monks from Drepung monastery confer with the General (centre) under a flag of truce on 8 August 1904.

Monks of Sera monastery. The men with the padded shoulders are proctors charged with maintaining discipline. Photo by Claude White.

The monk assailant under guard before his hanging, the chain-armour he wore lying beside him.

The four Shapés of Tibet, on the far right Younghusband's 'evil genius' Lobsang Trinley.

Left The front steps of the Potala Palace, photographed by Claude White.

Below The Royal Fusiliers march into Lhasa on their way to the signing of the Convention in the Potala on 6 September 1904.

awaited the Tibetan delegation, which they now knew had been joined by the Dalai Lama's Grand Secretary, Lobsang Trinley, already known to Younghusband from his earlier talks at Khamba Jong and regarded by him an 'evil genius . . . capable but evil-minded'. After an hour had passed without any sign of the Ta Lama and his delegation, Younghusband rose from his seat and declared the Durbar closed. It was a classic example of cultural confusion: the one party used to working by the clock and regarding lateness as an offence against good manners, the other with no concept of specific times of day other than those signalled by the position of the sun, and regarding undue haste as impolite.

At 1.30 p.m., just as the officers were sitting down to lunch, the Ta Lama's retinue was seen approaching and the Durbar was 'on' again – but not till lunch was over, and very much to the Tibet Commissioner's timetable: 'I kept them in a tent till 4 and then received them in full Durbar,' noted Younghusband in his letter to Emmie. 'I received them seated in dead silence and very coldly. I still kept silent for a long time while they squirmed. Then I said very slowly and sternly that I presumed from the disrespect they had shown me that they were not in earnest in desiring to effect a settlement and would expect us to advance to Lhasa. They vowed they did not mean any disrespect and were really anxious to make a settlement. I told them that as a preliminary they must clear out of the Jong: they wd be given 36 hours to go, after that military oper-ations wd commence.'

As the official papers showed, Colonel Younghusband made no effort to negotiate. There was no talk of a settlement, only a demand that the Jong be evacuated as a preliminary. The Tongsa Penlop's efforts at mediation were brushed aside. Yet there was no good reason why the talks could not take place while the Tibetans held the Jong. Quite when and why Younghusband reverted to his original stance remains a mystery, but there can be no doubt that he knew from Lord Ampthill's manner and from the hints of Louis Dane, his one remaining ally in the Foreign Department at Simla, that a satisfactory settlement at Gyantse would be followed by his recall and replacement by a more compliant political agent prepared to take orders from Brigadier-General Macdonald. Thus he had nothing to lose and everything to gain by seeking to postpone any settlement until he had arrived in Lhasa. As he twice put it himself in his letters to his wife, 'It is a case of heads I win tails they lose.'

However, there remained one obstacle to all this, in the person of James Macdonald. That he and his senior staff were disliked by even the most recently joined officers can be judged from the views expressed by Captain George Preston in a letter to his wife written at this time. It is clear that garbled versions of the General's first run-in with Younghusband at Tuna in January were still circulating: 'They say that General Macdonald is losing his nerve from illness. He wants to move the camp back to the last place, which would be madness, but Colonel Younghusband has flatly refused . . . He is not quite what everyone expects. He has a weak-looking face. Is absolutely run by his staff, who are a poor lot, and smokes cigarettes till he is sick.' It can be no coincidence that on 3 July – the day after the General began to reassert himself – a letter-writing campaign with the single aim of bringing about Macdonald's recall was initiated. Some of the evidence for such a campaign is largely circumstantial, such as the curious gap between 4 July and 22 July in the otherwise regular weekly letters written by Francis Younghusband to his father throughout his term as Tibet Commissioner: two seem to be missing from the file. Although their contents are unknown it is clear from an earlier letter, written on 17 June, that Younghusband was using his father as a conduit for getting his views known to influential friends in Fleet Street at this time. A similar if less striking gap occurs in the surviving letters to Helen, which at this time Francis was writing on a daily basis – except between 5 and 8 July. Much more damning is an only partly legible but none the less revealing letter written by Frank O'Connor to Helen Younghusband on 3 July – the day of the grand Durbar. 'The Colonel', he began, was 'very fit indeed', but he could not say the same for 'Gen. M.' O'Connor went on:

> You ask me in your letter of June 2nd that I received yesterday whether 'we should agitate for his removal' & I reply most emphatically yes . . . To present the case frankly he funks the task [three words illegible] In justice to the poor man I must say that he is very ill. Has been suffering from gastritis & insomnia

& is taking opium wh on top of the indiscriminate quantity of tobacco he smokes has entirely destroyed his nerves. He was carried for several days in a doolie on the way here! His troops have fought 2 small but successful actions during the last week but his conduct of both affairs was deplorable. Very slow, vacillations, numbless [?], no proper orders given & the fight in each case abandoned before resistance had been properly crushed & since then we have been sitting out in the plain with our fine force, guns etc. looking at the Jong – & the more he looks the less he likes it. He has persuaded himself that he is doing this from [illegible] & if Col. Y. had asked him to refrain from hostilities one could understand it [illegible] it is in the last degree undignified to sit down more & attempt to negotiate practically under fire of their jingals & in danger of attack at any moment day & night. Can you conceive a more ludicrous situation? A sick & feeble general refusing to support a rigorous & able commissioner with the troops which have been given to him for this very purpose & supinely awaiting the great pleasure of the Tibetan delegates . . . The man is physically & mentally unfit for the conduct of active operations. *He should be removed & another & better man – a fighting general – substituted.* [My emphasis: C.A.] Otherwise I am firmly convinced that it will be impossible for this force to reach Lhasa.

This is, by any standards, an extraordinary letter for the closest aide of the head of a mission to write to his master's wife, and why he penned it defies simple explanation. That Helen Younghusband then mounted an anti-Macdonald campaign on her husband's behalf from her end can be deduced from letters written by an old friend of the Younghusbands in the Indian Political Service, Major James Dunlop-Smith, then based near Simla. Writing to Mrs Younghusband on 28 August, he declared: 'I had an idea that M. was anything but what was to be desired but I had no idea things had gone so far. Of course I will keep your letter absolutely confidential. This news about his gastritis & the opium is distinctly bad & suggests all kinds of possibilities. But Frank [Francis Younghusband] cannot leave now . . . He is the one man in India for this course . . . It is everything for the Empire that he should see this business through. If he goes now they will send someone else who will make a hash of it or what is worse M. will be given *political powers . . . I will do all I can to help.*' [My emphasis: C.A.]

Dunlop-Smith subsequently lobbied the Viceroy's Private Secretary and others at the Foreign Department, citing Macdonald's opium-taking and his apparent encouragement of looting as evidence of his unfitness – but seemingly to little avail: 'They know nothing of M. & his peculiar habits,' he subsequently wrote to Helen, '& are prepared to accept the Army verdict that he has managed the show fairly well. I told them as much as I dared but I could not go into details as I did not wish to be pressed for the source of my information.' Mrs Younghusband then arranged with Dunlop-Smith that she should go to Simla to take the matter further, but was prevented from doing so by a bout of illness. By the time she had recovered, the issue had resolved itself.

Meanwhile, on the ground at Gyantse the Tibet Commissioner was once more forcing the pace as hard as he could. The deadline set for the evacuation of the Jong was noon on 5 July. Twelve o'clock came and went with no signs of movement from the Tibetans. According to Younghusband, he then ordered a signal-gun to be fired from the Mission. In fact, this was no signal-gun but a burst of machine-gun fire from Arthur Hadow in his redoubt on the roof of the Mission House: 'I had naturally assumed that we were to continue the "War" at that hour, so sat at my gun with my watch in my hand. It was rather exciting, as there were a good many Tibetans exposing themselves on the Jong, and gradually as 12 o'clock approached they began to disappear. However, exactly at 12 o'clock I opened fire, but it was not long before a peremptory order reached me telling me to cease fire.'

Brigadier-General Macdonald had in the meantime moved half his troops and heavy guns out onto the plain, taking up a position midway between Changlo Manor and the ruins of Tsechen. His intention was to engage in a 'demonstration', a feint directed mainly against the western perimeters of Gyantse Jong and the town. This was partly intended to give the Tibetans the chance to get their non-combatants out of the way, but also to draw the Tibetan defenders away from the southern side of the Jong, against which the main attack was to be directed on the following day. At half-past twelve Younghusband sent a message by heliograph from Changlo Manor signalling the General to commence firing. Macdonald's response was to flash back 'all manner of questions'. Younghusband then waited another hour and a half, and was on the point of sending 'a peremptory message' when the General at last began his military operations. A letter written by Hatter Bailey to his father shows that he was in no doubt that Macdonald repeatedly refused Younghusband's requests to open fire: 'We had an armistice which the Tibetans broke by building walls on the Jong which they promised not to do, but the General would not fire – We extended the Armistice several times as the Tibetans did not settle anything but when Col Y. asked the General to open fire he wouldn't.' Bailey's letter goes on to describe his part in the military operations that followed:

> We went up a nullah [ravine or river-bed] N of the Jong & the Ghurkas [*sic*] and Fusiliers attacked some villages NE of the Jong & were fired on from the high monastery wall. We fired a few shots at some people in a monastery up the nullah we were in & they fired at us but did not hit anyone. The General thought that by making a feint on the side he was not going to attack from, it would bring their guns over there. From where we were we saw the Tibetan jingall bullets bouncing along the ground like a cricket ball. Some of them bounced 6 times – They hit one Ghurka & I saw him fall & a doctor came & tied him up.

While this feint was in progress, the ancient monastic complex at Tsechen – founded in the fourteenth century and formerly the seat of the first kings of Gyantse – was set on fire to prevent it being reoccupied by the Tibetans, resulting in a 'tremendous blaze' that burned throughout the night. Everything was now set for the assault on Khamba Jong itself.

'Have just received orders to be ready to march at midnight,' wrote Corporal Percy Coath in a late entry to his diary on 5 July. 'We are to leave our tents standing and camp fires alight to deceive the enemy.' Each man was issued with two days' rations and an extra fifty rounds of ammunition. Further entries to Coath's diary were added by matchlight over the next hours as the opportunity arose: 'My company with native troops and others paraded at midnight and making a wide detour marched silently in the moonlight to Gun Hill where we took up position behind Pahla village . . . 3 a.m. We have just got into position, C Company with the 40th Pathans and Ghurkas are in front waiting to advance . . . 3.30 a.m. The front line has gone forward, their objective being villages at foot of the south side of the hill.'

Henry Newman had been given the nod by an officer that he should get up early next day or he would miss the sight of his life, but as no further information was forthcoming he had gone to bed telling his Gurkha servant to rouse him at dawn with a cup of tea. He was woken in the early hours and told that the troops were forming up, but by the time he had dressed they were gone. He could find nobody to answer his questions so he stumbled past the sentries at the gate and made towards the Jong until he was close enough to see its outlines as the first streaks of dawn appeared in the eastern sky. 'I must have fallen asleep,' he wrote, 'for suddenly I was awakened by a tremendous roar. All the Tibetans in the jong were firing off their guns and rifles as fast as they could.'

The General's plan was that the infantry would advance on the Jong in three columns, from the south-west, the south and the south-east. Private Sampson's C Company of the Royal Fusiliers was in the centre column, headed by the 40th Pathans. Their objective was a large building known as the China House directly in front of the Jong's main gate, but as they advanced in the darkness the head of the column veered too far to the right. At the same time the column on their right, which was supposed to be attacking the houses on the eastern flank of the ridge leading up to the Jong, also went off course. The result was confusion – and near disaster. 'The dark outline of the Jong could just be seen perched on the rocks hundreds of feet above the village,' was how Private Sampson saw events unfold.

Here a dog barked, & one of the Sappers poked it in the ribs with a crowbar causing it to yelp, which sounded much worse owing to the stillness of the night. I am quite sure it was that dog that aroused the Thibetans & shall always blame it. After resuming the march after a short time we wheel to the right, bringing the Jong on our left with the Pathans between us & it. We had not gone far in this formation before a Volley rang out from the village. The Pathans promptly broke through our ranks knocking our fellows over like dolls. The rush was so unexpected their Officers drew their revolvers but could not stop them.

In the darkness the heads of the centre and right columns had run into each other, and it was only the precipitate flight of the centre column, set off by the 40th Pathans, that prevented the encounter turning into a major fire-fight. In the event, Sampson's column regrouped and then took shelter behind a small bank to wait for daylight: 'Meanwhile we were watching the flashing of their guns from the fort. This was a very pretty sight the whole Jong being lit up at times. The shots went screeching over our heads.'

The left of the three columns largely comprised elements of the 'old firm' – a company each of the 8th Gurkhas and the 32nd Pioneers – and it made better progress than the other two, first capturing the houses below the south-west face of the Jong and then pushing east to take the China House, where the sappers set to work with their charges of gun-cotton. An officer of the 32nd Pioneers, Lieutenant Gurdon, failed to take cover when the first fuse was lit, was hit in the temple by a flying stone, and died within minutes. Further charges cleared the way for the infantry to fight through the complex of buildings that made up the China House until they had reached the southern foot of the rock citadel. 'For some time we had a nasty time of it,' wrote Captain George Preston of the fighting here. 'The Tibetans are rather good at throwing stones & 4 or 5 of us were knocked over by them.' He himself suffered three wounds which, he assured his wife, were 'very light scratches. One was a stone which hit me in the back of the neck and bowled me over, but was no worse. Another was a slight graze on the left hand and another was a graze on the chin. They are only scratches.' Once the China House had been secured a medical team led by Major Wimberley erected a Red Cross flag over the building and set up a forward dressing post. 'The bullets were kicking up the dust all round us,' wrote the Major afterwards to his wife. 'How we escaped Lord only knows . . . My Tibetan Kahars [dhoolie bearers] really behaved splendidly.'

In the meantime, the two columns on the right and centre had reformed themselves into a single column which now began to batter its way through the outworks and houses to the right of the Jong's main gate with the help of Captain Seymour Sheppard and his men. 'I must mention the Bravery & coolness of Capt. Sheppard RE,' wrote Private Sampson, watching from cover as the sappers went about their business:

> He went about blowing up places quite coolly while bullets were puffing up the dust all around him. He must have a charmed life . . . He planted a charge of gun cotton under a large gateway blowing the lot in. After the dust had cleared a little we rushed in the Village, the Thibetans retiring across the housetops towards the Jong. We ('C' Coy) then took up position on top of a large Chinese house which was less than 300 yds from the Fort. We could see the enemy's guns being moved in & out of the port-holes nearest to us.

As soon as there was enough light the combined firepower of the ten-pounders and the Gurkhas' pair of light guns opened up from three positions, each battery initially firing shrapnel that exploded in the air above the Tibetan positions before turning common shell on the walls and earthworks at the base of the Jong. The Maxims – now doubled in number with the addition of the two manned by the squad from the 1st Battalion of the Royal Irish Regiment – also began to hammer away, seeking out targets wher-ever the defenders on the Jong's battlements appeared most concen-trated. All the houses at the base of the Jong had been cleared and the reserves now moved forward. A company of the 8th Gurkhas together with F Company of the Royal Fusiliers came up to seize a section of the outer defences of the Jong partially breached by the guns. 'We advanced over 1,000 yards of open ground in extended order,' noted Percy Coath in his diary, 'till we reached the villages which had been captured by the front line earlier in the day. Tibetan fire was very inaccurate while we were advancing and making a slight detour we managed to get across with no casualties. The Ghurkas [*sic*] going straight across met with a few killed and wounded. We had half an hour's breathing space, after which we started to climb the hill. We had to sling our rifles and use our hands and knees.' The attackers now held all the ground up to the edge of the rock on which the Jong was built. Above them a road, ascending from right to left, had been cut diagonally across the slope to a gateway, but it was overlooked by a high wall surmounted by three towers. This allowed the defenders to bring concentrated fire down from several angles and made progress impossible. By midday the attack seemed to have ground to a halt.

Henry Newman, meanwhile, continued to have a frustrating morning. He had very speedily abandoned his exposed position and, after a couple of hours spent with the Fusiliers as they waited under cover, walked across to the jumble of ruined houses which were all that was left of the mansion at Palla. Here he found the General and his staff gathered on a rooftop. He heard Major Iggulden, the chief staff officer, give an order for the guns to be brought forward. Soon afterwards he observed the General's telescope and his staff's field-glasses trained not on the main gateway but over to its right and directly below the upper line of defences, where there was nothing more than a large expanse of almost sheer rock face. 'They seemed to be waiting for something to happen,' he noted. ' "Aha," I thought, "that's where the real assault is to take place." ' Since no one would tell him anything and nothing seemed to be happening, Newman again went forward, until he reached a row of barrack-rooms directly under the rock face, now held by the Gurkhas. Poking about in one of the rooms Newman found a elegant Tibetan dagger and belt which he appropriated. He then learned that the Gurkhas had been given the task of climbing the rock directly under the upper ramparts and were now waiting for the guns to take up new positions to give them covering fire. The best place to watch the coming assault was the spot occupied by the General and his staff, so Newman hurried back to rejoin them.

It was now approaching two o'clock. Soon afterwards the repositioned guns opened up on the fort's line of inner and upper ramparts, all using common shell and concentrating their fire on the wall directly above the open rock face. After about half an hour of firing a tremendous explosion indicated that a powder magazine had been hit. Nevertheless, the return fire seemed as vigorous as ever. Suddenly Newman heard one of the officers cry out, 'The

Gurkhas have started', and he saw their glasses were once more focused on the rock face:

> I had at the time in my possession what was known as a binocular-telescope . . . It was with this glass that I watched the Gurkhas climb up that fissure. The first wall was easily scaled because it had been battered to bits by the artillery. The next one, about forty to sixty feet higher, offered more obstacles to the attackers, not that there were no gaping holes in it, but it was defended by as stout a company of Tibetans as you can imagine. They lined what was left of the wall, not only with rifles, but with every kind of firearm, and with them were about a dozen or twenty men who were occupied with nothing but throwing boulders and stones down on the attackers. I turned my glasses for a while on these people. It was like looking at a close-up in a cinema.

The only way the Gurkhas could reach the upper ramparts was to scale the rock face – 'catching hold of projections, putting their feet into crevices and helping each other up. One or two men had slung their rifles and were making their way up hand over hand. Some were lending their shoulders to others.' The first to get near the top of the cliff was hit by a stone and fell all the way to the bottom. Then the bulkier figure of a British officer could be seen inching up the wall. 'I heard several names,' reported Newman.

Then it was the General himself who said: 'I can see him quite clearly. He is Grant of the Gurkhas.' Suddenly there was a sort of groan from the spectators. I had seen a Tibetan, his face contorted with passion, show himself in the centre of the broken wall: over his head he carried a great boulder which he hurled down straight at Grant. The boulder did not strike him directly, but hit a rock first and then struck Grant a glancing blow. He lost his hold and was sent hurtling down. By an amazing chance he was caught on a ledge, and before he could fall further two or three Gurkhas had got hold of him. Our relief was presently turned to amazement when we saw that Grant again was painfully pushing his way up at the head of the attackers.

At the foot of the rock face Gurkhas and Fusiliers crowded together waiting for their turn to join the assault. 'Such a mob,' noted Private Sampson, whose company was providing covering fire from the China House. 'There was Fusiliers & Gurks all mixed up. All this time we are firing as hard as possible to attract the attention of the enemy. The Artillery are putting shrapnel into their trenches & all the maxims hammering away as fast as possible as the Tibetans retire.'

From his dressing-station at the China House Major Wimberley and his men also watched the extraordinary spectacle of men attempting to scale the cliff face as rocks came raining down on them, observing how misdirected fire from one of the Maxims inflicted more casualties on the Gurkhas than on the Tibetan defenders above them: 'Unfortunately a badly aimed maxim was playing on them and wounded several of them; but they stuck to it like heroes and eventually got up. I was only 150 yards away and saw the whole thing and I never wish to see a finer exhibition of pluck. When Grant got to the top I couldn't help shouting out for all I was worth.' The Gurkhas now stormed the breach with the Fusiliers hard on their heels, although as far as Wimberley was concerned, it was the former to whom all honours were due: 'Grant led the Gurkhas, and with him Humphreys and Franklin their doctor. And after them came Royal Fusiliers, but they weren't in it, right behind under cover, tho. doubtless for the sake of the British Public they will be made to share the honour of the day . . . I saw the Gordons at Dargai, and I can honestly say that of the two, the storming of the breach at Gyantse Jong by the Gurkhas was a far finer performance.'

Missing from this account is any reference to Havildar Karbir Pun, the first Gurkha to be dislodged from the rock face. He too recovered, and scaled the cliff alongside Lieutenant John Grant, the two men hoisting themselves over the breach of the wall together (in due course one was awarded the Victoria Cross, the other the Indian Order of Merit, 1st Class – Indian and Gurkha soldiers being then ineligible for the VC).

To transport officer Mark Synge, watching with the General and his staff, this final assault was a 'glorious spectacle' never to be for-gotten: 'The rapid ping-ping-ping of the Maxim sets your blood tingling and really excites you . . . The rush through the breach of those Ghurkas and their comrades into that frowning impregnable-looking jong to the tune of artillery, dynamite, and Maxims would have appealed to the veriest man of peace.'

On the rooftop at Palla, Henry Newman saw the General turn away from his telescope and say to those beside him, 'Well, gentlemen, I think it is all over.' From the roof of the Mission House at Changlo, Frank O'Connor watched the final moments with Francis Younghusband: 'Suddenly like magic the defence fell to pieces like a house of cards and the defenders began to flee, their fire slackened, and in a few minutes the whole thing was over. The Tibetans were escaping in hundreds, climbing and jumping down the far side, and making off across the country and into the hills as fast as their legs or ponies could carry them.' A great cheer went up from the troops gathered down below.

When Corporal Percy Coath finally scrambled over the breach at the heels of the Gurkhas he found 'only dead bodies inside'. Minutes later he and his companions were posing for a group photograph under the British flag, watched from the plain below by Private Sampson and others in C Company:

At last the Union Jack floats proudly in the evening breeze from the highest Tower & Gyantse is ours after being stormed since daybreak. Now comes the worst part as a long string of stretchers come slowly down the hill bearing killed & wounded. Our men were very fortunate indeed. Several are slightly wounded but only two seriously: Lieut. Bowden Smith C Coy., Pte Harrison F Company, the former through the shoulder, the latter through the arm & wrist. Not so the Gurkhas. They had many killed & any amount wounded. Most of them were hit in the groin & leg.

It was left to Major Wimberley and his teams of stretcher-bearers and medical attendants to bring in their wounded and dead. Once again, the casualties were astoundingly low: just three dead and seventeen wounded. Wimberley himself carried out what he referred to as the 'last honours', tying up Lieutenant Gurdon in a blanket prior to his funeral in the Mission cemetery that same evening. 'I have done the last offices now for 4 poor fellows,' he wrote to his wife that same day, 'Bethune, Garstin, Craster [killed by a matchlock ball at Tsechen], and Gurdon, tho. why I should say "poor" I don't know, for they all died gamely, and were killed almost instantaneously at the moment when they were excited and no doubt keenly happy.' Wimberley spent much of the day collecting casualty figures for the General, grumbling later to his wife that this was 'really old Waddell's work but as usual at 6.30 a.m. this morning I got a note from him asking me to do it for him. He himself went off on the loot.'

Perhaps part of Wimberley's irritation was due to his having missed the opportunity to pick up a souvenir or two from the 'heaps of things' he had seen in the China House, and having to make do with what he regarded as a few worthless trifles: 'I have brought in 2 China vases, common ones like 2 you had that you bought in a Tea shop in Southsea; also a little Chinese brass tea pot, a Lhassa pencase, and a brass cup-stand and cover. I must try to get them packed up.'

The taking of Gyantse Jong was, in the opinion of Dr Austine Waddell, 'one of the most heroic achievements in the annals of frontier warfare' – and owed a great deal to the way James Macdonald had 'planned and personally supervised the attack'. This was the view of a man who had stood with other members of the General's staff on the rooftop at Palla. Perceval Landon saw the matter from a different perspective, having watched the action from Changlo Manor – in Francis Younghusband's camp in both a literal and a political sense. In his published account he implied that victory was secured despite the General: that Macdonald had been reluctant to force the issue and was more or less pushed into ordering the afternoon assault by Colonel Campbell of the 40th Pathans, commanding the storming parties. The truth of the matter was that the General had anticipated that taking the fort might require two or even three days of fighting. He had expected the first day to be spent clearing the outworks and defences at the foot of the Jong, and there is nothing to show that he did other than seize the opportunity when told that an assault up the cliff face was possible. Had there been any wavering at this point, then one or other of the junior officers would surely have written of it, for the General had few friends among them. Hatter Bailey, never afraid to say what he thought, reserved his criticisms for Macdonald's refusal to allow the Mounted Infantry to harry the fleeing Tibetans as they streamed north towards Shigatse. And Bailey it was who dared to say what no regimental histories have cared to mention: that it was not only the 40th Pathans who behaved badly when the two columns blundered into each other in the dark. Fusiliers and Sikh Pioneers also 'bolted', some throwing away their rifles and running for it.

On the following morning the General led a small force round to the back of the Jong to take the town and the Palkor Chode monastic complex. No further opposition was expected and there was none, most of the civilian population and monks having fled. While this was going on Arthur Hadow toured the heights of the Jong in the company of Francis Younghusband and Frank O'Connor. After a brief inspection of the battlefield, the Colonel and O'Connor returned to Changlo Manor, leaving Hadow and one of his men free to descend into the town and walk up its main street to the monastery – unaware that Macdonald was advancing on it in some strength. Finding the monastery complex all but deserted, they and several other officers decided to do some looting, smashing down doors with the aid of a sledge-hammer:

> We broke into three large buildings or temples on the hillside, loading ourselves with loot. Then, thinking it desirable to try and capture a Tibetan, to help carry our things, I came outside. I then discovered the Army had moved up in battle array to capture the monastery but instead of finding the enemy there was only a small party of British officers looting. We were quickly hauled before an angry staff officer, and I had to leave without my loot. Pte Smith was even searched, but he managed to slip three brass images down inside his vest, and this was all we managed to bring away.

From the details on a long list of Tibetan items subsequently donated by the Hadow family to the Royal Norfolk Regiment Museum in Norwich it seems that Arthur Hadow managed to retrieve at least some of his loot, for some sixteen objects are described as having come from Gyantse. They include an apron made from human bones, marked 'looted after the capture of Gyantse Jong', two daggers 'taken from some large idols at Gyantse', a gilded model of a *chorten* ('looted at Gyantse'), two blue cloisonné Ming bowls ('found in cellar at Gyantse'), numerous weapons and a bead rosary ('picked up near the breach after the assault of Gyantse Jong').

For all Macdonald's published orders, and despite Dr Waddell's published insistence that there was no looting, considerable pillaging took place at Palkor Chode, Dongtse and other monasteries in the aftermath of the fall of Gyantse Jong. Lieutenant Carey of the Fusiliers recorded in his diary that he 'snaffled' some items which he hoped to send home to his parents. Similarly, in their letters home Lieutenants Harvey-Kelly and Bailey both wrote quite openly about their looting. The general view among officers seems to have been that, whatever General Orders and the Hague Convention of 1899 had to say on the matter, pillaging was acceptable where an army had been opposed or where, in the case of monasteries, there had been incitement to oppose it. And as far as the Indian troops were concerned, loot (itself a word of Indian origin) was traditionally a soldier's perk. Not everyone approved: George Preston grumbled to his wife that he wished he could send her some loot 'but there are very strict orders about it and it is only people who haven't any conscience at all who get it . . . It is awfully annoying to see fellows sending away loot, whilst you can't send any away at all.'

In cultural terms this looting was relatively insignificant when compared to the destruction of the monasteries in and around Gyantse by Macdonald's forces. Most of it was in the nature of petty souvenir hunting and – if Arthur Hadow's list is anything to go by – a lot of what was brought back to England amounted to little more than trophies found on battlefields and in abandoned camps. But there was at least one instance of serious looting that far exceeded these bounds. The Field Force's commissariat department searched all the buildings at Palkor Chode and found three thousand maunds of *atta* or ground flour hidden in the main monastery – a much-needed addition to the army's fast dwindling supplies. But according to Major William Beynon, its officers also unearthed a cache of hidden treasure. 'Yesterday I got two really good things,' wrote Beynon to his wife on 7 July.

Ross 2nd Gurkhas was in the big monastery here and was looking for grain with his coolie corps when one of his men was stoned by a Lama. They caught the beggar and tied him up & gave him 20 lashes on the spot and then told him if he didn't show where the grain was hid he would be shot. So he showed them two places very cleverly hidden – but when Ross began to get the things out he found instead of grain that the man had shown him where the monastery's plate & robes were kept. Ross reported to the General who told him he might keep what he liked and to send the rest to the man who collects for the British Museum [that is, Dr Waddell]. Ross & Wigram who were working together took something and asked me to help myself, so I selected a very nice hanging silver censor and a gilt one – neither of them very valuable but very quaint design – and I also took two lamas' robes & some silk embroidery, which I am sending home to you through King Hamiltons.

This case of sanctioned plundering was subsequently hushed up, and no wonder, for it is difficult to square it with the claims made by Dr Waddell, Brigadier-General Macdonald and his chief of staff, Major Iggulden, that monastic sites were 'most religiously respected'. The 'plate and robes' discovered at Palkor Chode probably made up the finest of the religious objects collected by Dr Waddell in Tibet, which may well explain why his subsequent reports spoke of books and manuscripts, together with 'paintings, religious and mythological, and epigraphic historical material, including an important inscribed tablet' – but made no mention of religious artefacts. In these same reports he stated that 'by the month of May in that year [1904] I had amassed the greater part of the collection, for circumstances subsequently became unfavourable for procuring many additions' – the implication being that most of his collecting was done before the siege of Changlo Manor began on 5 June. No doubt Waddell did indeed secure many items out of the budget of ten thousand rupees allocated to him by the Government of India for the purchase of manuscripts, but no statement of precisely how he spent the money was ever provided.

Up at the Jong the Fusiliers' F Company, which had guarded the citadel overnight, was relieved by Private Sampson's C Company. 'As we marched up here,' recorded Sampson, 'we passed dead Tibetans laying in heaps. They are a fearful sight but it is much worse in a trench which runs the whole length of the Fort. The shrapnall must have caught them as they were clearing off out of this trench. There is a big gang of Prisoners employed dragging the dead away. This is how they do it: they tie two ropes to the heels, two men dragging them, the third lifts the head with the pig tail & so they cart them away.' Several hours later the Fusiliers suffered their greatest loss of the entire campaign:

> Just as the men were lining up after the call of 'Tea ready' there was a terrific report, everyone being knocked back in a cloud of dust. The next I saw was men rushing about all alight. One chap had to be floored before the flames could be put out. Another was just stopped from jumping out of a window. Then someone shouted 'there is some buried here'. As soon as the dust cleared a bit I could see a large heap of bricks, beams & mud. We set to work & found Pte Dare. Buckley & I carried him out of the building to await the arrival of the dhoolies. We are all ordered down below. The mules that have been carrying water for us all day are terribly burnt & the native in charge of them was blown to pieces. On the roll being called there were several names not answered. I never want to hear another roll-call like that. The men who died were Ptes Dare, Gallimore & Maloney. Seriously injured: Sgt Owen, Cpl McCarthy, Ptes Gill, Phillips, Sewell. There were dozens slightly burnt but were only bandaged up.

After this disaster Sampson's company was relieved of garrison duty and the able-bodied marched back to camp. There was much talk of the explosion being the work of a Tibetan prisoner, but it was later established that the cause was a lighted match dropped by one of a crowd of Fusiliers gathered on the first floor of what was, unknown to them, a powder magazine.

Over the next few days the troops were employed in various clearing-up operations, the sappers blowing up what remained of the defences at Gyantse, Tsechen and wherever else there had been resistance, while the supply officers went out with mules and yaks to bring in provisions, among them Lieutenant Mark Synge, who wrote that the officers soon became expert at finding bricked-up store rooms: 'The towns and lamasarais of Gyantse and Tsechin were our happiest hunting grounds . . . Our way was strewn with corpses. The warriors from the Kham country, who formed a large part of the Tibetan army, were glorious in death, long-haired giants, lying as they fell with their crude weapons lying beside them, and usually with a peaceful, patient look on their faces.'

On 12 July, four days after the capture of the Jong, Private Sampson's company provided the escort for a commissariat train going to Tsechen monastery and fort, 'where the Sappers & Miners have found huge supplies as they are pulling down the buildings'. There was little to do so Sampson and his chum Bob climbed to the top of the ridge: 'On reaching the top saw two dead youngsters cuddling each other in death. Both had been shot by a shell. One had its leg blown completely away. It was a fearful sight & the smell was awful. The Miners have now pulled the whole show down level with the ground.'

On the following day, 13 July, the Royal Fusiliers were told to prepare to move within twenty-four hours. On that same day Francis Younghusband wrote to Helen in Darjeeling to confirm what she had long dreaded: 'We are going to Lhasa after all. Govt think it will bring matters to a finality quicker and so it will . . . Now I have the terms I can negotiate on the way to Lhasa and I hope have the settlement through very quickly.'

The terms of settlement the British Government now sought were, in his opinion, 'extremely mild & insignificant and not worth going to Lhasa to obtain. As long as they want so little my task shd be very easy.' Younghusband was bitterly disappointed, however, by the Government's refusal even to consider his proposal for a British Political Agent and a permanent British Residency to be established in Lhasa. Yet he was not to be outdone so easily. 'I have thought out a great coup,' he told Helen. 'The pledge Govt has given to Russia is that "so long as no other Power intervenes we shall not establish any protectorate over Tibet". I propose giving the Dalai Lama a pledge that if any power does intervene we shall protect him against it. We shall thus have Tibet in our hands in spite of the pledge Govt have given Russia. Werning [Vernon Magniac, Younghusband's new PS] went wild with excitement when I told him this & says it would be a great coup.'

Francis Younghusband's spirits rose once more. Macdonald – whom he had now taken to calling 'the Chowkidar', an Indian term for a watchman – was again suffering from his stomach complaint and 'altogether out of sorts'. Edmund Candler had just reached Gyantse, short of a hand but 'looking fitter than when he arrived in Tuna in March'. The only thing to spoil the day was the news that his old friends of the 23rd Pioneers would not be marching on with him, having been selected by the General to form the garrison in Gyantse: 'Poor Col Hogge is being kept here. Macdonald has always had a down on him because of his friendliness to the mission and our staying at Tuna . . . Some pretty hard swearing is in progress.' Also to be left behind were the telegraph men, who had advanced the line from Kala Tso to Gyantse but would be taking it no further: Simla and London would be even more out of touch.

On 14 July, under a heavy and unrelenting downpour that marked the onset of the summer monsoon in India, Brigadier-General Macdonald's force marched eastwards out of the Gyantse Valley on the Lhasa road. 'I sincerely hope we will get there,' wrote Lieutenant Thomas Carey of the Royal Fusiliers, 'and that the Dalai Lama will not make peace, and so prevent us reaching the Holy City.' His view was shared by practically everyone in the column other than the General and his chief of staff. 'Goodness knows', continued Carey, 'when we will return, some say in October, some December, and some say we might winter at Lhassa. I expect it will all depend on the Tibetans and how they give in. The Indian Govt would give anything to have the show over.'

II

The March on Lhasa

'NEVER WAS a more cheerfully confident body of men,' wrote supply officer Lieutenant Leonard Bethell, 'than that which stepped out from Gyantse into the northward wilderness on that August [*recte* July] morning of 1904. Fifteen hundred men, three thousand mules, every man and beast laden to ultimate carrying power with every necessity from a cartridge to a box of medical comforts. Saving only food, we were a marching Army and Navy Stores, and on the single file track, we measured eight miles from advanced guard to rearguard.' In fact, the column numbered rather more than that: 91 British officers, 521 British NCOs and BORs, 32 Indian Native Officers, 1,966 Indian and Nepali sepoys or riflemen, and approximately fifteen hundred orderlies, porters, transport drivers and other camp-followers – in all, just over three thousand men. Confident they may well have been, but not everyone was cheerful. 'The most miserable march I have yet done,' grumbled Corporal Percy Coath into his diary late at night on the second day. F Company, Royal Fusiliers was on rearguard duty and had been forced to follow in the wake of the baggage animals and a huge flock of sheep that made up their main meat supply, arriving in camp long after dark: 'We are thoroughly wet through and properly done up, having had scarcely any food the whole day.

Now we are to sleep as best we can in our clothes. The tents are pitched anywhere as the camp is really in a damp ravine.'

It had been agreed between Younghusband and Macdonald that the remaining hundred and fifty miles to Lhasa should be covered as speedily as possible and without the support of supply columns, it being the former's contention that the army could subsist on what it carried and what could be obtained from the country they passed through. Sheep would supply the meat and the monasteries would supply the grain, was Younghusband's argument, and the closer they got to Lhasa the more monasteries they would find. The column's flock of sheep became a major nuisance, waking the camp long before reveille with their bleating as they were driven off by volunteers from the ranks. They grazed as they went, so the head of the column soon caught up with them. 'Always, seemingly, at the worst and narrowest part of the route,' wrote Lieutenant Leonard Bethell,

> the advanced guard would come up with them, they going one mile an hour, we three. Then, for what seemed like hours, men, horses, mules waded knee-deep in a maa-ing, baa-ing, reeking mass of obstinately obstructive wool. Sheep in a drove, when interfered with, move in headlong panic rushes; or stop dead, crowd together into an impenetrable lump, and face all ways at once; and these sheep were no exception to the rule. They added miles, in sheer fatigue, to our march, and we grew to hate the sight of them.

The men also grew to hate the mutton the sheep provided, likened to 'violin strings and piano wire, and indiarubber and leather and what is left over when you have chewed (and chewed, and rechewed, and finally and definitely thrown away) a piece of string'. However, the staple diet of the column came from 'the rough barley of the country, loose grain, unground, intractable and uninviting', most of it taken from the monasteries along the way. As Francis Younghusband had predicted, there were quite a number of these on or near their route, and each had large stocks of grain in its storerooms. Ottley's Mounted Infantry having first scouted them out, in moved the supply and transport officers with their mule caravans. Lieutenant Bethell was among them: 'Down loads, off equipment, take shovels, sacks, and unladed mules. In five minutes a caterpillar of men and beasts was crawling up the rock face to the *gompa* . . . Beyond lowering looks, no opposition met us.'

One of the first monasteries encountered was Ralung, up a side valley five miles south of the main trail. 'At Ralung we got a fair haul,' noted Mark Synge, who led the operation. 'We found some whole barley, some tsampa, and a fair stock of straw . . . I really had a very pleasant time, being happily entertained both by the monks and also the nuns – especially the latter. They brought out "chang" to drink. A home-brewed light wine, made I believe from barley, and the carcass of a sheep that had been cooked whole, and from which you were expected to pick off your individual require-ments.' Ralung gompa was unusual in that it housed both nuns and monks, the former distinguished by the red mop-like wigs they wore over their shaven heads:

> They came and talked to me through the interpreter whom I had with me, and quite a youthful little nun in a picturesque woolly red cap came and sat beside me and did her knitting. Quite warm and cosy it all was, with ladies' society and all thrown in. I was quite sorry when, after several long hours of waiting, a long serpent-shaped line of mules slowly trailed up the valley and came for the grain, the tsampa, and the straw. We were paying for what we foraged and I remember doling out what seemed to the recipients a prodigious number of rupees.

Both here and elsewhere Synge noticed that rupees bearing Queen Victoria's head were always preferred to those with King Edward's: 'The former were preferred because they were Kampani rupees [that is, rupees issued by the East India Company, the ruling power in India prior to 1858] known and trusted since the 1830s, while the latter were viewed with suspicion.'

The raiding of monasteries for supplies became an established routine. The supply officers' arrival would cause 'a fluttering of red monastic skirts' and a deputation of monks armed with a white muslin flag would descend to meet the intruders:

Along with the rag would be carried peace-offerings, of which the most common would be a tray of whole-wheat parched and salted, or a small basket of eggs . . . With the aid of an interpreter a pleasant conversation would then ensue. The officer would then probably produce a camera and snapshot the head lama, after which he would try to get to business. He would ask how much of such and such article the monastery could sell us. The monks would shake their heads, flutter their skirts, jerk up their thumbs, and in a shrill falsetto repeat the word 'Mindok' (which means 'nothing'). After a little more parley they would confess to having, say, twenty bagfuls of tsampa or whatever was required. You would then, if you were the officer, proceed within the monastery and demand to be shown the said twenty bagfuls. You would be led with great pomp and circumstance upstairs and along dark passages and past rows of cells till you were ushered into a small pantry or storeroom where, with a gesture of pompous satisfaction at having so completely fulfilled your requirements, the head monk would point to a few handfuls of tsampa lying at the bottom of a trough. You would feel a little annoyance at this, and show signs of it. The head monk, as by a happy inspiration, would suddenly beckon you to accompany him, and, after another long meandering through the monastery, would lead you through a large doorway into a large darkened hall, which, when your eyes became accustomed to the dim light, you would recognise as the main 'gompa' or temple of the monastery. Here his hand would steal into yours, which he would caress, while with his free hand he pointed to the chief image of Buddha, which he was apparently wishing you to admire.

At this point 'British choler' would rise and threats be made: 'The threatening crack of a whip round the head of a "chela" [novice] or two would send the monks all skipping about in trepidation, and the door of the main storeroom would be opened to you.' But once payment had been made 'you were all friends. No ill-will was borne on either side. The junior monks or "chelas" would assist in bagging the flour, and in carrying it down to the place where the mules were waiting for it. The money would be doled out and counted with the greatest good humour. There would be another proffer of parched wheat and rotten eggs, and you would depart with the head lama's blessing.'

Whatever the official line, some supply officers refused on principle to pay the monks. Lieutenant Bethell was one of those who regarded the monks as 'self-indulgent parasites' living off the sweat and toil of the peasantry, and who shared the general misconception that their huge stocks of grain were exclusively for the monks' own consumption: 'Our very souls would have revolted at the idea of paying to the monks one penny for what . . . they should never have possessed.' If the monks tried to deceive him by hiding their grain behind bricked-up walls, then as far as Bethell was concerned they were fair game. At one site his attention was drawn by one of his men to a wall that bore a freshly drawn painting of the divinity Avalokiteshvara. Despite protestations, it was attacked with picks and shovels – 'and out streamed a cascade of dust, mortar, and bushel on bushel of golden grain – ceiling high. I took the abbot by the folds of meat which he called the nape of his neck. I am not ashamed to say it. I took him by the nape of his lubberly neck, drove him down on his knees, and r-rubbed his nose in it. Avalokiteshvara, indeed!'

The problem was that this barley grain proved almost indigestible. The Sikhs took to it, being used to the wholemeal *atta* grown in the Punjab, but the potato-eating British and the rice-eating Gurkhas did not:

The grains were parboiled, pounded between stones, worried about and all but stamped on; and they went down somehow. But then the circus began. The first incautious hearty meal by hungry men, and two hours afterwards . . . Ooooh! . . . In twenty-four hours the hospital had issued its last scrap of Epsom salts, and the pills were running low. The doctors, alarmed at the prospect of the expedition entering Lhasa bent double and groaning, dashed about giving advice, the gist of which was to eat little and to chew that little thirty-two times before swallowing.

The parched and ground barley flour known as tsampa proved a lot easier on the stomach, and the supply officers soon learned to trade the bulk of their supplies of barley grain back to the monasteries in return for tsampa, receiving one maund of flour for three of grain, which seemed to leave both parties happy: 'In the end, it was practically the mules alone who had barley au naturel, the men drawing meal and barley alternately. The meal we made into a porridge and, by the addition of more dried meal to the mess, made fairly portable but nauseous-looking stuff. These balls were carried in the haversack and nibbled en route.' In spite of occasional variations in the form of bread and yak meat, grumbling stomachs continued to be a feature of the march almost to the gates of Lhasa.

After Gyantse the army's numbers had been swelled by the addition of large numbers of Tibetans, including released prisoners, who filled various roles ranging from yak drivers and porters to dhoolie-carriers and general dogsbodies. Many brought along their wives, helping to brighten up the expedition 'Merry little souls these women mostly were, ever to be seen laughing or chaffing one another,' wrote Synge.

> I remember passing a knot of them one day as we climbed one of the worst passes . . . Hill people know better than any one the advantage of breathing rhythmically, and the Tibetan loves to acquire this rhythm by singing over any work that strains him at all. Tibetan men and women, as they thresh their corn with their flail, chant pretty ditties in unison, and the Tibetan boatmen on the Sangpo will sometimes sing at their work. And here was this band of women singing cheerily as they climbed that mountainside, and never pausing in their song. They were well up with the advance guard too, and the chorus could be heard all down the column – a novel sort of band with which to cheer a British army onwards on a toilsome march!

After three days of sodden marching through rocky defiles now covered in a wealth of wild alpines in full bloom, the column emerged onto 'a fine open moor, bounded by rolling downs and grassy uplands'. Here too the turf was thick with tiny, brightly-coloured flowering plants – 'pink primulas, striped blue gentians, yellow potentillas, cobalt poppies' – and the rarefied air was scented by fragrant wormwood. Directly ahead of them stretched 'a great snowy range which blocked our way to Lhasa', dominated by the peak of Nojin Kangsang, the Noble Glacier of the Genius. Cutting into its southern flank was the deep ravine that led up to the Karo La, the Wide-Mouthed Pass that had been the scene of Lieutenant-Colonel Brander's high-altitude battle two and a half months earlier.

It had been known for some days that the pass had again been occupied by Tibetan troops and that the wall stretched across it was once more manned, the enemy's numbers being put at two thousand. On 17 July the army marched into the gorge and camped under the glaciers in that same magnificent amphitheatre within which Brander had laid his camp-site, the Field of Milk. That afternoon Corporal Percy Coath jotted down several entries in his diary:

We have marched about seven miles into the Pass which is narrow and hemmed in by high and steep cliffs on either side. The hills are mostly covered with snow. This is an ideal position to make a stand . . . We have entrenched ourselves. General Macdonald and Staff have gone out with reconnoitring party to locate the enemy's position . . . The above party have just returned. We have got to know that the enemy are entrenched on the summit of hills on either side near the glacier, with also strong Sungers [sangars] stretched right across the pass.

Despite bitter cold everyone in camp was 'in high spirits for a brush with the enemy', for it was widely anticipated that 'a desperate battle was impending'. The word in the officers' messes was that if the Tibetans intended to make a last stand, this was the place to do it: to stage, in Leonard Bethell's words, 'one last huge and spectacular battle wherein the Tibetans, as a nation, would have risen up to bar our way to the Holy of Holies, dying in heaps in defence of their monks.' Nobody wanted this final confrontation more badly than the Fusiliers, knowing that it was probably their last chance to shine after their disappointments at the storming of Gyantse Jong.

The morning of 18 July dawned bright and clear and icy cold. The men were up early, Private Sampson recording that he ate his breakfast of yak meat and black bread walking up and down to keep warm. Soon afterwards bright sunshine poured into the valley, warming bodies and spirits. At 7 a.m. the line of advance was formed with, at Lieutenant-Colonel Cooper's pleading, three of the four Fusilier companies at the front and centre, and the 32nd Pioneers in support. An hour's march took them up to and over the pass, where they turned the corner to see the Tibetan wall stretched out before them a mile and a half away, again strengthened by forward sangars on both flanks: a position that, to those seeing it for the first time, appeared 'almost impregnable'. With Lieutenant-Colonel Brander's experience at the earlier battle in mind, the General lost no time in despatching flanking parties of Gurkhas, two companies to climb the heights to the left and two to the right. The battery of mountain guns and the Maxims were brought forward, and the Fusiliers were given the order to advance in open order up the floor of the valley towards the wall.

Long before they were in range, jingals and rifles opened fire from the sangars and along the wall, raising a curtain of grey smoke that extended right across the valley. The force responded with its heavy weaponry. This was Edmund Candler's first engagement since Guru, and after the horrors of that all-too-close encounter the spectacle appeared extraordinarily tame and remote: 'Stretched on a grassy knoll on the left, enjoying the sunshine and the smell of the warm turf, we civilians watched the whole affair with our glasses. It might have been a picnic on the Surrey downs if it were not for the tap-tap of the Maxim, like a distant woodpecker, in the valley, and the occasional report of the 10-pounders by our side, which made the valleys and cliffs reverberate like thunder.'

The Fusiliers' H Company spearheaded the attack, advancing at a steady walking pace up the centre of the valley: 'The approach was uphill & we had to halt for breath nearly every 20 yards of ascent,' noted Lieutenant Thomas Carey. To his surprise the Tibetans' firing seemed to slacken rather than intensify with every step they took, so much so that by the time they had come within matchlock range of the wall it had stopped entirely. As they closed, onlookers and the troops held in reserve watched with bated breath. 'The excitement was intense,' noted Dr Waddell, assuming like everyone else on their side of the wall that the Tibetans were holding their fire for the final assault. But the Fusiliers came on without another shot being fired – until they had reached the glacis and the foot of the wall itself. 'We advanced to the Sungars,' wrote Corporal Percy Coath, 'which stretched across the middle of the pass, and on reaching them found the enemy had left them and retreated to the hills to join their comrades.' The Tibetans had fled and the entire wall had been abandoned. 'We were very sick,' wrote Carey, 'as we felt we had a good fight in prospect.' However, his frustration was also tinged with relief, for 'if the wall had been held no doubt we must have had many casualties'.

A rattle of rifle-fire from far above told the observers that not all the Tibetans had fled. On the heights to left and right an extraordinary high-altitude shooting-match was now in progress – higher even than the one waged in early May. Out of sight of those down below and too high to be covered by the ten-pounders or the Maxims, the Gurkhas skirmished with a determined body of Tibetans over rock, snow and ice at an elevation of 19,000 feet and above. Despite a dogged resistance, the superior fire-power of the Gurkhas soon began to tell, and a slow retreat turned into the familiar rout and chase. Many Tibetan warriors found themselves trapped, their only line of escape cut off by the Nepali riflemen climbing up towards them. Some threw themselves over the cliffs and were seen to fall many hundreds of feet, but the majority continued to climb up and onto the snowfields, against which their black figures could be seen clearly. Through his binoculars Austine Waddell watched them ascend 'like a string of ants, threading their way into the eternal solitudes of ice, to an elevation of about 23,000 feet . . . where doubtless most, if not all of them, must have perished miserably.'

Lower down, a last stand was attempted by a small group of Tibetans forty strong led by an officer clad in blue silk, all of whom were annihilated by a company of the 40th Pathans. Here Edmund Candler witnessed an act of heroism that 'quite changed my estimate of these men': a Tibetan struggling to carry a wounded comrade up a cliff. Both were shot down. Several men of the Fusiliers had accompanied the Gurkhas into the heights as signallers. According to Private Sampson, they returned bleeding 'from the ears & nose' but quickly recovered.

The assault of the cliffs was followed by the usual harrying of the retreating army down the trail by Ottley's Mounted Infantry. 'I asked a native officer,' wrote Candler of this episode, 'how he decided whom to spare or kill, and he said he killed the men who ran, and spared those who came towards them.' The wall was taken apart and the abandoned Tibetan camp ransacked before the army moved on, making an easy descent alongside a glacier-fed river that led them in twenty-four hours to the shores of the great lake known as Yamdok Tso and the lakeside fortress of Nakartse Jong: 'The bold outline of Nagartsé fort shot into view at the end of a spur on our left, and beyond it the silvery streak of the great Yamdok Lake gleamed amongst dark blue hills, whilst the tall poles of the prayer-flags, projecting over the house-roofs of the village, looked like the masts of fishing boats at anchor on the lake – the famous "ring-lake" of the older maps of Central Asia, a vast inland sea without an outlet.'

The Yamdok Tso, or High Grazing Lake, was also known to Tibetans as the Yu Tso or Turquoise Lake, on account of the almost impossibly azure colour of the water when lit by sunshine – a colour, according to Lieutenant Mark Synge, 'unlike anything in water scenery that the most travelled of us had ever seen before'. It was also one of the most remarkable of the many thousands of lakes on the Tibetan plateau, having long before been a ring of water, with an outer circumference of a hundred and fifty miles and a mountain-like central island that was now linked to the surrounding land by an isthmus of boggy ground. Yamdok Tso was also among the most sacred of Tibet's lakes, being regarded by Tibetans as nothing less than a talisman, for its waters were said to be the life-blood of their nation, watched over by the goddess Dorje Phagmo, the Thunderbolt Sow, made flesh in the person of the abbess of Samding nunnery, the highest female *tulku* or incarnate in Tibet.

The fortress of Nakartse was found to be unoccupied save for a party of delegates from Lhasa, who came out to meet the first patrols of the Mounted Infantry with the usual white flag and declared themselves eager to talk terms. As soon as Colonel Younghusband's Union Jack had been raised they rode into camp, among them the two familiar figures of the Ta Lama and the 'evil genius', Lobsang Trinley, in their yellow silk robes, but now joined by a personage in blue silks who declared himself to be Kalon Yuthok Shapé, the most senior of the four ministers who made up the Kashag. The Shapé informed Francis Younghusband that the Kashag had met in Lhasa and had considered the terms for a settlement forwarded by the Tongsa Penlop of Bhutan on Younghusband's behalf. They were now prepared to discuss those terms – not here at Nakartse, but at Gyantse. Younghusband heard the Shapé out, then informed him that he would only discuss terms once the fort of Nakartse and its contents had been handed over. This was done and the two sides agreed to talk more fully on the following day in full Durbar. In the meantime, another ceasefire was declared.

On the morning of the Durbar, 19 July, Dr Austine Waddell rode out with his assistant, the Anglo-Sikkimese David Macdonald, and the *Times* man, Perceval Landon, to visit the home of the Sow Goddess incarnate, the small nunnery of Samding sited four miles away across the marshy isthmus on the central 'island'. Despite a sudden snowstorm, it was a delightful excursion:

> It was a pleasure to leave our warlike surroundings and enter again the world of dreams and magic which may be said to be ever with us in the mystic Land of the Lamas . . . We dismounted at the foot of the convent hill at the prayer-flags on the large Chorten, and walked in the slushy snow up the long zig-zagging dilapidated pathway . . . The building itself also had a rather decayed and neglected look and a small and altogether mean appearance, which was disappointing in one of the most reputed shrines of Tibet. We saw no signs of inmates, and on entering the main court of the building, found that the pig-headed divinity and all her sisterhood had fled.

It transpired that the present incarnate, a six-year-old girl, together with all the other occupants, had fled at dawn that morning – a blow to Dr Waddell because he had looked forward to thanking the Sow Goddess for nursing (in her previous life) the explorer-spy Sarat Chandra Das when he had fallen ill here in 1882. Missing from Dr Waddell's and Perceval Landon's accounts of their excursion was any reference to their encounter with two sepoys of the Mounted Infantry whom they caught red-handed 'fairly bulging with looted gilt images'. Dr Waddell ordered the stolen treasures to be returned to the nunnery and subsequently reported the two miscreants to Brigadier-General Macdonald. To the dismay of his fellow officers, the General ordered the men to be tried before a court martial. In his diary Thomas Carey of the Royal Fusiliers gave a brief account of the outcome: one of the sepoys received a sentence of two years' imprisonment, the other one year, his sentence being reduced on account of his distinguished conduct at the second Karo La engagement. The verdict of the court martial was read out to the assembled troops and they were reminded that looting in any form was forbidden. To Thomas Carey, Dr Waddell's behaviour smacked of hypocrisy: 'They [the two looters] were caught by Col Waddell, IMS, who by the way, is also noted for his looting propensities. Everybody rather sympathised although it was a flagrant case, as all the staff have taken any amount of loot in their time. Before, the sepoys generally got flogged, but General Macdonald wanted to make an example, especially as he had promised the envoys that nothing would be touched.' In Carey's opinion, the worst looters were the Mounted Infantry, of whom he was exceedingly envious: 'They get all the fun and have a fight nearly every day of their lives, and the pick of the loot. Some of the M.I. officers have very valuable loot, we only get the dregs and the same of curios. Of course, there are stringent orders against looting monasteries, unless they fire or make resistance.'

In fact, Macdonald's stern action had been promoted by more than Dr Waddell's chance encounter. Indian newspapers in Calcutta had begun to demand answers to rumours of loot piling up in Gyantse, prompting questions in the British press about whether this had been obtained legally. Lord Kitchener had defended his man, arguing that 'General Macdonald is very strict on the subject' and that 'no looting is allowed amongst the military', but he had also required Macdonald to issue fresh orders to prevent 'further looting'.

This was a bad day for the General, for that same morning, just as the three Tibetan envoys were making their way over to

Colonel Younghusband's tent for the Durbar, one of Captain Peterson's patrols of Pathans from the 2nd Mounted Infantry ran into a party of Tibetan cavalry escorting the Yuthok Shapé's baggage train. One of the Tibetans panicked and loosed off a shot and the Pathans immediately returned fire, despite the fact that the convoy was flying a flag of truce. 'They were at once pursued,' noted Carey, 'and after an exciting chase were captured with the baggage, 12 of them were killed. They had some first class mules & ponies – some very good rifles were also taken, among them was one Russian, one American, a Winchester repeater & a Mauser.' The first the Shapé knew of this was when he peered out of Younghusband's office tent during his discussions with the Tibet Commissioner and saw the Pathans trotting into camp loaded down with precious silks that he recognised as his own. A protest was made to General Macdonald, who set up a court of enquiry. Although it subsequently ruled against the Tibetans on the grounds that they had fired the first shot, the matter became yet another bone of contention among the younger officers, who felt the General should have brushed aside the Shapé's protests.

Francis Younghusband meanwhile conducted his negotiations with his customary composure. Although he found the Yuthok Shapé 'a delightful old gentleman . . . very hearty and genial', he still considered him and his fellow envoys 'absolutely impossible in the business way'. Writing to his father two days later, he described how he had devoted almost seven hours to listening to their excuses:

> Of course it is very hard to keep my temper with them when they go on for hour after hour with silly arguments but I managed to do it through two interviews, one of $3\frac{1}{4}$ & the other of $3\frac{1}{2}$ hours. I quietly answer their arguments & smile & give them tea & cigarettes and leave the solid fact of our advance to produce its effect . . . The cussed part is that they are such absolute children in the business of this world. When I told them that we considered it a grave insult that the representative of a Great Power shd. be kept waiting for a year they said 'Oh, do not let us think of the past. Let us be practical & think only of the present. Here we are now, anyhow, so let us negotiate.' I told

them this was all very fine now they had got the worst of it but though I was ready to negotiate I had to go on to Lhasa.

At the Tibet Commissioner's side through every negotiation sat Frank O'Connor, still with his 'tame lama' at his shoulder but himself now thoroughly conversant with the finer points of the Tibetan language and the diplomatic niceties. Here at Nakartse and again in the days that followed, half-hearted attempts were made to bribe him 'by the unostentatious deposit of little bags of gold dust (worth a few pounds each, a regular form of Tibetan currency) on my table'. These little incidents, he wrote, 'always tickled the Commissioner's sense of humour when I related them to him, and I can see him now, with his grave air and a twinkle in his eye, as he advised me to stand out for something really worth having. And to do them justice, the Tibetans' own sense of humour always kept our relations sweet, and they would laugh heartily at some little joke, or some manoeuvre which we had unmasked.'

During the march from Gyantse and the forcing of the Karo La, James Macdonald had been allowed to get on with his military business undisturbed. However, the supplies of grain extracted from the monasteries were failing to meet the army's needs and the mules were already on half-rations. The day after Younghusband's Durbar with the Yuthok Shapé at Nakartse the General went to the Tibet Commissioner's tent, set out the difficulties he was having with the food supplies, and urged him to settle the business at Nakartse once and for all. To Francis Younghusband, this was just one more example of Macdonald funking it. 'The very morning after my interview,' he wrote to his father, 'Macdonald came to me and suggested I shd settle with them here now I had the chance for we might not be able to reach Lhasa. A bird in the hand is worth two in the bush he said. But I knew all this was simply due to his having a pain in the lining of his waistcoat so took no notice of it. The poor man is on an invalid's diet & ought really to be on the sick list.' Soon afterwards, the General *was* on the sick list, so weakened by another bout of dysentery as to be unable to sit his pony. His symptoms were consistent with amoebic dysentery, almost certainly contracted in Africa, which was treated at that time with such patent medicines as Dr Collis Browne's morphia-based Chlorydine, which is a palliative but not a cure.

If a letter written in 1950 to Francis Younghusband's first biographer by Leonard Bethell (formerly Lieutenant Bethell of 8 Gurkha Rifles, on attachment to the Coolie Corps) is correct, a mutiny was now hatched by the senior officers. The General was to be deposed and replaced by the next most senior British officer below him (presumably Lieutenant-Colonel Brander rather than Colonel Younghusband). If there was such a plan it certainly came to nothing, and it has to be said that Bethell showed himself in print to be Younghusband's most ardent but also his most fanciful admirer. Furthermore, Bethell was a mere subaltern at the time, hardly likely to be privy to the private discussions of commanding officers, and a good two hundred miles away from the action. It is more likely that he picked up rumours of the widespread discontent in camp, for it is beyond dispute that Macdonald's badgering of Younghusband about the shortage of supplies and the need to negotiate – to say nothing of his harsh treatment of the two looters – had made him heartily disliked by the majority of his officers.

As the army marched northwards along the shore of the great lake, the Tibetan delegation made repeated attempts to parlay. 'The sight,' recorded Mark Synge, 'which first of all used greatly to tickle the fancy, of important Tibetan personages under bright umbrellas and riding mules splendidly caparisoned, and led by servants in gorgeous liveries, soon grew quite common. At every point of importance along the line of our advance, this or a similar cavalcade would come hurrying up . . . After a pleasant talk of many hours the purple and fine linen used to ride away baffled.' Every approach met the same unflinching response from Younghusband: that he would negotiate only at Lhasa. 'He sat through every Durbar a monument of patience and inflexibility,' wrote Edmund Candler, 'impassive as one of their own Buddhas. Priests and councillors found that appeals to his mercy were hopeless. He, too, had orders from his King to go to Lhasa; if he faltered, *his* life also was at stake; decapitation would await *him* on his return. That was the impression he purposely gave them. It curtailed palaver.'

In the light of these rebuffs it was inevitable that the Tibetans should resort to a scorched-earth policy, emptying villages and doing whatever they could to remove food and fodder from the path of the advancing foreigners. The mounted patrols found it increasingly difficult to locate monasteries or villages that had anything to offer, even in the way of barley. As for the lake, there were plenty of seagulls and redshanks but disappointingly few wildfowl to be shot. But it was well stocked with good-sized carp-like fish, with the result that the lakeside below every camp site became crowded with fishermen, all eager to bring some variety to their diet: 'The regular trout fishing appliances – greenheart rod, reel and silk-spun line, catgut cast and choice Zulu or March-brown fly – accounted for large numbers; but side by side with the sportsman so equipped would stand some sepoy or follower with a lengthy stick, a bit of string, and a bent pin baited with a bit of tsampa, whose efforts would be crowned with success quite similar.' Vernon Magniac, Younghusband's brother-in-law and private secretary, had become something of a joke among the officers on account of his pomposity, ceaseless complaining, and apparent inability to do the smallest thing for himself, but now went some way towards redeeming his status by becoming the camp's champion fisherman, with a daily catch of up to seventy. The fish, like the carp they resembled, proved to be repellantly bony, and in better circumstances would not have been worth eating. Since the fish had been long isolated, Austine Waddell collected several specimens and named them *Gymnocypris waddelli*.

On 22 July the Tibet Field Force camped under the walls of another great fortress, Peté Jong, deserted and in ruins. Here, as at Nakartse Jong, an unlucky officer was deputed to stay behind with a small garrison while the army moved on. This was only one of a number of picturesque, tumbledown castles that lined the shore: 'There they stand,' wrote Perceval Landon,

foursquare, reddish-brown bulks of native quarrying, crumbling everywhere and sometimes fallen, now laying bare the long abandoned economy of an upper storey through a shattered corner, now, lower down, betraying the emptiness of a bastioned courtyard at the base of the tower. The rock-cresses and the saxifrages have long established themselves between the crevices of the stones, and on their old, worn surfaces the sombre mosses and the vivid orange and black lichens spread themselves in the pure air and sunlight. Overhead, among the beflagged sheaves at the corners of the keep, the ravens hop heavily and cry.

This melancholy lakeside scenery reminded Austine Waddell of the lochs of his Scottish homeland, and he caught himself scanning the headlands for a steamer coming round the corner.

Four days of easy marching brought Macdonald's column to the northern shores of Yamdok Tso. On the fifth they left its bowl behind to go up to the saddle of the Khamba La, a steep but comparatively straightforward climb, for the lake was already 14,400 feet above sea level and the summit of the pass a mere two thousand feet higher. But for the Fusiliers on rearguard duty it was a trying experience, as the yaks and ponies clambering along the zigzag path above them brought rocks crashing down the mountain side. 'Large stones & boulders rolled down at a terrific rate,' wrote Private Sampson in his diary. 'We had to keep stopping or rushing forward to dodge them. Several mules were injured with them . . . We had a terrible job to get the poor old mules up. They were groaning & grunting the whole way. After a short journey along this road we passed a sort of temple with a lot of red & white bunting flying from several poles on top.' This was the summit of the pass, with breathtaking views to north and south: to their rear, the waters of the Turquoise Lake, with Bhutan's Himalayan ranges framing the horizon; before them, the great chasm through which ran Tibet's Great River, the Tsangpo, and on its far side the valley of the Kyi Chu, the River of Happiness, extending northwards to Lhasa itself, now barely forty miles distant as the lammergeier might fly.

For those who had long dreamed of Lhasa and had suffered so many setbacks on their journey, this was a moment of exaltation second only to achieving the goal itself. Few felt this more keenly than Edmund Candler – or expressed themselves better:

We looked down on the great river that has been guarded from European eyes for nearly a century. In the heart of Tibet we had found Arcadia – not a detached oasis, but a continuous strip of verdure, where the Tsangpo cleaves the bleak hills and desert tablelands from west to east. All the valley was covered with green and yellow cornfields, with scattered homesteads surrounded by clusters of trees, not dwarfish and stunted in the struggle for existence, but stately and spreading – trees that would grace the valley of the Thames or Severn. We had come through the desert to Arcady.

No less moved, but for more practical reasons, were the transport and supply officers, among them Mark Synge:

The descent for the first two thousand feet would be over bare bleak hillside: after that we would descend across the wood-line, below which firewood, at any rate, would be found in plenty. And below that belt of forest, and on either side of a broad river, we saw thick green crops that meant grazing galore, and here and there among the crops large prosperous-looking villages, or stately monasteries that should assuredly be well stocked with grain and tsampa and other delights. One thought of Moses when he caught his first glimpse of the promised land!

For Francis Younghusband, too, this was a never-to-be-forgotten moment – not least because he had pulled off another of his gambles and again bested 'Retiring Mac', by demonstrating that his fears about running out of food and fodder were groundless. To Helen he wrote that it was a day to be remembered. Caught up in one of those moments of ecstasy that came to him in high places, he sought to capture in words the beauty of the lake they had just left behind: 'Never have I seen such colouring or such rapid changes of colour. At one time it would be a deep liquid Prussian blue. Then you wd find it had changed to a lovely light turquoise greenish blue. And sometimes in the far extremity you wd see a band of the most brilliant blue which could not be matched in any turquoise or any sky you ever saw.'

Brigadier-General Macdonald had to be portered up to the Khamba La and down the other side in a dhoolie. What his thoughts were can only be guessed at – but if he was a reluctant

traveller, he was not the only one in the party. For Captain George
Preston of the 40th Pathans this was just one more stage on a long
and uncomfortable campaign, and the views left him unimpressed:
'When we got to the top of the Khamba La,' he wrote to his wife,
'instead of seeing a beautiful river with wooded banks we saw
nothing but a dirty muddy stream about 150 yards broad.' The
descent into the Tsangpo Valley only reinforced his earlier impres-
sions: 'It is most disappointing – a barren uninteresting rainy
unhealthy country. It is raining now. The snows too are most disappointing and the atmosphere is unbearable . . . Personally I
never want to visit the country again.'

The two squadrons of Mounted Infantry had pushed on ahead
to seize the crossing at Chaksam, the Iron Bridge, sited ten miles
upstream at a point where the great river was at its narrowest. Here
there was an ancient and exceedingly dangerous-looking suspension bridge, made of iron chains and slats of wood, said to be at
least six centuries old – but also a ferry, consisting of 'two large
rectangular ferry boats, capable each of holding about twenty
mules, a hundred men, or two hundred maunds of stores.' Each
boat was decorated with 'a roughly carved figure-head representing a horse. One horse had lost its ears, which rather detracted
from its otherwise imposing appearance.' The Mounted Infantry
arrived just as the last load of Khampa warriors from the retreating
army was being unloaded on the far side. Specifically for this crossing the Tibet Field Force had brought up from India four Berthon
boats, collapsible canvas and wooden-framed structures, each
made up of two parts. These were duly assembled on the shore and
then rowed across while the rest of the Mounted Infantry stood by
to provide covering fire. Once again the Tibetans missed an
opportunity, for each Berthon boat was capable of holding no
more than four men at a time. Their landing was unopposed,
allowing both ferry-boats to be taken without a shot being fired.

The riverside monastery of Chaksam Chori was then searched,
producing an abbot and about twenty terrified boatmen. 'I showed
them twenty rupees,' wrote Ottley, 'and told them that they were
theirs if they brought the two barges to our side of the river; but
no, they would not trust us, and were too much afraid of their own
people. Well, there was nothing left but to tell them they had got

to do it, and that we would shoot anybody who tried to interfere with them.' Within half an hour the two ferry-boats had been brought over to the southern side of the river and the boatmen were duly paid – but not allowed to go: 'I gave them their twenty rupees, and told the Lama to send me ten sheep, some tsampa and chung (country beer) for the boatmen, for which he would be paid. This won their hearts.'

Their fears allayed by this unaccustomed generosity, the boatmen then produced from hiding a number of large coracle-like skin boats, which were found to make extremely effective shelters from the rain: 'Everybody was now happy, especially the Mounted Infantrymen, as they were able to cut as much of the green barley as the ponies could eat, and although we had no kits or tents that night, yet we had reached the Brahmaputra and would cross next day – a fact sufficient to keep everybody in good spirits.'

The following day, 25 July, the army began to cross the Tsangpo in the wake of the Mounted Infantry. It was a painfully slow business because the river had to be crossed in two stages: first, from the south bank to a sandbank in midstream, using the two Tibetan ferry-boats; then, in the yak-skin coracles, across a shallower side-channel to the far bank. To speed up the crossing the engineers strung a steel hawser across the fast-flowing main channel, and at the same time Major Bretherton, the chief transport officer, experimented with the Berthon boats by lashing them together in pairs beneath a wooden platform. He and another officer, Captain Moore, along with seven Gurkhas and two Indian camp-followers, then began to cross the main channel on one such structure, all of them dressed in their heavy clothes and carrying their packs and rifles. Before they had even got out into the mainstream, a side eddy caused by the sharp jutting-out of a rocky headland caught the raft. It tipped and overturned. Captain Moore and five of the Gurkhas were able to struggle to the shore but Bretherton and the remaining four men were 'engulfed by the surging waters' and never seen again.

For many officers this was the most shocking moment of the entire expedition, because it was so unexpected. The loss of Bretherton was particularly mourned because he was viewed by one and all as the most popular officer in the column. 'Such a loss he is,' wrote Francis Younghusband to Helen, 'so cheery with all his difficulties & so hard working.' No one was more upset than a close friend, Mark Synge. 'A moment before we had seen him full of health, cheery and active,' he wrote. 'Here was one, full of life and ripe for honour, cut off in his prime . . . His body was carried down the Tsangpo, and we grieved at this, for we could not pay it the honour it deserved. But why should we have grieved? For there, a pioneer always, who had ever gloried in exploring the confines of the Indian Empire, he had but followed his bent, pursuing the mysterious course of that river whose outlet still baffles us.'

In accordance with the Army's time-honoured custom in the field, Bretherton's effects were auctioned that evening: 'A committee of adjustment assembles and, after reserving only such articles as will be obviously acceptable to his relations as mementoes and can easily be carried, puts up the remainder to auction.' Synge was appointed auctioneer, finding the adoption of the 'correct, breezy, business-like auctioneer's manner . . . up-hill work'. Again in accordance with custom, absurdly large sums were offered for the most trivial items, the proceeds to be sent to Bretherton's widow.

Once the engineers had done their work, each crossing could be completed within minutes. 'The boat first goes upstream by a back current,' explained Lieutenant Carey in his diary. 'Then as it gets into the full force of the stream a rope is thrown from the shore which is manned by coolies, who pull for all they are worth. The force of the current carries the boat to the other side, where the boat gets into a smoother back current and the rope is dropped.' He crossed with the rest of the Fusiliers on 29 July. 'Marched early to the ferry,' Private Sampson recorded in his diary, 'where they made everyone take off his boots in case of an accident. I don't think many men would get ashore if the boat did upset. The river is too swift & we are in full marching order with ball ammunition. We all landed safely.' From the Tibetan ferry-boats they transferred to coracles for the second stage of the crossing: 'These are the most peculiar boats I ever saw. They are made by stretching a Yak-skin across a framework of wood. Two men can carry them easily yet they will carry 12 men. It is a strange sensation crossing water in them. They are transparent. One can see through the bottom. I was glad to get ashore.'

As the entire operation took four days, everyone in the column got the chance to rest and restore their appetites. The Fusiliers camped in a village surrounded by fruit-trees and vegetable gardens, which they named Eden: 'There are peas, turnips, onions. Mint and an abundance of clear sparkling water,' wrote Corporal Percy Coath in his diary. 'This is the best camping ground we have had as yet, and after our starvation diet we are veritably "in clover". We are going to have some vegetable stews. I am told Lhasa is about forty miles from here.'

The Tibetan deputations were now becoming desperate in their entreaties. They no longer spoke of the risks to their own lives but to that of the Dalai Lama himself, who would surely die if foreigners entered Lhasa. While he waited at Chaksam, Francis Younghusband wrote home to say that he was getting signs of the Tibetans 'caving in'. To his father he wrote that he had actually received a letter from the Dalai Lama,

> the first of course that he has ever written to an Englishman or I believe to any European for the letter he is supposed to have written to the Czar was I fancy a bogus one – at any rate it did not have on it the official seal which mine has. I have replied on magnificently crested paper saying I trust His Holiness will appreciate the inconvenience it would be to me to halt short of Lhasa now that I have left Gyantse. I ended up – 'I hope I may be able subscribe myself with the highest respect & consideration Your Holiness' sincere friend.'

But Younghusband was still quarrelling with Macdonald, who had now written him a formal letter suggesting he exploit the Tibetans' fears to secure their signatures to his treaty. 'Of course I absolutely refused to stop,' Younghusband wrote to his sister on 26 July. 'So he wrote to me officially about [it] and I promptly replied officially informing him that the Mission would proceed to Lhasa & I relied on him to break down any opposition to its passage. It is the very dickens having a general like this to deal with and I am terribly afraid that even when we get there he will refuse to put pressure on the Tibetans if I shd. require it.'

This note from Brigadier-General Macdonald was one of the

few from him to Colonel Younghusband to be reproduced in the subsequent Blue Books published by Order of Parliament. In it, James Macdonald referred to an exchange with Younghusband in which the latter had informed him that 'the primary object of the Mission and the Force escorting it was to reach Lhasa, and that effecting a satisfactory settlement was secondary'. This was contrary to the orders Macdonald had received, and he wished to see such an order in writing. Younghusband, of course, had no such order, yet it is clear from a subsequent letter written by Macdonald that he backed down in the face of Younghusband's obduracy, to the extent of expressing regret that his 'well-meant suggestion' should have caused a misunderstanding. This was the second time the General had backed down following a direct confrontation with the Tibet Commissioner, and it suggests that Retiring Mac's real pusillanimity lay not in his reluctance to advance on Lhasa but in his failure to stand up to Younghusband.

While camped beside the Tsangpo, Francis Younghusband also received further details of the treaty he was to secure. A key element was an indemnity to be paid by the Tibetans towards the costs incurred by the Government of India in mounting the Tibet Mission. This indemnity could be paid in instalments spread over three years, but until such time as it had been paid in full the Chumbi Valley was to be occupied as security. As to the exact amount of the indemnity, Younghusband was to be 'guided by circumstances', but it had to be a sum that was within the power of the Tibetans to discharge. A British Resident in Lhasa was not on the cards, but a British Trade Agent in Gyantse was.

On 31 July, now thoroughly rested and well-fed, the army began the last stage of its long march. 'All villages seem deserted,' wrote Percy Coath in his diary. 'I am afraid the people are dreadfully frightened, having heard, no doubt, of our slow but sure advance against all obstacles.' Private Sampson admired some rocks beside the trail 'painted with some fine coloured pictures of Bhudda with writing under in the Tibetan language', while Perceval Landon made notes for what became a striking evocation (in his book *The Opening of Tibet*) of the Mission Escort as it wound its way northwards beside the Kyi Chu 'for all the world like a long worm upon a path': at its head, the Mounted Infantry, 'inquisitive and at wary intervals', followed by the Sikh Pioneers, 'striding with long legs', and the quick-stepping Gurkhas. Then 'nearly a mile of mountain battery', followed by the 'endless ammunition train'. After them 'you would always find the General, jogging along with bent shoulders – a mile away you could tell he was a sick man', and close at hand Dr Waddell with his 'strangely laden assistants'. The Tibet Commissioner had no specific place in the column. He liked to remain in camp working on his letters and despatches until the rearguard were on the point of starting. He would then ride up through the column in the course of the day's march, reaching the head of the vanguard as it arrived at the evening's camping-ground.

On the following day there was talk of Lhasa coming into view. Major Iggulden and Captain Ottley raced each other on their ponies to the top of a spur, Ottley winning 'by a head', but the buildings they saw were those of the great monastery of Sera, several miles north of Lhasa itself. The valley began to broaden and a gleam of gold was spotted in the far distance. 'One p.m. Note the time please,' jotted George Preston. 'I have just seen Lhassa. It is about 10 miles away. I am not impressed, nor is anyone else. I fancy that tomorrow many people will be disappointed.' What he had glimpsed was the roof of the Nechung Oracle – better known to the invaders as 'the Chief Magician's temple' – still a short distance from the holy city. Lhasa and the Potala Palace remained hidden from view beyond two low spurs.

A final deputation came out to meet them, the most imposing so far, including two of the four Shapés and the abbots of the three great monasteries around Lhasa. Hatter Bailey sat in on the Durbar that followed: 'They asked us not to go any further. We promised not to enter monasteries. There were representatives of the three big monasteries there Drepung (7,700 monks) Sera (5,500) & Ganden (3,300) – They said they had great difficulty in keeping their monks in hand & were afraid they would break out if we went on.' That night Francis Younghusband wrote to Helen that they would be in Lhasa on the morrow. Of his dealings with the Tibetan delegates he had little to say, other than that it was 'the same old story – please don't go to Lhasa'. He had found them 'very polite – but so unbusinesslike. If I had not to do business with them I could make excellent friends with them.'

At mid-morning on 3 August the column reached the village of Nethang (today Nyetang), where the front of the column was ordered to halt to allow the gaps between units to close up. 'It was with impatience that we waited the order to continue our march,' wrote Landon. 'Before us the two spurs of intervening rock still closed the view of the Plain of Milk completely . . . We had to possess our souls of patience still.' While they waited, Edmund Candler accompanied Dr Waddell to a nearby temple, within which he found a simple, square, ziggurat-like chorten. This, he learned from Dr Waddell, was the tomb of Atisha, the Indian reformer who in the late tenth century began the process known as the Second Diffusion, leading to the spread of Buddhism throughout Tibet:

> Never in the thousand years since the good monk was laid to rest at Nethang had a white man entered this shrine. Today the courtyard was crowded with mules and drivers; Hindus and Pathans in British uniform: they were ransacking the place for corn. A transport officer was shouting:
>
> 'How many bags have you, babu?'
>
> 'A hundred and seven, sir.'
>
> 'Remember, if anyone loots, he will get fifty *beynt* [lashes with the cat-o'-nine-tails].'
>
> Then he turned to me.
>
> 'What the devil is that old thief doing over there?' he said, and nodded at a man with archaeological interests, who was peering about in a dark corner by the tomb. 'There is nothing more here.'
>
> 'He is examining Atisha's tomb.'
>
> 'And who the devil is Atisha?'

An hour or so later the column moved off again, crawling forward under the rocky sides of the northern spur and then threading through the defile marking the entrance to the Lhasa plain. But even from here not a stone or pinnacle of Lhasa could be seen. They passed a great stone Buddha carved in relief on a rock-face and then crossed another two miles of plain until ahead of them they saw a mud-coloured chorten piled with prayer-stones standing isolated beside a field of barley. Word ran down the column that it marked the spot from which the Dalai Lama's Potala Palace might first be glimpsed. It was three o'clock in the afternoon and the sun shone brilliantly. 'Excitement rose to a high pitch,' wrote David Macdonald, Austine Waddell's Tibetan-speaking assistant. 'As we approached this vantage-point all who were not tied to their places in the ranks broke into a race as to who should be the first living Europeans to set eyes on the Forbidden City of Lhasa.' Who actually won the race is uncertain, Landon declaring it to be either Captain Peterson of the 2nd Mounted Infantry or his second-in-command, Captain Souter. But there it was: 'Gleaming in the sun were the golden roofs of the pavilions which crowned the Potala.'

Frank O'Connor was riding beside Claude White when they came up to the roadside chorten. 'He and I,' wrote O'Connor afterwards, 'since 1895 had often worked together, and we had of course discussed the possibility of our ever entering Tibet and reaching Lhasa, and often and often we had nearly despaired of ever being able to realise our ambitions. "Well, O'Connor," he said to me, "there it is at last", and we rode alongside each other in silence. There was not much to be said but it meant a great deal to us both.'

Dr Austine Waddell was equally moved: 'Our feelings can be imagined and must have been akin to the emotions felt by the Crusaders on arriving within sight of Jerusalem.' He and a group of officers trotted forward until they reached the Pargo Kaling, the Middle Door Barrier, an enormous whitewashed chorten with a gateway in its base that stood at the intersection of two ridges which together formed the western wall and boundary of the city of Lhasa: 'On climbing the ridge alongside the gate, which was crowded with several hundred inquisitive monks and townspeople thronging to see the white-faced foreigners, the vast panorama of the holy city in its beautiful mountain setting burst upon our view, and we gazed with awe upon the temples and palaces of the long-sealed Forbidden City, the shrines of the mystery which had so long haunted our dreams, and which lay revealed before our eyes at last.' The credit for getting them there, he added, was due most of all to Brigadier-General Macdonald, 'who by flawless arrangements had led his little band of 650 British and 4,000 Indian troops across the backbone of the world.'

All who crowded up on the ridge were struck by the contrast between the town spread out at their feet and the 'temple-palace of the Grand Lama' that overshadowed it. 'Simplicity has wrought a marvel in stone,' wrote Perceval Landon, 'nine hundred feet in length and towering seventy feet higher than the golden cross of St Paul's Cathedral. The Potala would dominate London, Lhasa it simply eclipses. By European standards it is impossible to judge this building; there is nothing there to which comparison can be made.' He could see something Egyptian in the austerity of its 'huge curtains of blank, unveiled, unornamented wall, and in the flat, unabashed slants of its tremendous south-eastern face', but nothing Egyptian about the contrast of colour and surroundings:

The vivid white stretches of the buttressing curtains of stone, each a wilderness of close-ranked windows and the home of the hundreds of crimson-clad dwarfs who sun themselves at the distant stairheads, strike a clean and harmonious note in the sea of green which washes up to their base. Once a year the walls of the Potala are washed with white, and no one can gainsay the effect; but there is yet the full chord of colour to be sounded. The central building of the palace, the Phodang Marpo, the private home of the incarnate divinity himself, stands out four-square upon and between the wide supporting bulks of masonry a rich red-crimson, and, most perfect touch of all, over it against the sky the glittering golden roofs – a note of glory added with the infinite taste and the sparing hand of the old illumination – recompense the colour scheme from end to end, a sequence of green in three shades, of white, of maroon, of gold, and of pale blue. The brown yak-hair curtain, eighty feet in height and twenty-five across, hangs like a tress of hair down the very centre of the central sanctuary hiding the central recess. Such is the Potala.

Not everyone was so thrilled. 'It didn't look much except for the large golden temple in the middle,' wrote Hatter Bailey, ordered to remain on guard beside the gate with his men while the rest of the force made camp a mile and a half away. 'We had to wait on this hill till 2 p.m. when the camp was pitched so I put up my rod & fished a stream just below & caught 34 with fly. I thought the Tibetans might object but they didn't & were very excited when ever I caught one.' The reason for this excitement was that no one fished at Lhasa, the taking of life in any form being forbidden within the city's environs.

Another disappointed officer was Mark Synge: 'An exciting climax to our march, such as a good fight in the Lhassa plain, would have been highly artistic. Here stood the Debun [Drepung] monastery, and there further on the Sara [Sera] monastery, full of monks who at that time hated us. A few good shells in those monasteries would have set the monks buzzing . . . But such wild schemes were not to be realised. We marched quietly into a swampy camp.'

'I am wondering how the Dalai Lama feels now,' wrote George Preston in his diary. 'He must be a bit sick about it all.' His fellow officer on the staff, William Beynon, also set down his thoughts: 'We – the military party – have done our job and brought the Mission, like so many Cook's Tourists, to Lhasa. Now they must wade in and settle the negotiations and I only hope they will hurry up and get them settled & then we can start home – the sooner the better.'

12

Lhasa at Last

ACCORDING TO the Royal Fusiliers' regimental roll, they had marched a distance of three miles short of four hundred since setting out from Lebong on 22 May. Before they had even settled into their camp the man they were escorting began to receive visitors: first, the Nepalese Consul, who warned that a faction in the city had declared themselves ready to die rather than allow foreigners to enter the sacred city; then the Chinese Resident, Amban Yu-t'ai, who arrived in as much state as he could muster. 'He was carried in a Sedan chair,' wrote Corporal Percy Coath, whose company provided the guard of honour, 'and was escorted by about fifty Chinese infantry who were picturesquely dressed in scarlet cloaks, and armed with mediaeval Billhooks and other like weapons.' Coath thought him a 'nice old man' but was unimpressed by the weaponry of his escort, which struck him as 'rather ineffective in the present day'. As the Amban departed following his courtesy call Coath observed how 'before getting back into his Sedan chair he paused and turning towards Colonel Younghusband he saluted him in the Chinese fashion. It was quite touching. He seems to be greatly relieved at our arrival here.'

The Amban's actions went down well with Francis Younghusband, who was pleased to observe that the Chinese Resident had come to him first, rather than the other way round as protocol customarily required, indicating that he acknowledged the Tibet Commissioner to be his superior. And he was himself once more holding the reins, even if he was dismayed by the news that the Dalai Lama had fled from Lhasa. 'The Tibetans seem to be taking it casually & don't seem to mind much,' he wrote to his father that night, 'but I shall have the dickens of a job getting the convention through with them.' Garbled reports of Younghusband's terse exchange of notes with Macdonald at the Chaksam ferry had by now spread to every mess, and the General's standing with his army was as low as it had ever been. 'They say that General Macdonald is losing his nerves, from illness,' Captain George Preston reported back to his wife in a letter dated 3 August. 'He wants to move the camp back to the last place, which would be madness – but Col Younghusband has really refused. Gen. M. also does not think it safe for the Troops to march through Lhassa.' Equally misleading stories of Macdonald's reluctance to initiate hostilities at Gyantse were also circulating, leading Preston to remark further, 'Whether these reports are true or not it is impossible to say – and if they are not true it is a scandalous shame. All the same he is not quite what everyone expects. He has a weak looking face, is absolutely run by his staff, who are a poor lot, and smokes cigarettes till he is sick. They say that he, Gen. M., never has a cigarette out of his mouth & certainly I have never seen him without one. Personally I should be glad if things could be settled amicably – and then the Force could return to India. It is not a White Man's Country.'

That first night outside Lhasa the camp buzzed with rumours of seven thousand monks drawn from the three great monasteries poised to launch an all-out assault on the camp, so that when two sepoys from Preston's regiment, the 40th Pathans, were caught absent from their posts while on sentry duty, an example was quickly made of them. Within hours they were court-martialled and sentenced to be flogged, the sentence being carried out in front of the assembled troops, with Preston an unwilling participant. 'We have just finished a parade to witness 2 of our men being flogged,' he wrote. 'It was a beastly business and I don't want to see another scene like it. They had left their Post when on sentry &

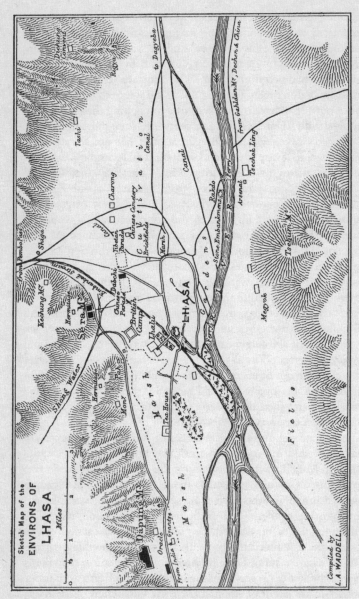

Lhasa and its environs, as mapped by Dr Waddell, showing the British camp and Lhalu Mansion nearby

Lhasa at Last

got 20 & 40 lashes each. I had to count each stroke & didn't appreciate it at all. It is a good example to the rest of them and I hope it will be the last.'

While this court martial was in still in session, Colonel Younghusband set out to return the Amban's courtesy call. Since the Amban's Residency was situated within the circular pilgrimage route known as the Lingkhor or Sacred Way that defined Lhasa's city limits, it gave him the opportunity to override James Macdonald's objections and stage a grand entry into the city. Nevertheless, just to be on the safe side, the General ordered his ten-pounders to be trained on the Potala and four companies of Sikh Pioneers to be held ready. The Tibet Commissioner's escort itself consisted of two companies of Royal Fusiliers and two of the 8th Gurkhas, preceded by the 2nd Mounted Infantry. The Colonel wore his best outfit: the Indian Political Service full-dress suit of a dark blue gold-embroidered morning coat with gold epaulettes, patent leather Court shoes with gold buckles, dress sword, and a gold-embroidered beaverskin cocked hat. Private Sampson, marching in the escort, thought he looked 'very smart'. Sampson, too, was fully aware of the historical significance of their entry: 'After going about ¼ of a mile we entered the gates of the Forbidden City of Lhassa. This is the first time that ever white men have walked openly into the city. On our right was the College of Medicine, on the left the Potala. These looked good buildings from the outside. We continued our way through dirty nasty narrow stinking streets with nothing to attract attention except the horrible stench of the slush we are walking through. It is knee deep. Eventually we arrived at the Amban's Residence. We were received by a salute of crackers or something.'

George Preston was among the small group of officers who accompanied Colonel Younghusband into the Chinese Residency. By his account, the meeting was gratifyingly civilised and cordial:

We were seated on chairs with crimson silk cushions and were given tea, cheroots, and Huntley & Palmers biscuits. There were about 10 followers to the Amban and besides ourselves, those were the only people admitted. The Durbar lasted about 2 hours & consisted of talking about the Tibetans, their ways &

manners, the terms to be imposed and a lot of other things. It was most interesting and one was able to judge what difficult tasks Colonel Younghusband & the Amban have to bring these people to reason. The Amban said that he intended to assist us as much as lay in his power – but as far as I could gather he has not much power. However, it was finally decided that unless they came to terms very soon, active hostilities would very soon begin again.

It was clear that the Tibetan Government was in a state of confusion. The Ta Lama was in disgrace and Kalon Yuthok, the most senior Shapé first met at Nakartse, had taken to his sick-bed. The Tsongdu or National Assembly was meeting in almost continuous session but was riven with dissension and unwilling to make any decisions without reference to the Dalai Lama, who was now said to be in religious retreat, although there was a rumour that he had been spirited away by Russia's agent, the spy Dorjieff. According to Francis Younghusband, 'Everyone was in fear, not now of us, but of his next-door neighbour: and each was working against the other.'

The Tibet Commissioner's immediate concern, however, was to find a residence for himself commensurate with his status as the representative of the King-Emperor Edward VII. The Amban already occupied the best house in the city, but there was the Norbulinka, the Dalai Lama's Summer Palace, set in its own park just below the Potala. Younghusband let it be known that this would suit him very nicely, which caused predictable alarm and resulted in the offer of a nobleman's large three-storey mansion just outside the city. 'With the object of getting into the next best house in Lhasa,' he later wrote, 'I made a pretence of wishing to go into the Dalai Lama's Summer Palace, which was in the plain close by, and eventually arranged that the house of the first Duke in Tibet should be at my disposal.' On 11 August he and his staff moved into their new accommodation, known as Lhalu Mansion. 'Though I pretend it is not nearly good enough for the British Envoy,' he told his sister Emmie, 'I am really only too thankful to be in a house at all . . . Both the Mission Staff and the officers of the escort have a room each besides two mess rooms and the escort of a company, and all servants have various tents in the court yard.

The rooms are very clean & roomy & have glass windows. They are rather in the Japanese style only not so artistic. The painting is more grotesque than beautiful. My room is about the size of the drawing room in the flat.' What was particularly pleasing was that his window looked directly out on the Potala Palace, no more than a thousand yards away.

In the same letter Younghusband informed his sister that he had just received from the Government of India the final draft of the Convention he was to secure: 'It is to be made between "Colonel F. E. Y. in virtue of full powers vested in him by His Brittanic Majesty's Govt and on behalf of that said Govt, and the Illustrious Dalai Lama, Nag Wang Lo-Tsang Theedan Gyatso Gyou Rimbrocay, Supreme Pontiff of the Great Buddhist Church." That's not so slow is it? But I don't know how on earth I shall get through it for no one will accept responsibility and the Dalai Lama has bolted.'

On the following day the Tibet Field Force upped tents and re-established itself on an open stretch of land just north of Lhalu Mansion known as the Plain of Wild Asses, after a number of *kiang* that had been tamed and presented to the young Dalai Lama and now grazed there. The official reason for the move was that Dr Waddell had declared the original camping ground dangerously unhealthy, but there were also sound strategic reasons, for the new site not only overlooked the Mission's quarters at Lhalu Mansion to the south but placed both the Potala Palace and Sera monastery within comfortable range of its artillery. Major William Beynon was in charge of the working parties that first laid out the new camp and then threw up a defensive wall of earth and sods round its perimeter. Nearby was a small grove of trees, within which he found, to his great delight, 'a pool of absolutely crystal clear water, so clear you could see every twig or pebble at the bottom & simply swarming with fish. I sent for my rod & caught them almost as fast as I could throw in the line.' Then to his dismay he discovered that many of the fish were diseased, and he threw them all back.

Over the next few days the troops continued to strengthen the camp's defences. 'Our little camp now looks more like a fenced city,' Corporal Coath was soon able to write in his diary. 'It is sur-rounded with an outer line of sentries ten yards apart during the night and [an] inner line which remains on the whole day. All the troops turn out and line the trenches at sunset every day. In case of alarm, the men fall into the trench immediately in front of their tent.' Port-holes were built into the turf wall for the big guns, which remained trained on the Potala.

Meanwhile, the General and his staff were doing what they could to procure supplies. The local authorities were given lists of what was required, but failed to provide anything like enough to meet the army's needs. After five days the shortage of grain and fodder had become acute, the mules were back on half-rations, and Macdonald was forced to take drastic measures. He ordered the compulsory requisition of 3,700 maunds (320,500 lb) of grain from Drepung monastery's food stores. On the morning of 8 August a strong force moved on the monastery to implement the order and was confronted by an angry crowd of monks who threatened Captain Frank O'Connor with stones and forced him to withdraw. A delegation then came forward with the usual white scarf tied to a pole and informed the General that they wished to discuss his demands among themselves and would perhaps bring the supplies over on the following day. Macdonald's response gave the monks one hour to comply, after which he would take the monastery by force. The big guns were now brought up and unlimbered, and Arthur Hadow's men set up their two Maxims. After sixty minutes had passed without any signs of activity from the monastery, the General's aide William Beynon was instructed to ride over to the 8th Gurkhas' positions on the slopes on the eastern side of the monastery and give the order to advance. Just as Beynon did so, a second aide galloped up with new orders countermanding the first: 'Elliott came up to say the supplies were coming and to hold on.' In fact, these supplies turned out to be no more than a hundred sacks of grain and tsampa and some butter: 'But as the abbots swore they would bring the remainder within five days the G.O.C. [General Officer Commanding] took four of them as hostages and the troops were withdrawn.'

This compromise by Macdonald infuriated even loyal supporters like Major Beynon. 'I think we should have gone into the monastery at all costs and helped ourselves,' he told his wife. 'We should have had no opposition to face, whereas they now think we can be put off with promises and next time we shall be in trouble and probably have to kill some score monks before they come to reason.' Others officers took a stronger line, among them Lieu-tenant Carey of the Fusiliers, who wrote in his diary that the General's behaviour was the 'most undignified that has ever hap-pened to our arms, in the annals of frontier warfare . . . How the monks, of whom there are about 700, must have laughed up their sleeves. Every one in the force is fearfully sick of him, & say he has no opinion of his own. Every one has for a long time thought him an awful rotter, but this caps everything.' Carey hoped the monks would 'remain obdurate, as we might have further scrapping instead of sitting on our hunkers'. In the event, the General's judgement was vindicated: the monks of Drepung kept their word and the remaining supplies of grain were duly delivered.

At Lhalu Mansion, meanwhile, the talks were not going at all well. At a bad-tempered meeting held on 13 December, attended by the Dalai Lama's private secretary, the secretary of the Kashag and two of the four Shapés who made up the Council, the Tibetans raised objections to every clause of the draft treaty but took particular exception to the idea of paying an indemnity. If anyone should pay an indemnity, they argued, it was the British, in reparation for all the damage they had wreaked on the country and its people. However, Younghusband now had two important allies in the persons of the Tongsa Penlop of Bhutan and the Nepalese Consul in Lhasa, Captain Jit Bahadur. During the march up from Gyantse Claude White had made it his business to cultivate the friendship of the Bhutanese chief, and even Younghusband had now to admit that this 'did much to bring the negotiations through'. As for the Nepalese Consul, Captain Jit Bahadur had already endeared himself to the troops by presenting each man, on behalf of his government, with two small silver coins known as *thankas*. Although worth less than half a rupee, these proved, in Private Sampson's words, 'very handy to many [as] we have had no pay since we were in Phari Jong'. A bazaar had sprung up almost overnight outside the main gate of their camp, but hitherto only those who had brought Indian rupees and annas up with them had been able to buy anything.

Now Captain Jit Bahadur initiated the first real breakthrough by turning up at Lhalu Mansion accompanied by 'a cultured, pleas-ant-mannered, amiable old gentleman, with a kindly benevolent expression'. He proved to be the acting Regent, a venerable lama known as the Ti Rimpoche, to whom the Dalai Lama had handed his seal before his departure. The old man was nominally the abbot of Ganden monastery but had spent most his adult life studying in monastic seclusion. He declared himself ignorant of public affairs and, much to the Tibet Commissioner's bemusement, opened dis-cussions by asking him if he believed in reincarnation, adding that he hoped 'both of us would be good during the negotiation. Then we might both go to heaven.' To this Younghusband replied that he had 'not the smallest doubt' that they would indeed go to heaven if they achieved a satisfactory agreement. He was clearly touched by the saintly nature of the Ti Rimpoche and later wrote of him as someone who 'more nearly approached Kipling's Lama in "Kim" than any other Tibetan I met'. But he remained unmoved. He had not come to Lhasa to bargain, and he left the Regent in no doubt that negotiation would be fruitless.

The first signs that the Tibetans were beginning to buckle came on 14 August when, at a hastily convened Durbar at Lhalu Mansion, two prisoners of the Tibetans were handed over to the Tibet Commissioner. These were the supposed yak-herds from Sikkim who had been caught spying by the Tibetans the year before and whose imprisonment had provided Lord Curzon with the excuse to adopt a more aggressive policy. Captain George Preston was among the officers called to witness the event. 'The Prisoners', he wrote to his wife, 'were brought in before Col Younghusband & had to state whether they had been threatened & how they had been fed, so it was most interesting. They said that when they were first taken they were beaten & not very well fed but latterly they said they had been treated well. Mr White (the Political of Sikkim) & I went off with the Prisoners to Capt. Ogilvie [Medical Officer] who inspected them to see if there were any signs of ill treatment. They were stripped but no marks were found on them. They were fat & in good condition except that they were very pale.' The two men were then taken back in to the Durbar and told they were free: 'It was quite good to see their smiles of pleasure.' According to Preston, Colonel Younghusband then gave the two Shapés who had surrendered the prisoners a 'wigging', telling them that 'this was the reason that the mission had come to Lhassa'.

On this same day Perceval Landon, the *Times* correspondent, together with Claude White and Mr Wilton of the Chinese Consular Service, went into Lhasa with a small escort provided by the Chinese Amban. Their purpose was to visit the Jokhang, described by Landon as the 'Cathedral of Lhasa'. It lay at the very heart of the city, which was fitting enough, for it was here rather than on the Potala that the spiritual life of Tibet was centred. The Jokhang temple had been positioned where it was for geomantic reasons, to pin down the demon ogress that dominated ancient Tibet, and within the dark sanctum behind its great central hall was Tibet's most revered icon, an image that symbolised the arrival of Buddhism in Tibet. This was a four-foot-high statue of Gautama Buddha known as the Jowo, said to have been brought to Tibet from Buddha's birthplace in India in the seventh century but much damaged and much restored since. It was this Jowo image – in Landon's words, 'beyond question the most famous idol in the world' – that the *Times* correspondent was intent on seeing, and he was evidently much moved:

In the darkness it is at first difficult to follow the lines of the shrine which holds the god . . . Before him are rows and rows of great butter-lamps of solid gold, each shaped in curious resemblance to the pre-Reformation chalices of the English Church. Lighted by the tender radiances of these twenty or thirty beads of light, the great glowing mass of the Buddha softly looms out, ghostlike and shadowless, in the murky recess. It is not the magnificence of the statue that is first perceived, and certainly it is not that which makes the deepest and most lasting impression. For this is no ordinary presentation of the Master . . . Here there is nothing of the saddened smile of the Melancholia who has known too much and has renounced it all as vanity. Here, instead, is the quiet happiness and the quick capacity for pleasure of the boy who has never yet known either pain, or disease, or death. It is Gautama as a pure and eager prince, without a thought for the morrow, or a care for today. No doubt the surroundings, which are effective almost to the verge of theatricality, account for much, but this beautiful statue is the sum and climax of Tibet, and as one gazes one knows it and respects the jealousy of its guardians.

This was only a brief visit, but when the three Englishmen and their Chinese escort emerged from the Jokhang they found the great square before it filled by a 'dense, growling crowd . . . pressing upon our horses and men'. As they mounted their ponies a stone was thrown 'missing Mr White's head by a few inches'. This first stone was 'the signal for a hundred more. Great jagged pieces of granite, weighing two or three pounds . . . crashed from the house-tops and the street upon our little party, and it was interesting to notice that the stones were directed obviously against our Chinese escort rather than against ourselves . . . We rode out slowly, trying to look as dignified as we could.'

When the news of this highly provocative visit to Tibet's most sacred shrine reached Brigadier-General Macdonald he was understandably furious, for he had given orders placing the city and all its religious sites out of bounds to all except those engaged in official business – and even they must be accompanied by a full military escort. It led to what Younghusband termed a 'battle royal', another of those by now all too familiar rows about who was in charge – and once again it was the General who came off worst. 'He wrote me an official letter,' explained Younghusband in his regular weekly despatch to his father, 'complaining that White & Wilton had gone into the city and asking me "to impress on members of the Mission that they must obey Force orders". I wrote back asking him to come & see me. I then told him my officers obeyed my orders not his & that he himself had to conform to my wishes. I told him plainly that there could be only one head up here and that I intended there shd. be no mistake that that head was myself. He blustered a good deal about referring to Govt. I said he was welcome to. But today he came round & said he would not if I would not. He now understands his position in the Universe.'

This row had number of consequences. It prompted the Tibet Commissioner's aide, Frank O'Connor, to write another of his curious letters to Mrs Younghusband, some of it in French for fear of it being intercepted and read, and largely taken up with an extended diatribe against Macdonald and 'the incredible infirmness' of his staff, who did nothing but 'try & devalue the Commission'. The General, it seemed, was causing Colonel Younghusband far more trouble than the Tibetans. 'I cannot tell you all his misdeeds in a letter,' O'Connor concluded.

More dramatically, there was the abrupt departure of Perceval Landon from Lhasa before dawn the next day. By his own account Landon carried important despatches from the Tibet Commissioner 'both to the Viceroy and to the Home Government', although Francis Younghusband later made light of this claim by saying that he had merely humoured Landon by giving him 'in a sealed cover copies of letters I was sending to the Foreign Office by the ordinary dak [mail]'. What is certain is that hours before his departure, the *Times* man wired the Acting Viceroy to say that he was coming to see him in Simla, adding, 'Hope you completely disengaged'. Landon and Lord Ampthill had been at Oxford together and were old friends, but this was still an odd message for a newspaper man to send to the most powerful man in India. Landon covered the four hundred miles between Lhasa and the Siliguri railhead in twelve days – an impressive feat made possible by the fact that, with the Tibet Commissioner's connivance, he used the Mounted Infantry's staging-post service of fresh ponies, on the grounds that he was carrying urgent official despatches.

But why would the special correspondent of *The Times* leave Lhasa just before the climactic moment, when the entire success of the Tibet Mission still hung in the balance – and at the risk of losing his £350 fee for covering the Mission? When asked by Lord Ampthill for an explanation as to why Landon should have left Lhasa 'before the end of the show' and why he had claimed to be on 'some mysterious mission from you', Younghusband's answer was that there was no mystery: 'He wanted to get home and get his book out first. From *The Times*'s point of view I think he was very unwise to leave Lhasa when he did . . . From the Government point of view it was distinctly advantageous that he should get to Simla and give you and the India Office and Lord Curzon the benefit of personal discussion with an intelligent man who had come straight from Lhasa.' But of course, it was also distinctly advantageous to

Younghusband to have Landon put his case in person to Lord Ampthill – and part of that case undoubtedly involved the removal of Macdonald. Ampthill, however, seems to have been less than impressed. Immediately after his meeting with Landon in Simla on 30 August the Acting Viceroy wrote to Lord Curzon to warn him that Landon was coming to London full of 'strange delusions' about what was going on in Lhasa: 'He will reveal himself as a hero-worshipper of Younghusband and a bitter despiser of Macdonald.'

With or without Younghusband's connivance – and the apparent removal from the files of the usual weekly letter to his father from the period between 14 and 30 August would seem to tip the balance of probability towards the former – Perceval Landon went to Simla (and subsequently to London) as Younghusband's man, intent on getting Macdonald recalled. And he might well have succeeded but for a robust defence of *their* man by the military every time the subject came up in the Viceroy's Council. Even so, Lord Ampthill was sufficiently alarmed to propose that Brigadier-General Macdonald be recalled to his base in New Chumbi, his place in Lhasa to be taken by Younghusband's old ally, the doughty Lieutenant-Colonel Herbert Brander. In the event, by the time Lord Kitchener had seen and approved the Acting Viceroy's proposal, the question of who should remain in command of the Mission escort in Lhasa had become academic.

Soon after Landon's departure two further acts of violence threatened what little progress the talks had made. A Sikkimese interpreter attached to the Fusiliers was found unconscious and badly wounded in a Lhasa street. 'He was left for dead,' noted Private Sampson in his diary, '& found this morning by a Chinaman who took care of him until the arrival of the ambulance & escort. He was operated on by the doctors. He had several fingers amputated. It is entirely his own fault. He has strict orders not to go into the City on any pretext.' Since no culprits could be found, no action could be taken. But on 18 August a far more serious incident occurred when two medical officers, Captains Kelly and Cooke-Young, were attacked by a sword-wielding monk just outside the main gate of the camp as they were making their way over to Lhalu Mansion for breakfast. The assault was witnessed by Herbert Brander:

He rushed at them from behind and cut Capt. Cooke-Young on the back of his head with his sword. Luckily, the blow fell on that officer's forage-cap which, although it was cut through, served to protect his head from serious damage. Capt. Cooke-Young, however, fell forward on his face, and Capt. Kelly, seeing a man of the 23rd with a rifle and fixed bayonet, seized it and went for the Lama. He drove the bayonet through the man's arm, bringing him to his knees, and with a second thrust, directed at his face, he pinned him by the cheek to the ground. Capt. Kelly then withdrew the bayonet, whereupon the lama charged, head downward, and brought him down. Seizing the rifle, the Lama made for camp, with it in one hand and his sword in the other. Capt. Cooke-Young now rushed at him again, only to receive a second, and severer sword-cut on the side of the head. Immediately after this our men closed on the fanatic, and Havildar Buta Singh brought him down with a blow with a stick aimed at his knees.

The monk was stripped and found to be wearing a suit of ancient chain-mail. He had come from Sera Gompa and claimed to have acted alone, in revenge for a brother killed at Gyantse. However, the Anglo-Sikkimese interpreter David Macdonald talked to him shortly before his execution and learned that he was a *dap-dop*, a member of a fighting order of monks who served the larger monasteries as guards, and had been encouraged to mount his assault 'to find out what would happen to the perpetrators of such wanton attacks'. If this was indeed the case, then the instigators soon got their answer, for the monk was tried the next day by a special commission and hanged at four in the afternoon 'in sight of the city as an example'. According to Arthur Hadow this unnamed monk died bravely, if not as a Buddhist monk might have been expected to depart this life: 'Truculent to the last, he kicked a Tommy in the face as he was going up the ladder, and spat at another's face; but hanged he was, dangling like a blot against the sunset.' He was left hanging for 24 hours, 'as a warning to others'.

The Tibet Commissioner was determined to exact full vengeance. 'Col Younghusband was very annoyed & sent at once for the Delegates,' wrote George Preston to his wife on 17 August. 'When they came in they were informed that a fine of Rs 5000 was imposed upon them, they were to send in 4 monks as hostages and in default of payment the monastery of Zara [Sera] – which is a very big & important one – would be burnt down. They have gone away to think over it.'

When the monks of Sera replied that they had no money to pay the fine, the monastery was promptly invested by a large punitive force. The Reuters man Henry Newman accompanied it, and many years later set down the only detailed account of what was very nearly a second massacre to rival that at Chumik Shenko: 'When we were about six or seven hundred yards away the monks poured out from a gateway in their thousands, and lined up. Our mountain guns got into action and the troops deployed. Everyone thought there would be a fight.' But as Newman prepared for the worst, the abbot and a group of lamas came forward and interposed themselves between the troops and the monks. The abbot repeated that there was insufficient money in their treasury to meet Younghusband's fine but said that they could pay in kind, in the form of silks and embroideries. Newman's account implies that the Tibet Commissioner was either on the scene or close at hand: 'To this Younghusband agreed, and in due course there emerged from the monastery monks carrying a certain amount of silver, and a number of bales of embroidered silks. These garments were afterwards sold in the camp by auction. I bought a lovely silk robe myself.'

A letter to Helen Younghusband dated 21 August provides further details. 'I . . . see my way to getting you some fine silks,' her husband wrote. 'A beastly lama ran amok the other day and slashed at two officers with a sword. So besides having the man hung I demanded a fine of Rs 5000 from the Tibetan Govt & hostages for future good behaviour. The fine I said could be paid in either cash or kind so today they brought me masses of beautiful Chinese silk dresses. I am putting them up for auction open to all not like Macd's – and will buy in some for you.'

This same letter gave news of 'daylight' in the talks: the Amban had advised the Chinese Emperor to depose the Dalai Lama, and both the Kashag and Tsongdu, the Council of Ministers and the General Assembly, were beginning to give way on the terms of his proposed Convention – on all terms, that is, save for the matter of the indemnity, which they declared to be impossibly high. They were insisting that Tibet was a poor country, and the sum proposed by the Tibet Commissioner simply beyond its means to pay. As for the Dalai Lama, it was now confirmed that he had fled north. Unknown even to the members of his Council, he had slipped out of the Potala under cover of darkness as long ago as 30 July, and was said to be heading for Mongolia. But he had sent a message to the Tsongdu informing the assembly that he had gone away to protect the Buddhist religion, and warning them to beware of the English, who were 'very crafty people' intent on binding them tight. The deposition of the Dalai Lama as proposed by the Amban would resolve the need to have him present to sign the Convention. 'This will be a most splendid stroke if it comes off,' thought Young-husband, 'and we shall have fairly done the Russians in the eye – wh. is always pleasing.'

But for those not directly involved in the negotiations, the days were beginning to drag. The monsoon rains had given way to regular autumn showers that brought the first light scatterings of snow to the lower slopes of the surrounding mountains. The mail and supply relays brought news that heavier snowfalls now covered all the higher passes. The days were still warm, but temperatures at night were once more starting to drop towards freezing point. It was clear to all that winter was just round the corner. As Thomas Carey put it to his wife, 'Everybody is rather fed up, & we long for civilisation once more.'

A series of sporting events was organised to keep the troops happy: football matches – 'like playing the game at an ordinary level, but with an eighty-pound load on your back' – a three-day rifle-meeting and, on 25 August, a race meeting organised by the officers. 'There was a good attendance from all corps,' wrote Private Sampson in his diary that day. 'I was on armed picquet in case any-thing turned up . . . there was no bookmakers but there was a Totalisator who did a roaring trade.' In camp, food and shopping now became the two most popular topics of conversation. With supplies of flour running low the cooks were reduced to adding tsampa flour to the bread they baked, the resulting loaves being 'hardly palatable'. The delicacies many officers had contrived to have transported up to Gyantse had long since been consumed and the result was that they became, in Mark Synge's words, 'frankly greedy in thought, word, and deed', spending many hours discussing 'the ideal menu at a first-rate London restaurant'. For spirits they were once more having to make do with regulation Army rum, while the smokers had been forced to turn to a hitherto unknown brand of cigarette known as Pedros – 'the produce of an enterprising firm whose custom extended to Lhassa. The Lhassa bazaar abounded in this article, getting it, I suppose, through China . . . By a rough estimate it would appear that for two months at least four thousand souls smoked an average of ten Pedros daily.' Shopping in the camp bazaar, run by Tibetan, Chinese and Nepali traders, was now 'the ladylike way in which we often spent our mornings', and once it became known that the *pelings* liked Tibetan novelties a thriving market in second-hand goods quickly developed: 'The vendors . . . discovered our childish mania for curios, and brought with them each morning such trinkets as would attract our fancy. Skins of all kinds including the lynx, wolf and snow fox. Also objects such as the heavy earrings, necklaces, waistbelts and charm boxes set with turquoises.' Among these locally produced articles were some that caused the buyers to puzzle over how they might have reached this remote corner of the earth: looking-glasses from Austria, penknives from Germany, quart bottles of Bulldog stout, a Rover bicycle and 'tradesmen's pictorial almanacs . . . usually in the form of a royal family group'.

Although Lhasa remained out-of-bounds to all except those on official business, a second visit to the Jokhang was authorised in order to facilitate the religious enquiries of the expedition's so-called archaeologist, Dr Austine Waddell, who brought with him a pilgrim's guide book that he himself had translated and published some years earlier, as well as a map of the city that he had drawn based entirely on travellers' accounts – both of which turned out to be gratifyingly accurate. This time there was a proper military escort for Dr Waddell, made up of a full company of Royal Fusiliers. Other than marching to and from the residencies of the Amban and the Nepalese Consul, the regiment's officers and men had seen little of the city, so there was eager anticipation to start with, but it soon gave way to disgust as it became clear to the marching men that the streets leading to the Jokhang were as filthy and rubbish-filled as everywhere else. The temple's massive outer doors were thrown open by a sullen monk and then Dr Waddell, his assistant David Macdonald and his two guests – a brace of unnamed colonels – filed through, together with a section of Fusiliers with fixed bayonets.

Lieutenant Thomas Carey, second in command of the company providing the escort, attempted to join them but had not been in the building five minutes before he was 'hoofed out' by Dr Waddell, 'as my name was not down on the list'. However, he remained by the outer door until the main party had moved out of sight and then slipped in after them: 'I did get inside and saw something of the interior and am one of the few Englishman who have done so. I heard and saw thousands of monks surrounded by candles, singing in very low monotone, accompanied with cymbals, and various other instruments. The walls are beautifully painted with figures, but the effect is spoilt by the dirt. There are some beautiful gold vessels all chained and an immense Buddha covered with turquoises and other precious stones, with a high golden crown.'

While Carey managed no more than a peep into the central hall, Dr Waddell's party and escort were able to penetrate deep into the Jokhang's inner recesses, to a degree hitherto permitted to no other Europeans. But Dr Waddell had come expecting to have his prejudices confirmed – and he was not disappointed. The Jowo statue of the young Buddha that Landon so admired he thought 'a repellent image . . . with goggle eyes and coarse, sensual face and . . . very rude workmanship.' Having suffered many depredations over the centuries, the lamas kept their most revered images behind a mesh of iron chains which reminded Waddell of nothing so much as spiders' webs: 'In the lurid light and suffocating atmosphere of the smoky rancid-butter lamps, it seemed more like a foul felon in his prison, or a glaring demon in a web of chains, than an effigy of the pure and simple Buddha . . . From this revolting and bizarre spectacle of barbaric idolatry we hurried on through the rest of the dark passages.'

According to David Macdonald, Waddell was greatly taken by some suits of medieval armour kept in the upper storey of the

Jokhang. Using Macdonald as his interpreter he sought to add them to his now extensive collection, 'but the lamas could not be induced to part with any, at any price'. The guardians of the Jokhang showed no signs of hostility towards their visitors, but rather gave every appearance of indifference. It was the same with the crowds gathered in the open square fronting the temple, who might have been expected to show signs of curiosity but remained largely impassive.

As August drew to a close, James Macdonald grew increasingly concerned about the safety of his force in the light of continuing adverse reports on weather conditions and supplies. He asked Dr Waddell to consult with his medical officers and come back to him with the last date until which they considered it safe to remain in Lhasa, based on the existing conditions under which they were living. Dr Waddell's answer was 1 September. The General then called all his commanding officers together, gave them the doctors' opinion and asked them what they thought. The consensus was that it would be unsafe to remain in Lhasa beyond 15 September at the latest. Accompanied by Dr Waddell, Brigadier-General Macdonald then conveyed this news to the Tibet Commissioner, who took it badly, calling it 'the most mean-spirited & almost traitorous act I have heard of for many a long year . . . I have never felt such contempt for any man as I did for him when he came up whining to me about the cold & sheltering himself behind an old woman of a doctor.' His response was to subject the General to another furious tirade which ended with the warning that he was 'not going to allow an Imperial affair of extreme importance [to] depend upon the opinion of a doctor and allow all the results of the sacrifices made by the troops & of their bravery & endurance [to] be thrown away because they could not stay two or three weeks longer to secure those results.' All this Francis Young-husband conveyed in a letter to his father, written on 30 August. 'All my staff are with me tooth & nail,' it concluded. 'And if Macdonald is not cashiered before I have done with him I will eat that best top hat of mine.'

Macdonald's deadline had the opposite effect to that intended for, instead of concentrating the Tibet Commissioner's mind and encouraging him to reach a compromise with the Tibetans, it led him to dig in his heels. Far from lowering his demands on the Tibetans, he actually increased them. A weak earlier he had set out his negotiating strategy to his sister Emmie. 'I have been as hard & stiff as anything with both the Chinese & Tibetans,' he had written on 22 August,

> though I have a certain amount I intend to give way upon at the very end, for I am asking more than Govt have sanctioned. I am asking what Govt of India <u>proposed</u> not what Secy of State <u>sanctioned.</u> Consequently the Tibetans are giving way bit by bit before me and then at the end I will be liberal and have them thinking they have got a lot out of me & very pleased with themselves while Govt will be only too glad to have got what they asked. Dear old Macdonald is horrified at my firmness thinking it may provoke them to war or cause delay and he actually suggested that we shld pay them a subsidy instead of asking an indemnity as this wd make them more friendly! Little does he know the Asiatic! Or me!

By the time the General came to Younghusband with his 15 September deadline – it was on 30 August – only one issue on the proposed treaty was still being seriously contested by the Tibetans: the size of the indemnity they were asked to pay. The Secretary of State for India, St John Brodrick, had made it clear that this indemnity was to be 'within the power of the Tibetans to pay'. Brodrick had by his own admission no idea of the state of Tibet's national coffers. 'Our ignorance of the resources of the country make it impossible to speak with certainty,' he had written to Lord Ampthill. Accordingly, he had given the Tibet Commissioner a free hand to 'decide what will tell most', being 'guided by circumstances in this matter'. Initially the amount suggested remained imprecise, based on a rough estimate of half the financial cost to the Government of India of the Tibet Mission. It then took on a more concrete form as a sum of 50,000 rupees for each day that passed from the date of the attack on the Mission at Changlo on 5 May to the date of the signing of a satisfactory treaty in Lhasa. Thus by 30 August, 118 days after the attack, the sum amounted to 5,900,000 rupees, or just under £400,000. Brodrick had also given

Younghusband permission to extend the period of payment to five years, with the British occupation of the Chumbi Valley as surety until the payment was completed. A British Trade Agent at Gyantse was still to be part of the deal – but any sort of British presence in Lhasa, whether as Resident or Trade Agent, was not to be countenanced.

On 30 August – that is to say, directly following his confrontation with Macdonald over the dates of the army's withdrawal – Younghusband telegraphed the Government of India asking for permission to 'arrange for payment of the indemnity by instalments of one lakh of rupees [100,000 rupees or £6,666] a year'. What he did not spell out was that he had raised the indemnity demanded of the Tibetans to 7,500,000 rupees or £500,000. Nor did he say that he was now demanding for a British Trade Agent, based at Gyantse, the right to visit Lhasa 'for consultations'.

For all Younghusband's earlier protestations in his letter to his sister that 'at the end I will be liberal', when the moment came for compromise he was nothing of the sort. His subsequent actions suggest that, in defiance of the Secretary of State for India's orders, he was still set on following Lord Curzon's agenda, which was to extend British influence in Tibet, principally by securing the Chumbi Valley for Britain. If the Tibetans paid an indemnity of 7,500,000 rupees at the rate of a lakh of rupees a year it would take them seventy-five years to clear their debt – which meant that the Chumbi Valley would remain in British hands for that length of time.

This was clearly the tenor of the Tibet Commissioner's argument when he again met the Ti Rimpoche at Lhalu Mansion on 31 August. 'The Ti Rimpoche said that we were putting on the donkey a greater load than it could possibly carry,' Younghusband later wrote of this meeting. 'I replied that I was not asking the donkey to carry the whole load in one journey. It could go backwards and forwards many times, carrying a light load each journey. The Ti Rimpoche laughed again, and asked what would happen if the donkey died. I said I would ask the Resident [that is, the Chinese Amban] to see that the donkey was properly treated, so that there should be no fear of its dying.' His message was quite clear: he would not reduce the size of the indemnity, but he would give the Tibetans more time to pay. On the following day a grander Durbar took place, at which all the major parties were present for the first time under one roof. Again the Tibetans took the position that the indemnity was too much to pay, and again the Tibet Commissioner reiterated that he would give them time to pay, but pay they must. And this meeting ended with Younghusband delivering an ultimatum: unless the Tibetans agreed to his terms within the week, he would 'take measures to compel them'. The Tibetan delegates left the Lhalu Mansion in no doubt as to what these measures might be.

Within three days the Tibetans had given in. 'I have just sent off the joyful news that the Tibetans have agreed to our terms,' Francis wrote to Helen Younghusband, now in Simla, on 4 September. 'The Regent came up to me this morning and after much haggling eventually put his private seal to the draft convention. So now we only have to get the final fair copies signed & get the Amban's consent & then the job will be done.'

The nine articles of the Tibet Convention were agreed upon on 4 September. Article VI of the agreement now declared that 'Tibet having disobeyed the treaties and insulted the Commissioner by the wrongful commission of hostile acts, shall pay Great Britain an indemnity of Rs. 7,500,000 (£500,000), payable in seventy-five yearly instalments'; Article VII that, as security for the punctual discharge of its obligations on the part of Tibet, 'British troops will continue to occupy the Chumbi Valley until the trading places are satisfactorily established and the indemnity liquidated in full'. What was termed a 'Separate Agreement' outside the Convention gave the British Agent in Gyantse the right of access to Lhasa 'to consult with high Chinese and Tibetan officials on such commercial matters of importance as he has found impossible to settle at Gyantse'.

In the months and years that followed, Francis Younghusband's public line over these three clauses was that he knew he was not acting within his instructions but that, firstly, it was the Tibetans who had come to him with the proposal to extend the period of repayment of the indemnity to seventy-five years, and secondly, he had been forced to make a speedy decision because of Macdonald's pressure on him to leave by 15 September: 'I consented & explained to Govt that there was no time to refer the matter to them for sanction.' Neither defence stands up. In the first place,

Younghusband encouraged the Tibetans to regard the period of repayment as flexible, while at the same time making it quite plain that the size of the indemnity – the one area where he had specifically been given flexibility – was non-negotiable.

As to the question of lack of time, a messenger riding on relays of fast ponies could cover the hundred and fifty miles between Lhalu Mansion and Changlo Manor, the terminus of the telegraph line, in two days, which meant that the Tibet Commissioner could have despatched the agreed terms to Simla on 4 September and received an answer by 9 September, six days before Macdonald's deadline. Furthermore, Younghusband had made it plain to the Government of India after his row with Macdonald that if he still had business to do after 15 September, and if the General refused to give him protection beyond that date, he would stay on in Lhasa, placing himself and his Mission under the protection of the Amban. This was a childish threat that greatly perturbed his masters in Simla and London, but it showed that he was prepared to sit and wait if necessary. He knew, too, that the more robust officers among his escort would support him, for William Ottley had given him a pledge that 'if I lifted my little finger the whole force would stay with me'. Yet the moment the terms of the Convention had been agreed, Younghusband kept them to himself and made haste to arrange for the official signing of the treaty to take place on 7 September – in other words, *before* Simla and London could challenge its terms. He did so on the assumption that the Governments of India and Great Britain, once they had seen what he had done in their names, would accept the signed Tibet Convention as a *fait accompli* and fall into line; nevertheless, 'I am fully expecting a wigging,' he wrote to his wife – and in that, at least, he was proved right.

The Tibetans and the Amban wanted the Convention signed in the Chinese Residency. The Tibet Commissioner insisted on the Potala and, as usual, got his way. 'We paraded as strong as possible at 1.30 p.m.,' was how Private Sampson began his diary entry for 7 September.

About 2 p.m. the whole Brigade marched off. The pipers of the 40th Pathans & 8th Gurkhas played in turn en route to the City.

We marched to the Potala which is built on a rocky hill. It is a fine large building protected by a huge wall. From the foot of the hill to the entrance the road up the hill was lined on either side by troops starting at the bottom with the Gurkhas then Pioneers & then Pathans, last of all up to the entrance the Royal Fusiliers. A little before 3 o'clock Colonel Younghusband and the General arrived & went inside this huge building, then shortly afterwards the Tonsal Penlop [and the] King of Nipaul [that is, the Nepalese Ambassador] they also went inside.

The day before the ceremony Captain Frank O'Connor had been taken round the Potala by some reluctant monks, and at his insistence the site for the signing was moved from the great outer courtyard where public ceremonies were performed to the private audience room in which each successive Dalai Lama was enthroned, a 64-pillared hall that rose through three storeys of the administrative section of the Potala. To reach it, the participants and those invited to witness this historic moment – including every officer who could be spared from official duty and the remaining special correspondents – had first to negotiate the steep and slippery stairway that climbed the lower façade of the Potala in a series of zigzags. 'One had to walk crabwise to prevent falling,' reported Edmund Candler, 'and plant one's feet on the crevices of the age-worn flagstones, where grass and dock-leaves gave one a securer foothold.' At the top of the steps they were ushered through a large gateway and then along 'a maze of slippery passages, dark as Tartarus, but illuminated dimly by flickering butter-lamps held by aged monks, impassive and inscrutable'. Just to be on the safe side, British soldiers were posted at regular intervals along these corridors and more were crammed in at the back of the great hall itself, dimly lit from above by a skylight.

The Dalai Lama's throne had been moved back behind a row of pillars and hidden by a large curtain of crimson silk, supplied by the Amban, on which was embroidered a large Chinese dragon. In front of it, on one of a row of his own crimson-cushioned chairs, sat the Amban dressed in a dark blue silk jacket and black upturned rimmed hat, flanked on his right by Colonel Younghusband in his diplomatic uniform and on his left by the Regent, Ti Rimpoche, bareheaded and clad in a monk's simple red garb. Beside the Regent the four Shapés, other senior members of the Tibetan Government, the heads of the three great monasteries and representatives of the Tsongdu sat in a wide semicircle that ended with the Tongsa Penlop and the Nepalese Consul, all in silk robes of every shade. Behind them stood their attendants and guards, equally exotically dressed and wearing an array of headgear that, according to Candler, 'would be the despair of an operatic hatter . . . red lamp-shades, yellow motor-caps, exaggerated Gainsboroughs, inverted cooking-pots, coal-scuttles and medieval helmets'. A more sober note was struck by the British contingent in their drab khaki: James Macdonald, seated to the right of Francis Younghusband, and beyond him other members of his staff in descending order of sen-iority. The only splash of colour they brought to the proceedings came from the Union Jack covering Colonel Younghusband's camp table at the centre of the room, upon which was placed a long scroll prepared by Mr Mitter and his staff setting out the terms of the treaty in English, Tibetan and Chinese. Five more copies were placed on another five tables on either side, all awaiting the affixing of seals and signatures.

Colonel Younghusband had been the last to take his place, which was the signal for a troop of Tibetan servants to bring in cups of Chinese tea on salvers, together with plates of biscuits, sweets, dried fruits and Pedro cigarettes. 'Those dainties', grum-bled Mark Synge, 'did not extend to the outer circles. Those of us who were behind contented ourselves by lighting up our own Pedros.' A Tibetan clerk attached to the Mission then read out all nine articles of the treaty, together with Younghusband's Separate Agreement that gave the British Agent to be stationed at Gyantse the right to visit Lhasa for consultations. The Tibet Commissioner rose and asked the Tibetans present if they agreed to these terms, receiving in reply a low murmur of assent. The treaty was then unrolled and affixed with stamps by representa-tives, in turn, of the Tsongdu, the monasteries of Drepung, Sera and Ganden, and the Kashag. The penultimate stamp was that of the great seal of the Dalai Lama, which was touched lightly by the Ti Rimpoche before being applied by a monk to a pad of vermil-ion ink and then imprinted. Finally, Colonel Younghusband added his signature and his own official Government stamp in red sealing-wax.

The signing and sealing of the treaties took almost two hours to complete, and while it was in progress small parties of troops drawn from those lining the route were allowed inside by turns to take a peek at the proceedings, among them Private Sampson: 'Of course I could not stay very long because the others were waiting to come up but one thing I did see was some very disgusting pictures & carvings round the wall.' Not everything went according to plan. A number of officers had brought in their cameras to record the occasion, but only Claude White had brought one with a magnesium flash. With the help of two officers he had carried his large plate camera up the steps and into the Potala – but failed to warn anyone that he was about to take a flash photograph. Henry Newman was among those to whom it came as a surprise: 'There was a flash of light, a report and then a blinding glare, in the light of which I saw a number of pallid and frightened faces. Then came a cloud of smoke. Everybody had half-risen from their seats, but no word was said . . . Luckily, after a minute or two, the room was still again. The smoke disappeared, and the Tibetans, reassured, became all smiles once more.'

Once the signing was completed Francis Younghusband again took the floor to address the assembly, each line being translated twice, first into Tibetan by Frank O'Connor, and then into Chinese by Mr Wilton of the Chinese Consular Service. 'I remember the thought passing through my mind,' wrote Frank O'Connor of this moment many years later, 'how I had examined the map of Asia years ago as a youngster, and wondered if I should have the good fortune to ever visit this mysterious country and play a part in great events.'

Younghusband's speech was later said to have been all about putting the misunderstanding of the past behind them and how the foundations of friendship had now been laid and must be built upon. But this was not how it came across to Lieutenant Mark Synge, who remembered it as being mostly directed at the four-man council of ministers: 'The latter sat bobbing their heads deferentially at each sentence, and looking thoroughly ashamed of themselves while Colonel Younghusband addressed them from his chair . . . The speech was emphatically "straight talk", the key-note seeming to be that the Tibetans had been very foolish in opposing and flouting us in the past, but that they were now going to be good boys. They were going to be well treated when they came to visit us, and were not going to misbehave themselves in any way, should we again come near them . . . The "council of three" [*sic*] seemed to take it all "lying down".'

Then it was all over and, after a great deal of handshaking, more cups of tea and more Pedros, the delegates and spectators dispersed. A messenger had been standing by his pony at the foot of the Potala, a message from Younghusband with all the details of the signed Convention already folded away in his pouch. He was now given the signal to mount his pony to begin his forty-eight-hour ride to Changlo Manor, where the good news was telegraphed down the line first, followed by the exact terms of the treaty, clause by clause.

If getting up the slippery steps of the Potala had been difficult, it proved twice as hard going down. 'It was the funniest sight imaginable,' wrote George Preston in his letter to his wife, 'to see officers hanging on to the walls, Tommies, anything they could catch hold of.' One of the few officers who succeeded in retaining his dignity was the General, who had thought to wear a pair of India-rubber boots. Francis Younghusband's letter to Helen, written immediately after his return to Lhalu Mansion late that afternoon, was altogether more serious: 'Just one line to say I have completed the greatest success of my life – the signing of the treaty in the Grand Lama's palace. You will know up in Simla how it is regarded by Govt. There are no two opinions about it . . . Every one was in excellent temper & the whole thing went off splendidly.' To his father Younghusband wrote gleefully that he had been able to 'ram the whole treaty down their throats . . . I have thus secured trade marts at Gyantse & Gartok (in W. Tibet). I have got Chumbi for 75 years. I have got Russia out for ever, I have got permission for the Gyantse agent to come to Lhasa & I have got a lakh of rupees a year for Govt for 75 years the payment of which by the Tibetans yearly at Darjiling will gradually be looked upon as a tribute & be I hope the means of gradually tying them to us.' This, from Francis Younghusband's point of view, was what the whole treaty was about. The Chumbi Valley was, in his own words, 'the key to Tibet . . . the only strategical point of value in the whole north-eastern frontier', and he wanted his country to have it, so that Britain might order the future destiny of Tibet.

That night the Tibet Commissioner was the guest of honour at a dinner hosted by the General. Both parties could now afford to be magnanimous: Younghusband had got his treaty, and Macdonald could now bring his troops back within the time limit he had set. And the General was indeed magnanimous. Before the meal he approached Younghusband and, by the latter's account, apologised for overreacting: 'He quite recognises it & came round to me and said I had got the better of him and trusted that we should have no more "even apparent friction" in future.' And at the dinner itself the General stood up and, again by Younghusband's account, 'made a very nice speech in which he said that everybody admired boldness & no one could say that I was not bold'. What James Macdonald's private thoughts were on that occasion can only be guessed at.

13

Picking up the Pieces

As soon as it became known that an agreement had been reached between the Tibetan Government and the *pelings* and that the latter would soon leave Lhasa, the atmosphere in the city and in the surrounding monasteries changed. The hostility evaporated and even the monks professed friendship. On 8 September all the Tibetan prisoners-of-war were paraded in the courtyard of Lhalu Mansion and each was presented with five rupees before being released, while the Tibetans for their part set free a number of men gaoled for helping foreigners to enter Tibet. One of them was the now elderly steward of the Palla estate at Gyantse, sentenced to life imprisonment for showing hospitality to the Bengali explorer-spy Sarat Chandra Das back in 1884. His first moment of freedom was witnessed by Edmund Candler: 'The old man's chains had been removed from his limbs that morning for the first time in twenty years, and he came in blinking at the unaccustomed light like a blind man miraculously restored to sight.'

First the British officers and then the troops were allowed into the city in small parties, to shop in the bazaars and see the sights, although always carrying their arms and under escort. Private Sampson's turn came on 20 September and after his squad had been marched into the open square in front of the Jokhang and reminded of the alarm signal – 'a rifle shot or one long shrill whistle' – he and his pal Bob were allowed to wander down the bazaar-cum-pilgrimage circuit known as the Barkhor that surrounded the Jokhang: 'We then commenced to roam through the bazaars. I bought several small things broaches & rings. After rambling 2 hours Bob & I were going back to the square when we noticed a bottle of Guinness stout. The fellow wanted 3 Rs for it (4 shillings). No deal. We fell in & marched out of the city.'

News that Tibetan curios had fetched high prices at Christie's auction house in London encouraged many officers to buy whatever they could find in the city. 'I have collected about £10 worth of Lhassa Curios,' wrote Captain Mainprise of the RAMC to his wife. He had purchased 'rings, necklaces, ear-rings, chatelaines and cup holders', mostly of silver set with turquoise stones, while noting that the demand was driving up prices: 'Some of the officers are spending hundreds of rupees on really worthless things, but as they have come from Lhassa they consider they all are of value.' Curios acquired in the earlier stages of the campaign could also be bought from their own sepoys with no questions asked, 'often at an absurd price, much more than they are worth'.

The city's arsenal was visited and, to the disappointment of the forward-policy men, found to be devoid of Russian rifles. Lhasa's 'rifle factory' turned out to be little more than a cottage workshop run by two Indian Muslim renegades. 'During the whole campaign,' Edmund Candler had now to admit, 'we did not come across more than thirty Russian Government rifles, and these must have drifted into Tibet from Mongolia . . . The reports of Russian arms found in Tibet have been very much exaggerated.' The whole business of Russian influence and the Czar's ambitions was quietly dropped. The series of devastating defeats inflicted on the Russians by land and sea in the Russo-Japanese war begun in February of that year had in any case dramatically altered the balance of power in Asia, so reducing the Russian threat.

More football matches were played and race-meetings held, with the Shapés and other Tibetan dignitaries often appearing as guests of honour. A special *puggal* or mad gymkhana held for the troops included a mule-back race over hurdles that no one won because no one finished, a Tibetan stretcher-bearers' race that ended in a free fight between the participants, a wheelbarrow race for the Gurkhas in which the winning 'wheelbarrow' lost several teeth and part of his nose 'through the eagerness of his pusher', and a wrestling match in which the champion, a Pathan, was disqualified after he was found to have bitten through the tendons of his opponent's knee.

A traditional Tibetan play with masked dancers was staged in the central courtyard of Lhalu Mansion: it started at 7.45 in the morning and lasted all day, and 'It was still going on at 5 p.m. when I left,' wrote Hatter Bailey to his parents. 'I believe it takes several days to do it fully. The thing was mostly singing and dancing – During the dance they used to turn wonderful cartwheels – The plot which was very hard to follow was this. The King of India sent a boy to get pearls from the sea. He was met by demons who ate him but as he was an incarnation it did him no harm and some fairies rescued him in a boat & he brought the pearls back.'

While encamped on the Plain of Wild Asses Bailey had at first been unable to satisfy his seemingly inexhaustible appetite for *shikar*, but was then recommended by Younghusband for a place on an expedition to the lower Tsangpo. He thus spent his remaining days in Lhasa in the company of Captains Rawling and Ryder of the Survey of India as they worked to map the surrounding countryside.

Sightseeing visits to some of the nearby monasteries were arranged, and the Nechung Oracle's residence just outside Lhasa proved a popular draw. The current incumbent had fled the city after the disastrous outcome of his predictions regarding the defeat of the Great Elephant from the South, but Dr Waddell and other visitors were received 'with smiling affability' by the monks who served the oracle, and found the shrine surprisingly neat and clean, and disappointingly free of displays of devil-worship. Waddell and the other doctors also toured Lhasa's famous medical college, dramatically positioned on the high summit of the city's second hill, Chakpori. Here Waddell questioned the 'high priest of the Temple of Medicine' at length about the philosophy underlying the Tibetan system of diagnosis and treatment, and found it to be 'saturated with absurdity'.

What did finally impress Dr Waddell, however, was the Regent, the Ti Rimpoche, who invited him to tea at his monastery in the north-eastern outskirts of Lhasa after hearing that he was the foreigners' leading authority on Tibetan religion. With David Macdonald acting as their intermediary, the two men sat sipping tea together while each questioned the other about his religion, seeking to find common ground – but with little success. The Regent was disappointed to learn that the Buddha was not to be found in the pages of the Christian scriptures and, when Waddell replied that the two creeds had much in common, particularly on the doctrine of 'peace and goodwill to all men', complained bitterly that the English had no religion at all. 'On my enquiring why he thought so,' wrote Waddell, 'he replied deliberately and emphatically: "Because I know it! Because I see it for myself in the faces and actions of your people! They have hard hearts, and are specially trained to take life and to fight like very giant Titans who war even against the Gods!" ' When Waddell expostulated that a military expedition was not a fair test of a nation's religiosity, the Ti Rimpoche again forcefully expressed his feelings: ' "It is not only your military, but *all* your people, even those who are not military! Your are all the same, except (here he added somewhat apologetically, probably out of deference to my feelings) you doctors, of whose humane work I have heard; but all the others are utterly devoid of religion!" ' One might wonder how the Regent had come to this conclusion, for the only Englishman he had met face to face who did not wear military uniform was Francis Younghusband. For all their differences, Dr Waddell took away from his meeting with the Ti Rimpoche 'the remembrance of a noble personality'.

On 13 September the first telegraphed replies from Simla arrived at Lhalu Mansion. 'It was a great day for me,' Francis was able to tell Helen, for all the telegrams were full of congratulations: a personal message from the Acting Viceroy, Lord Ampthill, another from Lord Kitchener, a third from the Government of India's Foreign Secretary, Louis Dane, and a fourth, forwarded by Lord Ampthill, from the King himself – 'an unprecedented honour for a political mission I believe'. Three days later came the telegram Younghusband had been waiting for most eagerly, from the Secretary of State for India, St John Brodrick. It, too, glowed with praises. 'They are all pleased as Punch,' Younghusband wrote to tell his father, '& think I am a great diplomatist.' It looked then as if his extraordinary gamble had come off. A second celebratory-cum-farewell dinner was held at Lhalu Mansion that night, to which all the officers were invited. The meal consisted of Potage Potala, followed by Dalai Lama Cutlets, Penlop's Poulet and Oeufs à la Shapé, ending with Amban Apricots. What was drunk that night is not recorded, but since a supply convoy had arrived from Chumbi on 14 September with a load of whisky it was certainly not commissariat rum.

Brigadier-General Macdonald's deadline of 15 September had now come and gone. Although plans for the return were ready to be implemented, the necessary permission from Simla was unaccountably delayed as Army Headquarters and the Political Department argued over whether the Mission's objectives had indeed been achieved. Overnight rain had become noticeably heavier, leaving the camp flooded most mornings, and the snow on the surrounding hills no longer melted in the afternoon sun but had become a permanent blanket. Twelve degrees of frost were reported from Gyantse. An urgent bulk order went out to the seamstresses of Lhasa for the heavy, long-sleeved Tibetan outer garment of yak and goat wool known as the *chuba*, worn hitched up round the waist but extending almost to the ground when released.

At last, on 22 September, permission to move came through and the General was able to give orders that the army was to pack up and leave on the following day. 'We shall have to move quickly before the winter snows commence,' Corporal Percy Coath noted in his diary. 'Chinese Amban had farewell tea with General Macdonald and Colonel Younghusband today. Everyone is laughing and jolly.'

That same night, as the temporary incumbents of Lhalu Mansion were completing the last of their packing, a messenger arrived with the first frantic telegram from London conveying the news that the British Government had woken to what the Tibet Commissioner had done on its behalf. It included a request that Colonel Younghusband delay his departure from Lhasa for three weeks so as to renegotiate the treaty, removing the three unauthorised sections relating to the payment of the indemnity over seventy-five years, the occupation of the Chumbi Valley for that length of time, and the Separate Agreement giving the British Trade Agent in Gyantse the right to visit Lhasa. This was couched not as an order but as a request, and Younghusband's response was to put the telegram to one side and continue his preparations for departure in the morning.

It was evidently the Tibet Commissioner's intention to leave quietly and travel fast, taking only a squadron of Mounted Infantry under the command of Hatter Bailey by way of escort. In the event his plans were forestalled by the unexpected appearance of the Ti Rimpoche, come to bid him and his escort commander farewell. To Younghusband's surprise and joy the old man presented him with a small bronze Buddha: 'As the reverend old Regent rose from his seat and put the present into my hand, he said with real impressiveness that he had none of the riches of this world, and could only offer me this simple image. Whenever he looked upon an image of Buddha he thought only of peace, and he hoped that whenever I looked on it I would think kindly of Tibet.'

Although still intending to set off without any sort of ceremony, Francis Younghusband was unable to resist a request from the 32nd Sikh Pioneers, the troops who had been with him almost from the first to the last moment of his Tibet adventure, that he should ride past their lines: 'When I reached them I found the whole regiment turned out – not on parade but quite informally – & as I passed they all shouted out their "Fateh" (victory) cry and then gave three cheers. All the native officers came rushing up to shake hands and the cheering went on till I was well out of camp. It was all most touching from being so spontaneous and so fervent ... I could have got the whole of that force to follow me anywhere and they would have stayed a dozen winters in Lhasa if it had rested with me to ask them.' Nor was this an end to the farewells, for a mile down the road a large tent had been erected overnight and here Younghusband found the four Shapés and a number of leading officials waiting to bid him and his officers farewell: 'Tea was served, and then, with many protestations of friendship, we shook hands for the last time, remounted our ponies, and rode away.'

Six years later, when Francis Younghusband came to set down his version of events, he wrote that at the end of that first day's ride he climbed to a high point above his camp and looked back up the Kyi Chu valley towards Lhasa. It was the first opportunity he had had for months to be entirely alone in the high country that meant so much to him. Despite the alarming telegram of the night before, he was still convinced that he had pulled off the greatest coup of his life, and he now experienced an overwhelming sense of peace that was almost in the nature of an epiphany:

> As I now looked towards that mysterious purply haze in which the sacred city was once more wrapped, I no longer had cause to dread the hatred it might hide. From it came only the echo of the Lama's words of peace, and with all the warmth still on me of that impressive farewell message, and bathed in the insinuating influences of the dreamy autumn evening, I was insensibly suffused with an almost intoxicating sense of elation and goodwill. The exhilaration of the moment grew and grew till it thrilled through me with overpowering intensity. Never again could I think evil, or ever again be at enmity with any man.

If the ever-fanciful Lieutenant Bethell's account of events is to be believed, he last saw the Tibet Commissioner some three weeks later as he surmounted the Jelep La and began the descent into the Indian plains: 'This scribe saw Younghusband at the top of the pass, looking southward, with who could guess what of thankfulness in his clean and steadfast heart. There and then it was borne in on us that the reality of leadership lies . . . in sheer dogged personality . . . and when, in addition, the leader commands the faith and affection of every man of his following, what, indeed, shall withstand him?'

But thankfulness must have been the last thing on Francis Younghusband's mind, for first at Gyantse and again at Chumbi he had opened a succession of telegrams each more dire than the one before. Finally, when he and his escort were one day's ride short of Darjeeling, where Helen and his infant daughter Eileen awaited him, Younghusband received the letter that destroyed all his hopes of a distinguished career taking him to the highest tiers of the Indian Political Service. Here he learned that the British Government, from a very angry Prime Minister and a 'quite frantic'

Secretary of State for India downwards, was preparing not only to repudiate the treaty he had worked so hard to achieve but also to 'throw over' its Tibet Commissioner. He was told that he had acted 'in direct disobedience of orders' in the matter of the three contentious clauses in the Convention and was, moreover, guilty of further insubordination in leaving Lhasa without attempting to amend the treaty as instructed. A letter from Lord Curzon, telling him that his name would live in history and that he had done his part 'skilfully and nobly', was small consolation.

In Lhasa, it had been announced that before Macdonald's army marched away, alms to the city's poor would be distributed on the Plain of Wild Asses. On the morning of 23 September, as the troops paraded in marching order, their tents struck and the mules loaded, a vast crowd streamed out from the city's western gate – intent not so much on bidding the foreigners farewell as on securing what they could in the way of handouts. 'They rolled up in hundreds and hundreds,' recorded Henry Newman, the Reuters man – so many, in fact, that the troops had to set to work marshalling them into seated rows. Chaotic scenes then followed, for 'as soon as the beggars in one row had got their money they all dashed round to the back and formed another row'. This was followed by a noisy mass protest staged by the women seamstresses of Lhasa, who had not yet been paid for the hundreds of *chubas* they had tailored. The mule-train bringing up the silver rupees due to them had by chance been delayed at the Chaksam ferry-crossing and they were understandably fearful that they were being fleeced. Asked to nominate a male representative to collect the money on their behalf, they refused, declaring vociferously that 'there was not a man in Lhasa who could be trusted'. The outcome was that the seamstresses tagged on at the back of the column. 'So the women marched with us also,' wrote Newman, 'not only the wage-earners but many others who came for the fun of the thing, and also a number of men who had heard from our Tibetan stretcher-bearers and doolie-bearers of the glories of civilisation . . . So when we started on our return journey what one saw was not a long, orderly column of troops and transport but what looked like the emigration of a nation, for strewn all along the road were parties of Tibetans, men, women and children, with all their household goods on their backs.'

Many of the troops had also acquired pets of various kinds. The gunners of the 7th British Mountain Battery had captured two of the Dalai Lama's wild asses that grazed in the fields surrounding the camp, and these two female *kiang* now joined the column as regimental mascots. But mostly it was dogs. 'It was a touching sight,' recorded Mark Synge, 'to see great bearded men sometimes leading, but as often as not carrying, on the march dainty little lap-dogs, of kinds that resembled the Pomeranian, the Skye terrier, or the King Charles spaniel.' Thus the Lhasa Apso made its first known debut on the Western stage. 'One or two Tibetan mastiffs – more like huge Welsh collies than mastiffs – also accompanied us.'

As the General, his Principal Medical Officer and several members of his staff led off the last of the three columns, an unexpected visitor rode up to them: the Ti Rimpoche. He presented James Macdonald with a small gilt image of the Buddha, just as he had Francis Younghusband, but then, to Edmund Candler's surprise, 'held his hands over General Macdonald in benediction, and solemnly blessed him for his clemency and moderation in sparing the monasteries and people'. He wished him and his men a safe return to India, and asked that they should always think kindly of Tibet. He then asked Austine Waddell to write to him, shook hands all round and rode slowly away, 'evidently oppressed by the cares of State which now, at this crisis, must weigh heavily on his shoulders'.

The men who marched off that day did so with mixed emotions – as did some of those who watched them go. 'Quite a number of us were loath to leave Lhasa,' wrote Henry Newman. 'I lingered among the last. Many Tibetans were weeping. Whether they missed us or their women and children I do not know, but I think the bulk of the inhabitants were really sorry to see us go.' For Lieutenant Thomas Carey, it was 'a treat not to have that Potala everlastingly staring one in the face', but as Private Sampson marched away he found that 'I kept turning round to look. I wondered how long it would be before White men visited this city again. Had the last farewell look as we turned to the right on the road which leads to the Daipung [Drepung] Monastery.'

More cables had been installed at the Chaksam ferry, which

meant that the entire army was across within forty-eight hours, the only mishap being the drowning of one of the Mountain Battery's two wild asses. A steeper but shorter route over the mountains west of the Khamba La brought the last of the three columns to Gyantse within twelve days. 'The country was happier-looking,' noted Corporal Percy Coath in his diary, 'with people who had disappeared on our advance, but had now returned to their homes and were busy getting their crops etc. into the granaries before winter came on them. They regarded us with kindly smiles, and seemed very happy that all was over.' Even in Gyantse, where the army had wreaked so much havoc, the local population seemed remarkably cheerful, even more so when it became known that the bulk of the supplies that had been so painstakingly and painfully brought up from the plains of India were to be abandoned. The troops, porters and camp-followers were allowed to take away as much tea, *ghee* or clarified butter and *ghoor* or molasses as they could carry. What remained was made up into packages and handed out to the local populace, who, according to Mark Synge, 'came up and, regarding the whole affair as a huge joke, went away laden with bundles selected at random from, as it were, a huge bran-pie. Rum was withheld from them, but I should have liked to see the effect of their consumption of some of the things they got, as, for instance, of an unsuspecting draught of neat lime-juice, or a mouthful of chillies.'

Before they moved on from Gyantse a final parade was held, at which Brigadier-General James Macdonald made what was his farewell speech to the troops. He, too, now knew that he was going back to face many questions and possible charges relating to his condonation of looting and the two occasions on which he had threatened Younghusband with the withdrawal of his escort. Whatever his officers thought of the General, little word of his weaknesses seems to have filtered down to the BORs. This last speech of his so impressed one soldier that he noted down its highlights in his diary. 'He said he was proud to have had command of the men for the Expedition,' wrote Private Sampson, '& it was only owing to the way in which all had worked together that the object of the Expedition had been gained. He said we had beaten all records by crossing over & through Passes higher than the Mtns of Europe & had reached an altitude never reached by civilized troops. He has communicated with the King through the proper authorities asking for some special recognition which he had reason to believe would be granted to them.'

The army left behind in Gyantse a Trade Agent in the person of Captain Frank O'Connor, together with a surgeon and a small military escort drawn from the 40th Pathans. It also left behind a small survey party under Captain Rawling. It had been hoped to send a much larger exploration party eastwards down the Tsangpo to resolve the mystery of how and where the great river entered India, but this plan had been vetoed at the last minute after a mail convoy was ambushed by what were presumed to be Tibetan bandits. Instead they would be travelling westwards up the Tsangpo to its source and beyond, mapping as they went. With them went Lieutenant F. M. 'Hatter' Bailey, now full of hopes again, for Colonel Younghusband had promised to do what he could to get him into the Indian Political Service and, what was more, the crossing of Tibet from east to west promised much in the way of *shikar*. 'There ought', he wrote to his parents, 'to be very good shooting on the way.' By a quirk of fate, one of Bailey's first discoveries was made at the scene of the ambush of the mail party: he examined the frozen bodies of the Tibetan mule-drivers and found they had been killed not with Tibetan weapons but by British-made rifles. His conclusion, never publicly acknowledged, was that the murders had been committed by Indian troops frustrated by the lack of looting opportunities, the most likely culprits being a section of Pathans from the 2nd Mounted Infantry.

The route from Gyantse south to the Tibetan border had now been transformed by the engineers and sappers. As well as the line of telegraph posts stretching away to either horizon there was what amounted to Tibet's first grand trunk road, upon which had trundled daily long convoys of Macdonald's yak- and mule-drawn *ekka* carts. This road would remain as the one permanent British mark on the Tibetan landscape. It also made the return march a very different experience from that endured six months earlier – until, that is, the last column was approaching the summit of the Tang La. Up to this point the good weather they had enjoyed had confounded the pessimists, but now it changed suddenly and savagely, a thick blizzard sweeping down on the men, mules and yaks as they laboured over this bleakest of passes. This same blizzard overtook the second column as it was leaving Phari, and continued south to strike the first just as the men were settling into their tents at Chumbi, beginning as a rain squall that flooded out every tent but turning to heavy, wet snow in the course of the night. 'We kept awake,' wrote Lieutenant Carey, '& smoked cigarettes & ate chocolate till daybreak. Just before daylight shouts were heard all over the camp, owing to the weight of snow. Four officers' tents and a good many of the men's bell tents collapsed.' Here there was only one casualty: a camp-follower found suffocated under a tarpaulin. But higher up the situation was far more serious. Three sepoys died of hypothermia in the second column and seventy-two were brought in to Chumbi in a state of collapse.

The third column, caught on the Tang La, suffered worst of all, and Henry Newman secured the expedition's last exclusive for Reuters, which appeared under the headline 'The picturesque suffering of the troops'. He later recalled how, as his pony struggled over the pass along with the rest, 'an officer who had ridden up to me cried suddenly: "Look! The Retreat from Moscow!" And, indeed, looking back, one saw those struggling and forlorn groups almost exactly as shown in the famous picture. There were animals being pulled along, half dead, there were men with bent heads, stumbling as they walked, and other men leading their companions who, having lost their snow-glasses, were now beginning to lose their sight.' Forced to make camp on the exposed plateau above Phari, the column remained snowbound for two days before finally struggling down through deep snow and in blazing sunshine. Many of the men had lost their snow-goggles months before and wore darkened bandages over their eyes, but even those who still had their goggles found them all but useless, so bright were the sun's reflections on the snow.

Among those caught up in this agonising march was Austine Waddell: 'Every one tramped on painfully with bent head through the deep snow, shading his eyes at intervals with his hand, and possessed by the one thought, to escape snow-blindness . . . About 200 of the men were snow-blind, and it was pathetic to see them led helplessly along by their fellows.' The sun's reflected rays also burnt any exposed flesh, leaving faces severely blistered and raw. It was the Tibetan Chang Tang's final demonstration of its capacity to chastise those who failed to show it the respect that was its due, and it caused many to reflect on how very different things might have been had the expedition not been so extraordinarily lucky in its brushes with the Tibetan winter. James Macdonald was among those in the second column, and it can hardly have escaped his mind that here was vindication of his judgement in setting the deadline of 15 September as the last safe day to leave Lhasa.

There were delays in Chumbi as each regiment and unit awaited its turn to be released. All beards were shaved off and hair was trimmed to regulation length. Yak-wool *chubas*, battered Gilgit boots, frayed sheepskin coats and other winter garments were exchanged for the smart uniforms that had been held in store for their return. A heroes' welcome of bunting, brass bands, guards of honour and applauding crowds greeted the Royal Fusiliers as they marched into Darjeeling on 28 October. Two days later they were back at their depot at Lebong, finding the air they breathed strangely oppressive and constantly scalding their lips and tongues in drinking tea made with water at normal boiling temperature. 'We were glad to get back,' noted Corporal Percy Coath in his diary, 'but equally glad were we to have had such a wonderful experience, in being privileged to have visited one, if not the most, mysterious country in the world, and the most wonderful.'

As the members of the Tibet Mission and the army that had escorted it went their various ways, its two main protagonists acted entirely in character. James Macdonald was reunited with his wife Alice in Darjeeling and then sat down to write the final despatch that every army commander has to compose at the end of a campaign. It was as bland and neutral a document as it was possible to produce, the only hint of personal opinion lying in the General's commendations for military decorations and mentions in despatches, of which members of his staff, the engineers and the supply and transport officers received the bulk of the citations. His old friend Colonel and Doctor Austine Waddell, judged by some to have been exceedingly remiss in fulfilling his duties as Principal Medical Officer, was recommended for and appointed a Companion of the Order of the Bath. Two officers who signally failed to receive the high marks of approbation widely considered their due were Lieutenant-Colonel Herbert Brander, who had commanded the unauthorised first assault on the Karo La, and Captain William Ottley, the man who had raised the Mounted Infantry and led them throughout the expedition.

The General's despatch also contained an official abstract of the casualties sustained by the force: 5 British Officers, 1 Native Officer and 28 Native Rank and File killed; 19 British Officers, 4 Native Officers, 11 British Rank and File and 116 Native Rank and File wounded. It omitted fatalities sustained outside the battlefield, such as those among the Royal Fusiliers in the explosion at Gyantse Jong, or the scores enlisted into the coolie corps, yak corps, PWD road gangs and other quasi-military support units who succumbed to exposure, frost-bite or other fatal causes in the course of the campaign. Tibetan casualties went unlisted because in many instances they were never ascertained. Lieutenant-Colonel Brander estimated that thirteen hundred Tibetans had been killed up to the capture of Palla, at which point he gave up; this was before the assaults on Tsechen and Naini monasteries, the assault on Gyantse Jong and the second battle of Karo La. The total figure of Tibetans killed or fatally wounded in fighting was certainly in excess of two thousand and possibly as high as three thousand.

Once the General had delivered his despatch on 11 November he took sick leave to recover his health. He appears to have made no official effort to defend his actions or to answer the charges laid against him by the Tibet Commissioner and others. Perhaps the mauling he received after writing of his African experiences caused him to stay silent. Francis Younghusband, by contrast, fought hard and fiercely for his Tibet Convention and, when it was clear that it was to be repudiated and renegotiated, fought even more fiercely to save his reputation. He travelled at once to Simla, where he was received with understanding by Lord Ampthill and his friends in the Government of India's Foreign Office and most unsympathetically by Lord Kitchener, whom he found to be 'more severe than any one'. Ampthill's understanding extended to allowing Younghusband to read through all the secret papers and correspondence relating to his Mission, from which he concluded that it was London and not Simla that was bent on throwing him over. His response was to catch the first train to Bombay and the first steamship home, halting only briefly at Port Said to confer with Lord Curzon as he returned to India to resume his Viceroyalty.

In England, meanwhile, Younghusband's relatives and friends had responded to his pleas by lobbying whoever would listen, so energetically indeed that their efforts provoked protests in Whitehall about undue influence being brought to bear. The Special Honours List for the Tibet Mission and Mission Escort due to be published in mid December now became a battlefield upon which the champions of Younghusband and Curzon on the one hand and Macdonald and Kitchener on the other manoeuvred on behalf of their respective candidates. Since James Macdonald was already a Companion of the Order of the Bath the logical promotion was to appoint him a Knight Companion of that Order (KCB), and Lord Ampthill argued that Colonel Younghusband could not well be given less. But Brodrick and others in the Cabinet were adamantly opposed to Younghusband being similarly honoured, declaring that since he was already a Companion of the Order of the Indian Empire (CIE) – distinctly inferior to the Order of the Bath – the logical progression for him was to KCIE. Despite Lord Ampthill's protests that this was a 'shabby and inadequate' reward for Younghusband's endeavours, and despite a final rearguard action by the King (kept fully briefed by an old friend of Younghusband *père* who was his aide-de-camp), this was settled as Younghusband's due. Francis Younghusband's ship docked at Tilbury on 2 December and he made haste to put his case. On 15 December, the day before the Special Honours List was due to be published in the *London Gazette*, the War Office was informed that the galley proofs must be amended. The name of Major and Brevet Colonel (Brigadier-General) James Ronald Leslie Macdonald, CB, Royal Engineers, was to be struck from the list of those appointed Knight Commander of the Order of the Bath and added to that for Knight Commander of the Order of the Indian Empire – joining that of Francis Younghusband. Even this, it seems, was not enough to satisfy one member of the Younghusband family, for it was afterwards reported that on hearing the news that the General was to receive exactly the same reward as her husband, Lady Younghusband – as she now was – 'burst into tears and had a severe heart attack'.

So far as one can judge, (now full) Colonel Sir James Macdonald, KCIE, CB, and Lady Macdonald took this public slap rather better than the Younghusbands. It has been said that the General ended his military career in deserved obscurity, but this was not the case. He retained Kitchener's support and was given command of the Bengal Presidency Brigade at Fort William, Calcutta, followed by that of the Lucknow Infantry Brigade in 1907. He was promoted to major-general at what his obituarist in the *Royal Engineers Journal*, 'H.H.A.', noted as 'the, then, early age of 46', and in 1909 made GOC Mauritius, a sinecure he held until 1912, when he resigned on medical advice and returned to Scotland. He volunteered for service in 1914 but was deemed medically unfit. 'Had his health and vigour not been unduly sapped by the ceaseless labours of earlier days, he would undoubtedly have risen to still loftier heights,' opined that same obituarist. Macdonald became Colonel-Commandant of the Royal Engineers in 1924 and was also Lord-Lieutenant of Aberdeenshire. Aside from his military interests, 'Retiring Mac' seems to have had a well-concealed passion for botany, as he spent the last fifteen years of his life engaged in what he hoped would become the standard reference work on the subject. 'His labours had nearly reached completion and he was contemplating the publication of his work', declared 'H.H.A.', 'when struck down by his last illness.' He died in Bournemouth in June 1927 at the age of 65. He and his wife had no children and his reference book was never published.

Macdonald's nemesis, Sir Francis Younghusband, KCIE, was fêted in England, lauded by the British press, received in private and sympathetic audience by the King, and greeted with rapturous applause when he lectured first at the Royal Geographical Society in London and again at the Scottish Royal Geographical Society in Edinburgh, where he stayed with that society's honorary secretary, Sir Frederick Bailey, father of young Hatter Bailey, who had much to thank him for. He received honorary doctorates from the universities of Edinburgh, Bristol and Cambridge, and was made an honorary member of the Alpine Club. Everywhere he went he was recognised and treated as a national hero. Meanwhile, in India his old friend and patron Lord Curzon was having problems of his own in what developed into a power struggle between himself on the one side and St John Brodrick and Lord Kitchener on the other. In August 1905 Curzon was provoked into offering his resignation, which was promptly accepted – but not before he had rewarded Younghusband with perhaps the juiciest of the few political plums open to him, the Residency of Kashmir, promoting him over the heads of more than thirty more senior political officers.

Though Kashmir was not the most important princely state in India, it was the largest and certainly the most mountainous, and it gave the Younghusbands three very comfortable years. But Sir Francis's judgement was no longer trusted, political decisions relating to Kashmir and the princely states were taken by Lord Curzon's successor without his opinion being sought, and it very soon became obvious that without Curzon's protection he had no future in the Indian Political Service. This was confirmed when in 1908 the one position he coveted, that of Chief Commissioner of the North-West Frontier Province, went to George Roos-Keppel, a true frontiersman whose dealings with the tribesmen of the border regions was based on a genuine respect for their customs and culture rather than the contempt that characterised Younghusband's dealings with the Tibetans and other 'lesser breeds without the law'. Younghusband retired from India at the age of 46 with no clear future but convinced that the 'greatest phase' of his life was about to begin. Yet despite the support of a wide circle of loyal friends from Curzon downwards, nothing seemed to work for him. He tried and failed to enter Parliament, Helen's nerves worsened and she fell into a deep depression from which she never fully emerged, their finances became increasingly precarious and, to cap it all, Sir Francis was run over by a motor-car in Switzerland and gravely injured. The end result was that he took to religion and began a spiritual crusade for a universal world faith that became the central feature of his life from 1912 until his death in 1942 at the age of 79. It was a journey full of surprises, chronicled most sensitively by Patrick French in his biography of Younghusband.

When Francis Younghusband was carried to his grave in Lytchett

Minster churchyard, the bronze Buddha presented to him by the Ti Rimpoche rested on his coffin. It subsequently became the focus of an unseemly squabble between his daughter Eileen and the family of Lady Lees, with whom he had taken up. Patrick French subsequently tracked it down to a biscuit box in the basement of the Royal Geographical Society.

As Patrick French also discovered, Francis Younghusband at his death left two other women besides Dame Eileen Younghusband (as she became) who regarded it as their duty to preserve and protect his reputation. Compared with some of Younghusband's more private correspondence his Tibet papers appear to have come off pretty lightly — but that filleting did take place is undeniable, if not by his daughter then possibly by the man himself. As French has observed, there were many Younghusbands, but among them the one who led the Tibet Mission was perhaps the least attractive.

The other members of the Tibet Mission had equally mixed fortunes. Frank O'Connor, now a major and the Trade Agent in Gyantse, was the man charged with renegotiating the Convention, which he did successfully from Changlo Manor. The sum of the indemnity was reduced to a third of the amount set by Younghusband, the period of the occupation of Chumbi Valley was reduced to three years, and the extra clause allowing the Trade Agent to visit Lhasa for consultations was dropped altogether. One of O'Connor's first actions as Trade Agent was to order a Baby Peugeot, which was carried over the Himalayas in pieces and reassembled at Phari Jong. It was said to have made a number of successful runs between Phari and Gyantse, and O'Connor often took Tibetan guests in it for spins, although always with a number of ponies following on behind to tow it back to Changlo Manor — for it almost invariably broke down, its carburettor unable to adjust to the thin air. At the end of O'Connor's tenure the car was again taken to pieces and conveyed to Lhasa, where it was subsequently found many years later in someone's back yard.

What is puzzling about Frank O'Connor is his long silence in the aftermath of the Tibet Mission and the British Government's repudiation of its leader's actions. This was the man who had witnessed every twist and turn in the negotiations from the first meeting with the Dalai Lama's delegates at Khamba Jong in July 1903 to the last at Lhasa in October 1904. No one was more intimately associated with Francis Younghusband or championed him more fiercely – in private at least – and no one was in a better position to defend him with chapter and verse. More than a quarter of a century passed before O'Connor set down his version of events, and when he finally did so he added disappointingly little to what was already in the public domain, merely reinforcing the received image of Francis Younghusband as 'at once a philosopher and a man of action . . . an ideal leader of men'. By the time *On the Frontier and Beyond: a Record of Thirty Years' Service* appeared in print O'Connor's *bête-noire* James Macdonald had been dead five years, so here was an ideal opportunity to set the record straight – yet the General is barely mentioned, with not a word about his alleged 'misdeeds'. Was this a case of forgive and forget, or had O'Connor learned discretion as the Government of India's man in Tibet? Not the latter, certainly, for where Anglo–Tibetan relations were concerned, O'Connor continued to march dangerously out of step.

O'Connor was always the forward-policy man. He became friendly with the young Panchen Lama in Shigatse – too friendly, as far as his neighbour in Sikkim and early patron, Claude White, was concerned. White later made it known that he thought O'Connor's behaviour 'quite improper for a British officer to adopt under any circumstances'. His main complaint was that O'Connor was plotting a madcap scheme whereby the British Government would supply the Panchen Lama with arms to enable him 'to throw off the yoke of the Lhassa Government, a measure calculated to create civil war in Tibet and a distinct breach in our Treaty obligations'. Relations between the two men eventually deteriorated to the point where White denounced O'Connor to the Government of India as 'highly excitable, easily biassed, very ready to lose his temper, often overbearing in his manner and apt under any strain to become hysterical and alarmist' – and quite unfit to hold any political post, 'especially in the frontier station of Tibet where, in dealing with both Tibetans and Chinese, the greatest tact, patience, and evenness of temperament combined with sound judgement are absolutely essential'. The words were uncannily similar to those which had been applied to Claude White himself by Francis

Younghusband four years earlier. Now, however, the Foreign and Political Department decided it had had enough of both White and O'Connor. The former was more or less ordered to retire, which he did in 1908, and died soon afterwards in Bhutan while working for his old friend the Tongsa Penlop as his agent. Frank O'Connor was moved to a less sensitive post, and his place as Trade Agent was taken by the young officer who was as much his own protégé as Francis Younghusband's, Frederick M. 'Hatter' Bailey.

Over the next two decades Captain and then Major Bailey matured into British India's most daring player of the Great Game, as well as becoming a distinguished explorer, naturalist and plant-hunter, although he never quite threw off his predilection for shooting whatever wild creature crossed his path. The Tibetan blue poppy, first noticed by him flowering abundantly in a meadow above the Field of Milk, the army's camp site below the Karo La, carries his name, *Meconopsis betonicifolia baileyi*. He and Claude White share joint honours as pioneer breeders of the Lhasa Apso.

Dr Austine Waddell took a path hardly less curious than that followed by Francis Younghusband, both men developing into what many would regard as cranks. His moment of glory came in Calcutta, when the four hundred mule-loads of 'rare and valuable manuscripts of Lamaist sacred works, images, religious paraphernalia of all descriptions, armour, weapons, paintings and porcelain' collected by him and his assistant David Macdonald were put on display at the Indian Museum in Calcutta. All but the porcelain was then divided between the Indian Museum (now the Calcutta Museum) and the British Museum, the Bodleian Library and the India Office Library (now the Oriental and India Office Collection of the British Library). The bulk of the porcelain was despatched to Lord Kitchener but, according to David Macdonald, 'many pieces of this consignment arrived at their destination damaged beyond repair'.

The exhibiting of the Tibet booty brought the issue of looting once more to the fore, with the vernacular press in India taking a hostile attitude towards the apparent official sanction of plundering. This resulted in a general closing of ranks. Dr Waddell let it be understood that the 'greater part' of his collection had been assembled before the attack on Changlo Manor in May 1904, noting that 'circumstances subsequently became unfavourable for procuring many additions': the implication was that he had bought much of his material using the ten thousand rupees allocated to him by the Government of India. He chose to stay silent on his role in the distribution of items taken from Gyantse Jong and Palkor Chode, and later claimed that much of what he had amassed for his own private collection was 'lost on the journey back from Lhasa'. However, in 1905 the Berlin Museum bought his 'Collection of Indian Antiquities' for a considerable sum, and in 1909 an incomplete set of the Kanjur belonging to one L. Austine Waddell was auctioned at Sotheby's. As it happened, quite a number of articles besides Waddell's were lost or damaged in transit between Gyantse and Darjeeling. According to Captain Mainprise, the RAMC surgeon, 'all the parcels were lost for weeks in an open shed, got thoroughly rotted in the rain and practically destroyed, labels, addresses, everything, and now nothing can be deciphered . . . The P. O. says it was the General's fault because he wouldn't provide transport.' Whether Macdonald really was responsible for holding back transport or not, the losses were considerable. Among those who suffered was Francis Younghusband, who never recovered photographs and other material he was planning to use in his book.

Although preceded by Perceval Landon's *The Opening of Tibet*, Edmund Candler's *The Unveiling of Lhasa*, Mark Synge's *To Lhassa at Last* (written under the pseudonym 'Powell Millington') and William Ottley's *With Mounted Infantry in Tibet*, Austine Waddell's *Lhasa and its Mysteries* was far and away the most authoritative of the many books written about the Younghusband Mission and the civilisation it broke in upon. It led to Dr Waddell's appointment as Professor of Tibetan at London University in 1906, which was followed after two years by his retirement to Scotland. At his meeting with the Ti Rimpoche in Lhasa, Waddell had been greatly disappointed to learn that there were no teachings of ancient wisdom preserved there by the 'Mahatmas' after the sinking of Atlantis. This Theosophical bent remained with him throughout his life and reappeared after the Great War (in which he lost his only son) in the form of a quest for evidence of the existence of an Aryan master race. This led to the publication of a series of books with such titles as *The Aryan Origin of the Alphabet*, in which he claimed that 'the Aryan Race, already known to be the foremost & and most highly evolved of the five races of mankind, was also in fact the Originator, Chief Developer & Chief Diffuser of the world's civilisation down the ages'. The outcome was his marginalisation as a serious scholar and, almost inevitably, identification in the 1930s with the Imperial Fascist League, the British version of Germany's Nazi party, a process only halted by his death in 1938. Perhaps his happiest memorial is the name given to the striped laughing thrush, *Babax waddelli*, collected by him near the Chaksam ferry in September 1904 along with two other Tibetan birds hitherto unknown to ornithologists.

If Dr Waddell gathered his booty with official sanction, more or less, others did not. Within weeks of the initial possession of Gyantse Jong, Tibetan curios were being offered for sale at the main London auction houses and elsewhere. In May 1905, for example, Major Iggulden, Macdonald's chief staff officer, sold no fewer than 169 artefacts to the British Museum. That looting took place in and around Gyantse is beyond dispute. By and large, it was indulged in with enthusiasm and without qualms wherever senior officers were prepared to turn a blind eye, and it extended beyond the battlefield to a number of monasteries. For this Macdonald, Waddell and Younghusband must all take a share of blame, the first for condoning it, the other two for perpetuating the belief that the lamas were oppressors of their own people and therefore the 'real' enemy.

How much of what was brought out of Tibet was looted and how much picked up on the battlefield or bought quite legitimately in the bazaars of Changlo, Gyantse and Lhasa will never be known, but a number of attics up and down Britain must hold such esoteric objects as thigh-bone trumpets or mahogany tsampa bowls whose purpose and origins are a mystery to their present owners. Captain Arthur Hadow's curios in the Royal Norfolk Regiment Museum are probably as representative as any of the collections brought back from Tibet in 1904. There are some sixty items, of which a third are weapons of one sort or another, battlefield trophies ranging from cannon balls fired by 'the big gun' at Changlo Manor to matchlocks 'captured at the fight at Tuna'. Of the remaining items more than half are of minor importance as artefacts: small brass bowls, handbells, wooden printing blocks, prayer-wheels, and the 'foot of a lammergaier eagle'; objects that could as easily have come from a local bazaar as anywhere else. Of the remaining items, perhaps half a dozen can be considered valuable objects of cultural importance. They include the apron of human bones looted after the capture of Gyantse Jong and such diverse articles as a set of carved book covers, the head of a statue 'broken off as image was too large to carry away' and a number of small statuettes. This pattern is repeated in the British Museum's and the V&A's collections of Tibetan artefacts: quite a number can be traced back to the Younghusband Mission, but none is among the better items on display. It suggests that looting, however distasteful as a practice, was far less damaging in cultural terms than the expedition's destruction of religious buildings and religious objects in and around Gyantse by shell-fire, demolition and fire.

In February 1905 it was announced that a campaign medal was to be awarded to all members of the Tibet Mission and to those who had served at or beyond Siliguri between 13 December 1903 and 23 September 1904, with in addition a clasp for those who had fought at Gyantse. In June 1906, at a parade at Windsor Castle, King Edward VII presented the Tibet Medal to eleven officers and 150 Other Ranks of those Royal Fusiliers who had seen service in Tibet and were still with the battalion. For some years afterwards the Royal Fusiliers lobbied to have 'TIBET 1904' listed on their colours as a battle honour, but although the campaign fulfilled all military criteria, it was denied them. Many of the officers and men who had been with the 1st Battalion, Royal Fusiliers in Tibet were young enough to fight and die in the First World War. Their CO, Lieutenant-Colonel Edward Cooper, commanded an infantry brigade and then a division in France. Lieutenant Walter Bowden-Smith, wounded in the assault on Gyantse Jong, was wounded again at Mons in August 1914 and died in a German hospital. Private Hannington, also wounded at Gyantse Jong, was awarded the DCM for gallantry at Fontaine-au-Bois in 1918. Lance-Corporal Alfred Dunning, extracts from whose diary appear briefly in these pages, was killed in action on the Western Front in October 1914. Corporal Percy Coath, another diarist, became the battalion's Regimental Sergeant-Major in 1916 and survived the war. Of Private Sampson, the liveliest of the Fusilier diarists in Tibet, nothing more is known after his service in India with the regiment. Probably the last surviving participant in the Tibet adventure was Jack Scarlett, who fought at Gallipoli and the Somme. He was wounded and discharged in 1917 – but lived on until 1977, when he died at the age of 96.

The one surviving *kiang* brought out of Tibet by 7th British Mountain Battery survived the sea-voyage home to England and was presented to the London Zoo. To the gunners' disgust she was briefly kidnapped by the Royal Fusiliers and paraded as a mascot when, after its return to England in January 1905, the regiment exercised its right to march through the City of London with 'drums beating, band playing, colours flying and bayonets fixed'. She died in 1915, having produced three foals – sire unknown, but most likely a wild ass from Mongolia – and her descendants are said to be alive and well in Whipsnade Zoo today.

Captain Arthur Hadow returned to England all too aware of the lethal powers of the machine-gun, for he had probably with his own hand on the trigger of his Maxim killed and wounded as many Tibetans as the rest of the force combined. He embarked on a personal crusade to impress upon the higher echelons of the War Office that this was the weapon of the future. The German Army drew the right conclusions, the British Army did not.

Of the two Indian Army officers selected by Francis Younghusband as destined for distinguished careers – William Ottley, who raised and ran the Mounted Infantry, and Seymour Sheppard, the explosives expert – only the latter lived up to his billing. Returning to England from Tibet, Sheppard, now a Brevet Major, entered and won the Singles Amateur Rackets Championships; he continued to compete well into his old age, winning the Army Singles Amateur Rackets Championships in 1921, aged 52. He retired from the Indian Army as a major-general after a long and successful career, and died in 1957 aged 88. William Ottley, however, did not fare so well. He returned to the 23rd Sikh Pioneers, but the rapid promotion he and many others must have seen as his due failed to materialise. Although he was never officially censured by Macdonald there can be no doubt that he was seen in some quarters as having been a little over-enthusiastic in his harrying of the enemy, and his men a little too close to free-booters for the Army's comfort. After a brief and apparently unre-warding interlude as a Political Agent in Perim he returned to the 23rd Pioneers and was with his regiment throughout the Great War. He ended in command of the two battalions of the 23rd in 1918, and finally retired from India with the rank of colonel in 1923. John Grant, who was awarded the Victoria Cross after his gallant scaling of the rock-face at Gyantse Jong at the head of the 8th Gurkha Rifles, fought with his regiment in the Great War in Persia and Mesopotamia, retired as Colonel-Commandant of the 10th Gurkha Rifles, and died in 1967 in his 89th year.

All the Indian units that went to Tibet fought in the two World Wars. After the Great War the 23rd and 32nd Sikh Pioneers were merged to become the 3rd Sikh Pioneers, which still serve in the Indian Army today. Similarly, the 40th Pathans were merged with other regiments drawn from the Punjab to become the 14th Punjab Regiment – now part of the Pakistan Army. The 8th Gurkha Rifles continued to serve the British Raj until 1947, their hour of glory coming in 1943 when their riflemen made a great name for themselves as exponents of jungle warfare against the Japanese in Burma. After Indian Independence the regiment remained an important component of the Indian Army, serving under Indian instead of British officers. The record for high-altitude warfare established first by the Pioneers and then by the Gurkhas at the first and second battles of Karo La lasted for the best part of ninety years. It has almost certainly been broken by Indian and Pakistani troops as they fight to secure the heights along the Line of Control in their apparently endless struggle for Kashmir.

That the Younghusband Mission inflicted considerable material damage on Tibet and its people is undeniable, but it was damage on a scale that pales into insignificance when compared to the invasion of Tibet by the Chinese People's Liberation Army in 1951 and the genocidal Cultural Revolution of 1966–7. Far more serious is the claim that the British invasion did incalculable politi-cal damage by laying Tibet open to a reassertion of Chinese authority. The leading proponent of this claim was Charles Bell, an assistant political officer in Sikkim under Claude White who later became an administrator of the Chumbi Valley during its brief period under British rule. Bell also became a close friend and ally of the 13th Dalai Lama, and it was his belief that 'By going in and then coming out again, we knocked the Tibetans down and left them for the first comer to kick. We created a political vacuum, which is always a danger. China came in and filled it, destroying Tibetan freedom, for she feared that if we came again we should keep the country. And Russia, in conformity with her warning, advanced into Mongolia, without any intention of retiring as we had retired from Lhasa.' The opposing argument put forward by Bell's critics is that the political vacuum created by the British invasion ended with the 13th Dalai Lama's final return to Lhasa in 1910. The Tibetans then turned against the Chinese, threw out the Amban and declared their country independent. Perhaps Tibet's real tragedy is that it then failed to build on that independence. Despite the 13th Dalai Lama's best efforts, Tibet's monastic and aristocratic hierarchies refused to modernise, clinging to their privileges and their isolationism. During the later years of the 13th Dalai Lama's rule, Britain came to be seen as a friend of Tibet and her influence was maintained through the person of the Trade Agent in Gyantse. But after the 13th Dalai Lama's death in 1933 the old Tibet very quickly reasserted itself and the links with British India were cut. A series of ineffectual regents who ruled Tibet during the 14th Dalai Lama's infancy and minority allowed China to reassert its control, culminating in the 'liberation' of Tibet by the Chinese People's Army in 1951.

The Younghusband Mission failed to bring Tibet into the twentieth century, but it did help to end Tibet's isolation. For Dr Waddell, this was its most important achievement: 'The earthly paradise of "The Living Buddha" is no longer the centre of fabulous conjecture. Its ring fence of mysticism has been penetrated, and the full glare of Reality has dispelled the mirage of spurious marvels that gathered over this Far Eastern Mecca during its long centuries of seclusion.' Waddell hoped Western civilisation would 'dissipate the dense mists of ignorance and unhealthy superstitions that cruelly harass the people'. In fact it worked out the other way round, for what he and his contemporaries could never have foreseen was the way Tibet's Vajrayana Buddhism spread beyond its borders – not as a consequence of Younghusband but in the wake of the Tibetan diaspora that followed the Chinese occupation of Tibet, the fleeing of the 14th Dalai Lama to India, and the Cultural Revolution of 1966–7. What might have been expected to lead to a breakdown of faith among the Tibetan exile community actually led to an extraordinary revitalisation, accompanied by a revival of religious scholarship that brought about many reforms in religious teaching and practice. This reformed teaching spread to the West, where the Diamond or Thunderbolt Path now has many thousands of adherants. If the Younghusband Mission did nothing else, it helped to lay some small part of the foundations for this Third Diffusion of Chos, by awakening Western interest in Tibet and its culture.

In Tibet itself the British intrusion has left little trace of its passing. In Gyantse, there is really nothing to show that the Tibet Mission remained here for more than six months, followed by a British Trade Agent and military escort for nearly three decades. The little British cemetery behind Changlo Manor was washed away in a flood in the 1930s and Changlo Manor itself is said to have been pulled down soon afterwards. What appears to be an electricity sub-station now stands in its place.

Today Gyantse is still the most Tibetan and least Chinese of Tibet's larger towns, its townspeople open-hearted and hospitable. The Jong still dominates the town and surrounding plains as it always did. Its walls, blown up once more during the years of the Cultural Revolution, are slowly being rebuilt. At the Museum of the Anti-British visitors can learn the basic, shameful facts of the Younghusband invasion – with a few understandable embellishments, such as a successful outcome to the night attack on Changlo Manor, resulting in the deaths of hundreds of English soldiers. A particularly fortunate visitor might get to see the Chinese-made film about the Younghusband Mission, which peddles the line that it was only through the heroic intervention of Tibet's elder brother, China, that the invaders were ousted. These absurdities notwithstanding, it cannot be denied that the memorial recently erected at the summit of the Jong has a certain poignancy, despite its comic English. It glorifies those who leaped to their deaths rather than surrender during the storming of the fortress on 6 July 1904, but it can equally be said to commemorate the many wretched conscripts killed by shrapnel, cordite, machine-gun and rifle fire in defence of their land and, as they believed, in defence of their faith.

Outside the walls of the Jong there is one surviving trace of the events that took place hereabouts in the year of the Wood-Dragon: a folk song commemorating the battle of Naini monastery, which tells how its last defenders continued to resist even after the walls of the monastery had been finally battered down by enemy guns. By this account two brothers fought on after all the rest had perished: 'The Ardus Gunbu warrior brothers charged the enemy with their swords and cut the British chieftan Zasaha into two parts. The courtyard of Nainiying monastery became a pond of blood.'

Naini, Tsechen and all the surrounding gompas were rebuilt after the British left, only to be destroyed again in the years of the Cultural Revolution. Some have been restored in part, others abandoned. Part of the Palkor Chode complex was pulled down – but not the magnificent Kumbum stupa, which remains one of the artistic glories of Tibet. The Chumbi Valley (now Dromo county) remains closed to foreigners, so as yet it is impossible to visit the killing-field at Chumik Shenko beside the Bam Tso lake or to cross the Tang La to Phari Jong and Chumbi. But it is possible to drive through the Red Idol Gorge as far south as Kangmar and to follow the invading army's route from Gyantse up and over the Karo La. The camping site under the huge glacier is exactly as it was a century ago, and Hatter Bailey's blue poppies still grow in profusion over the nearby alp. Traces of the great wall laid across the valley that was twice outflanked can still be seen, as well as the high snowfields across which so many vanquished Tibetans trudged to their deaths. The monastic town of Nakartse, against which the waters of Yamdok Tso then all but lapped, is now a rather squalid Chinese town with concrete streets laid out in a grid. The present incarnation of the Sow Goddess is once more in residence at Samding nunnery, although the great lake over which she presides, and which is believed by Tibetans to make up the life-blood of their country, is slowly draining away into the Tsangpo down a hydroelectric tunnel drilled through the intervening mountain range – much to the distress and anger of most Tibetans.

Lhasa, of course, has been utterly transformed, with a sprawling Chinese town now extending far across the Lhasa plain and over the Plain of Wild Asses where the British invaders camped. Although much of the old city has gone, the Jokhang and the area round it known as the Barkhor remains much as it was when Private Sampson and his pal Bob went shopping in 1904. It is still possible to see Tibetans from every walk of life buying and selling there, among them nomad families on pilgrimage as poor and dirty as they were a century ago. The great majority, however, while still as picturesquely dressed as ever, are now prosperous to a degree that would have amazed their great-grandparents. After many decades of brutal repression the three great monasteries of Ganden, Drepung and Sera are largely rebuilt and restored and functioning once more as religious centres, though the numbers of monks are carefully restricted and measured in hundreds rather than thousands, and their liberties are still curtailed. Not altogether surprisingly, it was the monks of these three monasteries who initiated and led the brief Tibetan uprising against China in 1959.

The Potala Palace still stands as one of the architectural wonders of the world, but as a dry shell rather than the dynamic heart of the country that it once was. Yet it is still visited by more pilgrims than tourists – and many of them, surprisingly, are Chinese. And, despite the six-lane highways that have to be crossed, the pilgrimage road that once enclosed the city continues to draw many thousands of pilgrims who circumambulate it every morning, just as the Jokhang and other places of worship in the city still hum with mantras and the unceasing turning of thousands of prayer-wheels throughout the day.

Austine Waddell believed the British invasion of Tibet would 'dissipate the dense mists of ignorance and unhealthy superstitions that cruelly harass the people' and inaugurate instead 'a veritable dawn, to herald the rise of a new star in the East, which may for long, perhaps for many centuries, diffuse its mild radiance over this charming land'. The journalist Edmund Candler took a more pessimistic view:

Hundreds of years ago a Buddhist saint wrote it in his book of prophecies, Ma-ong Lung-Ten, which may be found in the Lhasa bookshops. He predicted that Tibet would be invaded and conquered by the Philings (Europeans), when all the true religion would go to Chang Shambhula, the Northern Paradise, and Buddhism would become extinct in the country. And now the Lamas believe that the prophecy will be fulfilled by our entry into Lhasa, and that their religion will decay before foreign influence.

It remains to be seen which of those two predictions will turn out to be the more accurate.

The Players

Names asterisked are those whose written testimonies have been drawn upon in the writing of this book.

The Tibet Frontier Commission

*Colonel Francis Younghusband, CIE, Indian Political Service, explorer, British Resident in Indore Princely State, Joint then Senior Commissioner to the Tibet Frontier Commission: letters to his wife Helen, his father, his sister Ellie, as well as to others in high places; official despatches; *India and Tibet*

*Claude White, ex-Public Works Department engineer, British Resident in Sikkim since 1889, initially Joint then Assistant Commissioner to the Tibet Frontier Commission, keen photographer: letters and despatches (published his photographs in *Sikkim and Bhutan*)

*Captain Frederick 'Frank' O'Connor, ex-Royal Field Artillery, ex-British Mountain Battery in India, Intelligence Branch of the Quartermaster-General's Branch, Intelligence Officer, joint Assistant Commissioner to the Tibet Frontier Commission, Tibetan interpreter and private secretary to Francis Younghusband: *On the Frontier and Beyond*, and *Things Mortal*; letters to Mrs (Helen) Younghusband and others

*Mr Mitter, Bengali head clerk: letters to Mrs Younghusband

Vernon Magniac, brother-in-law of Francis Younghusband, joined Mission late as his Private Secretary

Military Escort to the Mission

General Staff
*Brigadier-General James Macdonald, CB, Royal Engineers, Escort Commander to the Tibet Frontier Commission: official despatches and notes

The Players

*Major H. A. Iggulden, Sherwood Foresters, chief staff officer to General Macdonald and his second-in-command: article for *Journal of the Royal United Services Institute*
*Major William G. L. Beynon, DSO, 2nd Gurkha Rifles: diary and letters to his wife
Majors George Bretherton, DSO, Supply and Transport Corps, OC transport; A. Mullaly, Supply and Transport Corps; M. R. E. Ray, Intelligence
Captains J. O'B. Minogue, C. A. Elliott, Royal Engineers
Lieutenant B. H. Bignell, ADC

32nd Sikh Pioneers

*Lieutenant-Colonel Herbert Brander, Commandant, commanded Mission Escort at Gyantse: *Regimental History of the 32nd Sikh Pioneers*
Major H. F. Peterson, DSO, 2nd in command
Captains J. B. Bell, H. Bethune and H. F. Cooke, company commanders
Lieutenants G. P. Gurdon, G. C. Hodgson, H. S. Mitchell, D. C. Home and F. M. Bailey (transferred to 1st Mounted Infantry)
Lieutenants L. G. Hart, H. St G. H. Harvey-Kelly, E. Marsden, A. E. S. Fennel (attached officers)

23rd Sikh Pioneers

Lieutenant-Colonel Arthur Hogge, Commandant, commanded garrison at Tuna
Major R. Lye, 2nd in command
Major A. Wallace Dunlop and Captains H. F. A. Pearson and G. H. F. Kelly, company commanders
Captains William Ottley (transferred to form 1st Mounted Infantry), *G. H. Sawyer, amateur artist
Lieutenants R. Nicholas, B. C. H. Drew, A. G. C. Hutchinson, E. P. A. Melville, B. Turnbull, E. L. Crosleigh
*Lieutenant Norman Rybot, amateur artist: article for *English Illustrated Magazine*, (1904), drawings in newspapers and magazines (attached officer)

8th Gurkha Rifles

Lieutenant-Colonel M. A. Kerr, Commandant
Major G. R. Row, commander at Changlo Manor
Major F. Murray, deputy commander of escort at Changlo Manor
Captains L. H. Baldwin, G. L. S. Ward, C. Bliss and D. W. H. Humphreys, company commanders
Lieutenants John Grant, J. F. S. D. Coleridge, G. P. Sanders, E. H. Lynch, L. G. Hart
Captain Luke, Royal Artillery, commanding seven-pounders 'Bubble' and 'Squeak'

40th Pathans

Lieutenant-Colonel F. Campbell, DSO, Commandant
Captains *George Preston (letter-diary to his wife), J. R. Maclachlan
Lieutenants R. N. Macpherson, R.N. Currie

1st Mounted Infantry (drawn from 40th Pathans)

*Captain William Ottley, 32nd Sikh Pioneers, unit commander: *With Mounted Infantry in Tibet*

The Players

*Lieutenant Frederick M. 'Hatter' Bailey (known as 'Eric' to his parents), 32nd Sikh
    Pioneers, detachment commander: letters to his parents, diary and other papers

2nd Mounted Infantry (drawn from 40th Pathans)
Captain C. H. Peterson, 46th Punjabis, unit commander
Captain H. M. Souter, 14th Bengal Lancers
Lieutenant F. Skipwith, 24th Punjabis

1st Battalion, Royal Fusiliers (4 companies)
Lieutenant-Colonel Edward Cooper, DSO, battalion commander
Major S. Menzies, 2nd in command
Captains S. F. Legge, C. V. Johnson, J. L. Fisher, C. A. H. Palairet, L. G. T. Stone
Lieutenants W. G. T. Currie, E. G. S. L'Estrange Malone, N. W. Gardner, W. A. B.
    Daniell, W. A. C. Bowden-Smith, R. E. Alston, A. C. S. Chichester, *Thomas de
    B. Carey, 2nd in command A Company (letter-diary to his wife), A. C. Hewitt,
    M. I. Wyvill
*Lance-Sergeant Alfred Dunning: diary
*Corporal Percy Coath: diary
*Private H. A. Sampson, C Company: diary entitled 'From Lebong to Lhassa with the
    Sikkim Thibet Expedition, 14 May to 20 Oct 1904'

1st Battalion, The Norfolk Regiment: Maxim Gun Detachment
*Captain Arthur Hadow, unit commander: letters to his parents, lecture on the Maxim
    gun in Tibet, contributed article to regimental journal, *The Britannia* (1933)

Royal Artillery: detachments from 7th and 30th British Mountain Batteries
Major R. W. Fuller
Captain F. A. Easton
Lieutenants G. A. Yates, C. C. Marindin, W. P. Bennett, F. E. Spencer, H. G. Boone

Royal Engineers
*Captain Seymour Sheppard, DSO, commanding No. 3 Company, 1st Bengal Sappers
    and Miners: article for *Royal Engineers Journal* (1905)
Captains Charles Ryder, RE, Survey of India, H. M. Cowie, RE, Survey of India, C. G.
    Rawling, Somerset Light Infantry (joined Mission to lead survey party)
Lieutenants E. F. J. Hill, A. D. Walker, H. L. Lewis, C. F. Birney

Supply and Transport, Coolie and Yak Corps
Captains H. Roddy, E. E. Preston, C. A. E. O'Meara, J. A. P. Manson, R. C. Moore, A.
    P. D. C. Stuart, J. B. Pollock Morris, H. E. Price, F. G. Ross, F. T. T. Moore,
    *C. H. G. Moore (article for *Journal of the Supply and Transport Corps Indian Army*,
    1912)
Lieutenants F. Shuttleworth and W. B. Dunlop, 108 Infantry, A. Vickers, 48 Pioneers,
    *Leonard Bethell, 8th Gurkhas ('A Footnote', published in *Blackwood's Magazine*,
    February 1929, under the pseudonym 'Pousse-Cailloux'), *Mark Synge, 6th Jat
    Light Infantry (*To Lhassa At Last*, 1905, under the pseudonym 'Powell

Millington'), *F. Holdaway (article for *Journal of the Supply and Transport Corps*, 1912); also attached officers from 2nd and 8th Gurkha Rifles

Mule Corps

Captains A. Gabbett, 5th Mule Corps, O. St J. Skeene, 6th Mule Corps, G. Gilbertson, 7th Mule Corps, F. I. T. Moore, 10th Mule Corps, A. R. Saunders, 11th Mule Corps; H. E. Price, 12th Mule Corps

Lieutenants J. E. Home, 8th Mule Corps, G. Merchant, 9th Mule Corps

Conductor T. Rogers, 13th Mule Corps

Medical Officers to the Mission

*Lieutenant-Colonel Austine Waddell, IMS, Principal Medical Officer, antiquarian and authority on Tibetan Buddhism: *Lhasa and Its Mysteries* (1905), and 'Tibetan manuscripts and books collected during the Younghusband Mission' in *Quarterly Review* (1912)

Majors *C. N. C. Wimberley (letter to wife published in *Tibetan Review*, 1904), A. W. Dawson, attached to 1st Bengal Sappers and Miners

Captains H. G. Walton, IMS, Mission Medical Officer, naturalist and ornithologist, *C. W. Mainprise, RAMC (letters to his family), W. H. Ogilvie, E. P. Connolly, T. B. Kelly, W. H. Leonard, A. Cooke-Young

Lieutenants Gerard Davys, IMS, surgeon, G. D. Franklin, *A. R. Aldridge (article for *Journal of the Royal Army Medical Corps*, 1905), John Murray, attached to 32nd Sikh Pioneers, L. Franklin, attached to 8th Gurkhas

Civilians attached to the Mission

*Edmund Candler, Special Correspondent representing the *Daily Mail*: despatches and *The Unveiling of Lhasa* (1905)

*Perceval Landon, Special Correspondent representing *The Times:* despatches and *The Opening of Tibet* (1905) and *Lhasa* (1906)

*Henry Newman, Reuters Correspondent and Special Correspondent representing *The Englishman* of Calcutta: despatches and autobiography, *A Roving Commission* (1937)

C. B. Bayley, Special Correspondent representing *Daily Telegraph* and *Pioneer*

*David Macdonald, Anglo-Sikkimese assistant to Colonel Waddell: *The Land of the Lama* (1929), *Twenty Years in Tibet* (1932), and *Touring in Sikkim and Tibet* (1934)

Mr Hayden, geologist

In Tibet

Tibetans

The Dalai Lama, Nawang Lobsang Thubden Gyatso, 13th Dalai Lama, leader of the Gelugpa school and spiritual ruler of Tibet

The Panchen Lama (Tashi Lama), residing at Tashilunpo monastery in Shigatse, spiritual partner and political rival of the Dalai Lama

Dorjieff (Kambo Agvan Dorzhiev, also known as Tsenyi Khenpo), Tibet's Envoy to Russia, thought by the British to be an agent of the Czar

The Players

Ti Rimpoche Ganden Lozang Gyaltsen Lamoshari, abbot of Ganden monastery, appointed Regent of Tibet in Dalai Lama's absence

Sengchen Lama, Abbot of Tashilunpo Monastery, representative of the Panchen Lama

The four-man Kashag or Council of Ministers made up of four Shapés: latterly, Kalon Serchung, Kalon Yuthok, Depon Tsarong Wangchuk Gyalpo (also known as Lobsang Trinley; negotiated with Younghusband at Khamba Jong) and Kalon Lama Chamba Tenzin, commander of the Tibetan forces

The Nechung Oracle

Depon Ladang (Lhading), 'the Lhasa General', commanding the Tibetan troops at Guru

Depon Mamseling, his deputy

*Tseten Wangchuk, junior officer and eye-witness of the Guru massacre: recorded deposition, later published in Tsepon W. D. Shakabpa's *Tibet: A Political History* (1984)

Dapon Tailing, commander of the garrison at Gyantse Jong

Ta Lama, lama from Lhasa representing Tibetan government in talks before and after Gyantse

Chinese Emissaries and others

Yu-t'ai, Amban or Manchu Resident in Lhasa

General Ma and Colonel Chao, Amban's representatives

Ernest Wilton, Chinese Consular Service

Captain Parr, Chinese Customs Service

*Ts'an-Chih Chen, young son of the secretary to the Amban in Lhasa: verbal account of the Younghusband Mission given in *Three Himalayan Autobiographies* (1998)

Ugyen Wangchuk, the Tongsa Penlop, prime minister and *de facto* ruler of Bhutan

Captain Jit Bahadur, the Nepalese Consul

*Miss Annie Taylor, Protestant Missionary, based at Yatung: letter in the *Morning Post*, 1903

In India

At Headquarters, Calcutta and Simla

*Lord Curzon (George Nathaniel Curzon), Viceroy and Governor-General of India: letters and despatches

*Lord Ampthill (Arthur Russell), Acting Viceroy in Curzon's absence: letters and despatches

*Lord Kitchener (Horatio Herbert Kitchener), Commander-in-Chief in India: despatches

*Louis Dane, Indian Political Service, Secretary of the Government of India's Foreign Department: letters and despatches

*James Dunlop-Smith, Political Agent, Sikh States: letters

Elsewhere in India

*Helen Younghusband, wife of Francis Younghusband: letters to him and others

Lieutenant-Colonel George Younghusband, brother of Francis Younghusband

The Players

In England

Lord Balfour, Prime Minister

*St John Brodrick (later Viscount Midleton), Secretary of State for India, close friend and later enemy of Lord Curzon: letters and despatches

General John Younghusband, retired ex-Indian Police, father of Francis Younghusband

Emmie Younghusband, retired ex-Indian Forestry Service, elder sister of Francis Younghusband

Colonel Frederick Bailey, retired ex-Indian Forestry Service, father of Frederick M. 'Hatter'/'Eric' Bailey

Acknowledgements

For their enthusiastic support and generous sharing of ideas I am especially grateful to: Dr Alex McKay, Research Fellow for Indo-Tibetan History at the Wellcome Trust Centre for the History of Medicine, UCL; John Falconer, Curator of Photography, Oriental and India Office Collection, British Library; and Jim Kelleher, Royal Fusiliers Regimental Museum. My particular thanks to Teddy Hadow for allowing me to quote freely from his father's papers (now lodged at the Royal Norfolk Regiment Museum), and to Jonathan Buckley for allowing me access to the letters of Captain C. W. Mainprise, RAMC. Many thanks also to the following for their assistance: Craig Bowen, Registrar, Maggie Roxburgh, Assistant Librarian, and staff at the Royal Engineers Library, Chatham; G. J. Edgerley-Harris, Assistant Curator, trustees and staff at the Gurkha Museum, Peninsula Barracks, Winchester; Julie Gardham, Assistant Librarian, Special Collections, Glasgow University Library; the Director and Trustees at the Royal Fusiliers Regimental Museum, Tower of London; Kate Thaxton, Assistant Keeper, trustees and staff at the Royal Norfolk Regiment Museum, Norfolk Museums & Archaeology Service, Norwich; Lieutenant-Colonel W. H. Clements and Terence Nelson, curator of The Royal Irish Rifles Regimental Museum,

Acknowledgements

Belfast; the Director and staff at the National Army Museum, Chelsea; the Director and staff at the Oriental and India Office Collection, British Library. Finally, thanks first of all to my new indexer, Drusilla Calvert, then my continuing gratitude to the 'old firm': Roger Hudson, who read my manuscript at an early stage and proffered much valuable advice and correction; Liz Robinson, whose magic pencillings turn straw into gold; my editor Caroline Knox who together with John Murray, Caroline Westmore and Katy Mahood saw to it that 50 Albemarle Street was more a home from home than a publisher's office; my agent and long-time bulwark Vivien Green; and, lastly, Dick and Liz for coming with me to Tibet.

Glossary

Note: Tibetan–English unless specified

Amban:	Chinese Resident in Tibet, representing Manchu government
ani:	nun
Atisha (Sanskrit):	Buddhist guru from India who initiated reform and so-called Second Diffusion of Buddhism in Tibet in 11th century
Avalokiteshvara (Sanskrit):	lord of compassion, patron deity of Tibet; in Tibetan, Chenresig
bharal, bhurrel (Hindi):	Blue Sheep, *Pseudos nayaur*, species of mountain goat; in Tibetan, *nawa*
chang:	barley beer
Chang-Tang (Jang-Thang):	great Northern Plain of Tibet, with an average elevation of 14,000 feet
chapatti (Hindi):	unleavened wheat bread baked on a griddle
Chenresig:	see *Avalokiteshvara*
Chi-Kyap Khempo:	Lord Chamberlain
chiru:	Tibetan antelope, *Patholops hodgsoni*
chorten:	see *stupa*
Chos:	the Buddhist Dharma or Law
chu (chhu):	flowing water, river
chumik:	spring
Dalai Lama:	All-Embracing Teacher; Mongolian title for the spiritual reincarnate *lama* (q.v.) and leader of the *Gelugpa* religious school; see *Gyalpo Rinpoche*

Glossary

Depon (*Dapon*):	senior military commander or governor, so-called 'general'
dhoolie (Hindi):	Indian covered stretcher, carried like a palanquin
dorje:	ritual implement representing thunderbolt
Dorje Phagmo:	Adamantine Sow, female consort of deity Demchok
dri:	female yak
gelong:	fully ordained monk
Gelugpa:	the Virtuous Order, so-called Yellow Hats; school of Buddhism founded by Tsongkhapa in the 15th century
geshe:	monk with highest spiritual qualifications
gompa (*gonpa*):	place of solitude, thus monastery
Guru Rinpoche:	Blessed Teacher; Tibetan name for the Indian guru Padmasambhava, traditionally said to have brought Buddhism to Tibet in 8th century
Gyalpo Rinpoche:	Tibetan name of Dalai Lama, embodiment of *Chenresig/Avalokiteshvara*, leader of *Gelugpa* school
jezail (Arabic):	long-barrelled smooth-bore matchlock; in Tibetan, *mendah*
jingal (Arabic):	small long-barrelled cannon similar to swivel-guns
jong (*dzong*):	fort, but also district headquarters, governed jointly by a monk-official and lay-official; see *Jongpon*
Jongpon (*Dzongpon*):	district governor; joint commander of a fort or district; see *jong*
kadakh:	ceremonial white scarf
kangri (*gang-ri*):	snow mountain
Kashag:	Council of four ministers; see *Shapé*
kiang:	Tibetan wild ass, *Equus hemonius pallas*
la:	crossing-point of mountain or river
lha:	gods
lhakang:	house of gods; temple or shrine
lama:	religious teacher; in Indian, *guru*
lapcha (*lapche*):	cairn of stones on pass
mandela (Sanskrit):	symmetrical diagram of the Buddha-mind depicted in art, sometimes in three-dimensional form
mane:	prayer, thus the mantra *Om Mane Padme Hum*
mani-wall:	wall on which rocks inscribed with prayers are piled
mantra (Sanskrit):	mystic formula or incantation
maund (Hindi):	Indian unit of measurement, weighing 88 pounds
mendah:	see *jazail*
nawa:	see *bharal*
nyan:	Great Tibetan Sheep, *Ovis ammon*
peling:	foreign barbarian, later used specifically for Europeans
phurbu:	ritual dagger
pundit (*pandit*) (Sanskrit):	Indian religious teacher of Brahmin caste, used by British to describe scholars
raj (Sanskrit):	kingdom or rule, later used to describe British government in India
ri:	mountain

Glossary

rupee (Hindi):	Indian equivalent of the English shilling; in 1900, 15Rs were worth £1 sterling
sahib (Arabic):	master; latterly used to describe European gentleman
sampa (*zamba*):	bridge
sangar (Pushtu):	stone breastwork
Shapé:	Councillor or Cabinet Minister, one of four making up the *Kashag*
Shata Shapé:	chief minister of *Kashag*
shikar (Hindi):	Indian term for hunting; thus *shikari*, hunter
stupa:	Buddhist monument containing religious reliquaries; in Tibetan, *chorten*
tang:	plain
thangka:	painted scroll
trapa:	monk, usually novice
tsampa:	barley roasted whole and ground into flour; staple diet of upland Tibet
Tsang:	district of Tibet centred on Shigatse
Tsang-Po:	Great River; the upper course of the Brahmaputra
tso (*tsho*):	lake
Tsongdu:	National Assembly
tulku:	reincarnate lama
U:	district of Tibet centred on Lhasa
yak:	Tibetan ox, *Bos grunniens*, domesticated from the wild *dong* and cross-bred with cattle to produce *dzoom*
yu:	turquoise

Bibliography

Unpublished sources and manuscripts

Note: OIOC = Oriental and India Office Collection at the British Library, London; NAM = National Army Museum, Royal Hospital Road, London

Bailey, Lieutenant Fred. M. 'Eric' or 'Hatter': the following papers from the Bailey Collection, OIOC, MSS Eur. F157, were consulted:

F157/145 and 150, misc. letters to Frederick Bailey Senior

F157/144-146 and 150, letters from Frederick Bailey Senior to (Sir) Francis Younghusband, 1889–1910

F157/163, Letters from 'Eric' to parents from Rawalpindi, Sikkim, Tibet, 1903

F157/164, Letters from 'Eric' to parents from Tibet, 1904

F157/197, Personal diary, 1901–09

F157/198, Notebook containing calculations, 1903–4

F157/199, Notebook containing observations on Tibet, 1903–4

F157/218, Letters to Lt-Col Sir William Frederick Travers O'Connor, 1901–9

F157/256, Letters to Peter Fleming in 1960

F157/324b, Military Report on Sikkim and the Chumbi Valley with some notes on Tibet, by Captain W. F. O'Connor, *c.* 1903

F157/380, Sketch Map to Show Routes Leading from Sikkim to Lhasa, reduced by Captain W. F. O'Connor, RA, Gangtok, 3 Feb. 1903, Int. Branch

F157/381, Skeleton Map of Tibet from the Sikkim Frontier to Lhasa, reduced by Capt. O'Connor, 12 Feb. 1903

F157/382, Road Sketch, Gyantse to Karo La and Tibetan Wall, from road sketches by Capt. H. M. Cowie, RE, Survey of India, May 1904

F157/383, Map of Changlo, near Gyantse, the defences, May–June 1904

F157/509, copy of J. C. White's *Tibet and Lhasa*, volume of photos, published 1905

F157/809, Notes on the Blue Poppy

Beynon, Major William G. L., OIOC, MSS. Eur. D830:

D830/17, Tibet Diary

D830/31–2, Letters to his wife Nora, 1903–4

D830/40, Scrapbook

D830/12, *Man of Iron,* manuscript biography of Major-General Sir William Beynon by his son-in-law T. L. Hughes

Carey, Lieutenant Thomas, Expedition to Tibet: Letters, being extracts from Diary of T. de B. Carey, 1st Battn Royal Fusiliers, 1904, Royal Fusiliers Museum, Tower of London

Coath, Corporal Percy, Royal Fusiliers, Tibet Diary, Royal Fusiliers Museum, Tower of London

Dunning, Lance-Sergeant Alfred (James), Royal Fusiliers, Tibet Diary, Royal Fusiliers Museum, Tower of London

Hadow, Lieutenant Arthur. C., Letters to his parents and journal, List of items presented to Royal Norfolk Regimental Museum, Norfolk Regiment Museum, Norwich

Harvey-Kelly, Lieutenant H., 64th Pioneers, Diary, NAM, Acc. No. 6612/2 MFN (not accessible)

Iggulden, Colonel H. A., Chief Staff Officer, OIOC, MSS Eur. C270: An Account of Lhasa and its Inhabitants

Legge, Captain Septimus Frederick, Royal Fusiliers, Tibet Diary with press cuttings from *The Pioneer,* June–October 1904: NAM, Acc. No. 8308–27

Mainprise, Captain C. W., RAMC, Letters from his family, private collection

Preston, Captain George, 40th Pathans, Letters to his wife, NAM, Acc. No. 6510–11; also scrapbook and photo album

Rybot, Lieutenant Norman, Drawings, OIOC, WD1160–1221

Sampson, Private H. A., C Coy, Royal Fusiliers, 'From Lebong to Lhassa with the Sikkim Thibet Expedition', diary from 14 May to 20 Oct 1904, NAM, Acc. No. 8005–149

Younghusband, Colonel Sir Francis:

the following papers from the Younghusband Collection, OIOC, MSS Eur. F197, were consulted:

F197/78, Memorandum on our Relations with Tibet, Aug. 1903

F197/79, Note on the Present unsatisfactory situation in Tibet with proposals for the measure necessary to remedy it, Oct. 1903

F197/80, Correspondence with Lord Curzon relating to the Tibet Mission, 1903–4

F197/81, Correspondence with Lord Amptill, ditto

F197/84, Papers relating to Tibet 1889–1904, Cd. 1920

F197/87, Copies of ultimatum sent by Younghusband to Tibetan General, June 1904

F197/96, Correspondence relating to razing and rebuilding of Tibetan forts

F197/100, Letters from S. Mitter, 1903–4

F197/101, Letters from Capt. William Frederick Travers O'Connor to Mrs Younghusband

Bibliography

F197/102, Letters to Col and Mrs Younghusband from Major James Robert Dunlop-Smith

F197/103, Papers relating to Tibet, Cd. 1920

F197/105–6, Further Papers relating to Tibet, Cd. 2054

F197/109, Notes by Lady Younghusband on the Tibet Mission in 1930s

F197/145, Letters from Col Younghusband to his father relating to the Tibet Mission, 1903–4

F197/158, Letters from Col Younghusband to his sister Emily, 1901–8

F197/161, Letters from Col Younghusband to 'Jack' (Maj-Gen Sir George Younghusband), 1891–94, 1904

F197/173-7, Letters from Col Younghusband to his wife, May 1903 to Sept. 1904

F197/178, Telegrams from Col Younghusband to his wife, 1903–4

F197/270, Rough Notes passing through Sikkim on my Mission to Tibet, June–July 1903

F197/271, Lists of kit taken to Tibet, July 1903

F197/272, Note for book on 'The Religion of the Traveller', Jan. 1904

F197/273, Notes for interview with Lord Curzon, Nov. 1904

F197/301, Notes on the British Purpose in India, c. 1917

F197/465, The Dalai Lama, undated

F197/476, The Holy Himalaya, undated

F197/506, The Spiritual Basis of the Indian Connection with India, undated

F197/651, Photographs of Tibet and the Tibet Mission, 1903–4

F197/524, Press illustrations

F197/527, Press cuttings of Tibet

F197/328, Notes and fragments

F197/551, Correspondence of (Dame) Eileen Younghusband

Periodicals and newspapers

Anon, 'A Story of Struggle and Intrigue in Central Asia', in *Journal of the Royal Central Asian Society*', Vols 14 & 15, 1927 and 1928

'H.H.A.', 'Major-General Sir James Ronald Leslie Macdonald', in *Royal Engineers Journal*, September 1927

Aldridge, A. R., 'With the Tibet Mission Force', in *Journal of the Royal Army Medical Corps*, Vol. III, pp. 272–3 (1904); Vol. IV, pp. 235–40 (1905)

Barakatullah, M., 'British Invasion of Tibet', in *Forum* 37, July 1905, pp. 128–40

Bethel, Lt-Col L. A. (writing as 'Pousse Cailloux'), 'A Footnote', in *Blackwoods Magazine*, Feb. 1929

Cotton, Sir Henry, Letter to *The Times*, 2 December 1903

Dillon, E. J., 'Tibet: the California of the Future', in *Contemporary Review*, Jan. 1904

Ferrier, J. A. and Spinks, A. R., 'Letters' in *Royal Engineers Journal*, N.S. 33, 1921

Holdaway, F., 'Random recollections of the Tibet Expedition', in *Journal of the Supply and Transport Corps, Indian Army*, No. 6, 1912

Iggulden, H. A., 'To Lhasa with the Tibet Expedition', in *Journal of the Royal United Services Institute*

Bibliography

International Studies, 'Special Issue on Tibet', Vol. 10, No. 4, April 1969

Lamb, Alastair, 'Some notes on Russian intrigue in Tibet', in *JRCAS* 46 (1), Jan. 1959

Mehra, L. P., 'Tibet and Russian Intrigue', in *JRCAS*

Molesworth, E. K., 'Obituary on Lt J. A. Garstin', in *Royal Engineers Journal*, No. 34, 1904

Moore, C. H. G., 'A few personal experiences with transport in Tibet', in *Journal of the Supply and Transport Corps, Indian Army*, No. 7, 1912

Neame, P. L., 'Tibet and Russian Intrigue', in *JRCAS* 45(1), Jan. 1958

Rybot, Norman, 'With the Tibet Expedition', in *English Illustrated Magazine*, N.S. 31, 1904 (account of his stay in Phari)

Sheppard, S. H., 'No. 3 Coy 1st Bengal Sappers and Miners on the Thibet Mission', in *Royal Engineers Journal*, N.S. 2, 1905

Ular, Alexander, 'The Tibetan Puzzle', in *Contemporary Review*, Jan. 1904

Waddell, L. A., 'Tibetan manuscripts and books etc collected during the Younghusband Mission', in *Imperial Asiatic Quarterly Review*, 34, 1912

Wimberley, C. N., letter to his wife from Gyantse, quoted by Colin Narbeth, 'The Story of Gyantse Fort: An Unpublished Letter', in *Tibetan Review*, June 1996

Younghusband, Sir Francis, 'Our Position in Tibet', in *JRCAS*, 1910

Published primary sources

Austin, Herbert, *With Macdonald in Uganda*, reprint with new introduction by A. T. Matson (1973)

Bailey, Col F. M., *China, Tibet, Assam* (1945)

Bell, Sir Charles, *Portrait of a Dalai Lama* (1946)

——*Tibet, Past and Present* (1924)

Bower, Capt. Hamilton, *Diary of a Journey across Tibet* (1894)

Lt-Col H. Brander, *32nd Sikh Pioneers: Regimental History; Vol. II, Sikkim and Tibet 1903–04* (1905)

Burleigh, Bennet, *The Khartoum Campaign* (1898)

Candler, Edmund, *The Unveiling of Lhasa* (1905)

——*Youth and the East; an unconventional autobiography* (1932)

Carey, William, *Adventures in Tibet*, 1902

Curzon, George Nathaniel, Baron Curzon of Kedleston, *Russia in Central Asia in 1889* (1889)

——*Frontiers* (Romanes Lectures) (1907)

——*British Government in India* (1925)

——*Leaves from a Viceroy's Notebook* (1926)

HMSO, East India (Tibet), *Papers relating to Tibet, presented to both House of Parliament* (1904)

Holdich, Sir Thomas, *The Indian Borderland 1880–1900* (1901)

Indian Officer, *Russia's March Towards India* (1894)

Landon, Perceval, *The Opening of Tibet* (1905)

——*Lhasa* (1906)

Macdonald, David, *The Land of the Lama* (1929)

——*Touring in Sikkim and Tibet* (1931)

——*Twenty Years in Tibet* (1932)

Bibliography

Macdonald, J. R. L., *Soldiering and Surveying in British East Africa 1891–1894*, reprint with new introduction by A. T. Matson (1973)

Midleton, Lord (St John Brodrick), *Records and Reactions* (1939)

Millington, Thomas Powell (Mark Synge), *To Lhasa at Last* (1905)

Newman, H., *A Roving Commission* (1937)

O'Connor, Sir William Frederick, *Memorandum dated 10 June 1901* (pamphlet)

——*Report on Tibet* (1903)

——*On the Frontier and Beyond: a Record of Thirty Years' Service* (1931)

——*Things Mortal* (1940)

Ottley, William J., *With Mounted Infantry in Tibet* (1906)

Rawling, Captain C. G., *The Great Plateau* (1905)

Scott, Alexander Macallum, *The Truth About Tibet* (1905)

Waddell, Lt-Col Dr Austine, *The Buddhism of Tibet or Lamaism* (1897)

——*Among the Himalayas* (1898)

——*Lhasa and its Mysteries* (1906)

White, Claude, *Sikkim and Bhutan* (1909)

Younghusband, Sir Francis, *Memorandum on Our Relations with Tibet* (1903)

——*India and Tibet* (1910)

——*The Light of Experience* (1927)

——*The Heart of a Continent*, revised (1937)

Younghusband, Maj.-Gen. Sir George, *Indian Frontier Warfare* (1898)

——*Forty Years a Soldier* (1923)

Published secondary sources

Carrington, Michael, 'Officers, Gentlemen and Thieves: the Looting of Monasteries during the 1903–4 Younghusband Mission to Tibet', in *Modern Asian Studies*, 37, 1, 2003

Chopra, P. N., *Social, Cultural and Political History of Tibet* (1989)

Das, Taraknath (ed. N. M. Ray-Chowdhury), *British Expansion in Tibet* (1927)

Dilks, David, *Curzon in India* (1970)

X Fleming, Peter, *Bayonets to Lhasa* (1961) X *[handwritten: Gave this book to Dad for a present]*

French, Patrick, *Younghusband: the Last Great Imperial Adventurer* (1994)

Gilbert, Martin, 'Tibetan Tragedy', in *History of the Twentieth Century*, Vol. 1, No. 2, 1984

Gilmour, David, *Curzon* (1994)

Gould, Tony, *Imperial Warriors: Britain and the Gurkhas* (1999)

Govt of the Tibet Autonomous Region, *A Complete History of the Tibetan People's Struggle Against the British Invasion*, c. 1980

Holdich, Sir Thomas, *Tibet the Mysterious* (1906)

Hopkirk, Peter, *Trespassers on the Roof of the World* (1982)

Huxford, Lt-Col H. J., *History of the 8th Gurkha Rifles, 1824–1949* (1960)

Jones, Kathleen, *Eileen Younghusband: a Biography* (1984)

King, Peter, *The Viceroy's Fall: How Kitchener Destroyed Curzon* (1986)

Lattimore, Owen, *Studies in Frontier History* (1962)

Li, Tieh-tseng, *Tibet Today and Yesterday* (1960)

McKay, Alexander, *Tibet and the British Raj* (1997)

Magnus, Philip, *Kitchener* (1958)

Bibliography

Marshall, Julie, *Britain and Tibet 1765–1947: annotated bibliography* (1977)

Mehra, Parshotam, *The Younghusband Mission: An Interpretation* (1968)

Meyer, Karl and Brysac, Shareen, *Tournament of Shadows* (1997)

Morris, Jan, *Farewell the Trumpets* (1978)

Namseling, Paljor Jigme, *The History of a Man's Life and Other Matters* (1988) (as quoted in French, *Younghusband*)

Richardson, Sir Hugh, *Tibet and Its History* (revised 1984)

Robson, Isabel, *Two Lady Missionaries in Tibet* (1909) (photo of Annie Taylor in Tibetan dress opp. p. 104)

Royle, Trevor, *The Kitchener Enigma* (1985)

Sandes, E. W. C., *The Royal Engineers in Egypt and the Sudan* (1937)

Seaver, George, *Francis Younghusband* (1952)

Shakapba, Tsepon W. D., *Tibet : a Political History* (1967)

Snellgrove, David, and Richardson, Hugh, *A Cultural History of Tibet*, 1968.

Snelling, John, *Buddhism in Russia: the Story of Agvan Dorziev Lhasa's Emissary to the Tsar* (1995)

Society for Anglo-Chinese Understanding, 'The Question of Tibet', in *China in the News*, No. 6., 1968

Taring, Rinchen Dolma, *Daughter of Tibet* (1970)

Tsering, Phuntsog, *Annals of the All-Revealing Mirror* (1987) (as quoted in French, *Younghusband*)

Verrier, Anthony, *Francis Younghusband and the Great Game* (1991)

Waters, Major R. S., *History of the 5th Battalion (Pathans), 14th Punjab Regiment, formerly 40th Pathans* (1936)

Whitehead, John, *Far Frontiers: People and Events in North-East India 1857–1947* (1959)

Unpublished secondary sources

Kelleher, J. P., 'The 1st Battalion, Royal Fusiliers and the Tibet Military Escort: a Short Account and Biographical Medal Roll', Royal Fusiliers Museum, Tower of London

Index

Index

FY refers to Francis Younghusband; references to maps are in italic

Index

Gyantse Jong, *138*, 203, 312; demand from
 FY to evacuate, 211, 214; attack on,
 214–22; looting after attack, 225, 306,
 307; *see also* Gyantse
Gymnocypris waddelli, 245

'H.H.A.', 149, 301
Hadow, Captain Arthur, 16, 42–3, 78,
 318; booty, 20, 224–5, 307–8; on
 Tibetans, 66; on diet, 74; in Tuna,
 80–3; on Sikh deaths, 84; details of
 battle plan, 104; on order not to fire,
 107; in advance on Guru, 108, 109; on
 dummy attack, 113; in Chumik
 Shenko massacre, 117; and Candler,
 124–5; on Tibetan weapons at Guru,
 124; in Gyantse, 148; in Changlo
 Manor, 150, 186; in advance on Karo
 La, 159; in battle at Karo La, 168, 170,
 171, 173; attack on Gyantse Jong, 214;
 in Gyantse Jong, 224; on execution of
 Sera monk, 271; career after
 Younghusband Mission, 309;
 promotion of Maxim gun, 309; *see also*
 Maxim guns
Hannington, Private, 308
Harrison, Private, 222
Harvey-Kelly, Lieutenant H. St. G. H.,
 225, 317
hats: worn for signing Convention, 282
Havildar Karbir Pun, 221
Hayden, Mr (geologist), 80, 150, 319
health *see* illnesses
high-altitude warfare: records, 176, 238,
 310
Hodgson, Captain C. G., 156, 317
Hogge, Lieutenant-Colonel Arthur, 41,
 78, 81, 196, 317; as FY's supporter, 41;
 concern over safety of Mission, 85;
 reprimand over escort for FY, 87; and
 Bailey, 92; threat of court martial,
 96–7; on dispute over command of
 Mission, 101; in charge of Gyantse,
 229
Huc, Évariste Régis, 27
Humphreys, Captain D. W. H., 221, 317
Hunterian Museum, Glasgow, 38

Iggulden, Major H. A., 38, 89, 102, 126,
 219, 226, 253, 317; sale of Tibetan
 curios, 307

illnesses, 83–4, 92, 198; Macdonald, 140,
 206–7, 212–13, 229, 243–4, 253, 259,
 299, 301; Sampson, 198; *see also*
 mountain sickness
indemnity to be paid towards costs of
 Younghusband Mission, 252, 265,
 272–3, 277–9; repayment, FY's terms,
 279–80, 284, 290–1; renegotation by
 O'Connor, 303
India: Buddhist collections, 40; *see also*
 Government of India
Indian Museum, Calcutta, display of
 Waddell's collection, 305
Indian troops: in invasion of Tibet, 179
interrogation of prisoners: massacre at
 Chumik Shenko, 121–2

Jameson Raid, FY's involvement, 19
Jelep La, 9–10, 15, 91, 182–3; descent into
 Tibet, 44, 62, 64, 183
Jeluk, 181
jingals (weapons), 132–3, 164; 'Chota
 Billy', 192
Jokhang temple (Lhasa), 50, 267–8, 274–5,
 314
Jongpon of Gyantse: as hostage, 160,
 165–6; wife, information from, 166
Jowo (statue of Gautama Buddha), 267, 275
Juba Mission, 36, 37

Kala Tso, 130, 196
Kalon Yuthok Shapé *see* Yuthok Shapé
Kanchenjunga massif, 9
Kangmar, 131, 195–6, 313
Kanjur (Tibetan Buddhist Scriptures), 71,
 143–4, 306
Karo La, 156, 157, *169*, 313; battle at,
 168–75; battle plan, *169*; booty taken,
 175; second battle, 236–8
Kashag (Tibet cabinet), 24, 53, 76, 240,
 320; deputation to Phari, 76, 80, 81;
 and draft treaty, 265, 272–3;
 representatives at signing of
 Convention, 282; *see also* Shapés; Ta
 Lama
Kashmir, Residency: FY promoted to,
 302
Kelly, Captain T. B., 270–1
Khamba Jong, 25–6, 32; as trade meeting
 place, 3; British presence, 52
Khamba La, 246–8

340

Index

Macdonald, General James Ronald Leslie, (*cont.*)
81, 89, 95–6, 99–101, 103–4, 196–7, 206, 209, 243, 251–2, 268, 285, 300–1; road-building, 43; in China, 45–6; preparation for attack on Phari Jong, 67–8; on advance to Tuna, 74–5; return from Tuna, 80; troops' opinion of, 89, 95, 184, 212, 259, 265, 268–9, 295–6; and supplies for Mission, 96–7, 99, 243, 264; threat to Hogge of court martial, 96–7; relations with press, 101–2; in advance on Guru, 105, 109; order not to fire, 107, 109; dummy attack, 113; in Chumik Shenko massacre, 115, 116, 123; report on Chumik Shenko massacre, 123–4; in advance on Gyantse, 129, 139; advance towards Kangmar, 132; as chain-smoker, 140, 207, 259; in Gyantse, 140, 146; illness, 140, 206–7, 212–13, 229, 243–4, 253, 259, 299, 301; booty from Gyantse Jong, 145; return to Chumbi, 149; and advance on Karo La, 159; in New Chombi, 184; on keeping troops in Lhasa, 196; Kitchener's support for, 196–7; in Naini, 202; attack on Tsechen monastery, 207; unpopularity with officers, 212, 213, 244, 259, 264–5; opium-taking, 213, 214; in attack on Gyantse Jong, 214–15, 223–4; and looting, 214, 225, 226, 241, 295, 307; advance to Lhasa, 229, 247–8; and attack on Yuthok Shapé's escort, 242; credited for success of Mission, 255–6; and advance on Drepung monastery, 264–5; ban on religious sites in Lhasa, 268; proposal by Ampthill for replacement in Lhasa, 270; proposed withdrawal from Lhasa, 276, 277, 279–80, 290, 298; at signing of Convention, 282, 284; dinner to celebrate signing of Convention, 285; farewell tea with Amban, 290; departure from Lhasa, 294–6; farewell speech to troops, 295–6; final report on Mission, 298–9; after expedition, 299; in Special Honours List for Younghusband Mission, 300; career after Younghusband Mission, 301;

passion for botany, 301; reaction to Honours List, 301; in O'Connor's memoirs, 305; and losses of material in transit from Lhasa, 306

Magniac, Vernon, 31, 155, 205, 229, 245, 316

Mahmood Isa, 161, 165

Mainprise, Captain C. W., 121, 125, 319; booty from Tsechen monastery, 208–9; collection of Tibetan curios, 287; on lost and damaged artefacts, 306

Manchu Resident in Lhasa *see* Amban

Manchus: control of Tibet, 27–8, 58

Manning, Thomas, 27

massacre at Chumik Shenko, 111–28, *118*; reports, 114–20, 123–4, 126–7, 128; stimulus for, 115–16, 120, 123; weapons, 117–19, 120, 122; Tibetan reports, 119–20; casualties, 120–2, 123–4, 125; interrogation of prisoners, 121–2; treatment of wounded Tibetans, 121, 125; pursuit after, 122; items taken on battlefield by troops, 124; arguments over sequence of events, 126; Tibetan forces, 127; British reaction, 154

Maxim guns, 10, 16, 32, 117; problems with cold, 81–2; in advance on Guru, 108; in Chumik Shenko massacre, 117, 119; in Karo La, 159, 169, 170, 171, 173, 174, 237; in defence of Changlo Manor, 186; in attack on Gyantse Jong, 218, 221–2; promoted by Hadow, 309

Meconopsis betonicifolia baileyi, 168, 305

medical conditions: treatment of wounded Tibetans, 121, 125; surgery in Gyantse, 151, *see also* mountain sickness

Medical Officers, 319; *see also* Field Hospitals

medicine: Tibetan, 288

mendah 'fire arrows', 54

Midleton, Lord *see* Brodrick, St John

Millington, Thomas Powell *see* Synge, Lieutenant Mark 'Thomas Powell Millington'

Mitter, Mr S., 24, 150, 163, 164, 282, 316

monasteries: destruction, 225; grain taken from, 231–4; payment for grain, 232, 233, 234

342

Index

Index

88–9; 'The Religion of a Traveller'
(book outline), 94–5; and supplies for
military escorts, 96–7; threat of court
martial for Hogge, 96–7; opinion of
press representatives, 103; in advance
on Guru, 105, 155; ultimatum to
Tibetans, 106, 194–5, 207; order not to
fire, 107, 109–10; on Chumik Shenko
massacre, 112, 126–7, 128; dummy
attack, 113; official report on Chumik
Shenko massacre, 123; on Tibetans,
126–7, 139, 242, 253, 259, 284; on
Tibetan monks, 127; and Landon, 130,
206; on battle at Red Idol Gorge, 136;
booty from Gyantse Jong, 145; in
Changlo Manor, 149–50; proposed
advance to Lhasa, 154–5; treatment of
Tibetan monks, 155; and Brander, 157;
and march on Karo La, 158; and
Brander's advance on Karo La, 160–1;
and Macdonald's demand to return
from Karo La, 160, 165; on failure of
Gurkha sentries, 162; and attack on
Changlo Manor, 163–4, 177; on
Bethune, 176; return from Gyantse,
185; on Ottley, 189; on Sheppard, 189;
summoned to New Chumbi, 193–4;
on negotiations with Tibetans, 194–5;
'farewell' dinner at Gyantse, 195; in
Kangmar, 195–6; on keeping troops in
Lhasa, 196; as Macdonald's subordinate,
196–7; offers resignation, 206; and Ta
Lama, 209–10; in attack on Gyantse
Jong, 215; move towards Lhasa, 228–9;
negotiations with Yuthok Shapé,
242–3; first view of Lhasa, 247; on
Bretherton, 249–50; details of
proposed treaty and, 252, 263, 265,
277; in march on Lhasa, 253; meetings
with Amban, 258–9, 261–2; grand
entry into Lhasa, 261; accommodation
in Lhasa, 262–3; proposed Convention
between FY and Dalai Lama, 263; and
Sikkimese prisoners, 266–7; and Ti
Rimpoche, 266, 278–9; and ban on
religious sites in Lhasa, 268; and
disappearance of Landon, 269;
vengeance for killing by Sera monk,
271–2; and proposed withdrawal from
Lhasa, 276–7, 280; and repayment of
Tibetan indemnity, 277–80; and

Chumbi Valley, 278; and signing of
Convention, 281–4; achievements in
Convention, 284, 299; congratulatory
telegrams, 289–90; farewell tea with
Amban, 290; request from British
Government to renegotiate treaty,
290–1; farewell gift from Ti
Rimpoche, 291, 303; farewells, Lhasa,
291; on leaving Lhasa, 292; repudiation
of treaty by British Government,
292–3; guilty of insubordination, 293;
attempts to save reputation, 299; secret
correspondence read, 299–300; return
to London, 300; in Special Honours
List for Younghusband Mission, 300;
honours after Younghusband Mission,
301–2; life after Younghusband
Mission, 301–3; promotion to
Residency of Kashmir, 302; religious
faith, 302–3; in O'Connor's memoirs,
305; loss of material in transit from
Lhasa, 306; and looting, 307
Younghusband, Lieutenant Colonel
George 'Jack' (brother of FY), 31, 43,
320
Younghusband, Helen (wife of FY), 19,
320; campaign against Macdonald,
213; correspondence with Dunlop-
Smith, 213–14; decline into
depression, 302; letters from FY (on
White, 25; on crossing of Tang La, 77;
on Macdonald, 79, 80, 96, 103–4, 130,
149–50, 206–7; on negotiations with
Tibetans, 86–7, 206; on Chumik
Shenko massacre, 126; on Landon,
130; on Tibetans, 136, 253; on life in
Gyantse, 149–50; mocking of Indian
staff, 164; on attack on Changlo
Manor, 177; on British Government,
194, 228, 280; gaps in, 212; missing
letters, 212; on view from Khamba La,
247; on Bretherton, 249–50; on
acquisition of silks, 272; on signing of
Tibet Convention, 279, 284; on
congratulatory messages, 289); letters
from O'Connor, 86–7, 101, 212,
268–9; and Magniac, 155; reaction to
Macdonald's knighthood, 300–1)
Younghusband, General John (FY's
father), 19, 321; letters from FY (on
White, 21, 25; on interview with

349